❖ ❖ ❖ ❖ ❖ ❖ ❖ ❖ ❖ ❖ ❖ ❖ ❖ ❖ ❖ ❖ ❖ ❖ ❖ ❖ ❖ ❖ ❖ ❖ ❖ ❖ ❖ ❖ ❖ ❖ ❖ ❖ ❖ ❖

# *FDR's Good Neighbor Policy*

Franklin D. Roosevelt speaking with Mr. Reuben Appel, Hyde Park, New York, November 4, 1930. Photographer unidentified. UPI/BETTMANN.

*As governor of New York in 1930, FDR displays his ability to establish rapport with the nation's "underlings." Whether of old stock or of recent immigrant extraction (as seems likely in the case of Mr. Appel), America's little men and women tended to remain feisty and unbowed. They responded to a national leader who could seem solicitous without being condescending. Before long, Depression-ravaged Latin Americans demonstrated their own responsiveness to this sort of North American leader.*

Fredrick B. Pike

# FDR's
## Good Neighbor Policy

❖ ❖ ❖ ❖ ❖ ❖ ❖ ❖ ❖ ❖ ❖ ❖ ❖ ❖ ❖ ❖ ❖ ❖ ❖

Sixty Years
of Generally
Gentle Chaos

University of Texas Press
Austin

#30979459

Requests for permission to reproduce material from this work should be sent to Permissions, University of Texas Press, Box 7819, Austin, TX 78713-7819.

∞ The paper used in this publication meets the minimum requirements of American National Standard for Information Sciences—Permanence of Paper for Printed Library Materials, ANSI Z39.48–1984.

Library of Congress Cataloging-in-Publication Data

Pike, Fredrick B.
    FDR's Good Neighbor Policy : sixty years of generally gentle chaos / Fredrick B. Pike. — 1st ed.
        p.    cm.
    Includes index.
    ISBN 0-292-76557-6
    1. Latin America—Relations—United States.   2. United States—Relations— Latin America.   3. United States—Foreign relations—1933–1945.   4. Roosevelt, Franklin D. (Franklin Delano), 1882–1945.   I. Title.
    F1418.F553   1995
    327.7308′09041—dc20                                                    94-29811

To the memory of my mother and father,
June Braun and John Pike;
for my sister Barbara,
and for Pachita's and my granddaughters,
Paulita and Margaret,
and our grandsons, Beto and Fredi;
and for my wife, Helene

# Contents

❖ ❖ ❖ ❖ ❖ ❖ ❖ ❖ ❖ ❖ ❖ ❖ ❖ ❖ ❖ ❖ ❖ ❖ ❖ ❖ ❖ ❖ ❖ ❖ ❖ ❖ ❖ ❖ ❖ ❖ ❖ ❖

### Illustrations

# *Preface*

To his thoughtful 1959 book that surveyed hemispheric relations since 1930, historian Donald Dozer gave the title *Are We Good Neighbors?* Obviously that title could not have been chosen had it not been for the "Good Neighbor policy" that originated . . . Well, just when did it originate?

The majority of scholars who have written on the topic contend that the policy actually originated toward the end of the 1920s, during Herbert Hoover's presidency. Often they find reasons even to credit Hoover's predecessor, Calvin Coolidge, with planting some of the policy's seeds.[1] Their claims cannot be lightly dismissed. To me, though, it seems that historian Bryce Wood makes a compelling case in arguing that the real essence of the Good Neighbor policy emerged during Franklin D. Roosevelt's first term.[2] However that may be, it was FDR who made the Good Neighbor policy known to Americans and managed to popularize it among a great many of them, whether those Americans resided north or south of the Rio Grande. That's why I've chosen to call my book *FDR's Good Neighbor Policy.* Quite aside from the issue of who originated it, was there much of genuine substance to the Good Neighbor policy?

Getting back to the Donald Dozer book: were we in the United States good neighbors, specifically during the years between 1933 and 1945, when FDR presided over the Good Neighbor policy? By and large, following the lead of Roosevelt himself, we were, it seems to me, no better neighbors than we had to be. To me, that seems the most one could expect. We might, after all, have been a good deal worse as neighbors.

What drove North Americans, between 1933 and 1945, at least to go through the motions of becoming better neighbors than they might have been, or than they actually wanted to be? The attempt to answer this question has not yet yielded a broad consensus. I doubt that it ever will.

To some careful students of these matters, the desire to create a hemispheric environment more propitious to the U.S. investors lay behind the Good Neighbor policy. Lloyd Gardner and David Green figure in the forefront of writers who have ascribed economic motivation to those who originated the Good Neighbor policy, whether under Roosevelt or his two immediate predecessors in office.[3] They belong to a school of diplomatic historians perhaps most notably and honorably exemplified by William Appleman Williams and more recently by Walter LaFeber. This school also includes more ideologically rigid historians, some of whom are Marxists of one stripe or another and many of whom subscribe uncritically to "dependency" analysis. So-called *dependencistas* see behind U.S. diplomacy little more than the calculated endeavor to render the entire hemisphere, maybe even the whole world, dependent upon the whims and purposes of the American capitalist system, ostensibly based on free enterprise but actually relying on state protection.

On the other hand another school of historians, including Dana G. Munro, Samuel Flagg Bemis, and J. Lloyd Mecham, have seen U.S. hemispheric policy, whether before, during, or after the Good Neighbor era, as dictated primarily by security considerations. It seems to me, as readers with sufficient patience to make their way through this book will discover, that security and economic pursuits are so intimately intertwined as to be inseparable. Nevertheless, historians continue to break lances over the matter, convinced they confront an either-or issue.

The one school of diplomatic history that comes closest, in my mind, to encompassing the complexities of the Good Neighbor era, as FDR helped shape it, is the realpolitik school—which, in the Cold War era, would find its ablest proponent in Hans J. Morgenthau. To those of the realpolitik persuasion, the United States (or any other country for that matter) should attend principally to maintaining the military *and* the economic strength needed to defend its vital interests—meaning ultimately, I assume, the fundamental, underlying values of its national culture. In pursuing realpolitik objectives, according to proponents of the school, the United States should not fret unduly about imposing the values of its national culture, including democratic procedures and human rights, on other countries. Crusades to spread the "American way" allegedly accomplish little beyond inciting resentment in countries whose support is useful, even essential, to U.S. strategic interests.

FDR's concern to establish nonintervention as a fundamental building block of his hemispheric policy points to his realpolitik approach. While he might pressure his old friends among the British to relinquish their imperialism, convinced this would ultimately make for the sort of more peaceful world in which American interests could thrive best, he was not inclined to pressure Latin Americans into abandoning political and economic, cultural and moral habits that were antithetical to what was assumed to be the U.S. way of life. Eventually, Roosevelt believed, hemispheric convergence would come about; eventually, Latins would recognize the advantages—economic, cultural, and moral—of basic U.S. values. In the short term, however, attempts to speed the process up would probably prove counterproductive: counterproductive to hemispheric relations and perhaps even to the internal stability of individual Latin American states. Basic to FDR's approach was the assumption that Latins had a lot of growing up to do before they could adjust to U.S. culture.

Most sympathetic toward realpolitik approaches, FDR was least sympathetic to the romantic primitivism school that contributed its grain of sand to a U.S.–Latin American rapprochement in the 1930s. Encouraged by what they took to be the death blow that the Depression had dealt self-seeking materialism, the romantics envisaged a return in the hemisphere to some sort of Edenic "peaceable kingdom," cleansed of avarice and greed and excessive individualism. American romantics (who included more than a few Marxists) liked to assume that Latin Americans, relatively uncorrupted by material progress, could actually serve as role models for their northern neighbors, trapped in the ruins of their modernity. While contemptuous of these attitudes, which actually found expression in a good many books that his countrymen—and -women—published in the Good Neighbor era, FDR was willing to take advantage of the sophomoric goodwill they occasionally fomented in order to serve his own hemispheric purposes.

Unlike the romantics, FDR accepted human nature as it was, while still hoping occasionally to smooth off some of its roughest edges. Unlike Charlie Chaplin in his 1936 movie destined to become a classic, FDR knew that *Modern Times* were here to stay and that the more indulgence the Yankees displayed toward Latin Americans the sooner they would embrace modernity. For FDR modernity meant not untrammeled laissez-faire capitalism, but rather some form of social capitalism. Most assuredly, though, it did not mean Marxism or other varieties of utopian socialism that many dreamers thought at hand once the Depression struck. To this day, critics on the left tend to condemn Roosevelt for not having seized the moment to lead the hemisphere to its live-happily-ever-afterward redemption. Beyond this, they are likely to charge that behind a smoke screen of reformist rhetoric FDR actually permitted U.S. capitalists to steal the store both from their less advantaged fellow citizens and from Latin Americans in general.

On the other hand, critics on the right remain to this day equally put out with Roosevelt for not having seized the moment to bolster untrammeled free-enterprise capitalism within the United States. The Depression, they insist, did not result from any basic flaws in free-market capitalism; and had the president cooperated with rather than harassed businessmen, they could quickly have led the country out of its hard times. Above all, they contend, a worthy leader would have confronted the crisis by bolstering, not by assailing, America's hallowed economic traditions. Beyond this, he would have insisted that Latin Americans adapt themselves fully and at once to the ways of the market; and he would have left them to stew in their own juices if they proved recalcitrant. Instead, so the critics on the right maintain, FDR coddled antimarket socialist types both in the United States and in Latin America. He gave the store away to deluded radicals and to wastrels and ne'er-do-wells both in the United States and in Latin America.

Appraisals of Roosevelt's Latin American policy grow out of appraisals of his domestic policies. Those to the left and those to the right will never agree in evaluating FDR's New Deal, and this means they will never agree, fundamentally, in assessing his Good Neighbor policy. It means, too, they will lie in wait, ready to pounce on anyone who attempts this assessment either from the pole opposite to the one they defend or from the perspective of the center: the perspective that—properly, it seems to me—always most appealed to FDR himself.

Even though knowing the perils, why do I add my assessment of FDR's Good Neighbor policy to all those that have already appeared in print, many of which I cannot hope to match in quality? In the remainder of this preface, I'll try to explain why.

In a 1992 letter to my friend and former student William Sammon I mentioned my foolhardy intention to venture into the Good Neighbor thicket. By way of explanation I told him it was my intention to end my publications on Latin America with a book on the era in which I'd first become aware of that region. He, being the civilized person that he is, responded with some lines from T. S. Eliot's *Little Gidding:* What we call the beginning, Eliot observed, is often the end, "And to make an end is to make a beginning. The end is where we start from." Those lines help explain the book at hand: at the end, I've been irresistibly drawn to the beginning.

Born in 1926, I began in the early to mid-1930s to become a bit aware of a few things going on in the world, in part by listening to the radio a great deal more than a kid my age ordinarily would. Mainly this was because I had been confined to bed for almost three years by a misguided doctor. My choice of programs must have driven my sister Barbara crazy, but she has always been patient and indulgent with me and with others. My favorite radio entertainment came from the western music programs of Stuart Hamblen, the broadcast descriptions of Joe Louis fights, "Amos 'n' Andy," Eddie Cantor and Jack Benny and Bing Crosby, and above all else from FDR's Fireside Chats. While I didn't necessarily understand much of what he was saying, there was something about the man's voice and presentation that made me feel good and secure, providing a sleepy blanket in which I could serenely doze off for the night. My grandfather and mother were aghast at my esteem for the president they regarded as a dangerous radical, but somehow their warnings about him didn't register with me. I've never repented my youthful fixation, even though in later years I've discovered that my hero had huge feet of clay.

Vaguely in the 1930s I became aware that FDR had an interest in certain neighbors to the south called Latin Americans, and that he had initiated a Good Neighbor program through which he hoped to establish better relations between them and us. Well, that sounded like a decent enough idea. At the time a lot of Latin songs were in vogue; I listened to them on the radio and liked them and began to sing them myself, almost as often as the cowboy songs I'd learned from Stuart Hamblen. The Latins had begun to intrigue me about as much as cowboys. By the end of the 1930s, moreover, the Latins took on an appeal the cowboys couldn't match. They were sexy. Dolores del Rio and Carmen Miranda provided all the proof of that one needed. Obviously FDR was right in wanting Americans to get closer to Latin Americans.

Beyond this, the story of how and why I became interested enough in Latin America to spend my life studying it is long and dull, and probably by now embellished by fiction. Suffice it to say that toward the end of 1949 my Salvadoran wife, Pachita, and I arrived in Austin, the University of Texas having accepted me for graduate studies in Latin American history. Without Pachita's influence, I would never have initiated my career as a Latin Americanist. Without her presence later in Chile and Peru as I plunged into research projects, I could not fruitfully have furthered that career. Ultimately, though, had it not been for FDR, who had died less than five years before Pachita and I arrived in Austin, I might very well have been embarking on a different career in a different place.

The University of Texas proved a marvelous choice for a young graduate student in my chosen field. I doubt I could have found a better place to begin my advance along what has turned out to be a circular trek. The university's recently established Institute of Latin American Studies was staffed by men and women who were giants in the field, each one of whom I revere to this day, each one of whom I sorely miss nearly every day of my life: Charles Wilson Hackett, Nettie Lee Benson, J. Lloyd Mecham, and Carlos Eduardo Castañeda.

Charles Hackett was the best narrative classroom lecturer I ever encountered. Three times a week through some magical process he made the history of Mexico come alive in a crowded classroom in Garrison Hall. With his students he was warm and encouraging. Nettie Lee Benson was inspiring, and intimidating. The first time I wandered into her library domain she, in effect, asked me what right I thought I had to use her books and papers. She was altogether justified in wondering if I had a deep enough commitment to merit use of her facilities. Eventually she seemed to think that I earned that right, and I've always treasured her for having concluded this, and for treating me as an equal—of whom, in truth, she had none. Of course what I and hundreds of others treasure her most for is building the fabulous collection of Latin American materials that comprise the collection that now bears her name.

J. Lloyd Mecham would hem and haw his way through a fifty-minute class period. Then, when the bell rang and as some students worried about making their next class, he would launch into some of the most marvelous, rich, concise, well-organized eight-to-nine-minute lectures I've ever heard. To this day his studies of U.S.–Latin American relations remain among the best ever written; and just as significant is his trailblazing monograph on church and state in Latin America. Eventually the quality of my exams, or maybe it was just my physical energy, earned me the right to toil with him on some of the rock projects along the creek that ran through his property; and during those hours I fell all the more under his spell, and that of his beloved wife, Mabel. And I thought all the more about his conviction that FDR had gone too far in extending concessions to Latin America during the World War II years, though to this day I'm not sure my mentor was altogether right.

One lesson above all others that I learned from Mecham (though for a time I resisted it) was that a Yankee could like Latins, and like to study their culture, without romanticizing them. FDR, it turns out, had felt that way, too. He never took seriously the edge of romanticism that, for public relations reasons, he sometimes imparted to the Good Neighbor policy.

Carlos Castañeda (who would become my *compadre* in 1952) was simply one of the most decent, warm, generous, open human beings I've ever known, though every now and then a bit of the hurt he had to have accumulated as a result of growing up Mexican in Texas would surface. Every now and then, too, he lamented that the religious trappings (a rosary was embossed on the cover of each volume) and title of his seven-volume *Our Catholic Heritage in Texas* impeded recognition of it as the finest available history of Texas. Fellow graduate students, like Max Maisel, often joined me in helping Don Carlos haul the boat he acquired late in life from lake to lake in Austin, cursing that boat and yet blessing it, too; for once the sun set, we had the prospect of taking Don Carlos to some favorite spot for a few beers. In the classroom and out, Don Carlos awakened in me an undying love for the history of imperial Spain and colonial Latin America.

Though for some reason he chose to remain somewhat reticent on the subject, Carlos Castañeda could have told me a great deal about his wartime role in the Southwest in implementing Roosevelt's fair employment practices policies. Perhaps if I'd had sense enough to ask the right questions he would have fleshed out his occasional hints that FDR's interest in a domestic Good Neighbor policy, one that involved fair treatment of Mexican and other minority workers in the Southwest, extended no further than expediency demanded.

At the University of Texas, many of the students seemed almost on a par with my mentors in providing inspiration. I think primarily of Vic Niemeyer, who went on to a distinguished career in the United States Information Service, and of Leonard Masters, who deepened my love and understanding of that other great passion in my life which often has quite eclipsed history: music. I suppose my love of classical music must be traced back ultimately to my mother, who used to take me as a very small boy to hear the Los Angeles Philharmonic, conducted at the time by Otto Klemperer, who had been hounded out of Hitler's Germany.

On the recommendation of Carlos Castañeda to his friend Thomas T. McAvoy, then head of the history department at the University of Notre Dame, I landed a job there in 1953. Six years later a Doherty Foundation grant came my way. In consequence, my wife and I and our three children (Paulita, June, and Fred) arrived in Santiago, Chile, in September. Chile provoked a real scholarly awakening, and amid less straitened circumstances than would have obtained but for the generosity of my father and his wonderful wife, Caroline.

Shortly before leaving for Chile I had read the first two volumes (published in 1957 and 1958) of what would become Arthur Schlesinger, Jr.'s three-volume study, *The Age of Roosevelt*. I found these volumes interpretively convincing, enormously exciting, and beautifully written—and they still seem exciting and well-written. They strengthened my liberal leanings and put me on the alert for Chilean counterparts of FDR who might pull the country out of the difficulties and social injustices that, so it would soon seem to me, afflicted it as the 1950s gave way to the '60s.

During a year of obsessive research I managed to learn a fair amount about Chile's history, though not nearly as much as I at first thought I had learned. However, the marvelously stimulating year had a downside for the intellectual development of a young historian; for I became increasingly partial to rather unilateral, leftist interpretations of the Latin American reality. Already the forces that would bring Salvador Allende to the Chilean presidency ten years later were gathering force and velocity. Resisting their intellectual momentum was almost as difficult for an impressionable young historian as saying no to Marxism was for intellectuals in Paris in 1968. And so, in Santiago, I began to wonder if Chile, and much of the rest of Latin America, might need leaders even to the left of FDR as portrayed by Arthur Schlesinger, Jr.

Shocked by conditions of poverty in Chile that quite eclipsed anything I had yet witnessed, I was drawn toward those leftists who, sometimes smugly and glibly, insisted there were easy solutions, rather than toward the rightists who, sometimes smugly and glibly, insisted either that there were no problems or no solutions. In a way, in Chile I went through the sort of intellectual experience many Americans had gone through in their own country about a quarter of a century earlier. Confronting the Great Depression, they had placed their faith in New Deal statism, convinced that concentrations of power in the hands of bureaucrats posed less menace than concentrations of wealth in the hands of plutocrats.

A partiality to leftist-statist viewpoints, heightened by a visit to Cuba in 1960 shortly after Fidel Castro took over, remained with me for about a decade. It resulted, among other things, in a conviction (widely shared by my compatriot scholars of the era and not altogether abandoned since then by many of them) that we gringos had been notoriously bad neighbors to Latin Americans. Therefore, we deserved whatever nasty things it might occur to Latins to do in dealing with us. So, more power to Castro!

For a while, then, I ignored all that the mellifluous-voiced radio celebrity who brightened my childhood had done to suggest that we norteamericanos were resolved to become good neighbors. For a while I may even have begun to wonder if FDR's denunciation of the abuses of capitalism and of economic royalists was, as so many of my fellow gringo Latin Americanists had begun to charge, just a smoke screen to cover his collusion with plutocrats, both north and south of the border. I would have to find out more about that man, and his policies.

The bureaucrat-plutocrat dichotomy continued to fascinate me. About a decade after Castro took over Cuba I began to suspect that the bureaucratic approach was not necessarily so wonderful after all, while what leftists reviled as the "plutocratic" approach was not necessarily so vile as they pretended. Why, I wondered, could not these opposites be combined, in some sort of harmony? Many years later it dawned on me that FDR had addressed the same question back in the 1930s. Indeed, as readers will discover, it is Franklin Roosevelt's dream of synthesizing opposites, one of the noblest of all impossible dreams, that has most fascinated me. Surely this dream lay at the heart of the Good Neighbor policy and of the entire New Deal. Or so it began, at first very dimly, to seem to me; and this is one reason I kept on thinking about the Good Neighbor era and the man who presided over it even while focusing on other research projects.

Four years after the Chilean experience came a year's grant from the Social Science Research Council for research in Peru. I never really figured Peru out, not even to my own satisfaction, though I did love my time spent in the archives (superbly administered by Graciela Sánchez Cerro), tramping through the Andes, boating down the Amazon, and enhancing my appreciation for the tragic sense of life through attendance at the Sunday afternoon *corridas de toros* at the Plaza de Acho and shouting olé as "El Viti" and "El Cordobés" and Paco Camino (and many a lesser torero) reenacted the drama of death the inevitable.

Though I didn't realize it at the time, the year in Peru helped advance me a bit on the circle that would bring me back to Franklin Roosevelt. In that country I became intrigued by Víctor Raúl Haya de la Torre (1895–1979). Shortly I'll explain the connection between interest in Peru's Henry Clay, the perennially unsuccessful seeker after the presidency, and in FDR, the man who won twice as many presidential elections as any other person in his country's history. Before that, though, there are other matters with which to complicate the tale.

After Peru came a move in 1965 to the University of Pennsylvania, where I was engaged to replace Arthur P. Whitaker, who had reached the age that at that time mandated retirement. No one, of course, could replace Arthur P. Whitaker, who to this day I revere as the noblest figure his field (a broad one, but primarily hemispheric diplomatic history) has produced—although in recent years Lester D. Langley at the University of Georgia has in my estimation begun to rise to that level. Knowing Whitaker personally, a man whom previously I had reverenced from afar, inspired me to reread his *The Western Hemisphere Idea* (1954), and references to that book appear several times in the pages that follow.

To his study of the Western Hemisphere Idea Whitaker gave the subtitle *Its Rise and Decline*. As of the early 1990s, the Idea—one that pertains partly to convergence between North and South America—may actually be on the rise. In the concluding section of the present book I touch on some of the evidence that suggests the Idea's resuscitation by pointing to signs of late-twentieth-century hemispheric convergence around the values of modernity, embourgeoisement, and market capitalism. Perhaps Arthur Whitaker would have been surprised.

However, there's another side to this story. The Western Hemisphere Idea posits not just convergence but a *unique* degree of convergence among New World republics. In this respect, Western Hemisphere Idea assumptions remain as far-fetched as ever. Certainly events in 1993 underlined this fact; and Whitaker would not have been surprised.

In the fall of that year opponents of freer trade with Mexico assailed their neighbors to the south with far more ethnically prejudiced nativist rhetoric than ever they would have resorted to in opposing freer trade with Canadians or Europeans. Moreover, the rancor of their anti-Mexican tirades may even have exceeded that so often vented by American isolationists against Asians. As it turned out the opponents to freer hemispheric trade went down to defeat in 1993. However, congressional approval of the U.S.-Canadian-Mexican North American Free Trade Agreement (NAFTA), even assuming that this agreement may eventually be expanded to include the other Latin American countries clamoring for admission, does not suggest any unique Western Hemispheric destiny of convergence. Potentially far more important than NAFTA in pointing the way toward free-trade ideals are U.S. interaction with the European Union (formerly designated the European Community) and U.S. participation within the fifteen-member Asia-Pacific Economic Cooperation forum (APEC).

Could he have foreseen it, this situation would not in any way have surprised or discomfited the Hyde Park architect of Good Neighborliness. Despite the aplomb with which he donned the Good Neighbor mantle, Roosevelt had no sympathy with mystical concepts about unique ties, whether economic or cultural, that bound the Americas together and set them off from the rest of the world. This, at least, was what I concluded on the basis of frequent conversations with Arthur Whitaker in the mid-to-late 1960s, conversations during which he persuaded me that the Good Neighbor policy essentially did not fit into the scheme of the Western Hemisphere Idea. Once again, without having directly, consciously willed it, I was learning more about the man who stood at the beginning and awaited me at the end of the circle I was traversing.

Three years after relocating in Philadelphia, the family and I were off for Spain, thanks to a Guggenheim grant. Living in Spain, I was fascinated by the transition the country was making in the late 1960s, rather more gracefully than Chile and Peru I thought, from traditionalism to modernity: the sort of transition that North Americans under Roosevelt in the Good Neighbor era, and much more so in the years after that, for better and for worse but above all just simply inevitably, tried to hasten throughout Latin America.

Here is what I took for a sure sign that Francisco Franco was dragging Spain into modernity: the corridas in 1969 were dreadful. As a country modernizes, I conjectured, it loses interest in reflecting on death the inevitable. Manolete makes way for Elvis Presley and Andy Warhol. Oh, well, better Presley and Warhol as icons than statues of Lenin and "La Pasionaria." And it was the latter icons that might have been foisted on Spaniards had FDR succumbed to pressure from his country's more liberal voters and also from its most blatant leftist ideologues to intervene in Spain's Civil War (1936–1939) on the side of the Loyalists. At least this is the way it began to seem to me; and in consequence, while living in Spain I became ever more curious about the man I had once thought wrong not to intervene in Spain. Wherever I went, I could not escape the FDR presence.

Meantime, Spain, to my surprise, has (like FDR) learned to combine opposites. As of the early 1990s, the epic go-go-go culture personified by the likes of Presley and Warhol and their successors was still all the rage; but simultaneously, the classic sun-*and*-shade, success-*and*-tragedy drama of the bulls was making a spectacular comeback as a new generation of toreros mastered the ancient art. For this I have no pat explanation, though I do derive a moral from it: avoid sweeping generalizations on the confrontations of modernity and traditionalism.


After Spain, it was back to Notre Dame rather than Pennsylvania. By that time the Fidel Castro phenomenon had revived U.S. interest in Latin America. Specialists in the field were much in demand in North American universities. Sometimes we received offers we didn't deserve but couldn't refuse. Once more at Notre Dame I had occasion to be grateful to the administration for leaving me alone to "do my own thing," which was mainly to experiment with new courses. Once more I had the opportunity to serve under outstanding department chairmen, among them Father Marvin R. O'Connell, Father Tom Blantz, and Vincent P. DeSantis. Once more I benefited from some of the splendid students the university has always attracted. They provided more intellectual stimulus for me than I for them. Most especially, I think of Mike Ogorzaly, Blake Pattridge, Juan Ramón García, Martha Lamar, Tom McCaffery, Patrick Timon, Tom Krieg, Cynthia Watson, and the already-mentioned Bill Sammon. They continued the good-student, good-friend precedent that David Valaik and Maurice Brungardt had established back in the 1950s, before going on to become members of the history faculties of Canisius College and Loyola University of New Orleans, respectively. Moreover, there were plenty of good colleagues at Notre Dame, above all Tom Stritch. My dear friend Steve Kertesz, who for many years headed the university's Committee on International Relations, once observed (when frustrated by some particularly tardy contributors to an edited volume) that there are few gentlemen in the academic profession. He has a point. In the Notre Dame history department, though, I found an unusually high percentage of gentlemen—

and gentlewomen. From other universities as well I've known many exceptions to the Kertesz rule; and I am grateful to these exceptions for their long-term friendships. I think especially of Tom Davies (San Diego State University), Larry Clayton (University of Alabama), Jim Henderson (Coastal Carolina University), and Marilyn S. Ward (Brookhaven College).

From the early '70s on, my new books were not researched abroad but rather at the many-splendored Benson Collection of the University of Texas. One of these books (for which research was supported by a National Endowment for the Humanities grant) was a study of Peru's Víctor Raúl Haya de la Torre, a man who, as mentioned, has fascinated me since my year in Peru: fascinated and utterly baffled me. To this day I remain uncertain as to which of my interpretations of him is closer to the truth: the hostile one contained in a 1967 book, the friendly one in a 1986 intellectual biography, or the middleground judgment rendered in a 1977 volume. At least in studying Haya de la Torre, especially in his extrarational hopes to combine opposites in harmony and also in his frequent lack of scruple as to how he pursued his dream, I had the chance to observe a thwarted, would-be Andean FDR. No wonder Haya held Roosevelt in reverence. They were birds of a feather. In this particular instance, the American eagle seems to me to have soared to loftier heights than the Peruvian condor; but observing the condor certainly prepared one to glimpse the eagle.


For the first time in 1992 the University of Texas Press published one of my books (*The United States and Latin America: Myths and Stereotypes of Civilization and Nature*). In this book that brought me back to the Latin American program at Texas—and initiated a warm friendship with Theresa J. May, the Press's Assistant Director and Executive Editor—I developed a thesis about some of the underlying attitudes that have shaped U.S. relations with neighbors to the south. While writing the book I discovered I was more fascinated than ever by FDR. Obviously the time had come to go back all the way to where I'd begun as a Latin Americanist.

With this last book, as in all of the previous ones, parts of the text just wouldn't shape up to say all that I wanted them to say. At least, though, I found some illustrations that are eloquent in depicting conditions in the United States during the Great Depression—conditions (as I argue in this book) but for which there could never have been the sort of Good Neighbor policy that FDR managed to shape. Larry David Perkins, curator of collections at the University of Florida's splendid Samuel P. Harn Museum of Art, helped me select these illustrations. They are taken from the museum's rich holdings (the result of a gift from Dr. and Mrs. Corbin S.

Carnell) of graphics produced by artists sustained by one of the New Deal's many inspired programs: the Federal Art Project (FAP) that fell under the umbrella of the Works Progress Administration (WPA). Unhappily, the haunting scenes that some of the FAP artists depicted are as revealing of times in the 1990s as they were of those in the '30s. That's a point I return to in this book's final section. But I'll play with it just for a moment now, before ending this preface.

As already mentioned, I had my first sustained look at poverty while in Chile, as the 1950s gave way to the '60s. The experience prompted my conviction that there had to be an effective way to mitigate poverty, a way that probably involved massive state-administered programs. Americans en masse had a similar first-time exposure to poverty, but poverty within their own country, during the Depression era. To a large extent they responded as I had in Chile, which meant they supported Roosevelt's socio-economic interventionist policies.

Those Americans who did not personally view, at first hand, the social and economic ravages wrought by the Depression on individual lives could not turn, in the 1930s, to television for the surrogate experience. By the hundreds of thousands, though, relatively sheltered Americans could and did flock to exhibits of graphics produced by WPA-subsidized artists. They could and did flock, moreover, to exhibits of the heart-rending pictures of impoverished citizens taken by photographers employed by the Farm Security Administration (FSA). In museums and in high school auditoriums and in libraries and other public and private buildings across the land Americans looked, generally with dismay and compassion, on the artistic testimony to the suffering of their fellow citizens. Just as great art of earlier centuries in Europe had inspired faith in ultimate salvation, so America's secular art of the Depression era sparked faith in deliverance from the temporal suffering it depicted.

Appalled by what they saw, either at first hand or by means of graphics and photographs, Americans tended in the majority to support the New Deal; for they believed it would help banish poverty and suffering amidst people who, only yesterday, had thought themselves a people of plenty.

Their social conscience awakened to a degree that probably was unique in all their history, Americans for a while tended, by and large, to support not only the New Deal but the Good Neighbor policy. The latter, they concluded, might help succor needy and suffering people who shared the New World and who, in consequence, were just not supposed to endure the outrages that the Old World had grown accustomed to enduring.


At the end of the 1950s Chilean friends from the accommodated and satisfied classes were alternately annoyed and amused by what they considered my immature response to their country's poverty. Unlike the Marxist and "do-gooder" friends I made in their country, they tended to shrug their shoulders in the face of problems that, they assured me, had no solution. Perhaps through the decades, through the generations, they had succumbed to compassion fatigue. Nowadays North Americans, too, have fallen into compassion fatigue. In the wake of the largely futile wars on poverty that succeeded the only partially successful one that FDR had waged, they have begun to assume that if human problems do not somehow solve themselves, then perhaps they may be insoluble. Would that I knew, for certain, whether their attitudes reflect mature wisdom as much as, or more than, self-serving callousness.

However that may be, compassion was relatively robust and unfatigued back in the '30s when a majority of Americans supported New Deal and Good Neighbor initiatives. Perhaps even then, and perhaps not, compassion was naive and misplaced. In any event, rediscovering it in more or less pristine estate has refreshed me as I circle back to the times of FDR.

In this book that grows out of the journey back to beginnings I've made no attempt to be comprehensive in endnote citations. Often in the pages that follow I toy with ideas I've lived with for too many years to be able to recall their sources. What notes there are attest to a very few of the many impressive monographs and essays that I've used in the past few years, in hopes of getting some of the details right. Without those sources I'd not have dared begin this book at all. The citations bear witness to at least a few of the dedicated persons who by their labors in the archives have turned up the data that informs me as to what lay beneath the surface I began to observe back in the '30s.

About the subtitle, *Sixty Years of Generally Gentle Chaos:* my reasons for choosing it may not become apparent until the final, brief chapter. Along the way, though (beginning almost at once, in fact), I provide some hints. What about the main title, *FDR's Good Neighbor Policy?* Already I've indicated the belief that FDR rather than his two immediate predecessors in the Oval Office deserves primary credit as the father of the policy. Beyond that, though, does the policy really belong to the man, or to the times?

Many observers feel that circumstances peculiar to the era rather than Roosevelt the man shaped hemispheric policy in the 1930s and early '40s; and often in the pages that follow I subscribe to their view. Moreover, during the Good Neighbor era there was often an ad hoc, ad lib, fortuitous quality to the shaping of relations with Latin America. In consequence, policy frequently did not bear the identifiable mark of the president or of any one person. All of this I concede, along with other objections to assigning primary responsibility for the Good Neighbor policy to the president.

Roosevelt himself as often as possible turned his back on what he regarded as the side show in Latin America. He let his underlings stage-direct that show, always being careful, though, as was his wont in virtually all matters, to choose underlings with different, even irreconcilably different, approaches to hemispheric issues. But, when the chips were down, when he absolutely had to do something to resolve bureaucratic chaos and synthesize irreconcilable positions, Roosevelt would assert himself, often with a deft, improvisatory hand that seemed to hold not so much the trademark cigarette-holder as a wand. Out of the bureaucratic chaos there could well have issued relatively harsh policies toward Latin America, especially with Mexico in 1938, if FDR had not bestirred himself to resolve matters, gently.

Under Roosevelt's hand, policy would emerge out of chaos, at least for a brief moment before being overtaken by the next crisis. Then the chronically distracted master would have to try once more to apply his magic touch. The method—if one can call sporadic crisis control a method—didn't always work. But it worked often enough to allow Roosevelt to place his own, unmistakable stamp on the overall Good Neighbor policy, to make that policy his policy. The Roosevelt "method" also established a precedent for sporadic crisis control in hemispheric affairs that remained largely in effect for the following sixty years. During the Cold War years, though, the Roosevelt gentleness sometimes gave way to harshness, perhaps necessarily so, perhaps not. Be that as it may, by the early 1990s, by one path or another, Latin American republics had arrived by and large at the point FDR always expected them to reach. Undergoing embourgeoisement, they had begun to achieve more dynamic economies intimately linked to the economy of the United States. Dependency theory to the contrary notwithstanding, Latin Americans probably derived as much advantage from this linkage as North Americans. Ultimately, though, how beneficial the mania for individual material aggrandizement and for freedom bordering on license will prove to them and to us remains to be seen.


For encouragement and counsel in preparing this book I am especially grateful to Professor Lester D. Langley, author of what I consider the finest book on hemispheric relations to appear in many years: *America and the Americas: The United States in the Western Hemisphere* (1989). Lester was kind enough to read my manuscript, and to make enormously helpful suggestions. Moreover, one day over lunch in Gainesville, Florida, the only occasion when we have met personally, he introduced me to a few of the rudiments of chaos theory. That introduction helped lead to some of my concluding assessments of Roosevelt and the Good Neighbor policy and influenced my choice of a subtitle for this book. Not even Lester, though, could save me from the sort of interpretive lapses and factual flaws that none of my books escapes. For these, the fault is mine alone.

The fault for stylistic lapses lies also with me. I am only thankful that these lapses are fewer, by the hundreds, than if I had been left to my own devices. Paul Spragens, as fine a copyeditor as I have ever worked with, labored heroically to put a better face on my work, and I am enormously grateful to him.

Helping prod me into writing this book was a granddaughter. Young Paulita, perhaps ten at the time, asked one night over a restaurant meal in South Bend, Indiana, whether I would someday dedicate a book to her. The present book provides at least a partially affirmative response to a request delicately phrased as a question. Without it, I might never have undertaken this final book.

Above all others, one person enabled me to return to origins by writing this book. For her patience and understanding in the face of neglect, for her unflagging encouragement and good spirits I thank Helene, my wife for the past quarter century. Had she had better clay to animate, this work could have been more worthy of her and also of its central protagonist.

❖ ❖ ❖ ❖ ❖ ❖ ❖ ❖ ❖ ❖ ❖ ❖ ❖ ❖ ❖ ❖ ❖ ❖ ❖ ❖ ❖ ❖ ❖ ❖ ❖ ❖ ❖ ❖ ❖ ❖ ❖ ❖ ❖ ❖

# *FDR's Good Neighbor Policy*

# SECTION

# I

❖❖❖❖❖❖❖❖❖❖❖❖❖❖❖❖❖❖❖❖❖❖❖❖❖❖❖❖

*The Great
Depression
and Better
Neighborliness
in the Americas*

# 1.

❖ ❖ ❖ ❖ ❖ ❖ ❖ ❖ ❖ ❖ ❖ ❖ ❖ ❖ ❖ ❖ ❖ ❖ ❖ ❖ ❖ ❖ ❖ ❖ ❖ ❖ ❖ ❖ ❖ ❖ ❖ ❖ ❖ ❖ ❖ ❖

It may seem bizarre, even demented, to begin a book on the Good Neighbor era with a reference to two operas. Nevertheless, here goes! The works in question are Claude Debussy's *Pelléas et Mélisande* and Alban Berg's *Wozzeck*.

Inspired by Maurice Maeterlinck's 1889 play of the same title, Debussy had completed a preliminary version of his opera *Pelléas et Mélisande* in 1895. Rather than celebrating the dawn of a new century, the opera that premiered in 1902 after extensive revision to the early score suggested a fin-de-siècle perspective. Almost by definition, fin-de-siècle works must be gloomy in outlook, and *Pelléas* fits this mold. It projects a vision of human foibles and suffering, current and to come. Following Maeterlinck's vision, Debussy depicts a poor, lost, wandering waif of a woman, perhaps no more than a teenager, who obviously has been the victim of abuse in the never identified, presumably troubled land whence she comes. She is an alien seeking solace in a new land. Golaud, the royal-blooded man who rescues and marries her, at first showers her with solicitude and attention. Then, he discovers grounds to doubt her fidelity as she and Golaud's half-brother Pelléas become interested in each other. Increasingly Golaud, wracked by suspiciousness about what is going on, turns insensitive, oppressive, and bullying toward his wife. Ultimately he resorts to the murder of his half-brother in order to retain possession of the alien waif to whom he had initially afforded protection. At the end of the opera Arkel, the archetypal wise old man who is the grandfather of Pelléas and Golaud, observes, just after Mélisande has died giving birth to a daughter, that now "it's the poor little one's turn" to suffer—one of the classic downers in all of opera.

The United States managed to escape the avalanche of tragedy apparently foreseen by Maeterlinck and Debussy that did indeed overtake most of Europe beginning in 1914. But America escaped tragedy only until the Great Depression struck in 1929. Then, it was America's turn to suffer.

As *Pelléas et Mélisande* unfolds, Debussy deals with a situation peculiarly attuned to the United States of the Depression years. Specifically, an Act II scene in which the protagonists fall deeper into their ill-starred infatuation takes place outside a grotto and against a background of social tragedy. Suddenly into the misty night comes a shaft of bright moonlight. It reveals three old beggars, victims of famine, asleep on the floor of the cave.

To some extent, the famine and the beggars issue out of the old order, personified by Golaud, replete with good intentions but utterly ineffectual in the face of puzzling new developments. Golaud, like many Depression-era Americans who persisted in their traditional love affair with capitalism and its traditional rules of the game even as the system collapsed about them, watched uncomprehendingly as matters spun out of control.

While some Americans clung to what seemed for the moment to have become a doomed romance shaped by outmoded prescriptions, other Americans—even as Pelléas in the opera began to do—faced the temptation to develop a new kind of romance that set old standards on their head. They began to toy with the notion of abandoning or at least temporarily modifying their respect, reverence, and love for an old order shaped by a male ethic of possessive individualism, whether applied to money and goods or to women.

Like Pelléas and Mélisande, Americans, from President Franklin Delano Roosevelt on down, faced the temptation to abandon traditional ideas about an old love affair and to experiment with some new type of relationship. Like the two operatic protagonists, though, many Americans, again from the president on down, felt guilty about abandoning the old mores in order to flirt with new ideas anathema to the sort of traditionalists that Golaud, along with conventional American masters of capital, personified. At the same time America did not lack citizens who, like Arkel, perceived little ahead save misery, regardless of how they conducted themselves. In most un-American fashion, they abandoned hope in the bourgeois ethic and contemplated the necessity of resigning themselves to a tragic destiny. Often, though, they expected to grow in inward treasure even as they declined in outward measures of affluence.

Most Americans held out against the tragic sense of life. Some who spurned dalliance with the muse of tragedy flirted and even fell in love with one sort or another of alien temptresses who promised their favors only to utopian dreamers who dared to renounce mates who had grown churlish and brutish in their obsessive dedication to superannuated values. Unlike Pelléas and Mélisande, these American adventurers entered into new affairs without any sense of remorse, without any holding back.

The vast majority of Americans, though, found it as difficult as Pelléas and Mélisande to abandon, without enormous pangs of guilt, the old norms of conduct. They hoped that somehow they could continue to love in the old way, to cling to the essential features of the old romance with capitalism, introducing just enough slight alterations in the way they pursued the romance to transform starving persons into a chorus of well-fed and contented observers. These Americans, the majority, might flirt with potential new lovers, but they would not allow the flirtation to get out of hand.

FDR suited the mood of these Americans, the majority of Americans. Not for him the wise old man's resignation to the inevitability of tragedy, in the mold of Arkel. Not for him, either, not necessarily at least, the perpetuation of an old love gone sour. Instead, why not persuade or force Golaud to change, to become more like the graceful and gracious and accommodating Pelléas. Golaud could discard the possessive individualism that rendered him insensitive to the needs of others, whether spouse or social underlings. His Neanderthal ways, just as those of primitive capitalism, had served their purpose. Appropriate to a man like Golaud who initially had to concern himself with providing security in what had been the wilderness, frontier circumstances in which he had found his bride, Neanderthal capitalism could now give way to a more refined and caring and solicitous code of conduct. Out of this new conduct would issue neither unemployed and starving men such as those who lurked about in the dark nor daughters fated to suffer what abused mothers had endured. In the new dispensation, these victims of an order that had served its purpose and become anachronistic would give way to secure citizens and children with happy futures.

To FDR it seemed possible, likely, even almost foreordained, that Americans would not abandon totally their old love affair. Golaud, the power wielder, and Mélisande, the dependent waif, would remain together. But the rough Golaud would mend his ways and become more solicitous to the needs, economic and emotional, of those who depended upon him. Although remaining the upholder of old traditions, Golaud would bend a bit as he faced the needs of dependents and not permit them to sink into the abyss of dire poverty and hunger.

This is the sort of solution FDR could hope for in domestic matters. At the same time, as he faced the domestic challenge of the Great Depression, he found unusually propitious circumstances for improving relations with Latin America, the sort of region from which poor abused and bewildered refugees, real-life Mélisande types, had sometimes sought escape in the United States, only to find gruff, even abusive, new masters.

Meantime, as the Great Depression tightened its grip Latin Americans within their home countries showed an increasing desire to terminate their forced hemispheric marriage with the Yankee colossus. Increasingly the Latin bride in coerced or what had initially seemed advantageous unions began to interest herself in new suitors in far-off lands. Some of these promised all kinds of previously unknown bliss: bliss to be found in houses built according to the blueprints of socialism, whether of the national or Marxian variety. If he hoped to maintain the old marriage, the Yankee Golaud had to change his ways.

Before moving on to read into my second opera, *Wozzeck,* meanings that may shed light on the Good Neighbor era, I want to squeeze some final meanings out of *Pelléas et Mélisande.* First, I want to emphasize anew that Golaud can be seen as the upholder of traditional values, a person who is kindly so long as he is obeyed, so long as the values he incarnates are not challenged; but, he can resort to bullying and brutal vengeance when those values are challenged. Thus his initial kindness, patience, and forbearance with Mélisande and Pelléas give way to terrible retribution when they appear to challenge his entire corpus of traditional values. This is what happens when Mélisande, either in her *grande innocence* or in her wanton sexuality (depending on what particular stage directors and protagonists feel about the matter), rewards Golaud's kindness by entangling Pelléas in her snares.

In a way Roosevelt's secretary of state Cordell Hull, who although often thwarted in his designs by rival foreign affairs advisers did set many of the Good Neighbor policy's parameters, can be seen as a Golaud-like defender of traditional mores. Kindly when operating within the guidelines of the traditional, free-enterprise, free-trade capitalist order and when interacting with people who essentially respected and abided by the tenets of that order, he could turn livid and reveal a dreadful temper when confronting those who spurned or questioned the underlying validity of his own cherished moral universe.

There were other Americans, however, for whom the Great Depression experience fundamentally undermined faith in the old order, in the Protestant Ethic as revered by Hull, and in the bourgeois set of values so often assumed in the past to have emerged out of that ethic. Often those Americans most alienated from the old order thought of discarding traditional restraints, among them sexual restraints, and adopting a more uninhibited approach to life. After all, the old inhibitions had not worked in the way the Protestant Ethic had posited: they had resulted not in ongoing progress and development, but in a crunching economic catastrophe that threatened to sweep aside the old economic system and in the process annihilate the values that had girded that system. So, why not think of starting anew, of seeking renewal through the liberation of that great drive of renewal, the sexual urge? In this frame of mind, Americans could identify and sympathize with Latin Americans, prevailingly dismissed by traditional Yankee Protestant moralists as uninhibited perpetual teenagers in their refusal to place adult restrictions on their libidos. In this frame of mind, too, rebellious Americans intent on fashioning a counterculture would have cheered on the Pelléas-Mélisande infatuation and wasted no sympathy on Golaud.

In the course of this book, we shall encounter many Americans—men and women as well—who dreamed of liberation not necessarily from the old sexual taboos but certainly from the sort of channeling of the libido into the pursuit of private wealth as commanded by the Protestant Ethic. Sumner Welles, who as a close personal friend of the president's and as an under secretary of state helped shape the Good Neighbor policy, was a person of private means who saw little need to channel the libido into the pursuit of additional private wealth. And, when it came to hemispheric policy, so far as he was concerned much more was involved than the defense of hard-bitten, rough-edged Yankee capitalists. If the Latins sometimes acted as star-struck teenagers in the Pelléas and Mélisande mode, let them have their fun. Bisexual and something of a hedonist himself, Welles brought to his evaluation of Latin American affairs an entirely different perspective than Hull's. I rather fancy that if he had seen the opera, Welles would have sympathized with the two youthful protagonists. Hull, in the unlikely event he'd have been able to sit through a performance, would have identified with Golaud. Or so I would imagine. In any event, on matters we can document, such as the shaping of Latin American policy, Hull and Welles seldom saw eye to eye as they contemplated people living in a largely precapitalist milieu.

And what of FDR? Where did he come down on the Hull-Welles face-off? Or, to put it another way, would his sympathies have lain with Golaud as the militant defender of the old system, or with the two teenagers who shattered his tranquility? Well, that would have depended on what day or what hour of the day one happened to catch the president. At times as he heeded the advice of Welles he would have identified with the teenage fecklessness of Pelléas and Mélisande and with Latin Americans in their stereotyped guise of perpetual adolescents ready to thumb their noses at the stuffy and the traditional. At other times, he would have identified with Hull and Golaud in defending the old order. At such times, he would have looked upon the Latins as utterly irresponsible and much in need of the firm hand. Bipolar if not multipolar, incapable of being a single- or simple-minded bigot, always beset by inner dissensions and positively exulting in them, FDR needed men about him to champion each of the poles that attracted him. No wonder Latin Americans, even as the American public, were at times confused. And the president thrived on their confusion.

Briefly, now, I turn to the second opera. In its own and distinct way, *Wozzeck* proved prophetic in depicting how a traditional, bourgeois power structure had grown inhuman and, in its inhumanity, produced a mass of suffering underlings actually far more human than the callous creatures who controlled and manipulated society. At the same time the opera delivered, by implication at least, an appeal for the sort of changes in society that would elevate and reward the victims and punish their oppressors. Here was a theme that many Germans could take to heart in the troubled days of the Weimar Republic when the opera premiered in Berlin in 1925. A handful of years later, here was a theme that many Americans, even though never having heard of *Wozzeck,* could take to heart. In the midst of a Depression that cast doubt on the capabilities if not the moral vision of the leading classes, Americans could sympathize more than ever with those whom they regarded as the innocent victims of an oppressive and dehumanizing power structure.

Often described as the first great truly modern opera, with music tending consistently toward the atonal rather than the melodic, *Wozzeck* explores the notion that in a brutalized, materialistic society the social outcast, the marginalized being, the misfit who not only is down and out but whose whole personality borders on what conventional souls consider insanity, is actually the only sort of person who is decent, humane, and sane. In the 1960s, British psychiatrist R. D. Laing attracted considerable notoriety by advancing this thesis.

*Wozzeck* reflects the fact that whenever conventional bourgeois society begins to founder, to show signs of serious malaise, then those persons once dismissed as losers, as marginal—whether mentally or economically—suddenly begin to appear not so abnormal after all. Indeed, when a once flourishing society show signs of collapse, then that society's oppressed underlings replace the power wielders as heroes; for it is the power wielders who seem to bear responsibility for the collapse. At such a time dreamers in great profusion emerge, predicting a new order in which the previously reviled will become the focus of attention and solicitude, in which the last shall be first.

So long as the American capitalist system had flourished, its beneficiaries and directors had consigned persons who failed to flourish to the ranks of marginal humanity. Marginal, presumably barely human persons, as defined by the prospering sectors, included not only the poor and ne'er-do-wells in general but certain groups defined by their race or ethnicity: American Indians, African Americans, and to the south the vast majority of Latin America's populace—especially its dark-skinned Indian, African, and mestizo-mulatto masses.

Then, the Depression struck. Suddenly the revising of old assumptions and attitudes became the order of the day. As Americans under Roosevelt began to reassess their evaluations of winners and losers, now that the old-time winners seemed to have thrown the entire system into disarray and despair, traditionally poverty-stricken groups within the United States itself and indeed within the entire American hemisphere came in for re-evaluation.

Against this background, the Good Neighbor policy came into being. But for the Depression, Americans could not have learned to empathize with the hemisphere's losers, the poor, the dark-of-skin, the primitive. But for the Depression, the vast majority of them could not have opened their hearts to the sort of perplexed and bewildered souls that Pelléas and Mélisande personify, or to the afflicted beings symbolized by Wozzeck. Nor, in real life, could they have begun to reevaluate the comparative merits of winners and losers, whether in America itself or in the entire American hemisphere. Under the new set of circumstances people once assumed to be backward and even perhaps mentally deficient emerged as the innocent, childlike victims of unjust oppressors. Americans could say to the dispossessed, both in their midst and in Latin America as well: blessed be your backwardness, which attests to the innocence you have preserved.

America's Great Depression, though, was double-edged in the attitudes it encouraged toward marginalized people on the part of those who stood—or had until very recently stood—among the accommodated and privileged sectors. Faced with diminishing prospects of their own, some of these latter persons thought only of clinging to what resources they still possessed and grew more hostile than ever to seeing their government share diminishing resources with "wastrels," whether in their midst or south of the border. And they justified such hard-heartedness by resorting to old clichés and repeating old stereotypes about the moral failure that allegedly underlay economic failure. In this, they resembled the Doctor in *Wozzeck,* who is cruelly scornful of the poor demented Everyman whom Berg made the hero of his opera.

Throughout the Great Depression and the era of the Good Neighbor, many Americans refused to be neighborly with fellow citizens. Even more adamantly they refused to be neighborly with Latin Americans, although they might find enjoyable distraction in light-hearted Latin rhythms or movies set south of the border, just as they found amusement in dim-witted, stereotyped blacks as conveyed by the white actors who created the popular radio-drama duo Amos 'n' Andy. Throughout the Good Neighbor era, many accommodated Americans resented keenly social assistance programs that in their view portended the redistribution of money within the United States or the sharing, in however niggardly a manner, of American resources with the hard-pressed governments of Latin America. To these Americans, their fellow citizens caught up in hard times and Latin Americans in general represented feckless Pelléas and Mélisande types or, even worse, mental defectives and moral degenerates of the Wozzeck sort. Any soft-heartedness toward them smacked of weak-minded do-goodism, and perhaps also of communism or some other variety of un-American thought.

In urging Americans to act more neighborly with each other, and even with Latin Americans, FDR played to a mixed audience and would have had to proceed with caution even had he himself not so often been of two minds. When it came, however, to helping anyone who was disadvantaged, his wife Eleanor was never of two minds. Even to the point of recklessness that might threaten a system's economic security, she would help the person in want. And this brings me to my final topic for this section: Eleanor attends *Simon Boccanegra*.

Not until recent times have *Pelléas et Mélisande* and *Wozzeck* become popular among American opera goers. In the early-to-mid 1930s, however, with the Depression at its worst, they flocked to the Metropolitan Opera to hear a revival of Giuseppe Verdi's *Simon Boccanegra* with an all-star cast that featured Lawrence Tibbett in the title role. In many ways, the opera was appropriate for Depression-era America. It takes place in fourteenth-century Genoa, traditionally a rich maritime republic but suffering at the time from economic difficulties and rampant social discord. Whenever Tibbett sang the great aria toward the end of the first act begging Genoans to put aside their social dissension and unite for the country's well-being, he seldom failed to reduce sensitive persons to tears.

Either Eleanor Roosevelt knew opera or her aides chose wisely for her. As First Lady–elect, she attended a Metropolitan Opera performance of *Simon Boccanegra*. Between Acts I and II, just after Tibbett had sung the great aria, she appeared before the audience and stated: "When you come face to face with people in need, you simply have to try to do something about it. . . . After all, this is the richest country in the world. We cannot allow anyone to want for the bare necessities of life."[1]

Given her way, within the United States the First Lady might have spent even more than the country could afford to succor those in need. Generously disposed himself toward those in need, her husband was more cautious and also more realistic. He seldom underestimated the tenacity with which many privileged Americans clung to every penny that had rewarded, so they believed, their virtue; he never discounted their reluctance to share the fruits of alleged virtue with those whose misfortune sprang, supposedly, from moral shortcomings. Franklin Roosevelt knew he would have to proceed cautiously. In his own way, though, just as much as the First Lady, he hoped for an American rebirth.

Like the protagonist in *Simon Boccanegra,* a somber-hued opera in which the sea is constantly present in the background, FDR throughout his life remained enamored of, fascinated by, the ocean. Roosevelt's love and fascination must have sprung in part from a penchant to perceive the sea, like poets and artists since time immemorial, as a symbol of healing and regeneration. Like Verdi, who drew on sea symbolism to promise an eventual Risorgimento to an afflicted patria, FDR throughout his presidency drew on the sea to animate his hopes for an American Risorgimento or resurrection. Just like fourteenth-century Genoa's, America's resurrection would come in part from the sea, specifically from trade and commerce with those neighbors immediately to the south.

How stunningly fortuitous that Eleanor chose *Simon Boccanegra* for her visit to the opera, all the more so because in a way the opera could serve to underline the differences between the First Lady and her husband. Eleanor inclined toward the social and political romanticism, even millennialism, that shaped Verdi's hopes for Risorgimento as revealed not only in *Simon Boccanegra* but many other operas as well. For his part, as he looked forward to national regeneration, Franklin turned for inspiration to the realist from Florence, Machiavelli.

They were a formidable combination of opposites, Eleanor and Franklin, a veritable microcosm of the romantics and realists who did battle in the Depression era over how to revitalize not only the United States but the American hemisphere.

# 2. Depression: The New World's Great Equalizer

✧ ✧ ✧ ✧ ✧ ✧ ✧ ✧ ✧ ✧ ✧ ✧ ✧ ✧ ✧ ✧ ✧ ✧ ✧ ✧ ✧ ✧ ✧ ✧ ✧ ✧ ✧ ✧ ✧ ✧ ✧ ✧ ✧ ✧

For some eleven months in 1959 and 1960 while living in Chile I had my first immersion, in situ, in the culture of a Latin American country. What struck me above everything else that seemed novel was the wild diversity of opinion, the lack of consensus about national values. Newspapers afforded one example of this. Every day I read perhaps ten different dailies, each with totally different perceptions of the national reality, of aspirations for the future, and interpretations of the past. So many different outlets of the press and the publishing industry in general gave voice to so many outside-the-mainstream opinions that the novice gringo historian had to conclude that really there was no mainstream at all. Only in Chile did I become aware of just how much the mainstream to which the American press had accustomed me was something peculiar, in the New World hemisphere at least, to the United States.

Suddenly the American press of the Eisenhower consensus years to which I had grown accustomed began to seem bland, utterly without the tang of the Latin spices that sometimes clashed with each other but occasionally combined to produce a pleasing if totally undefinable flavor. It would take a while before it began to sink in that variety was not necessarily the spice of life, and that blandness is the reward of nation-states that have been most successful in approximating some at least temporary agreement as to the basic problems that afflict a broad array of the citizenry and the parameters within which government should approach those problems. Only later still did it become clear to me that one generation's approximation to solutions is likely to become unworkable for future generations and that nation-states have to work constantly to forge new sorts of consensus if they are to remain nation-states, with access to all the rewards that such status has made available at least to many peoples in the modern era.

Chile at the time I experienced it was coming unglued. Whatever sense of national cohesiveness might once have existed was disintegrating. Already the harbingers of the veritable civil war between left and right that would overtake the country late in the early 1970s were unmistakable. They were on display each day in the national press.

Up to mid-twentieth century, Chile may not ever have achieved anything approximating widespread, fundamental accord as to the underlying values that shaped and defined national identity, and as to the contrary values that most threatened that identity. But it had at various times in its past come close to that accord, and some of its old and yellowed newspapers (microfilm was not then much in use in its national library) reflected a near–national consensus. Indeed, in 1959 it seemed likely to me that many Latin American countries had never come even as close as Chile to forging a deep and enduring national consensus on what their citizenry should most seek, treasure, and preserve, and what values and aspirations they should most reject, discard, and stifle. Chauvinistically, perhaps, I began to speculate as follows: countries that had never achieved much success in advancing toward the indices by which "civilized" countries liked to measure success, indices that included political stability and steady economic advance and the knack for not allowing religious disagreements to spill over into civil strife, never came close to the best rewards that modern culture, however flawed it might be, had to offer.

Consensus on the main ingredients that comprise the national culture and civil religion, and agreement over just what characteristics attest both to national success and failure, are among the hallmarks of successful nation-states. This consensus is missing among countries that, animated by wildly conflicting visions of national goals and identity, have never achieved genuine nation-state status. Nevertheless, on some days back in the late '50s I found it difficult to decide whether Latin America's failure, as I saw it, to achieve consensus constituted a curse or a blessing.

Later, in Spain, I would discover that the great philosopher Miguel de Unamuno saw nationalism and national consensus in some ways as curses. Could people, he wondered, ever feel compelling loyalty, a willingness to sacrifice personal, individual interests, to anything so nebulous as the nation-state? Unamuno doubted they could. He took pride in the strong sense of devotion to family, to region, and to corporate entities that animated Spaniards, so he believed, and made them more willing to sacrifice claims to individual ego satisfaction than citizens of "advanced" countries who defined themselves in terms of membership in that over-arching reality called the nation-state.

Faced with the Great Depression, Americans became less certain about an overarching sense of national identity. In compensation, they retreated into perhaps more profound identification with familial and local and corporate or functional-interest-group values; as they became less caught up in the nebulous demands of and responsibilities to national well-being, they became more capable of ego-effacing actions that served the cause of something more immediate than the nation-state. Did they become better or worse people as a result, better or worse citizens? Unamuno surely would have found much to commend in America's Depression-era reassessment of values.

FDR, as was his wont, hedged. Why did Americans have to decide at all, he might well have wondered, between two approaches to life? Americans should be able to intensify loyalty to smaller entities than the nation-state *and* to the nation-state as well. In many respects, providing Americans with two opposing options was what the New Deal was all about. One of these options was to conform at least a bit to the premodern, pre-nationalist values that Unamuno treasured in the Iberian world—both in the Iberian peninsula and in Ibero-America.

Confronting the Great Depression's assault on national prosperity in the 1930s, Americans did become in some ways more like Latin Americans. A people of plenty (to borrow the title that David Potter gave to a splendid book on national character), whose national consensus had generally been held together by the plentitude of their economic security, suddenly faced an economic calamity of such magnitude as to call into question the way in which they and their ancestors had believed and acted. Suddenly the jeremiads that self-styled prophets had been issuing since literally the birth of Britain's New World colonies took on the ring of genuine prophecy. The Jeremiahs out of the American past had warned their countrypersons that unless they changed their ways they faced catastrophe.

As the Depression tightened its grip on American life, Jeremiahs appeared from sea to shining sea, each explaining why it was that the once proud nation had been humbled and each proferring advice on which sins of the past to discard in order to reap future rewards, whether material or spiritual.

Virtually every geographic section of America, every interest group, and every political, religious, and ideological camp, produced its own prophets, detailing why things had gone wrong and what must be done to set them right. Each prophet was likely to produce his or her own pamphlets, bulletins, and even newspapers; many had access to radio stations

Anton Refregier, *Mine Accident,* between 1938 and 1940, woodcut, image: 9 ×
12 in. Gift of Dr. and Mrs. Corbin S. Carnell, in memory of E. Muriel Adams.
Collection of the Harn Museum of Art, University of Florida. 1992.11.175
*No longer reviled as victims of their own vices, the poor and the afflicted come
increasingly to be perceived as victims of a savage capitalist system.*

and church pulpits. To live in the United States with the bombardment of
wildly diverse diagnoses of malaise and prescriptions for cures had become in a way like it was to live in Chile at the end of the 1950s, or in
most Latin American countries at virtually any time in their historical past.

Early in the 1930s historian Herbert Eugene Bolton had advanced the
thesis that Americans and Latin Americans had a common history and a
common destiny. The Bolton thesis, it has always seemed to me, was
largely without merit as a tool for analyzing the historical past of the republics of the Americas. However, as of the early 1930s, Americans of the
North and the South did indeed seem to be involved in the common destiny of seeking institutions and policies, whether social, political, economic, or spiritual, that would point them toward the path to stability and
security. And most agreed that, Unamuno to the contrary notwithstanding, the nation-state and nationalistic devotion to it were objectives worth

pursuing, even though in the immediate future less grandiose entities might elicit the citizen's primary concern.

For arguably the first time in the hemisphere's history the United States and Latin America had become immersed in a common culture: the culture of economic adversity. And where economic adversity prevailed, could social instability be far behind? As one perceptive American put the matter as he contemplated the possibilities of a nation in decline in the early 1990s: "Are we still a society, even if we are no longer an economy?"[1] With a far greater sense of urgency, Americans on both sides of the border faced this question in the 1930s.

When EuroDisneyland opened near Paris in 1992, novelist Jean-Marie Rouart grimly warned: "If we do not resist it, the kingdom of profit will create a world that will have all the appearance of civilization and all the savage reality of barbarism."[2] In Depression-era America, the country's intellectuals found it easier than ever before to convince a broad cross section of the public that those tycoons dedicated to the pursuit of the kingdom of profit had indeed created a reality of barbarism. Latin American intellectuals, rightists and leftists alike, had been saying the same for at least two or three generations; in fact, this was the closest those intellectuals could come to consensus.

The common ground that American and Latin American intellectuals found in condemning business civilization was just one indication of a hemispheric convergence in the 1930s. Without that convergence, there could have been no Good Neighbor policy. And this meant that when the convergence ended, so—in many ways, at least—would the Good Neighbor policy. At the very least, much of that policy's general gentleness would decline. When Americans returned to the national identity of a people of plenty, when they resumed, at least to their own satisfaction, their ever-upward ascent toward political and economic grandeur even as Latin America seemed to them to remain largely prostrate in its lingering social, economic, and political malaise, then the Good Neighbor policy in its full panoply could exist no more.

# 3.

## Depression in America's Cities, Depression in the Countryside, and a Rapprochement with Latin America

❖ ❖ ❖ ❖ ❖ ❖ ❖ ❖ ❖ ❖ ❖ ❖ ❖ ❖ ❖ ❖ ❖ ❖ ❖ ❖ ❖ ❖ ❖ ❖ ❖ ❖ ❖ ❖ ❖ ❖ ❖ ❖ ❖ ❖ ❖

### Portents of Disaster in America's Cities

Visitors arriving by train to most large American cities in the early 1930s might well have felt they were traveling in a Third World country—even though that specific terminology had not yet come into use. They alighted from the train virtually in the midst of hoboes, warming themselves by fires as they sought shelter in makeshift quarters in or near the switch-yards. Nearby, hundreds might await their turn in breadlines or in front of soup kitchens or before unemployment offices. Visible to any discerning eye were the hungry who combed through garbage dumps or who waited outside restaurants and hospitals hoping for handouts. Everywhere in evidence were panhandlers and beggars, of the sort American visitors to Mexico and other Latin American countries had once complained about even as they assumed their country was somehow immune from such annoyance. This smugness vanished in the 1930s. American beggars might be more embarrassed and less importunate and include fewer children than their south-of-the-border counterparts. Nevertheless, they had become an inescapable fact of urban life. So had the homeless.

American visitors to the lands below the border once habitually commented on the backward conditions that forced armies of the destitute to cluster under the one shelter they could find: highway bridges. But now those backward conditions appeared in America itself. A Chicagoan observed, "You can ride across the lovely Michigan Avenue bridge at mid-

Harold Faye, *Old Apartment House,* between 1935 and 1939, lithograph, image:
11¾ × 14⅞ in. Gift of Dr. and Mrs. Corbin S. Carnell, in memory of E. Muriel
Adams. Collection of the Harn Museum of Art, University of Florida. 1992.11.48
*Not only in Latin America but in the Depression-gripped United States desolation
and destitution lurked beneath magnificent bridges.*

night," while lights all around made a "dreamy city of incomparable
beauty." At the same time twenty feet below, "on the lower level of the
same bridge, are 2,000 homeless, decrepit, shivering and starving men,
wrapping themselves in old newspapers to keep from freezing, and lying
down in manure dust to sleep."[1]

When visiting Haiti during the World War I era in connection with his
duties as assistant secretary of the Navy, the young Franklin Delano
Roosevelt had observed scenes of destitution and starvation. In 1939,
viewing a special White House showing of *The Fight for Life,* a film that
Pare Lorentz had just completed based in part on Paul de Kruif's book of
the same title, Roosevelt the president had the chance to observe Haiti-
like scenes filmed in Chicago. One scene was shot against the Chicago
Maternity Center, established before the turn of the century in the city's
slums. In front of the hospital Lorentz's camera caught the faces of mothers on relief, lined up to receive life-sustaining handouts for themselves

and their families. Nor did Lorentz spare the president the sight of Chicagoans scavenging for food in garbage piles.[2]

No more adequate than the Michigan Avenue bridge was the shelter to which other down-and-out Americans were reduced, and about which the president and his wife learned through reports submitted by the corps of private observers they had sent into the American heartland to report on its plight. In St. Louis armies of the destitute lived in "refuse dumps along the river." Here they built shacks and dug in the dump for food. Visiting the dump in Youngstown, Ohio, a journalist reported that in the stench of decaying garbage he found "more women than men—gathering food for their families." However, neither begging, panhandling, soup kitchens, nor restaurants or hospitals willing to share scraps with the indigent, not even garbage dumps, sufficed to save some Americans from starvation. *Fortune* magazine conceded that starvation had become a factor in certain cases of urban mortality.[3]

Urban blight had once been associated with Bombay, India, or with Mexico City or virtually any other large urban center in Latin America. Now it spread in the American heartland. City after city suffered from a lack of money; and municipal fiscal impoverishment became "a cancer that ate away at the cityscape itself. Building virtually ceased, and slums spread into previously respectable areas. The construction of residential property declined by 95 percent from 1928 to 1933."[4] How it must have grated on their sensibilities for Americans with income enough for travel in the 1930s to have to concede that Buenos Aires, Santiago, or Rio de Janeiro in many respects appeared in better repair than any number of cities back home.

Only yesterday Americans had been assured by President Herbert Hoover that, thanks to the wonders of the free-enterprise system, they stood on the threshold of banishing poverty. Now with municipal and state governments facing financial collapse, they placed their last good hope in massive federal government intervention, precisely the sort of social and economic intervention to which they had tended in the past to attribute Latin America's chronic underdevelopment. Only yesterday Americans had scorned the ineptitude that, so they assumed, lay behind Latin America's unemployment and underemployment. Now they had occasion to wonder about themselves, about the entire economic, social, and political system they had created. From all walks of life men and women across the country wondered if the American system teetered on the edge of total breakdown.

Americans had once associated bank closings with the primitive economies of Latin America, with ingrained Latin economic fecklessness and deviousness. Not so long ago they had applauded as giants of American finance, with State Department encouragement, moved to try to straighten out the financial morass of Central America and the Caribbean and as they dispatched missions to help even the relatively advanced countries of South America put their banking structures in order. But now, as President Hoover prepared to surrender his office to the newly elected Roosevelt, banks in the United States had closed their doors or were about to do so. The first closing occurred in Nevada in October 1932, and others soon followed. Early the following March as the country prepared for FDR's inauguration "all remaining states declared their banks officially closed."[5] How could it be, many an American must have wondered, that virtually overnight their country had undergone Latin Americanization? How foolish now seemed all those turn-of-the-century dreams about extending a beneficent American sway over Latin America so as to uplift those unfortunate enough to reside south of the border.

When FDR took the oath of office in March of 1933, nearly fifteen million people, comprising one-fourth of the labor force, were unemployed. National income "was half what it had been in 1928." The banks soon began to reopen, and some economic confidence returned to the country, but conditions remained grim. "Across the nation, a million Americans in broken shoes were on the move, 200,000 of them children." On average, some fifteen hundred vagrants passed daily through Kansas City alone. Across the nation internal migrants, many of them boys and girls, "moved from town to town, from state to state, . . . from door to door, seeking a meal, shelter for the night, a day's—even an hour's work." For a time after the new administration took over, the economy showed some signs of being on the mend. But in March of 1938 Americans faced a new economic dip, with national unemployment hovering around 20 percent as the stock market again plummeted.[6]

Americans, on the whole, had long assumed the existence of the undeserving poor—of people, that is, who because of their bad habits and perhaps their genetic flaws deserved to be poor. If such people existed in America, they existed by the droves in Latin America, or so smug Americans assumed. In the years following the First World War, more and more Americans assumed they could solve the problem within their own country by reducing immigration while at the same time introducing programs of eugenics that would keep the poor, especially the presumably racially inferior African American poor, from reproducing so profligately. What Americans found it hard to accept in the 1930s was that now some of the country's apparently most deserving citizens had fallen into poverty. Indeed, those Americans who just possibly suffered the most (psychologically, at least) during the Depression years were "middle-aged white-collar workers, men and women, who had played the game according to the rules."[7] Now they were out of work, their security suddenly gone.

No longer was virtue a guarantee of security. There must be something

Don Freeman, *Money Magnet*, 1936, lithograph, image: 9⅜ × 7⅞ in. Gift of Dr. and Mrs. Corbin S. Carnell, in memory of E. Muriel Adams. Collection of the Harn Museum of Art, University of Florida. 1992.11.49
*The impoverished man "fishing" for coins that have fallen beneath a sidewalk grate is depicted with far greater empathy than the haughty and affluent passerby.*

unfair about the system, even about life itself. Possibly, just possibly, prosperity was not a sign of virtue, of God's approbation, and possibly poverty was not a badge of vice and of God's scorn. The gritty survivors of an unfair system, whether economic and social or even theological, deserved respect—whether they lived in America or in Latin America. If the fault lay in the economic and social system, some of Latin America's anti-Yankee intellectuals and populist politicians perhaps deserved to be taken seriously. They had been in the forefront of critics alleging that by its very nature America's capitalist system gouged and shortchanged and exploited not only dusky-skinned Latins caught in the tentacles of expanding imperialism but American underlings as well. Perhaps it was time that American and Latin American populists and progressives and Marxists and radicals of every stripe joined forces.

Black writer Richard Wright, who like many African Americans toyed with communism in the 1930s, produced his first masterpiece, *Native Son*, in 1940. The novel's central character is Bigger Thomas. As Wright saw him, Bigger "was not black all the time; he was white, too, and there were literally millions of him everywhere." In America there was "a vast, muddied pool of life," composed of people of all colors so hopelessly mired in poverty that they could never realistically hope to escape its clutches.[8] In Wright's analysis, one that came in the Depression era to be shared by a broad array of Americans of all skin color, lurks an implication of vast importance to hemispheric relations. When it came to socioeconomic, and perhaps even moral and religious indices, many a Caucasian American began to think the unthinkable: we American Caucasians are not so distinctive in our whiteness, in our national identity; we all share in the plight of the underprivileged; we are all of us as the black and the brown; we are all of us as the Latin American.

### Rural Blight in America

Not just in the disintegration of urban civilization but in the blight that descended over their farmlands, Americans found occasion to doubt the chosen-people assumptions that had so long prevailed. Rural America, not yet altogether removed from the pristine nature that according to frontier mythology had always provided Americans the opportunity for renewal, to be born anew and thus to remain different and a breed apart from ordinary mortals, suddenly became as hostile as the economically collapsing cities. No longer could Americans delude themselves about a frontier that would save them. The frontier, or what was left of it, was no longer the solution; it had become part of the problem. This fact could only have contributed to a national perception, whether acknowledged or lurking somewhere just beneath the level of full consciousness, that Americans were not altogether distinct from those Latin Americans whose rich farmlands had somehow produced chronic losers rather than winners in modernity's sweepstakes.

More movingly perhaps than any other author, John Steinbeck in his 1939 novel *The Grapes of Wrath* described the plight of American farmers on the move from Dust Bowl disaster in the nation's farming heartland to California. However, even in the Golden State they failed to find adequate opportunities for starting anew. Meantime, though, America's farm-sector losers had replaced losers from south of the border, who until the Depression struck had provided California's and the entire Southwest's farm sector with its steady supply of migratory workers. Now, in the 1930s, down-on-their-luck Americans sought opportunities to do what Mexicans and Central Americans had done in California and neighboring states, or what immigrants from the Caribbean had done in Florida. In the rural sector, Americans and Latin Americans had become interchangeable as migratory laborers.[9] Once more the proud Anglo-Saxon people of plenty had to face the possibility that they were—some of them, at least—as the black and the brown, and as the Latin American. No longer did a sacred hierarchy necessarily assure them a higher place than that of traditionally disparaged underlings from below the border.

Whether the victims of the Dust Bowl catastrophe or other types of disaster, farmers were driven to seek federal succor. Through 1934 and 1935, federal relief funds sustained more than two-and-a-half million residents of Oklahoma, Arkansas, Missouri, and Texas. By the end of 1936, more than half of the rural families in these states were on relief. And not even the assistance received from the Agricultural Adjustment Administration or the Farm Credit Administration or the Resettlement Administration could salve their pride or restore their confidence.[10]

Many down-and-out rural Americans appear in the haunting photographs assembled by the Resettlement Administration/Farm Security Administration and published in, among other books, Archibald MacLeish's 1938 volume *Land of the Free*. An outstanding poet whom FDR appointed Librarian of Congress in 1939, MacLeish sought to present in his book "a series of pictures which will portray the people left behind after the empire builders have taken the forests, the ore, and the top soil." Not very subtly, MacLeish questioned the extreme individualism in which Americans once took pride. That individualism, as MacLeish and so many other observers of Depression-era America saw it, had produced not only ecological disaster but human disaster, not only in the farmland but in the cities as well. Along with earth stripped of its topsoil, America now had to reckon with way-of-life farmers who, with their families, were "ill fed, ill clothed, ill housed," and in need of federal assistance. In the illustrations of numerous books in addition to MacLeish's briskly selling volume Americans could find graphic, moving testimony to the victims of a heartland turned spiteful. Nor was the testimony confined to books. Resettlement Administration/Farm Security Administration photographs were featured in mass circulation magazines and newspapers and exhibited in

Mac Raboy, *Migratory Workers,* between 1935 and 1939, color woodcut, image:
6¹³⁄₁₆ × 10⅞ in. Gift of Dr. and Mrs. Corbin S. Carnell, in memory of E. Muriel
Adams. Collection of the Harn Museum of Art, University of Florida. 1992.11.118
*Not only for African-American sharecroppers in the South, but for white yeoman
farmers in the West, once hailed as the backbone of the nation, grinding poverty
had become a way of life.*

various museums throughout the land. They suggested the existence of a
people who faced not just a momentary defeat but absolute disaster.[11]

With the relief checks that farmers began to receive came "the humiliating realization that . . . America had a new dependent class. Nature's
bombardment during the mid thirties sent many a western farmer running
for the nearest fiscal foxhole, desperately seeking aid from any and all
sources."[12] Traditionally, Americans had looked down upon the hordes of
dependent peoples who—at least in Yankee stereotypes—had always constituted a good percentage of the Latin American population. Now Americans had themselves become dependent. And, even as Latin America's
privileged classes throughout their history, the minority of the Depression-
era privileged Americans who managed to preserve status and wealth
throughout the crisis years looked down on their fellow citizens sunk in
dependency, whether in the cities or in the farm belt.

In California and in Texas, Americans who managed to retain at least
a toehold in the status of privilege began to refer to the hordes of struggling farm laborers, whether local in origin or migrants from nearby

states, as *Texicans*.[13] Much of the ethnic-cultural prejudice that lay behind traditional hatred of Mexicans in the American Southwest was encapsulated in the word Texicans; and that hatred now was directed toward fellow Americans who had lost out in the struggle for individual security, dignity, and independence. The losers in the great American drama were no better than Latinos. Like Latin Americans throughout their history, North Americans now made it a point to distinguish between the *gente decente* (decent people) and those who constituted a *mala raza* (a bad race or breed).

Perhaps, though, the mala raza in the United States would be less quiescent than its Latin American counterpart. North Americans seemed ill inclined to look upon their misfortune as the will of God and to bow their heads resignedly to the divine scheme. Not even in Mexico, for that matter, had exploited rural sectors remained stoic, as the revolutionary events touched off in 1910 seemed to prove. Now the revolutionary spark threatened to ignite a social conflagration among American farmers. In 1932 midwestern farmers laid plans for a protest meeting in Washington. They climbed into their jalopies and headed for the capital. Along the way they received food and lodging from the Salvation Army and a variety of church groups "as well as from unions and the Communist-inspired Unemployed Councils." In Washington, they called for "a moratorium on mortgages, interest, taxes, and indebtedness for marginal farmers." And they demanded an end to evictions. In many instances they and those who cheered them on, even as their populist ancestors of the 1890s, blamed capitalism and unfettered economic individualism for their plight.[14] Capitalism was no longer sacrosanct in the United States.

Just as Latin Americans had tended to blame exploitive Yankee capitalism for their difficulties, so Americans from the agricultural South and West, joined in many instances by the urban indigent whose ranks seemed to grow by the month, blamed Wall Street, the bankers, the captains of industry for their plight. In a way, they were blaming free-enterprise capitalism itself for the divisions that had appeared between the self-styled decent people and those whom the decent dismissed as a bad breed of men, women, and children.

As struggling Americans saw the situation, the source of their trouble lay in an amorphous region that they termed the "North." Historian Walter Prescott Webb caught this spirit when in his 1937 book *Divided We Stand: The Crisis of a Frontierless Democracy* he charged the North with having gained undisputed command over the rest of the American nation. "At the present time the North owns 80 or 90 percent of the wealth of the United States." The North had perfected industrial capitalism, and this fact had enabled it to exploit and indeed to colonize, economically, the rest of the country.[15] Webb spoke for many Americans outside of the metropolis, outside of the North, when he blamed it for the problems of the periphery. His charges were interchangeable with those that ever so many Latin Americans had for half a century or so raised against the land that to them represented the North: the United States. The anticapitalist, anti-North virus that had since colonial times seldom existed at less than epidemic proportions among the Latins had now swept northward and found a propitious environment among Americans undergoing the novel experience of impoverishment. Behind the Good Neighbor spirit about to make inroads both north and south of the border lay the ongoing Latin Americanization of the United States.

# 4. Americans Reassess Capitalism and the Hemisphere

❖ ❖ ❖ ❖ ❖ ❖ ❖ ❖ ❖ ❖ ❖ ❖ ❖ ❖ ❖ ❖ ❖ ❖ ❖ ❖ ❖ ❖ ❖ ❖ ❖ ❖ ❖ ❖ ❖ ❖ ❖ ❖

## Americans Lose Faith in American Capitalism

Accepting the Republican Party's presidential nomination in 1928, Herbert Hoover referred to the nation's "magnificent progress" during the past eight years, attributing it to the "fundamental correctness of our economic system." He went on to associate American success with the "high sense of moral responsibility in our business world." Hoover conceded that Americans had not yet achieved the full panoply of economic success they coveted for their nation, but they were getting closer. If the nation persevered with the policies shaped since 1921 by Republican administrations, then "we shall soon, with the help of God, be in sight of the day when poverty will be banished from this nation." Less than two years after his acceptance speech came the stock market collapse that presaged the Great Depression. Not long after that, President Hoover observed: "The only trouble with capitalism is capitalists. They are too damned greedy."

Greed was not the only problem. When Hoover summoned business leaders to a White House conference on the crisis, it became increasingly evident that they were "as bankrupt of ideas and as demoralized as the President himself." Throughout the land, more and more Americans came to the conclusion that business leaders had destroyed capitalism through a combination of greed and stupidity. If anything historian-journalist Claude Bowers, who would serve as American ambassador to Spain and to Chile during the New Deal, understated the matter when he wrote that the national economic collapse disillusioned average Americans "about the superhuman wisdom of the great financiers."[1]

Even the apologists of industrialism had to admit, according to a band of southern intellectuals who called themselves the Agrarians, that economic evils followed inevitably in the wake of machines. The evils included overproduction, unemployment, and a growing inequality in the distribution of wealth. Leaving aside for the moment the critique of capitalism expressed by the growing number of American communists and socialists of one stripe or another, many an observer of the American scene found the southern intellectuals too mild in their critique of the country's business society. In his influential and widely read 1937 book *America's Sixty Families*, Ferdinand Lumberg, a one-time financial reporter for the *New York Herald Tribune*, brought a new urgency to the old populist-muckraking tradition of excoriating the affluent business class. America, he charged, was owned and dominated by a "hierarchy of its sixty richest families, buttressed by no more than ninety families of lesser wealth." Outside this charmed circle of plutocracy, "perhaps three hundred and fifty other families" accounted for "most of the incomes of $100,000 or more that do not accrue to the members of the inner circle." Essentially, a mere sixty families comprised the "living center of modern industrial oligarchy" in America. They functioned discreetly "under a *de jure* democratic form of government behind which a *de facto* government is actually the government of the United States—informal, invisible, shadowy. It is the government of money in a dollar democracy."[2]

Lumberg was only the most effective and the most recent in a long line of crusaders against the perceived inequities of American capitalism— inequities that now loomed especially large because of the social and economic catastrophes that its *de facto* rulers had brought to the country. From the late nineteenth century onward, investigative reporters and so-called muckraking novelists—some of them persons of genuine literary eminence such as Upton Sinclair, Sinclair Lewis, Frank Norris, and Theodore Dreiser—had created a growth industry out of exposés of American capitalism's rotten core; and more than a few of those who excelled in the genre had waxed romantic and misty-eyed as they beheld the new social experiments of the 1920s in the Soviet Union.

If exposés, whether legitimate or propagandistic, of American tycoons helped sell books in the 1930s, they also helped sell tickets to the movies; and Hollywood moguls quickly learned this lesson. They turned out a rich offering of movies that attributed the undermining of American innocence to a cynical and corrupt alliance between politicians and businessmen. Typical of a new genre of film was *Corsair,* produced in 1931. Its not very subtly conveyed message was that in the American rush for success, "it doesn't matter how you make your money, it's how much you have when you quit." Piracy and American capitalism were one and the same. Very much in the new Hollywood spirit were Frank Capra's *An American Madness*, released in 1932, and his smash hit of 1936, *Mr. Deeds Goes to Town*. The first depicted the directors of a small-town bank as greedy capitalists who placed their own personal ambitions above the interests of depositors. The second dealt with what had already become Hollywood stock figures: greedy politicians and amoral capitalists on one hand, the heroic and virtuous poor on the other.[3]

Similar stereotyping found its way into the 1932 song "I Don't Want Your Millions, Mister," written by Kentucky union activist Jim Garland. The song concerns a down-and-out laborer who doesn't want the rich man's Rolls Royce or his pleasure yacht; all he wants is food for his children. He and his fellow laborers worked to build their country, while the rich enjoyed their lives of ease, and stole all that the workers built; so now the workers' children starve and freeze. It doesn't matter if the rich man calls the laborer green or blue or red; all that matters is food for the worker's children. Then there was the rhyme about Andrew Mellon (secretary of the treasury, 1921–1932) and Herbert Hoover presiding over a country that had become a derelict locomotive. Its gist was that Mellon pulled the whistle while Hoover rang the bell; and, with Wall Street giving the signal, the country went to hell.[4]

By no means was it just leftist literati and Hollywood movie makers and labor activists and humorous lampoonists who fomented and nourished suspiciousness of American capitalism. Already in 1912 Louisiana Representative Arsene Pujo, chairman of the House Committee on Banking and Commerce, had presided over an investigation that turned up considerable evidence about the dangerous extent to which the country's financial resources were concentrated in the hands of a few. Even conservative newspapers conceded "there was a potential danger in the growing consolidation of money and credit, and that it was up to the government to do something about it." Drawing on some of the Pujo Committee findings, Louis Brandeis in 1914 published his carefully documented *Other People's Money and How the Bankers Use It*. "We must," Brandeis concluded, "break the Money Trust or the Money Trust will break us."[5]

Americans failed to break the trust, and by the early 1930s the unpleasant alternative foreseen by Brandeis was at hand—or so an increasing army of Americans concluded, among them the Democratic president Franklin D. Roosevelt, who delighted in railing against the "economic royalists." Protestant theologian Reinhold Niebuhr warned that capitalism in its full maturity threatened to create a Marxian proletariat in America. Niebuhr saw little chance for social decency in his country so long as a business leadership class remained virtually unchallenged.[6]

In 1934 a new edition of Brandeis's *Other People's Money* appeared, and it became required reading for newly elected lawmakers as they launched fresh investigations of the sins of the capitalist class and the role of these sins in bringing on a national economic collapse. The principal investigation in 1934 was carried out by the Senate Banking and Currency Committee. New York attorney Ferdinand Pecora served as the committee's counsel, and because of his prominence in conducting the proceedings and the attention lavished upon his every utterance by the press, the investigation came to be known as the Pecora hearings.

In the course of the hearings "leading bankers admitted shocking breaches of ethics and exceedingly stupid decisions." As a result, businessmen sank to a new low in public esteem, and along with them the Republican presidents of the 1920s who had lavished such praise on the economic statesmanship of the masters of capital. At first not particularly interested in the Pecora hearings, which he feared might upstage some of his own pronouncements, President Roosevelt soon recognized a good thing and began to capitalize on the work of Pecora and the Senate investigators in trying to neutralize the opposition that business groups waged against most New Deal reform programs. In part because of the groundwork done by such respected figures as Pecora, Roosevelt was on safe ground when he charged the banking community with egregious errors of judgment and gross irresponsibility and when he castigated "that unfortunate decade" of the 1920s for its "mad chase for unearned riches and an unwillingness of leaders in almost every walk of life to look beyond their own schemes and speculations."[7]

## Declining Sympathy for American Business, Rising Empathy for Latin America

One particular piece of dirty business that the Pecora hearings brought to light was the degree to which U.S. bankers had resorted to bribery and other questionable means of persuasion to induce Latin American governments in the 1920s to contract huge loans: loans that because of total lack of planning could not have been expended wisely; loans that had no decent prospects of repayment should the slightest economic downturn develop. As more and more Latin American governments defaulted on loan repayments in the 1930s, the American public that had followed the highly publicized Pecora hearings decided that culpability lay not so much with the Latins as with Wall Street manipulators.

The sympathy for Latin Americans that developed among Americans informed as to Wall Street's nefariousness in hemispheric economic dealings contributed significantly to the early popularity of the Good Neighbor policy. Recognizing this fact, FDR found it expedient to devote more publicity to his new hemispheric policy, and to praise the Latins as good neighbors even as he excoriated American economic royalists as unworthy citizens set upon abusing not only laborers within the United States but also within any Latin American country where they operated. In particular the president went after Republican bankers in New York City, charging them with extortionate loans to Latin American governments.[8]

In his populist stance Roosevelt found an unlikely ally in the arch-isolationist from Montana, Sen. Burton K. Wheeler. Rather than on Wall Street capitalists, Wheeler blamed the impoverishment of his state and also to some degree the impoverishment of Chile on the machinations of Anaconda Copper. Any attempt of the Chileans to wrest more of the profits from Anaconda would meet with Wheeler's blessings. The U.S. Senate and House included many a person like Wheeler who thought the worst about American companies based in their states or precincts and were ready to curb those companies not only in their local operations but in their Latin American ventures as well. In many instances, the president of the United States stood ready to extend his blessings to Latin governments that sought to hold Yankee firms to higher accountability. The American electorate, he well understood, would approve his stance.

Another set of congressional hearings contributed further to the rapprochement between the United States and Latin America that the Pecora investigation had, indirectly at least, helped to initiate. Holding its hearings between September 1934 and April 1936, the Nye committee was chaired by Republican Senator Gerald P. Nye of North Dakota. A defender of heartland, agrarian America who had arrived in Washington wearing yellow shoes and sporting hair that looked as if a barber had used a bowl to shape it, and displaying an attention-grabbing distaste for industrialists and bankers as well as monopolies, chain stores, and the rich in general, Nye caught the public fancy in the Depression era. He proved a formidable isolationist propagandist, one the president had to take very seriously indeed.[9]

The Nye hearings churned up material seeming to indicate that American munitions makers, many of them locked into intimate relationships with European counterparts, had to some considerable extent been responsible for pressuring the United States into entering the World War against Germany. Thus Democratic President Woodrow Wilson's so-called crusade to make the world safe for democracy allegedly, in the final analysis, had been a war to make the world safe for the investments of a nefarious international cartel of munitions makers, the so-called "merchants of death." The Nye hearings, which rivaled those of Pecora for press attention, nourished American resolve never again to be drawn naively into crusades in Europe that were really crusades to swell the profits of American munitions makers and their overseas partners. Indeed, Senator

Nye's hearings played a crucial role in inspiring the Neutrality Act of 1935 that prohibited the sale of arms and munitions to any belligerent.

Pundit Walter Lippmann was among the many American internationalists who bitterly regretted the effectiveness of the Nye hearings in seducing Americans into the embrace of isolationism. Because Americans, with an all too effective nudge from Nye, had come to believe their entry into World War I had been manipulated by British propaganda and by U.S. bankers and munitions makers, they would steadfastly resist efforts to involve them anew in the affairs of the Old World—however much enlightened self-interest, to say nothing of high-minded international statesmanship, counseled participation in those affairs. So, at least, Lippmann feared; and events would prove his apprehension justified.

## Isolationism: The Monroe Doctrine Lives Anew

The Pecora hearings had helped arouse sympathy for Latin America, and the Nye investigations had encouraged an isolationist spirit vis-à-vis Europe. The two developments went hand in hand. To some considerable degree, American interest in Latin America that made possible the Good Neighbor era grew out of disillusionment with Europe and a desire to isolate not only the United States but all of the Americas from Old World contagion. Moreover, the Good Neighbor policy in its origins represented a return to one of the earliest themes of hemispheric policy as sounded by the 1823 Monroe Doctrine: America for the Americans.

A century plus a decade after it had first become a factor in shaping their country's foreign policy, Americans heartily reaffirmed the principle of America for the Americans. Because it arose out of deeply felt public conviction, the reaffirmation won firm backing from the president, a man who had a uniquely sensitive finger for testing the winds of public opinion. However, the reaffirmation did not necessarily sit well among Latin Americans. In particular, Argentines were suspicious. Most Argentine statesmen had always tended to look askance on the spirit of Monroeism. In fact, they had tried to counteract it with a "let America be for humanity" pronouncement, by which they implied their preference for close ties with the humanity of the Old World rather than with the presumptuous upstarts to the north who claimed the right to define the spirit of the New World. The renewed Monroeism implicit in America's revitalized isolationism cum hemispherism set Washington at odds with many an Argentine intellectual and statesman.

Already, then, from the very inception of what FDR proclaimed as a Good Neighbor era, Washington and Buenos Aires were on a collision course. As some south-of-the-border countries tended to line up with Buenos Aires rather than Washington, the Roosevelt administration would find it necessary to devise ever more conciliatory and also expensive devices to woo them into Washington's orbit. Many of these challenges, though, lay ahead. What mattered for the moment as a new administration took up the reins of power was that a good part of the politically aware American public was beginning to reassess traditional attitudes toward Latin America, beginning to view the Southerners as decent neighbors after all.

## Some Americans Begin to Reassess Latin Americans

Caught in the throes of a humbling economic crisis, many Americans had begun to lose confidence in their exceptionalism. Once they had disdainfully dismissed Latin Americans for their inability to solve economic and social problems and thereby attain development and political stability. Now Americans faced economic and social problems of their own that might well defy all their time-tested remedies; and they began to wonder just how revolution-proof their institutions actually were. Not just in Latin America but on many a U.S. Main Street there was speculation about revolution and dictatorship. Whereas a history of political and economic success confined largely to the region above the Rio Grande had driven gringos and Latins apart, mutual adversity helped bring them—some of them, at least—together.

"Democracy," Walt Whitman wrote, "looks with suspicious, ill-satisfied eyes upon the very poor, the ignorant, and those out of business. She asks for men and women with occupations, well-off, owners of houses, and acres, and with cash in the bank." [10] Many Americans continued to look with distrust and moral disapproval on the economically afflicted, and to resist with all the fervor at their disposal the New Deal's whole array of welfare programs. More than ever before, though, a good number of them were willing to recognize the virtue of the poor and the afflicted and to extend a helping hand to them, even if they lived below the border. They could agree with diplomat Jefferson Caffery, who as the Depression tightened its grip on the Americas suggested that hemispheric harmony would ensue once "American business concerns . . . act toward the Governments and peoples South of the Rio Grande in the same manner as . . . towards people and concerns in the United States." [11] For many Americans, the time had come to put Caffery's analysis to the test.

Indeed, it might be necessary to deal rather more leniently with Latin Americans than with some North Americans. One well-known political writer in the 1930s suggested that Washington could no longer contemplate the old type of intervention in what had once been referred to as banana republics. The only real banana republic in the hemisphere was

Wall Street. Here was where intervention was needed, not in Central America or the Caribbean.[12]

What I'm suggesting is that the Depression produced a virtual revolution in American attitudes, and that out of this revolution issued the public attitudes that enabled FDR to forge a Good Neighbor policy.

## The Quest for Renewal: Americans Turn to Internal Frontiers

The principal revolution Americans underwent during the Depression was inward. It did not produce blood on the streets, or even an enduring change in the political and socioeconomic order. What it did produce, at least among a fair number of citizens, was inward change. In the course of the inward revolution many citizens learned they could be happy without some of the material trappings that in the past they thought essential to happiness. Moreover, they acquired, some of them did, a penchant for fraternity that weakened their old obsession with individualism. The new-found sense of fraternity, for some Americans at least, extended across the border to encompass many Latin Americans: a people who like America's own down and out were poor, but not to be reviled just because of that. The revolution, it is true, generally did not broaden the parameters of Caucasian-American fraternity enough to include the black of skin, on either side of the border. Nevertheless, there was a revolution: a cultural revolution, a revolution in values—a revolution as real as it was ephemeral.

American movies reflected and nourished the revolution. Americans, in large numbers at least, were poor, but most of them could still go to the movies; and they did, in unprecedented numbers. Watching, for example, Bing Crosby on the silver screen in 1938, they could emphathize with him as he crooned, "I'm no millionaire, but I'm not the type to care, 'cause I've got a pocketful of dreams." [13] Without money in their pockets, they could still feel contented, at least part of the time; they could like themselves and others even when all of them together seemed economic failures.

For a minute in America's twentieth-century history, the lust of consumerism was curbed. As they looked inward, many Americans learned how to settle for the "simple gifts" Aaron Copland celebrated in one of his compositions based on a Shaker melody. Or, in the grip of a new kind of American dream that Hollywood and much of the American media sought to sell (for a profit, of course) in the Depression era, they could share with Bing Crosby in appreciating the always close-to-hand rewards that nature offered: they could rejoice that every time it rained, they received "Pennies from Heaven." Or, as they listened to the Depression era's great classic "Brother, Can You Spare a Dime?", they could content themselves with the thought that poverty was no disgrace.[14]

Albert James Webb, *Book Worms,* between 1935 and 1943, drypoint, image:
11¼ × 8⅞ in. Gift of Dr. and Mrs. Corbin S. Carnell, in memory of E. Muriel
Adams. Collection of the Harn Museum of Art, University of Florida. 1992.11.158
*Americans who in the 1920s had sought more glamorous distractions often had
to settle in the '30s for the simpler pleasures of reading, finding their sources of
escape and uplift in dingy racks of used books.*

Chuzo Tamotzu, *East 13th Street,* between 1935 and 1937, lithograph, image: 17⅜ × 11½ in. Gift of Dr. and Mrs. Corbin S. Carnell, in memory of E. Muriel Adams. Collection of the Harn Museum of Art, University of Florida. 1992.11.137 *Depression-era children of once affluent parents had to settle for the simple pleasures customarily reserved for children born into poverty. The artist somehow makes a thing of rare beauty out of the simple pleasure afforded by water spouting from a hydrant.*

In giving Americans confidence to pursue a dream not associated just with material aggrandizement, Hollywood moguls and American songwriters and other creators of popular culture may have been as important—and also as self-interested and phony—as many of Washington's New Dealers. Be that as it may, in Bing Crosby Hollywood discovered a gold mine in its campaign to turn Americans to dreaming about simple pleasures. With his relaxed, golden tones, Crosby succeeded, almost as much as the mellifluous-voiced Roosevelt, in selling the idea of nonmaterial rewards to Americans, and in making them feel good even in the midst of economic uncertainty—not only good, but morally superior to those who remained affluent throughout the Depression.

Fidel Castro and Che Guevara themselves could scarcely have aspired to accomplish more in the way of creating "new persons" when, a generation later, they sought to induce Cubans, and then—so they vainly hoped—the rest of Latin Americans as well, to abandon materialism and take up the pursuit of nonmaterial rewards. Not even Mao Zedong could have aspired to much more of an inward, cultural revolution. But, as Mao would soon discover, revolutionary change of heart is ephemeral at best. Just as China's cultural revolution ultimately disappeared beneath a wave of consumer appetites, so America's making-a-virtue-of-necessity attempt to contain those appetites in the 1930s ultimately failed. Just like mammoth Depression-era projects to dam mighty rivers in the West, the attempt to dam consumerism temporarily halted a great force of nature, only to release it later in a monumental avalanche. But, while the acquisitive mania was momentarily checked, Americans had a unique opportunity to begin to appreciate those Latin Americans they had previously disparaged because of their inability to produce consumer societies.

At the same time that it turned many Americans inward in quest of alternatives to vanished material abundance, the Depression inspired others to dream of blazing new trails on which they could resume their interrupted trek toward that abundance. Historically, a favorite American myth associated the frontier with economic bonanzas, with redemption from the ills and afflictions of already settled and civilized regions. Longing for new frontiers with payoffs rich enough to lift their civilization out of its economic doldrums, many Americans cast their eyes southward. Nonmaterial rewards held no charm for them. By playing their cards right in a new Latin American frontier they hoped to fulfill the old national dream of ever expanding private and national material enrichment.

### Americans Eye the Latin American Economic Frontier

Despite the myth of the frontier's unique contribution to American economic development, that development had always depended every bit as much, perhaps even more, on economic ties with the Old World. However, the failure of the London Economic Conference that followed close on the heels of Roosevelt's inauguration reinforced the isolationist sentiments that the Nye hearings had fomented. Indeed, by late 1933 "American foreign policy had shifted to a more isolationist stance than anything seen since the late nineteenth century."[15]

The new president in some ways welcomed the collapse of the London Economic Conference, for it gave him a chance to rail against London bankers and thereby cement his support among Irish voters. FDR struck a chord that resonated not just among the Irish but among a broad national cross section. Americans might or might not believe former president Hoover's contention that the Depression had originated in the economic foolishness of Europe and from there had reached out to envelop an American economy that was basically sound; by and large, though, they certainly sensed that they could not rely on the Old World to pull them out of the financial emergency. In this time of crisis, it appeared that Americans would have to rely on the resources of the New World, a world that happily still contained—especially in the undeveloped reaches of Latin America—vast, untapped frontier resources. By no means for the first time in the New World's history, assertions of a common destiny among the nations of the Americas implied, and indeed rested upon, a sense of separation from Europe.

Few men attested so clearly to the sense of isolation from Europe, together with a feeling of connectedness among the New World countries, as Gen. Robert E. Wood, a West Pointer and a vice-president of Sears, Roebuck. Looking back years later on his attitudes in the early 1930s, he told interviewer Studs Terkel: "I was an isolationist. . . . I still think it was a mistake for us to have gone into the [first world] war. We've got an empire here, and we've got two great undeveloped continents, North and South America." Under these circumstances, why, he wondered, "should we get mixed up in the affairs of Europe which is an old-time continent? We've got unlimited room to expand, and why we should get mixed up in an old, tired Europe, I couldn't see."[16]

Liberal Democrat Adolf A. Berle, Jr., an early New Deal brain-truster and an important architect of the Good Neighbor policy, felt much like the Republican general and business magnate. He believed Americans should seek their destiny in the largely undeveloped reaches of Latin America. If he had had his way, Americans in the mid- and even late 1930s would have sealed the hemisphere off from Europe.[17]

Their original western frontier, or so Americans liked to delude themselves, had been virtually an unoccupied frontier. Nurturing this delusion helped them to forget about, or at least to minimize, the extent of the mayhem and slaughter that had accompanied their move into the frontier.

But when they had pretty well overrun their own empty spaces and had then turned to those far to the south, they could not dismiss the fact of that new frontier's previous occupation. Latin Americans might not be much, in the American estimation, but there were a great many of them; and some of them, in Yankee perceptions, had at least a bit more of the accoutrements of civilization than Indians.

In turning originally to the frontier to their south, Americans at the turn of the century and on up through the World War I era had to face up to a fact they had not liked to acknowledge when dealing with mere Indians in an "unoccupied" frontier: they, the Americans, were an imperialist people, ready to use gunboats and strong-arm tactics to open the southern frontier to the expansion of economic activities. They, the Americans, had also to acknowledge, at least before long, that strong-arm tactics often goaded the Latin American natives into opposition, into making extreme nuisances of themselves.

Like the North American Indians, Latin Americans victimized by American frontiersmen sought to league themselves into confederations so as to present a stronger resistance to the expansionists, or at least so as to force them to pay more equitably for the opportunity to exploit the abundant resources. Faced with growing and ever more concerted Latin American resistance to their economic incursions, severely strapped for funds with which to finance strong-arm tactics in the southern frontier, and encountering strong opposition among their own taxpaying citizens to footing the bill, would-be frontiersmen in Latin America had to develop a new sensitivity to the feelings of the natives. They had to make themselves welcome within the homes of the natives, not batter down the doors. In one way, this is what the Good Neighbor policy was all about. Old habits died hard, though; and it was not in the American tradition to knock politely on the doors of "lesser" people. Without the crisis of confidence spawned by the Great Depression, Americans would have been a lot slower to become more mannerly in their imperial, frontier demeanor.

Subtle psychological factors may also have been at work to induce Americans simultaneously to cast off from Europe and seek their destiny in Latin America's frontier. For all their protestations of disgust with the economic, social, and even moral malaise into which Europeans allegedly had fallen during the 1930s, Americans still felt a tinge of cultural inferiority as they measured themselves against Old World citizens. In the Depression era, when their confidence lay shattered, Americans relished the opportunity to deal with people to whom, by and large, they felt clearly superior. Paradoxically, then, the Good Neighbor era grew in some measure out of American disdain for Latin Americans. Sometimes the more things changed the more they remained the same.

# 5. A Clint Eastwood Cinematic Epilogue

❖ ❖ ❖ ❖ ❖ ❖ ❖ ❖ ❖ ❖ ❖ ❖ ❖ ❖ ❖ ❖ ❖ ❖ ❖ ❖ ❖ ❖ ❖ ❖ ❖ ❖ ❖ ❖ ❖ ❖ ❖ ❖

## The Depression and the Frontier, America and Latin America

Facing the financial panics that occurred during his presidency at the beginning of the twentieth century, Theodore Roosevelt quite understandably cast his eyes toward Latin America, impressed by the economic possibilities of trade and commerce. In this, he followed the advice of the historian he so admired, Frederick Jackson Turner. Contemplating the significance of the closing of the frontier, about which he had written so eloquently and influentially in 1893, Turner speculated that in seeking frontier substitutes, Americans were likely to turn more and more to commercial opportunities in Latin America.[1] All the more likely, then, was it that President Franklin D. Roosevelt, facing the greatest economic crisis in his country's history, would turn toward Latin America as a source of stimulus to the foundering American economy. Times had changed, though, between the presidencies of the two Roosevelts. The second Roosevelt would approach Latin America, as well as frontier mythology, in a different mood from the first.

Early in the twentieth century, President Theodore Roosevelt, taking as his point of departure the widespread conviction among Americans that the frontier had come to a close, suggested that the individualistic values inculcated among pioneer settlers of the wilderness might now have to be reassessed. Unbridled individualism, he suggested, "was incompatible with the realities of a more complex, postfrontier America."[2] In this belief, the president reflected Progressivism's analysis of America and its ills. The theme of the disappearing frontier, and the reshuffling of traditional American values that the disappearance mandated, ran like a leitmotif through much Progressive political analysis and propaganda. Above all, Progressives suggested the need for increased government social and economic intervention in the face of diminishing resources in a frontierless society.

As for himself, though, TR was not altogether ready to write off the individualism to which heroic frontier settlement had, in his view, contributed significantly. True, a reevaluation of individualism might be in order now that the frontier had closed. But might not a few last flings for the old frontier spirit still be possible? As it turned out, Americans just before TR ascended to the presidency had indeed enjoyed a last-gasp opportunity to play the role of cowboys or "Rough Riders" (as Col. Roosevelt called the western cowhands and eastern polo players he led into Cuba in 1898). The Rough Riders helped Cuba obtain its independence from Spain. In their derring-do bravado they also opened the island's resources to Yankee capitalists. In consequence, the newly liberated islanders virtually surrendered their economic freedom to their liberators. For a brief moment at century's turn, the frontier had worked its old miracles of rewarding its conquerors with the opportunity to build character and fortunes. Soon, TR found similar opportunities for Yankees in Panama; and, for a time, he toyed with seeking still more opportunities of this nature in Venezuela.

A third of a century or so later and in the midst of an economic crisis that completely eclipsed what his cousin had faced, another Roosevelt listened to advisers and brain-trusters who insisted no more time could be bought for beleaguered frontier values. The moment had come, they insisted, for government socioeconomic intervention on such a scale as to banish forever from the pantheon of national values the unfettered individualism supposedly spawned by and appropriate to frontier settlement. FDR himself might not have felt altogether comfortable with such an assessment. Still, the Hyde Park aristocrat had always been somewhat dubious about the frontier virtues that his rugged outdoorsman cousin extolled. So, he could be swept along upon occasion by brainy urbanite advisers, especially if they seemed attuned to the wishes of the electorate.

In the course of his election campaign in 1932 Roosevelt delivered an important address, written principally by future brain-truster Adolf A. Berle, Jr., at San Francisco's Commonwealth Club. As noted in the previous chapter, Berle favored relative isolationism from the Old World and a strengthening of ties with America's New World neighbors. He recognized that in strengthening ties with the new frontier to their south, Americans would have to cast aside their tough-guy, gunslinger approach to the old frontier; and this recognition helped shape the speech he wrote for Roosevelt.

To his San Francisco audience FDR observed that Americans had reached their last frontier. There was no more free land. In the setting of reduced opportunity America's great "industrial combinations" could no longer be permitted the "uncontrolled and irresponsible . . . power within the state" that had seemed acceptable in an earlier age of unbounded individual opportunity. It followed, in the Roosevelt-Berle analysis, that a reappraisal of values was imperative. Government would have to play a greater role in assuring "everyone an avenue to possess himself of a portion of that [remaining] plenty sufficient for his needs, through his own work."[3]

As Americans continued to expand southward, FDR, like Berle, realized they would have to recognize, especially in an era of economic hardship, that Latin Americans needed access of their own to the plenty their lands possessed. Unlike American Indians in an earlier frontier experience, Latin Americans would have to be guaranteed a decent share of the wealth that accrued from their untapped or underdeveloped resources. Referring to Latin Americans, FDR once admonished: "Give them a share." This is what much of the Good Neighbor policy was all about—which is to say that the Good Neighbor policy represented the attempt to live by a new kind of frontier credo. Unlike the Sitting Bulls and the Crazy Horses, the Pancho Villas and the Sandinos henceforth would not be dealt with by the Custers and the Sheridans.

## Clint Eastwood's Frontier

Clint Eastwood's Academy Award–winning 1992 movie, *The Unforgiven,* provides a classic presentation of what, during the Depression era, came to be a widely held view of the frontier as the incubator of socially destructive individualism. In the Eastwood perspective (which also shaped many of his earlier westerns), individualism as nourished on the frontier led to violence and utter disregard for the social consequences of a person's actions. Toward the end of *The Unforgiven* one unforgettable scene epitomizes the notion that frontier individualism undermines the basic social fabric. In this scene the movie's hero, who in so many ways is an antihero, unleashes bloody havoc as the U.S. flag flutters in the background. The implication, of course, is that American patriotism is vitiated by a misguided set of values that arose in the frontier—and later transferred to the marketplace.

Not surprisingly, as the movie ends the audience is informed that the hero/antihero eventually made his way to San Francisco where he had gone into business. Viewers are left with the inference that the same ruthlessness that led him to excel in playing by the frontier's law of the jungle will also guarantee him success in the marketplace. In either instance, success is the reward of those willing to run the risks of becoming moral disasters. Here is the sort of interpretation that in the 1930s became identified with a left wing of the Democratic Party, and with ever-so-many political and ideological entities to its left.

Depression-era Democrats, many of them at least, tended to think frontier values were never much and had become less acceptable than ever. Republicans, on the other hand, whether before, during, or after the Depression, tended often to regard the individualism of the frontiersman and his modern-day descendant the captain of industry as heroic. By and large they resisted any attempts by an interventionist government to impose restraints on this individualism. John Wayne became their movie hero, certainly not Clint Eastwood. Both during the Depression and afterward, they reveled in the traditions of a "gunfighter nation."[4]

This sharp dichotomy between Democrats and Republicans in interpreting the frontier myth and gleaning from it lessons applicable to contemporary life lay behind some of the political warfare that raged during the Depression years. Democrats of that era (many of them, at least) moved to curb individualism through government programs aimed at mitigating the effects of economic adversity. In contrast, many staunch Republicans decided it was better to learn to live with adversity, however long it might endure, than to undermine the frontier-nourished individualism that accounted, ostensibly, for American exceptionalism. Even in 1932, former president Herbert Hoover saw no reason to revise the conclusions he had reached in his 1922 book *American Individualism*. In it Hoover condemned "the perpetual howl of radicalism . . . [which] assume[s] that all reform and human advance must come through government."

A widely prevailing interpretation has it that the Good Neighbor policy really began with Hoover. And this, in some ways, is true. But Hoover and his fellow Republicans could never have advanced that policy to the degree that Roosevelt and the Democrats did. Basically, Hoover and his political partisans distrusted and disliked the underlying Latin American approach to governance that was, and since colonial and even the preconquest times of the Maya and the Aztecs and the Incas always had been, based on intervention by the state in virtually every aspect of civic life. On the other hand, FDR and—at least during the Depression years—a major section of his political partisans saw little wrong with the statist traditions of Latin America—saw little wrong with them and could, indeed, go so far as to sometimes positively applaud and identify with them. Republicans in the 1930s simply could not have advanced as far as FDR in improving relations with Latin America.

Republicans by and large persisted in an inclination to denigrate Latin Americans for having failed to develop their own frontier in the Anglo-American style. They attributed this failure in some measure to corporatist systems of government that stifled individualism, not only on the frontier but in the urban marketplace as well, thereby permanently impeding development. On the other hand, Depression-era Democrats could look at Latin interventionist proclivities and applaud them not only for having been wise in the past but prophetic of the future as well. If the Latins had much to be ashamed of in their past, Americans had even more. Looking back to their past, a fair number of Democrats found America's original sin in the sort of self-centered, heedless violence that Eastwood portrays in *The Unforgiven,* and in much of his earlier oeuvre.

During the Depression years, with their massive influx into the Democratic Party, more and more Americans seemed predisposed to accept—for the moment, at least—the Clint Eastwood perspective on the American reality. More and more they were ready to agree with New Deal ideologues that America was in trouble because it had lived by a credo of excessive individualism. They were ready to believe that their country now faced the challenge of creating a stronger social fabric through government programs aimed at stifling individualism. To meet this challenge it might be necessary for Americans to create a society in some ways akin to the ones that so often in the past, in their moments of supreme self-confidence, they had criticized Latins for aspiring to.

In the Democratic purview, of course, there was as much chauvinism as in the Republicans'; for even the Americans most ardent in clamoring for a Good Neighbor policy seldom entertained serious doubts about the moral superiority of Anglo Americans and their ability to do a better job than Latins were capable of in forging honest and efficient statist institutions. Conviction among Democrats about American moral superiority had roots sunk deep in racist prejudices—prejudices that permeated the Democratic Party of the Depression era, with part of its power base deriving from white supremacist Southerners and rabidly racist northern factory workers.

For all their lack of genuine good neighborliness, however, Democratic leaders especially among northern intellectuals could sympathize with and even enthuse over Latin American predilections toward the interventionist state. They were even ready to adopt, convinced that they could then improve upon, some of Latin America's more collectivist and "medievalist" or Thomistic approaches to social, economic, and political organization. Although they might not employ the terms medievalist or Thomistic, many leading Democratic thinkers agreed that an interventionist government dedicated to achieving the common good was what the country needed in its desperate hour of economic collapse. Moreover, to the degree that they understood what was afoot, a good portion of the national electorate was willing to tolerate, or at least to contemplate tolerating, this sort of sea change in American values.

Even during the Good Neighbor policy's glory days, Republicans steadfastly resisted notions of hemispheric convergence arising out of shared faith in the interventionist state. Like the Republican Roosevelt, Republicans of the 1930s could not bring themselves altogether to doubt the virtues that, according to America's great national myth, arose on the frontier and in turn led to urban economic success. Could they have seen *The Unforgiven* back in the '30s, they would have hated it as a sample of Democratic propaganda. Furthermore, had Democrats been able to view the film in the late 1940s, in the postwar and post-Depression era, many of them would have hated it just as much as the average Republican. By then, the so-called American Century had begun, chauvinism was escalating, and only communists or "pinkos" could doubt the grandeur of America's past, its present, and its future. If the Latins wanted to share in that future, let them become as Americans were and, except for deviants, always had been.

For a brief moment, though, back in the Depression era, many Americans felt differently. In that brief moment the Good Neighbor policy flowered.

# SECTION

# II

❖ ❖ ❖ ❖ ❖ ❖ ❖ ❖ ❖ ❖ ❖ ❖ ❖ ❖ ❖ ❖ ❖ ❖ ❖ ❖ ❖ ❖ ❖ ❖ ❖ ❖ ❖ ❖ ❖ ❖

*Inducements
toward Good
Neighborliness*

# 6. Religion, Social Gospel, and Social Work

❖ ❖ ❖ ❖ ❖ ❖ ❖ ❖ ❖ ❖ ❖ ❖ ❖ ❖ ❖ ❖ ❖ ❖ ❖ ❖ ❖ ❖ ❖ ❖ ❖ ❖ ❖ ❖ ❖ ❖ ❖ ❖ ❖

### *Religion's Diminishing Role in Hemispheric Divisiveness*

According to Ray Allen Billington, in his classic study of religious prejudice in the United States, the average mid-nineteenth-century Protestant
was still, like his or her ancestors, "trained from birth to hate Catholicism." From infancy on, the minds of most Americans "were shaped to
believe that 'to be a Catholic, was to be a false, cruel and bloody wretch,'
and that Popery included everything that was vicious and vile."[1]

By century's end, fresh from their victory over Catholic Spain that had
liberated Cuba from the forces of darkness, Americans more than ever saw
themselves as the citizens of God's country, chosen to lead the world away
from papal obscurantism and toward regeneration, both spiritual and
economic. Indeed, they assumed that spiritual probity and economic grandeur went hand in hand, whereas those who worshiped falsely doomed
themselves to economic backwardness. Being chosen by God implied being chosen to be successful—temporally, economically successful. More
and more in the aftermath of the war that swept Catholic Spain off the
seas even more effectively than had British sailors at the time of the Spanish Armada, Americans saw themselves as "the great missionary race,"
destined now to lead backward peoples, especially those most immediate
unto them within their own hemisphere, away from false beliefs, away
from spiritual and economic underdevelopment. More and more, prominent Methodist clergyman James M. King seemed to have had it right

when in the immediate post–Civil War period he proclaimed that God had chosen the Anglo Saxon "to conquer the world for Christ by dispossessing feeble races, and assimilating and molding others."[2]

As Americans struggled to pull themselves out of the crushing poverty that had suddenly descended on so many of them as the 1930s began, they had to revise some of their old theological assumptions, and to rethink some of the religious prejudice that had led them to regard Latin Americans as decidedly second-class Americans, their religious inferiority attested to by their lack of economic success. The spirit of Manifest Destiny, based in part on assumptions of a divine right to dominate religiously blighted and economically retarded people, died at least a temporary death in the 1930s—rebirth of course being possible whenever American prosperity returned. In consequence of the temporary death of religiously inspired Manifest Destiny, the American hemisphere entered an era uniquely favorable to good neighborliness.

Further contributing to the diminution of religiously inspired, religiously justified American prejudice against Latin America was the splintering of Protestant cohesiveness. American Protestantism, of course, had always been riven by bickering and divisiveness. But something new was afoot in the 1920s and '30s. As Martin Marty, Distinguished Service Professor at the University of Chicago, points out, the feature story of American religion in those two decades is the fragmenting of the Protestant synthesis.[3]

Beginning in the 1920s, the real news in American religion concerned not Protestant animosity against Catholics but Protestant animosity against Protestants. With the Fundamentalist-Modernist split eclipsing the seriousness even of the North-South, abolitionist-slavery issue that had divided Baptists, Presbyterians, and Methodists in the years preceding, during, and immediately after the Civil War, Protestants beginning in the 1920s and continuing for decades to come devoted more energy to worrying about and harassing other Protestants than to fretting over the Catholic "menace." Indeed, some Protestants actually seemed more drawn to theologically conservative Catholics than to Protestant Modernists. With Catholics, the Fundamentalists shared a firm belief in revelation and dogma, a resolute rejection of evolution and biblical criticism, and more often than not a blanket condemnation of birth control. On the other hand the rampant religious individualism of Fundamentalists (with their stress on personal conversion experiences) set them at odds with Catholicism's rigidly hierarchical institutional structure. In contrast, Episcopalians and Presbyterians rather preferred this feature of Catholicism to Fundamentalism's stress on born-again experiences and private judgment of scripture that allegedly spawned virtual anarchism. However, when the communist issue flared in the 1930s, Fundamentalists tended to assume they had firmer anti-Marxist allies in Catholics, both north and south of the border, than in Modernist Protestants such as Episcopalians and Presbyterians and above all Unitarians.

In many significant ways, overt and subtle, the "P" in WASP (White Anglo-Saxon Protestant) began to lose some of its significance in defining true Americanism; for it became more impossible than ever before to define just what was represented by the "P." Furthermore, it was becoming more difficult to find one-dimensional Catholicism in America.

By the 1920s and '30s, not just East Coast working classes were of Irish or Italian Catholic descent. By then, more and more native-born Midwesterners were of Irish Catholic descent. Not only Irish-origin Catholics, but second-, third-, and fourth-generation immigrants of German and Slavic extraction swelled the numbers of midwestern Catholics; and they became increasingly powerful in shaping regional politics, all the while relegating to the historical past the once assumed connection between Protestantism and Americanism. The increasing amorphousness of American Catholicism and the loss of Protestant focus in opposing it helped persuade Democrats to do what would have been unthinkable at an earlier time when they nominated the Catholic Al Smith as their standard-bearer in the 1928 presidential election. True, Smith went down to defeat. But the general consensus among historians is that he would have lost even had he been a Protestant.

Professor Marty is on solid ground when he speculates that Catholics, and also Jews and humanists (among others once considered outside the pale by Americans), "would have been worse off had Protestantism kept a united front rather than dividing somewhere down the middle," beginning in the 1920s. Marty is also on solid ground in drawing attention to growing American secularism in the 1930s. To an increasing number of Americans, religion somehow just did not seem an important enough basis any longer on which to judge and condemn people. So, religious indifference joined with religious divisiveness among American Protestants in the Depression era to undermine old justifications for exclusionary policies vis-à-vis Catholics.[4] And the breakdown of old rationalizations for exclusionary policies had not just a national but a hemispheric dimension; this breakdown facilitated the rise of the New Deal *and* of the Good Neighbor policy.

Throughout the 1930s new factors kept surfacing that contributed to the weakening of the Catholic-Protestant dichotomy as a major source of divisiveness, whether on a national or a hemispheric scale. For example, Catholicism underwent at least a bit of the proliferation that had already made it more difficult to define just what a Protestant represented. In the Depression decade the Catholic Church in the United States ran the gamut from Dorothy Day's anarchism to Father Charles Coughlin's anti-Semitic crypto-fascism—a position that, incidentally, won him the support not only of a Catholic working class extending far beyond the Detroit region where the so-called "radio priest" was headquartered, but of widely dispersed Protestant workers as well.

In the Depression setting, it turned out that Catholics as well as Protestants were susceptible to Coughlin's attempt to out–New Deal the New Deal as he railed against America's uneven distribution of wealth and assailed bankers and successful capitalists in general as "financial Dillingers." Coughlin also spread a virulently anti-Semitic line, and this appealed to some Catholics. Other Catholics, however, took up the fight against a resurgent Ku Klux Klan that in the 1920s and '30s directed its wrath not just against black Americans but against Catholics and Jews. So, many a Jew and many a liberal Protestant incensed by Klan activities welcomed Catholic partners in the struggle against bigotry.

By 1937 when the Spanish Civil War became a divisive issue among Americans, the Catholic laity showed itself uncertain and divided, even though the hierarchy came out solidly in favor of the Nationalists under Generalissimo Francisco Franco. Furthermore, many Catholics toward the end of the 1920s had begun to ignore the admonitions of their bishops and to look with tolerance on the virulently anticlerical but social reform–minded Mexican administrations that had come to power in the wake of the 1910 revolution. These American Catholics judged the Mexicans not so much by their willingness to toe the lines that the hierarchy drew as by the extent of their concern for the poor and the powerless. Especially after the Depression's onslaught, the American Catholic laity, increasingly focused on the need for domestic socioeconomic reform, pushed sectarian issues into the background when judging events in Mexico.

Although the Mexican situation could be seen in terms of a clash between clericalism and secular reform, not even in that country was the issue cut and dried. From the papacy on down, the Catholic Church, rhetorically at least, had long since assumed a stance that placed it on the side of socioeconomic reform, and sometimes even in the vanguard of the struggle for social justice. From popes on down, Catholic leaders stopped preaching nostrums about poverty being the estate richest in the means of salvation. So, when the Depression struck, Catholic leaders in the United States as well as in Latin America were ready to speak out boldly for programs of basic reform. Indeed, many social-justice clerics in the United States, finding justification in the encyclicals of Popes Leo XIII and Pius XI (*Rerum Novarum* [1891] and *Quadragesimo Anno* [1931], respectively), advocated government interventionist programs very much in line with those devised by the most ardent New Dealers.

The U.S. clergy, of course, included also many a conservative bishop and priest ideologically to the right of Herbert Hoover. In this as in many other signs of diversity, the Catholic Church had become an elusive target for its foes. In fact, these foes had to accept the fact that their old bête noire now presented not one but several targets; and so they became confused as to where to aim their broadsides. Moreover, they had to reconcile themselves to the fact that to some Americans Catholicism had earned its place in the cult of muscular Christianity once confined to Protestants. Notre Dame football had acquired a bevy of Protestant fans, in part because it projected "a macho image, of good boys becoming good men."[5] What could be more American?

Seldom slow to detect a public trend, Hollywood awakened to the fact that movies portraying Catholicism, or at least Catholics, in a favorable light made for good box office returns. Moreover, by 1934 Hollywood had had a run-in with the Church when, through their Legion of Decency, the hierarchy enlisted vast Protestant support in launching a campaign against "sleazy" movies. Hollywood lost its battle to escape censorship and had to settle for production codes, often framed by Catholic clergymen and their Protestant allies. Unable to defeat the Church, Hollywood in effect joined with it, becoming downright sycophantic in depicting it in a number of movies. Patrick O'Brien was recruited to play the roles of empathetic priests in films such as *Angels with Dirty Faces;* Spencer Tracy assumed the role of Father Flanagan in *Boys Town,* a movie, incidentally, that stressed the social consciousness of the Church in working to correct the ills inflicted by capitalist society; William Gargan played Father Dolan in *You Only Live Once;* and in 1944 Leo McCarey "found his heart full of a moist mixture of music, religion, and patriotism" as he produced his biggest hit ever, *Going My Way.* The film depicted "cozily irreverent priests [played by Barry Fitzgerald and Bing Crosby] doing good deeds."[6]

South of the border, the Catholic Church during the Depression era was in many ways a house divided against itself as conservative and reformist elements battled for the upper hand, largely ignoring—as they had since colonial times—attempts from Rome to impose discipline. Church divisiveness was nothing new in Latin America, where Catholicism since the earliest days of conquest had seldom presented a united front, whether on social, political, economic, or theological issues. North of the border, though, a Protestant house hopelessly divided against itself and no longer united even in assessments of the Catholic Church was something new. This Protestant divisiveness contributed enormously to America's ability to assimilate Catholicism into the national mainstream; it also helped to

remove Catholicism as a major stumbling block to amicable relations with
Latin America.

## Roosevelt and Religion

Throughout New Deal days, acceptance of Catholicism as a main ingredient of the American reality began at the top. In the New Deal coalition,
labor was a key element; and American labor meant, to some considerable
degree, American Catholicism. Catholics made up nearly 50 percent of
members of the American Federation of Labor (AFL) during the 1930s; in
the Congress of Industrial Organizations (CIO) Catholics comprised an
even higher percentage of membership—probably appreciably higher. To
wed an administration to labor meant, in some ways, to wed it to the
Catholic Church, and this FDR proceeded to do—to his great political
advantage. In 1936 it is estimated that some 78 percent of all Catholics
voted for Roosevelt.[7] As Catholicism entered the mainstream, FDR welcomed it with open arms. And he took full advantage of the social-justice
ideology that, even as in Latin America, had entered the Church, in part
under the inspiration of the two papal encyclicals already cited.

Beyond expediency, FDR was attracted to the Catholic Church in
consequence of his own devotion to the Episcopalian Church, the two
churches being similar in many respects. What is more, FDR's attraction
to Catholicism extended to its south-of-the-border manifestations. Not a
regular church goer, FDR insisted upon being Episcopalian in his own
way. While he may not have warmed up to the priest-ridden Irish manifestation of American Catholicism, he could respond to the free-wheeling
ways in which Latin males approached their religion, ever insistent upon
being Catholic in their own way, in a way frequently at odds with what
priests and bishops might prescribe.

While some biographers maintain that FDR's concern with religion
was dictated primarily by expediency, others insist that he was profoundly
influenced by the "New Testament's emphasis on social responsibility,"
and had been ever since his student days at Groton when he fell under the
sway of its founder and headmaster, the Rev. Endicott Peabody. As is so
often the case with FDR the two appraisals, even if mutually exclusive,
may both be right. Whether sincere or not, FDR did frequently draw on
what appeared to be a biblical spirit as he stressed that social obligations
must supersede mere private interest, and as he blamed "selfish minorities" for having brought on America's economic collapse. Although ordinarily not given to conspicuous displays of religiosity, he "studded his
speeches with biblical metaphors" and "probably invoked God's name
and encouraged religious belief more often than any previous president."[8]

In many of FDR's social-justice pronouncements, there is little if anything to distinguish him from Leo XIII or Pius XI or from Latin America's predominantly Jesuit social-justice priests of the 1930s.

For that matter, the United States itself had more than its share of social-justice priests, and FDR utilized them fully in the New Deal. Perhaps he naively believed, like these priests and very much like their Latin American counterparts and also like the papal authors of social-justice encyclicals, that the private enterprise system in its old form was doomed by the exploitive greed on which allegedly it rested; perhaps, on the other hand, he believed that by assigning roles to such reform-minded priests as Francis Haas, James M. Gillis, and above all others Georgetown University's Monsignor John A. Ryan (who came to be called "Right Reverend New Dealer") he was outflanking the rabble-rousing Fr. Coughlin, whom the president recognized as a dangerous political rival and possible third party head. Probably overriding expediency, occasionally leavened by genuine religious leanings, underlay FDR's opening toward the Catholic Church, and his cultivation not only of labor priests but influential prelates, including George Cardinal Mundelein of Chicago, Archbishop Francis Spellman of New York, and William Cardinal O'Connell of Boston—who referred to the president as "a God-sent man."

An indication of just how much America had changed on the religious front came during the Spanish Civil War, when Roosevelt desisted from so much as seriously considering actions that might have aided the Republic against Franco's Nationalists lest in so doing he offend the Catholic hierarchy. Not too many years before this, offending the Catholic hierarchy would have earned an American president enthusiastic public plaudits. Moreover, not so many years before Roosevelt, no American president would have found it politically expedient to appoint fifty-one Catholic judges (his three Republican predecessors had appointed a total of eight). Nor could an earlier president have gotten away with assigning a personal representative (Myron C. Taylor) to the Vatican. Nor would an earlier president have waxed rhapsodic in referring to Rome (as FDR did in his June 5, 1944, Fireside Chat) as "the great symbol of Christianity." On this occasion, the president went on to declare the churches and shrines of Rome "visible symbols of the faith and determination of the early saints and martyrs that Christianity should live and become universal." Rome, he averred, was not only the republic and the empire; it was "in a sense the Catholic Church." He concluded that Americans could take deep satisfaction in the fact "that the freedom of the Pope and the Vatican City is assured by the armies of the United Nations."[9]

Not too terribly many years earlier, the public had applauded when journalists and politicians had referred to popes as great whores of Babylon, and to Rome as a latter-day Sodom and Gomorrah. American public opinion about Catholicism had changed, and but for this change there would have been significantly less public support for a Good Neighbor policy; and without significant public support, FDR was loathe to embark on any policy.

Meantime, American and Latin American thought had begun to converge on issues of Social Gospel and social work. The convergence represented no less dramatic a change in hemispheric relations than the removal of religion as a central source of divisiveness. Without a Depression-induced flowering of the Social Gospel in America, accompanied by a burgeoning respectability for social work, whether private, state, or federal, the common ground on which North and South met and embraced in the Good Neighbor era would have remained comparatively minuscule.

## Social Gospel and Social Action

A bit beyond midpoint in the nineteenth century, the influential clergyman Henry Ward Beecher gave voice to what had become a central, underlying assumption of the Protestant establishment. "No man in this land," he proclaimed, "suffers from poverty unless it be more than his fault—unless it be his sin."[10] Toward the end of the century, however, the Protestant establishment began to have second thoughts about Beecher's assumption, so comforting to the accommodated classes. Toward century's end, as Americans found it increasingly difficult to ignore the social problems that had begun to blight their cities, the Social Gospel movement challenged Protestant conventional wisdom.

In general, the social gospelers began to find sin not in America's impoverished classes but rather in the affluent power wielders who controlled and manipulated an industrial society that, allegedly, had gotten quite out of control and lost all semblance of having moral bearings. For social gospelers, poverty could no longer be seen as the badge of personal sin. Rather, it attested to an unjust society. At fault were huge industries and capitalist conglomerates that, as they grew ever bigger and more powerful, acquired ever more insatiable appetites for unskilled workers and ever greater proclivities to exploit those workers. It followed, in the logic of the social gospelers, that righteous, God-fearing citizens must begin to intervene in social matters, that they must become politically active in the attempt to curb the abusers of power, even as they sought to succor, assist, and ultimately uplift the innocent, childlike victims of an unjust system.

Students of the original Social Gospel movement in America have attributed various motives to the Christian "do-gooders." In the view of their defenders, the social gospelers acted out of the sincere desire to establish a more just society, to protect the abused, and to give them an adequate chance to develop their human potential. All of this, of course, required that the haughty money changers be driven from the American temple, over which they had acquired ownership, in the process debauching and perverting it. Through their machinations they had transformed the "city on a hill" into a redoubt for the greedy and corrupt; from there the unworthies looked down on worthy citizens consigned to the slums below.

More cynically inclined students of the social gospelers tell a somewhat different story. While conceding the pure, disinterested intentions often at work, they also detect the quest on the part of the clergy and the genteel, the respectable, and cultured elements in general, to reclaim the status and power that a band of purportedly money-grubbing barbarians had wrested from them. Moreover, say the cynics, the women who increasingly became active social gospelers and who then assumed dominant roles in the social work spawned by the religious movement coveted more than the opportunity to do good. Beyond this, they sought status and recognition; indeed, they aspired to assert over society's unfortunates the sort of control and power that up to now males had exercised over females and over society in general. Prevailingly, Social Gospel clergymen cheered the women on, perceiving allies who might help them reacquire the power, status, and influence they had once wielded in society.

Not surprisingly, the spirit of the Social Gospel soared anew in Depression-era America, as more and more citizens tended to blame their plight on callous, selfish plutocrats and as attribution of poverty to personal moral failings became ever more dubious. True, some religious Fundamentalists continued to connect poverty with sinfulness and to argue that only individual moral regeneration could bring about personal recovery from economic adversity and ultimately restore the whole nation to prosperity. Religious Modernists, however, tended to find more secular causes for America's economic collapse. Prevailingly, they attributed the collapse to the rapacity of those "sixty families" and their hangers-on whom Ferdinand Lumberg had castigated in his best-seller exposé of the depravity of the privileged. New Dealers, from the president and First Lady Eleanor Roosevelt on down through the ranks, tended to side with the Modernists; they blamed the mighty and the powerful, and the business society they had created to serve their own exclusive interests, for America's hard times.

For most New Dealers a pledge that a Methodist group began to circulate among its members went, just a shade at least, too far. The pledge began: "I surrender my life to Christ. I renounce the Capitalist system." If they generally refrained from going so far as to renounce the system altogether, New Dealers and American Democrats by and large seemed to agree with Protestant theologian Reinhold Niebuhr, who wrote in 1932 that society was developing a social conscience; and in consequence of this emerging conscience, society would no longer accept social and economic circumstances that the previous generation would have found normal and proper. In the Depression setting, what once passed for normal came to be regarded "as an intolerable scandal."[11]

Inspired in no small part by the spirit of the Social Gospel, Frances Perkins, a graduate of Mount Holyoke College, which produced many like-minded women dedicated to Christian social service, gained her first practical experience while working at Hull House—the Chicago settlement house founded by Jane Addams. Later, Perkins pursued her vocation in New York, and with Roosevelt's election became the first woman to hold a cabinet position: that of secretary of labor. For a moment it appeared that the burgeoning number of women she symbolized, who had during the preceding two decades or so begun to achieve position and status by doing good, stood on the threshold of achieving their ambitions: to achieve still higher position and status by doing still more good.

Then a funny thing happened. Now that women had helped popularize the Social Gospel, and now that they had pioneered a new field of social work that suddenly had passed from what many Americans had once considered the lunatic fringe into the political establishment, they began to lose the status and influence to which their pioneer efforts entitled them. With its importance and status-conferring role clearly recognized in the Depression years, social work began to be taken over by men. In the New Deal one thinks of Frances Perkins in connection with social and economic relief projects. But one thinks even more of Roosevelt's bureaucrat par excellence and personal crony, Harry Hopkins.[12]

In the American story of the birth and reflowering of the Social Gospel, and of the importance of the feminine role in establishing a veritable social work industry that once it flowered began to be taken over by men, one finds a remarkable parallel to events unfolding in Latin America. I am persuaded that this parallel helped the two Americas to find common ground during the Good Neighbor era.

In much of Latin America from mid-nineteenth century on, a rising class of business entrepreneurs began to challenge the old landowning and intellectual and church elites for social, economic, and political dominance. To a considerable degree, however much the phenomenon was dwarfed by corresponding developments in the United States, Latin America's new men wrested control away from the genteel, old-line aristocrats and set themselves, sometimes with striking success, to the pursuit of wealth in the business world; occasionally at least, their personal success translated into remarkable gains in national economic development. If anything, though, social problems grew more intense, even as in the United States during its days of economic takeoff when the great fortunes were created even as impoverished masses remained in misery.

At this point, I am going to oversimplify, vastly, a complex set of circumstances that varied enormously from country to country. Basically, though, I think there is some fair degree of validity to my generalizations. Here is the situation south of the border, around the turn of the twentieth century, as I see it.

As social problems intensified against a background of the rising fortunes of a new class of men on the make who classified themselves as modern capitalists, the displaced aristocracy took note of the social mayhem accompanying the process. Often encouraged by the Catholic clergy that had suffered a relative decline in influence as a new and secularly oriented class rose to power, old-line aristocrats professed concern about the increasing social unrest that accompanied what the new elites proudly referred to as the modernization of their republics. Sometimes genuinely concerned about the suffering of masses now being exploited in new ways by new master classes, the old-line elites, again encouraged by the clergy, began to advocate measures of social justice that would, supposedly, alleviate the plight of the suffering and at the same time, and not incidentally, curb the power of the new elites. With a base among the impoverished, the old elites might strike back and reverse their status decline.

With the encouragement of the Church, so often a dominant influence in their lives, women assumed leading roles in Catholic Action programs designed to alleviate the suffering of the poor and sometimes as well to mobilize them as a political force that could be manipulated by the old, traditional aristocracy against the interests of the new business-oriented bourgeoisie. In all of this, the Church and the upper-class women of Latin America were building on a tradition extending back to colonial times. Under the tutelage of the male-dominated, patriarchal Church, colonial upper-sector women often assumed the roles of *supermadres*. They served as mothers not only of their own families but of the extended family of the powerless and the dependent in society at large. Often the supermadres were mothers only to the poor, having resolved to remain single and celibate.

Although Americans and Latin Americans had followed different paths, in the 1920s and 1930s they had begun to arrive at the same point. Supermadres in the United States, exemplified by Jane Addams at Hull House (who like so many of her kindred social workers chose to remain single), by Frances Perkins, and by Eleanor Roosevelt, who had already carved out a social service career by the time she married and who never abandoned it, took up the challenge to restore social stability by succoring the lowly while curbing the exploitive potential of parvenu capitalists. As often as not, even as in Latin America, the American supermadres were inspired by the teachings of male-dominated churches. They were the spear carriers of clergymen, and in general of male elites who hoped to reap the major share of the gains that the women initiated.

So, both in America and in Latin America, the Depression era spawned a movement directed against the values and policies associated with a modernizing bourgeoisie, and in both areas women played comparable roles. What seemed suitable to many a Latin American male and female who for altruistic or self-serving reasons railed against an unjust capitalist order, seemed suitable as well to many a North American male and female also on the warpath against the old capitalist order.

The plot thickens a bit with the entry of leftist intellectuals, both American and Latin American, onto the scene in the 1930s. Faced with the crushing effects of the Depression these intellectuals, who receive more extended coverage in the next chapter, embraced remedies more radical, and they hoped far more efficacious, than those pursued by old-line aristocrats trying to parlay social problems into the restoration of status. According to leftist social critics, the plight of the lower classes stemmed from the fact that both the old and new elites alike sought merely to use them for their own purposes. Even if the old elites reacquired their former power, the underclasses would remain as dependent, as subject to exploitation, as ever.

In Latin America, these arguments took on a different twist than in the United States; for Latin American leftists began to castigate elites, whether old or new, for their alleged dependence on Yankee capitalists. According to this line of reasoning, which came more into evidence in the 1960s when "dependency theory" analysis emerged as a growth industry among leftist-leaning intellectuals throughout the world, the plight of the Latin American masses stemmed not just from the abuses historically heaped upon them by old and new elites alike. It stemmed also, at least from some point around the beginning of the twentieth century when American capital began its large-scale penetration of the southern hemisphere, from the ultimate dependence of Latin America's privileged sectors (old and new) on Yankee capital. In abusing native workers, Latin Americans were in the final analysis simply doing the bidding of their Yankee masters to increase profits, the lion's share of which ultimately wound up in North American coffers.

In the Depression era, when Marxian analysis made dramatic headway among North American intellectuals, Latin America's early spinners of dependency theories found many allies in the United States. In fact, the shared expectations of American and Latin American Marxists as to what the future held contributed to feelings of good neighborliness among leftist thinkers on both sides of the border—a point developed further in the next chapter. Then, when the Depression gave way to the spectacular resuscitation of North American capitalism, Marxism very nearly disappeared for a generation or so among U.S. intellectuals. In contrast, Marxism remained a formidable intellectual force among Latin American thinkers living in the midst of lingering economic failure. And so, at least until the 1960s, the Marxist convergence of Yankee and Latin intellectuals that had contributed however minimally to hemispheric good neighborliness passed virtually out of existence—the Yankees having defected from the convergence.

For a decade or two after 1945 North Americans, by and large, tended to discard the Social Gospel. Once again the spirit of Henry Ward Beecher stalked the northern half of the hemisphere: poverty *was* the consequence of sin. As they luxuriated in the postwar era of plenty and girded themselves for the Cold War, Americans could not forgive Latin Americans for their continuing poverty or for their ongoing flirtation with Marxist remedies.

Involving both men and women, the moment of American and Latin American convergence around a Social Gospel that sometimes spilled over into Marxist proclivities had been brief. But it had lasted long enough to facilitate the birth of the Good Neighbor era.

# 7. *American and Latin American Intellectuals as Good Neighbors*

❖ ❖ ❖ ❖ ❖ ❖ ❖ ❖ ❖ ❖ ❖ ❖ ❖ ❖ ❖ ❖ ❖ ❖ ❖ ❖ ❖ ❖ ❖ ❖ ❖ ❖ ❖ ❖ ❖ ❖ ❖ ❖ ❖

### American Intellectuals Become Pensadores

Among the many ways in which the Anglo and Latin halves of the hemisphere differed in their historical traditions, none was more pronounced than the divergent appraisal that each attached to the man of business affairs, the man who pursued economic aggrandizement as an end in itself. While norteamericanos tended to lionize the successful pursuer of affluence, Latins characteristically expressed disdain for persons whose only success lay in the accumulation of capital. Remember, it's the historical past, not the present, I'm referring to.

To some degree, the hemisphere's contrasting attitudes toward the businessman spring from the fact that in Latin America's political culture the intellectual has traditionally played an important role; he (and increasingly in more recent years, she) has had access to the levers of power and all the attendant opportunities to derive personal gain while ostensibly laboring for the commonweal. Until quite recently, Latin American politicians have permitted and even welcomed the arrangement, for it gave to their regimes the aura of respectability that has traditionally attached to the world of the intellectual, the person purportedly interested in the spiritual exaltation attached to the life of the mind. This approach to life is reflected in the saying that emerged out of medieval Spain: *las letras y las armas dan nobleza.* Nobility stemmed from letters, meaning belles lettres, and military excellence, not from mere pecuniary success. The latter was acceptable only if stumbled onto indirectly when seeking some higher goal—such as the conquest of Muslims in the Iberian peninsula or of Indian civilizations in the New World.

In the United States, on the other hand, where the values of modernity were enshrined relatively early, intellectuals and pursuers of the fine (rather than the applied) arts prevailingly have been looked upon with suspicion by the wielders of economic and political power, by the movers and the shakers; and even generals and admirals lacked the prestige of the millionaire. To successful modern men of affairs, the pursuit of purely intellectual concerns smacks of hopeless impracticality, and suggests lack of skills in doing what really matters, which is creating wealth. In general, at least until the Depression era, American intellectuals, in stark contrast to their counterparts in Latin America, found themselves excluded from influential roles in shaping national policy.

In a tradition harking back to colonial times, Latin American intellectuals, to say nothing of generals, have not confined themselves to ivory towers, or to mere battlefields. Their *nobleza* or nobility has entitled them to play an active role in politics. The intellectual who turned his attention to politics and who often gained an important, influential place of his own among political power wielders came to be known as a *pensador*: literally, a thinker. Latin American pensadores, then, were more than just thinkers; they were, in addition, political activists and doers, movers-and-shakers who operated not just out of street rallies or classrooms or libraries but out of offices in the citadels of power, rubbing elbows with if not actually serving as presidents and ministers, rubbing elbows, too, with generals turned politicians. Purely intellectual pursuits did not satisfy the pensador. If he happened to be a university professor for a few hours each week, the rest of the time he was a cabinet member or some other functionary involved in shaping and implementing policy.

In the New Deal era, American intellectuals to a degree previously unprecedented became pensadores. Often leaving the university behind them altogether, they accepted political appointments, moved to Washington, and played active roles in shaping government policy. It was a heady experience. Seldom if ever before in American history—at least not since the constitutional convention—had intellectuals been taken so seriously. American military officers in the 1930s were still expected to remain apolitical; but when it came to intellectuals in politics, the United States and Latin America began to converge. A fundamental reason for this was that in the Depression setting, businessmen in America fell into something of the same ill repute that had prevailingly dogged them in Latin America. North and south of the border in the 1930s, citizens tended to coalesce in the opinion that businesspersons were callow, shallow, on the make, as unconcerned with the commonweal as they were ignorant of how to achieve it.

Already by the 1930s Latin American pensadores had for quite some time tended to picture themselves, and also the national masses whose protectors they professed to be, as victims. Somehow the political policies that they, the intellectuals, advocated and sometimes actively helped to implement from the halls of government never produced the hoped-for results; their countries remained economic basket cases, seemingly altogether incapable of achieving adequate levels of development or political stability. Pensadores, of course, could not admit that the reason for this lay in their own ill-founded schemes, in a colossal impracticality often enough compounded by venality. No, the fault lay not in themselves that they and their fellow citizens were underlings: the fault lay abroad, centered among the Yankee capitalists who indulged their lust for profits in fields to the south, often abetted not only by their own government but by local politicians on the make—politicians, of course, with whom the pensadores happened to be at odds. Not only they, the pensadores, were victims; so, too, were the poverty stricken citizens for whom they proclaimed (often hypocritically) deep concern. Together, intellectuals, unsated for one reason or another in their power aspirations, and the masses, impoverished and exploited, were victims of outside forces manipulated by the Yankee money changers who in turn were abetted by Latin American stooges. The pensadores would not have agreed with the lines Shakespeare gives to Cassius in *Julius Caesar:* "The fault, dear Brutus, lies not in our stars but in ourselves that we are underlings."

To many a Latin American pensador, the fault behind their failure to rise as high in political circles as they had hoped, and the fault behind the failure of their policies to produce promised results, lay not in themselves nor even in their stars but in Washington and in those offices on Wall Street where unprincipled plutocrats planned how to sink their tentacles deeper still into Latin American flesh. As the Depression struck, more and more did Latin pensadores tend to blame their plight on the baneful effects of Yankee dollar diplomacy. And now, on the other side of the border, more and more American intellectuals tended to agree with this vastly oversimplified analysis.

American intellectuals, whether or not they ever got enough of a foot inside the doors of Washington offices to qualify as pensadores, tended—like the genuine pensadores to the south—also to see themselves and the impoverished citizens they claimed to champion as innocent victims of the cultural barbarians: barbarians who, especially during the post–Civil War Industrial Revolution and the corruption of the Gilded Age, had gained control over national destiny. Allegedly, these robber barons had turned politicians into mere lackeys who carried out their orders. If the intellectuals had their way, they would begin to issue the orders to politicians. Thereby the country would be saved; for the intellectuals understood how to devise the policies that would bring well-being to the masses—if not necessarily material well-being, then at least the sort of cultural fulfillment through which properly led and suitably inspired citizens would overcome their addiction to mere material comfort.

During the Depression years, the workers of the American hemisphere may not have arisen together to discard their chains, as the *Communist Manifesto* admonished. Throughout the hemisphere, though, intellectuals did begin tentatively to unite, or at least to find some common ground, as they savored the political power that would, so they modestly believed, enable them to forge a new and just and culturally elevated world in the American hemisphere, thereby making America truly a New World.

Some of the intellectuals in Washington dreamed on a relatively modest scale. All that immediately interested them was devising restraints on American businessmen that would end their ability to exploit the laboring classes both in the United States itself and in all those Latin American republics to which they had extended their operations. Others, more radical, more mystical and dreamy and lyrical, spurned or were never offered Washington positions. Often they envisaged not piecemeal reforms but radical, all-inclusive transformation. A fair number of those who dreamed on a heroic scale looked southward for allies who would join in the task not just of transforming individual countries but the entire hemisphere.

Among those in the United States who dealt in lyrical, utopian politics, a fair number turned to Marxism in one guise or another—helping to account for the fact that between 1928 and the late 1930s membership in the American Communist Party soared from a few thousand to somewhere between 75,000 and 100,000. Often American Communists, and the additional tens of thousands of fellow travelers, struck alliances with the burgeoning ranks of south-of-the-border Communists and Marxists, and dreamed of leading a great revolution of the proletariat throughout the hemisphere. Now that capitalism seemed to have self-destructed, its final demise might not even require violence, just the concerted will of right-thinking leaders who could direct the masses along the peaceful road to utopia. At a time when even *Business Week* could inform its readers that industrial gains under Soviet plans had become "real and significant—when compared with our own," it is not surprising that a fair number of intellectuals, whether in the United States or in Latin America, began to think they would not need to push very hard in order to speed the inevitable historical processes toward their final destination of socialism.[1]

## The Latin Americanization of American University Life and the Ongoing Radicalization of Intellectuals and Writers

Hemispheric accord among intellectuals came about for many reasons other than cross-border leanings toward Marxism. Among those reasons figured the Latin Americanization of the American university system during the Depression. Virtually since independence those Latin American intellectuals who had not been able to find university posts, government positions, or other suitably dignified niches suffered the discontents common to persons who are well educated but un- or underemployed. America's intellectuals faced similar discontents in the 1930s.

Between 1930 and 1934, private universities in the United States reduced faculty by nearly 8 percent, while public universities cut back by about 7 percent. Even professors who retained their positions suffered salary cuts. In their discontent and disillusionment, they began increasingly to assign as required readings books such as Matthew Josephson's *The Robber Barons* (1934), depicting America's most successful capitalists as out-and-out moral failures, and describing the whole American economic structure as vicious to the core. In line with what their south-of-the-border counterparts had been doing for decades, some of America's best-educated intellectuals, both within the universities and outside, began to rail against the economic system. Even when they stopped short of embracing socialism or communism, they built their case against capitalism on charges that the moneyed interests, by plundering the people and robbing them of effective liberty, violated the "libertarian beliefs of the founding fathers."[2]

All the while American writers joined in the intellectual revolt against capitalism, frequently turning their pens to propagandizing in behalf of socialism. Among such writers was critic-essayist-novelist Edmund Wilson. Granted, the Depression brought pain and woe, Wilson observed; but "one couldn't help being exhilarated at the sudden unexpected collapse of that stupid gigantic fraud": American capitalism.[3] Latin American writers had been predicting that collapse for many a year. Now, to their surprise, they discovered an abundance of like-minded writers to the north: writers ready to join with them, the Latin Americans, in applauding the collapse and concocting utopian rebuilding schemes.

Latin America's sensitive souls, its writers and poets who ostensibly transcended sordid economic pursuits, found another kindred soul in John Dos Passos (of Portuguese extraction). In his *U.S.A.* trilogy (1930–1936) Dos Passos presents the case that pre-Depression-era life in America had become shallow and selfish, so focused on gaining wealth as to preclude "principled conduct." Also figuring among the kindred souls was social novelist Josephine Herbst, born in 1897 in Sioux City, Iowa. In her estimation, formed during the Depression years, the only Americans who "made it" materially were those who became most adept "at capitalism's requisite selfishness"; and the "light" of acquisitiveness by which most Americans lived was in reality "no light at all." Then there was the disgruntled Yugoslav-born writer Louis Adamic, who became a successful novelist in America during the Depression years and who turned increasingly against what impressed him as the country's crass materialism. Seeking the companionship of higher-minded people, he retreated for a time to Guatemala.[4]

In huge numbers, other disgruntled American writers sought, and for a while came to believe they had found, their oasis of higher values in revolutionary Mexico—a utopia far more accessible than the USSR, to which only a relative handful of Americans who had abandoned hope in their native land made their way. While most American literary malcontents did not vote with their feet in favor of what they perceived as a less hectic, less selfish, less materialistic life in Latin America, they sympathized in their hearts with the stereotyped multitudes of virtuous Latin American primitives who had not succumbed, not sold out, to the wiles of modernity.[5]

At least a few American intellectuals instead of lashing out at the capitalist system attributed the Depression to some sort of tragic fate, perhaps related to the theological concept of Original Sin, that doomed human beings, regardless of what political and economic practices they chose, to suffering and earthly failure. In this, the American intellectuals (whether knowingly or not) forged common bonds with traditionalist, conservative counterparts in Latin America who had always derided the human quest for mere earthly comfort, advising that rather than questing after fortune humans should seek to build character by stoically shouldering the tragic burdens of temporal existence. Sometimes Ernest Hemingway wrote in this spirit. In *Death in the Afternoon,* his great book on bullfighting as the embodiment of the Spanish tragic sense of life with its focus on death the inevitable, Hemingway quotes the lines so intimately intertwined with the Anglo-Saxon epic sense of life: "Life is real and life is earnest, and the grave is not its goal." About the author of these lines, Hemingway asks: "And where did they bury him?"

### *American Jews as* Pensadores *and Activists and Some Hemispheric Implications*

The Latin American was not the only exotic Other with whom American intellectuals and writers, in their discontent with home-grown values and institutions, began to find common ground. A good number of Jews in America also benefited from the new mood of tolerance and inclusion into which at least an articulate minority of Americans entered as they came to doubt their traditional values and along with them their traditional prejudices.

By the 1930s, Jews in America were a power to be reckoned with. Although arriving as immigrants without material wealth as they fled Old World pogroms and generalized persecution, they brought with them either a superior education or a burning desire to obtain an education in their new homeland. By the 1920s they had established a proud ethnic literature, had founded newspapers, and organized "emphatically Jewish unions and fraternal orders." Moreover, a powerful Reform Judaism had established itself by the 1920s, its constituency not only eschewing much religious ritual while rejecting ethnic exclusivity, but at the same time cultivating a "modern civic consciousness and a feeling for secular social reform." In this particular manifestation of their New World activities, Jews had established their own "analog of the social gospel." Bent on contributing their grain to the reform movements unleashed by the Depression, they turned in many instances to socialist politics, while still keeping their attention focused on practical, incremental, bread-and-butter gains.[6]

Still other Jewish thinkers and activists assumed a millennialist-utopianist stance, mixing the Cabala and Marx as they agitated in favor of sweeping social transformation in America. Such a person was the writer and social critic Waldo Frank, who for a time gained a large following among Latin American utopianist intellectuals. Frank's significance as a Good Neighbor emissary was recognized in 1942 when the State Department sent him on a goodwill tour to Latin America.[7]

Latin America's more down-to-earth labor organizers, on the whole indifferent to Waldo Frank's spiritualist vision of hemispheric rapprochement, formed alliances with like-minded Jewish organizers in the United States. A particular hero to them was CIO leader Sidney Hillman, who, especially during the war years, became one of the most powerful figures in Washington. Increasingly, then, Latin American reformers of many different stripes came to see in American Jews their natural allies; and this fact contributed enormously to the popularity of the Good Neighbor policy south of the border. Many Latin American intellectuals, reformist and revolutionary, noted approvingly that while Jews constituted about 3 percent of the population, they made up approximately 15 percent of Roosevelt's top appointments.[8] This implied to them that FDR was turning to brainy rather than wealthy types, to those who inclined more to be pensadores than businessmen.

The importance of Jews in the New Deal won Roosevelt plaudits from south-of-the-border liberal intellectuals that actually he did not fully merit. At the same time, Jewish prominence in the New Deal garnered Roosevelt unmerited criticism from Latin American Catholic bigots and from anti-

Semitic politicians—especially in that country that would emerge as the main thorn in the side of Good Neighbor diplomacy, Argentina. The bigots, many of them overt or crypto-fascists in addition to being fanatical Catholics, believed Roosevelt had gone all too far in kowtowing to Jews.

FDR remained totally indifferent to the millennialist-utopianist cast that some Depression-era Jews brought to their social vision, perhaps an outgrowth of Old World Judaic messianism. But, ever on the lookout for allies in his endeavor to introduce social reform, the president moved to cultivate the support of more pragmatic Jews; and soon the Washington bureaucracy was, as noted, sprinkled with bright young Jewish intellectuals. Moreover, along with organized labor and African Americans and Catholics, Jews became an essential ingredient in the New Deal electoral base—so much so that some of FDR's more venomous detractors dubbed his program the Jew Deal and floated rumors that the president himself sprang from Jewish ancestry. Even FDR's firm supporters among Catholics of Irish and other immigrant backgrounds resented the president's courting of liberal Jewish intellectuals.

Ever the practical politician, FDR tried carefully not to go too far in his opening toward Jews. For one thing, he was impressed by the enormous popularity that Detroit's radio priest Fr. Coughlin garnered through his obscene anti-Semitism. (In one issue of his periodical *Social Justice,* Coughlin had stated that the "Jew . . . had no more business . . . in politics and government than had a pig in a China shop.") Above all, the president often allowed his moral posture to be set by opinion polls, one of which (conducted in 1938) found "58 percent [of Americans with an opinion on the issue] believed that persecution of Jews in Europe was either partly or entirely their own fault." Nor would he ignore a 1942 poll in which 44 percent of respondents indicated their belief that Jews already had too much power in the United States. Nor did he fail to take to heart other polls conducted between 1938 and 1942 revealing that only one-third of the populace would have opposed anti-Semitic legislation if the government had proposed it. Nor did he have the moral stamina to fly in the face of polls indicating that between July 1938 and May of 1939, "the worst period of open anti-Jewish excesses in Nazi Germany, from 66 to 77 percent of the American public was opposed to raising the immigration quota to help Jewish refugees, even children."[9]

Nor did the president deem it expedient to ignore FBI Director J. Edgar Hoover's conviction that wartime Jewish immigrants to the United States should be kept to a minimum, for they were likely to be infiltrated by communist and even fascist spies. This was one reason for FDR's shameful refusal to intervene when the Cuban government and the U.S. State Department turned away the liner that bore some 960 Jews to what they assumed would be a safe refuge in the New World. The *St. Louis* returned to Europe with most of the would-be refugees still aboard, and many subsequently met their fate in Hitler's gas ovens.[10]

On the whole, it just did not seem politically expedient to Roosevelt to challenge American anti-Semitism, or to lock horns with Breckinridge Long, an anti-Semitic assistant secretary of state who along with other department officials, and with J. Edgar Hoover's blessings, thwarted numerous efforts to rescue Jews and downplayed rumors about Hitler's extermination programs. Perhaps, too, FDR was piqued when Franz Boas, one of the leading Jewish intellectuals in America and one of the most important figures in twentieth-century anthropology, compared U.S. treatment of blacks to Nazi conduct toward Jews.[11] Given the New Deal's reliance on black support, here was a potentially damaging assessment of enormous magnitude.

Once over a White House lunch with Catholic economist Leo T. Cowley, the president betrayed the instincts of a born WASP when he observed: "You know this is a Protestant country, and the Catholics and Jews are here under sufferance; it is up to you [and here FDR intended his remarks to apply not only to Cowley but also to his Jewish secretary of the treasury and friends of sorts, Henry Morgenthau, Jr.] to go along with anything that I want."[12]

To a large degree FDR felt the same about Latin Americans as about Catholics and Jews within the United States. He might not especially like them, but he realized the important ways in which he could use them. Furthermore, unlike the intolerance that opinion polls revealed toward Jews, similar polls conducted in the late 1930s and early '40s revealed American empathy for Latin Americans and a desire for policies of hemispheric inclusion. The pollsters had spoken, and FDR, as always, was attentive.

Still, if Latin Americans did not respond favorably to his overtures, then Roosevelt would try to find ways to impress upon them that their admittance into hemispheric good graces was under sufferance and depended on their good conduct. Not until the threat of involvement in a European or Asian war became imminent would the president realize that, for the time being at least, he might sometimes have to suffer the Latin Americans patiently regardless of how insufferably they responded to his overtures of good neighborliness.

# 8.

# *Becoming Good Neighbors through Arts and Letters*

❖ ❖ ❖ ❖ ❖ ❖ ❖ ❖ ❖ ❖ ❖ ❖ ❖ ❖ ❖ ❖ ❖ ❖ ❖ ❖ ❖ ❖ ❖ ❖ ❖ ❖ ❖ ❖ ❖ ❖ ❖ ❖ ❖ ❖

### *The New Deal: Support for* Letras *and Art*

In New Deal days, government support for struggling literary artists went hand-in-hand with succor for unemployed manual workers and down-on-their-luck farmers. Surveying the plight of writers and artists, FDR and adviser Harry Hopkins concluded that they had to live, too—which meant the government had to help them live. Helping them in the hour of need when the private sector no longer provided an adequate number of purchasers and patrons of their work seemed the decent thing to do. Moreover, books and art might possibly substitute for circuses in diverting attention from the Depression era's lack of bread. Just possibly, too, there might be a political payoff. Conceivably, benefited writers and artists would wield their pens and brushes in defense of the New Deal. Maybe it was time for American political leaders to learn from the example of the Medicis and a long line of Latin potentates, whether in the Old or the New Worlds. These potentates had believed that practical benefits accrued from subsidization of the culturati, who, to hear them tell it at least, were molders of public opinion. Whatever the reason, New Deal relief programs soon came to include the Federal Writers' Project.

By the time its seven-year life came to an end, the Federal Writers' Project had been involved in publications that filled seven twelve-foot shelves, all of the books and pamphlets thereon subsidized in whole or in part by the approximately $27,000,000 that Washington allocated in order that writers might live, too. This sum represented about 1 percent of total expenditures by the Works Progress Administration, of which the Writers' Project was a part. Struggling writers supported by the Project included Conrad Aiken, Nelson Algren, Saul Bellow, John Cheever, Ralph Ellison, and Richard Wright.

The Writers' Project subsidized preparation of some of the finest guidebooks ever to appear in America. Beyond this, it supported publications that stimulated interest in America's rich traditions of folklore and regional cultures, promoted racial understanding and tolerance of diversity, and helped to make "articulate the lower third of the society."[1] Contributing toward these same worthy ends were the documentary films produced by Pare Lorentz with federal subsidization.

At the same time, though, the Writers' Project subsidized many an attack, subtle and not so subtle, against American capitalism; and more than a few of these attacks were inspired by the authors' communist sympathies or even party membership. When Texas congressman Martin Dies, chairman of the House Committee for the Investigation of Un-American Activities, complained in the mid-1930s that the Communist Party had a grip on 40 percent of participants in the Federal Writers' Project he may have exaggerated considerably, but he did have a point.[2] And FDR's political enemies made the most of it. Meantime, though, Latin America's intelligentsia had observed in fascination the spectacle of America doing what they had praised the Soviet Union for doing: subsidizing "intellectual workers." Here was a Yankee example that Latin intellectuals hoped might inspire their own governments toward greater largesse.

Still, many of Latin America's intelligentsia, to whom intellectual tolerance and freedom of expression remained virtually incomprehensible, must have puzzled over a government that actually subsidized attacks on the nation's basic economic foundations. What strange and unfathomable ways the Yankees had taken to in their time of economic woe. What the Latin intellectuals may have failed to realize was that in America few people took the writing classes, the intelligentsia, as seriously as Latin American authors and intellectuals liked to think they were taken in their own countries. Roosevelt, though, realized that for all their self-inflated pretensions, writers were not going to bring on a revolution. In his heart of hearts, Martin Dies probably knew this, too. Politically, though, it helped him and like-minded Americans to pretend otherwise, and to step up attacks on liberal Democrats as permissive, cultural weirdos at best and as dangerous subversives at worst.

Permissiveness reached new levels of absurdity, so far as America's defenders of old-time cultural values were concerned, with the Federal

Theater Program, conceived by Eleanor Roosevelt, that subsidized playwrights and performances of their plays. Howls of outraged protest greeted many of the plays performed under Program auspices, most especially in 1938 when its support facilitated production of the folklore-based ballet *Frankie and Johnny*. The work featured pimps and prostitutes and other "deviant types," all of whom "pirouetted onto stage with Federal backing."[3] This alleged encouragement of permissiveness was anathema to the protectors of "genuine," one-dimensional American culture, and from that time on the Theater Program's days were numbered.

Permissiveness, at least of one sort, was something Latin Americans long had looked for in vain among their neighbors to the north. Permissiveness of the sort they coveted meant tolerance of the Other, tolerance of the sort that might make it possible for Yankees to accept them, the Latins, for what they were, rather than looking upon them as human clay to be molded in the gringo image.

## The New Deal and Federal Support for Artists

Giving a boost to writers and artists and at the same time delivering a putdown to affluent capitalists who had tended to regard themselves as the only true Americans, FDR in one of his 1936 Fireside Chats affirmed that those who lived by their hands and brains were every bit as important as those who lived from the accumulation of property. Not surprisingly, the president soon lent his support to programs that aided artists, supreme examples of Americans who lived by their hands and their brains in addition to their intuition. When Secretary of Labor Frances Perkins, at the instigation of her daughter Susanna, approached Roosevelt with the suggestion that artists be hired at government expense to decorate America's dreary and gloomy public buildings, thereby imparting a note of cheerfulness to drab times, the president responded enthusiastically. "A lot of artists are out of work," he soon explained to his secretary of the treasury: "Let us hire these people and put them to work painting pictures on public buildings."[4] And that is precisely what government began to do, as it created within the Works Progress Administration (WPA) a division called the Federal Art Project (FAP). As it turned out, though, artists were far more likely to receive government checks for prints (graphics) or easel paintings or photographs then for murals. (A minuscule sample of the graphics produced by the WPA/FAP comprises the bulk of the illustrations for this book.)

For the statistically inclined, here are some statistics. During the duration of its activities (1935–1943) the WPA/FAP paid, in part or in full, for the production of 108,099 easel paintings, 250,000 prints, 500,000 photographs, 17,444 sculptures, and 2,566 murals. In all, some twelve thousand artists were hired through government relief projects. Moreover, they had the opportunity to display their work before hundreds of thousands of viewers "at the 450 [government-subsidized] exhibits which traveled to city halls and public schools."[5]

New Deal programs did not represent by any means the first instance of government support for the arts. Between the end of the War of 1812 and the outset of the Civil War, the federal government commissioned numerous statues, reliefs, murals, and fresco paintings to decorate the U.S. capitol. This subsidized artwork in general, so it has been convincingly argued, helped justify and reinforce America's imperialist inclinations by depicting, among other subjects, heroic and civilized and ethnically superior Americans bent upon the subjugation, or "uplift," of cruel and savage Indians. What was new was that now, in the 1930s, artists would be paid to create works that often ridiculed the imperialist mystique and the capitalist drives that allegedly spawned that mystique, works that also presented in a favorable light people, ranging from Indians to African Americans to Latin Americans, once portrayed—in line with prevailing national prejudice—as ethnically inferior. And, if the old form of arts patronage had served to glorify the old America, the support of the 1930s encouraged an art that sometimes disparaged the old, money-grubbing republic while conveying the image of a new and humanistic America that artists would help bring into being.[6]

If murals represented a numerically small proportion of New Deal–subsidized artworks, they did make up the most spectacular, most highly visible, and widely viewed art produced during the Depression years. To some Americans, the subsidized murals suggested that the Roosevelt administration hoped to produce in America the same sort of sweeping socialist revolution that Mexicans allegedly initiated in 1910 and subsequently propagandized by means of their "Bolshevik" muralists. Whatever their political leanings, and they were decidedly leftist, Mexico's muralists, headed by Diego Rivera, David Siqueiros, and José Clemente Orozco, just happened to be the most celebrated in the western world during the 1920s and '30s.

Many Americans traveled to Mexico to steep themselves in the work of the revolutionary painters. And Mexican muralists traveled north across the border, sometimes subsidized by U.S. federal funds, to make their contributions to the revolution that American conservatives feared and that radicals hoped was underway. To the resentment of Orozco and other Mexican artists testing America's cultural waters, north-of-the-border radicals took especially to Diego Rivera; indeed, they lionized him as the model for Yankee revolutionary artists to emulate. Various commissions took Rivera from San Francisco to Detroit, and finally to New York. In that city he created a sensation by depicting Lenin in one of the murals he did for the Radio City Building at Rockefeller Center. This touched off a heated legal battle that ended with destruction of the offending artwork, an act that contributed all the more to its creator's fame. Rivera became the model for many American artists who wanted to propagandize on the "big wall" against humanity's principal enemy: capitalism.[7]

The Mexican muralists did pack a strong cultural wallop north of the border. Black artists in particular, and also Native Americans who created a flourishing new art during the Depression, fell under the influence of the swarthy-complected Mexicans. They seemed to prove that the dark-of-skin and the humbly born who might lack social finesse could take their place in the front ranks of those struggling to launch the revolution that would usher in racial and every other variety of justice.

What was most striking, though, was the degree to which American artists did *not* fall under the revolutionary, Marxist sway of the Mexican muralists. If anything, what they admired in Mexican artists was their attempt to cast off from European traditions and develop their own autochthonous, New World art. Rather than for their ties to Moscow, American artists admired their Mexican counterparts for their widely proclaimed attempt to find inspiration in their country's Indian culture and rural, regional folklore in general. They, too, the North American artists, wanted to join in the move to create a genuine Western Hemisphere art, one that emerged out of the very bowels of the New World. They were no longer content to remain on the edges of European art.

Periodically, it seems, American artists feel obliged to declare their cultural independence from Europe. And artists of the Depression era afford one of the more striking manifestations of this phenomenon. In this spirit, they accepted some of their Latin American counterparts as allies, even role models of a sort. In this spirit, too, they simultaneously reflected and helped to shape the hemispheric isolationism out of which the Good Neighbor policy emerged. Theirs was the artistic equivalent of a Monroe Doctrine: America for the Americans.

The general American public remained largely unaware of what was really going on in American arts and letters. To the degree they thought at all about the issue, they tended to accept the charges of staunch conservatives that radical and government-subsidized American artists and writers, some of the former accepting Mexican communists as role models, were out to destroy the "real America"—however one might choose to define those terms. While largely not guilty of the un-American charges leveled against them, the U.S. culturati did contain elements that harbored the sort of delusions of grandeur that simultaneously isolated them from mainstream fellow citizens and united them with fellow savants below the border.

## Changing the World through Arts and Letters

During the Depression years, many an American intellectual, writer, and artist came to share in the hubris that some of their Latin American counterparts had exhibited through the decades, going back even to the colonial period. Out of this hubris sprang faith in the ability of persons of ostensibly unique artistic and cultural talent not only to change the course of history but to transform human nature itself. Representative figures among the North American culturati came to believe they could accomplish this modest undertaking by means of what they considered their singular sensitivity and perceptiveness, their understanding of the most exalted realms of human potential, their aesthetic prowess, their spiritual superiority, their unique ability to communicate with the masses, through their art, on levels both below and above mere rationality. Through all of these and other gifts that set them apart from ordinary mortals, they could produce a revolution that would change the world by changing human nature.

Not only writers and artists shared in this belief. The enormously talented African-American singer and actor Paul Robeson seems honestly to have believed that through his art he could inspire his audiences to change their whole set of values, to ascend to a higher stage of being in which they would no longer be influenced by racial prejudice. To some extent he ignored the efforts of more down-to-earth Negro intellectuals and activists who worked within the political and economic order to advance the cause of civil rights. Robeson believed he could accomplish more through the mesmerizing power of his art.

Undoubtedly, art critic and historian Robert Hughes is correct when he denies validity to the belief that it lies within the power of the arts "to change the moral dimensions of life." This delusion, he notes, first peaked in America between the deaths of Presidents Monroe and Lincoln. It soared even higher, both north and south of the border, during the Depression years. Taking note of the delusion at that time, British-American poet W. H. Auden observed that, though he did not mean to imply it didn't matter, art changes nothing.[8] Nevertheless, the shared delusion that art could change everything helped establish for the first time a genuine camaraderie among many of the hemisphere's writers and artists, among the culturati in general.

Beginning even just before the Depression era, utopianist visions of a new order sprouted in almost epidemic proportions among not only artists and writers but also among a fair number of Americans who regarded themselves as especially gifted in the esoteric arts. To help sharpen their perception and vision, such persons turned to gurus, among whom figured Georges I. Gurdjieff (the favorite spiritualist mentor of Frank Lloyd Wright and his wife, Olgivanna) and P. D. Ouspensky; they turned also to Helena Blavatsky and Annie Besant, those two remarkable women who helped establish Theosophy; and they turned to wise men from India, never in short supply during the first half of the twentieth century. In all of this American mystics (knowingly or not) entered into the flow of Latin American messianism, spiritualism, esotericism, and various outpourings of so-called popular religion. In a way they put themselves, too, in the tradition of the Plains Indians, who as they faced prospects of doom in the late nineteenth century dreamed of creating a new utopia by means of performing the Ghost Dance.

Times of crisis, it is said, induce the quest for utopian and otherworldly solutions to worldly ills. Not surprisingly, such quests have flourished in Latin America, so often a land of adversity and failed hopes. As hopes dropped even lower than usual among Latin Americans, who in many regions did not share in the general prosperity that much of the world enjoyed in the 1920s and who then faced still greater calamities in the 1930s, new millennialist visions flourished. The Magnetic Spiritual School of the Universal Commune, headquartered in Buenos Aires, won new adherents throughout the continent, including Nicaragua's Augusto César Sandino. And in Peru Víctor Raúl Haya de la Torre drew on a rich variety of esoteric, spiritualist, gnostic, millennialist, theosophical, and pre-Columbian aboriginal influences, seasoned by a dash of Einstein's relativity theories that appealed to so many unconventional thinkers at the time, as he formed one of the most powerful change-oriented political movements ever to emerge out of the southern hemisphere: the APRA (Alianza Popular Revolucionaria Americana).[9]

So, in the Good Neighbor era, not only material and worldly considerations but forces that transcended the world accessible to sensory perception drew Americans, North and South, together. Even highly placed American political figures who had some considerable input into the shaping of hemispheric policy were attracted by the currents of spiritualism they encountered in Latin America. Such a person was Henry Wallace, FDR's secretary of agriculture and later (1940–1944) his vice-president.

### The New Deal and Support of the Nobleza of Arts and Letters

While he tolerated the esotericists and the spiritualists, FDR reserved his most enthusiastic support for the more down-to-earth writers and artists who, while often enough having their own private spiritualist leanings, produced tangible works of art and did not rely on intangible, other-worldly forces to change the world. And, to some considerable degree at least, FDR managed to co-opt a good many artists, intellectuals, and culturati of every sort who might otherwise have devoted their energies to planting revolutionary sparks among the combustible materials of the unemployed. The president performed the feat of co-optation by seeming to take artists, writers, and intellectuals in general as seriously as Latin American political leaders had through the years seemed to take them. By doing so, Roosevelt contributed an important, often ignored, ingredient to the Good Neighbor policy: proof that even Yankees could take seriously and encourage the arts and the letters that conferred nobleza.

Among those taking note of the benefits, domestic and hemispheric, that might derive from support of the arts were American businessmen. When World War II ended and new administrations did not rush to assume the mantle of patron of the arts that FDR had worn, businessmen grabbed for it: they became large-scale patrons of the makers of American culture. This was an era, after all, when Americans had not yet been thoroughly corrupted by television and the commercialization of art, when many of them still took "high" culture seriously, and appreciated those firms that helped sponsor the art they craved—or at least thought they should act as if they craved in order to appear "civilized." Under such circumstances, support for the arts was good public relations.

So, however much they might have hated him during the New Deal years, businesspersons ultimately paid FDR the compliment of imitating him. Furthermore, entrepreneurs and financiers who operated across the border managed, even as Roosevelt had, to enhance their image by showing their concern for culture. In this, they followed in the wartime footsteps of Nelson Rockefeller. As coordinator of inter-American affairs in charge, among other things, of cultural exchanges, Rockefeller had demonstrated—at least to his own satisfaction—the usefulness of culture in serving the interests not only of the American government but of American business firms. This is a story briefly sketched in a later chapter. It's a story, though, that has its origins in domestic New Deal policies that supported the arts through federal programs, thereby leading many a Latin American to suspect that the gringos had begun to try very hard to transcend their old boorishness.

As far back as 1883 Walt Whitman had prophesied that Americans, once they had accomplished the economic development of their continent, would begin to transcend their material feats "by fulfilling their spiritual and aesthetic potential."[10] To the amazement of many Latin Americans, their gringo neighbors, with government support, seemed suddenly intent upon fulfilling their spiritual and aesthetic potential. Maybe they weren't such bad neighbors after all.

# 9. Krause, Sacco and Vanzetti, and the American Culturati

❖ ❖ ❖ ❖ ❖ ❖ ❖ ❖ ❖ ❖ ❖ ❖ ❖ ❖ ❖ ❖ ❖ ❖ ❖ ❖ ❖ ❖ ❖ ❖ ❖ ❖ ❖ ❖ ❖ ❖ ❖ ❖ ❖ ❖

### Krausism-Arielism in the American Hemisphere

In addition to the likelihood that he hoped to co-opt them, enlist them as allies, and blunt their possibly dangerous, revolutionary tendencies, Franklin Roosevelt approached artists and intellectuals with the very practical and humanitarian purpose of giving them some means of earning a living. In this latter respect, he approached them as he did farmers through the Agricultural Adjustment Administration (AAA) or Farm Security Administration (FSA), or as he approached down-on-their-luck and unemployed blue-collar workers, and youths who had never yet really broken into the labor market, through the Works Progress Administration (WPA), the Public Works Administration (PWA), and the Civilian Conservation Corps (CCC). However, many of the artists and intellectuals attached a far more portentous meaning to the fact that they had come to be included under government's security tent. They saw this inclusion as enhancing their ability to work a virtual revolution in American society and its fundamental values. They saw the opportunity to wrest from allegedly crass businessmen the power to establish national values, to forge a society dedicated to the pursuit of culture and nonmaterial rewards.

In their delusions, the American culturati resembled the turn-of-the-century Krausistas in Spain and the Arielists in Latin America. These Spanish and Latin American prophets of a new and better world took their names respectively from a relatively insignificant German philosopher, Karl Christian Friedrich Krause, who (through a fluke that need not concern us here) came to be lionized among Spanish liberal thinkers, and from José Enrique Rodó, an Uruguayan thinker convinced it was possible to spread Athenian values among Latin Americans and thereby save them from contamination by North American materialism.[1]

Krausism, it has been said, embodied the entire spirit of late nineteenth- and early twentieth-century Spanish liberalism. Its influence spread to Latin America, where it helped inspire the Arielist social philosophy associated with Rodó as unveiled in his sensationally popular book of 1900: *Ariel*. Krausism, passed along to Spanish American intellectuals mainly in its rechristened guise of Arielism, contributed also to the spirit of the university reform movement that gained vast intellectual influence in the 1920s and '30s. In some ways, the spirit of Krausism found its way also into various Latin American offshoots of Marxism, whose prophets, among them Peru's José Carlos Mariátegui, proclaimed the primacy of nonmaterial values, thus standing Marxist materialism on its head by glorifying the superstructure over the base, by exalting the importance of spiritual over economic determinants.

In essence, intellectuals of the Krausist-Arielist persuasion sought a means of social pacification not associated with Catholicism's otherworld-liness as interpreted and manipulated by a priestly elite. By insisting that poverty was the estate richest in the means of salvation and by seeking to instill in the masses an overarching concern for otherworldly rewards that would lead them happily to accept their misery in this life, the priestly caste of a purportedly outmoded and superstition-ridden religion had sought to guarantee social stability on this Earth by focusing the attention of the gullible masses on the alleged glories of the world to come. This, at least, was the way in which Krausists-Arielists regarded the Catholic priesthood. Indeed, the claim of Krausists-Arielists to the liberal label derived well nigh exclusively from their anticlericalism. Except for this, they tended to be staunchly conservative. For example, they detested the one-person, one-vote sort of democracy and resisted all leveling influences in society that might reduce elites to the level of commoners.

In the Krausist-Arielist vision of the good society, order and harmony would derive from nonmaterial rewards to the masses, rewards resulting from appreciation of art, good music, and the higher cultural and intellectual treasures in general available in this life, here and now. The ties between elites and masses, forged by a common appreciation of the higher things in life would, ostensibly, eliminate crass materialism and replace disruptive individualism with social solidarity: for the masses would appreciate the degree to which their fulfillment in life depended on the spiritual-aesthetic riches that intellectuals and artists, the culturati in general, created and then shared with the masses, to whatever extent the masses were capable of coveting and appreciating such riches. Generally Krausists-Arielists also sought to encourage among the masses an appreciation of natural beauty. In short, they endeavored to instill respect, love, and veneration for all that refined, elevated, cleansed, refreshed, and uplifted the spirit—here, on this Earth, in this life.

Krausists-Arielists often advanced the same populist credo that from some point early in the nineteenth century both Spanish and Latin American intellectuals had proclaimed. Iberian populism stressed the unique ability of certain select souls to enter into the very psyche of the masses, to intuit, and then to articulate, the innermost longings of the masses, and thus enlightened, to devise and implement the measures that would lead to satisfaction of those longings. Not surprisingly, Krausist-Arielist populism helped pave the way for a later generation of thinkers raised in the school to warm to the concept of the dictatorship of the proletariat—which of course inevitably meant the dictatorship *over* the proletariat by those who understood what the masses truly desired, even though the masses themselves might not yet have become conscious of just what it was they did want and might have suffered from the delusion that their chief desire was for mere material rewards.

In the economic hard times of the 1930s, a fair number of the North American culturati established bonds of empathy with Latin America's anticapitalist prophets of nonmaterial rewards. Indeed, the success of the Good Neighbor policy depended, in some small measure at least, on the uniquely propitious climate that the Depression created for Yankees and Latins alike who wanted to lead their fellow citizens in the quest for nonmaterial rewards. As the Latins watched their kind of Krausist-Arielist value system spreading among the Yankees, they had to feel that the Colossus of the North was reinventing itself.

In the course of this reinvention, culture seemed to thrive as never before throughout what Latins had once disparagingly called *Yanquilandia*—a word they intended to connote crude materialism. Not only did literary figures emerge whom Latins admired enormously (with Hemingway and William Faulkner perhaps heading the list), but artists flourished and seemed to garner more prestige in the era of economic hard times. What is more, American classical music entered its golden age, producing composers such as Samuel Barber, Aaron Copland, George Gershwin, Howard Hanson, Roy Harris, David Diamond, Vincent Persichetti, William Schuman, Virgil Thomson, and many others. No longer could Boston be dismissed as the home of uncouth Irish immigrants and economic piracy as exemplified by, for example, Joseph Kennedy. Instead, it was home to the Boston Symphony and to its conductor Serge Koussevitsky, who delighted in commissioning new works from American composers.

Some of these composers, moreover, advanced good neighborliness by incorporating Latin themes and rhythms into their music, even as they established warm ties with such Latin American musical figures as the Brazilian Heitor Villa-Lobos and the Mexican Carlos Chávez.

Even "colored" composer William Grant Still began to carve out a reputation for himself, suggesting to some Latin Americans at least that through art, and a newfound public appreciation of art, Americans might move to overcome the race prejudice that all too often they had directed not just at African Americans but at Mexican immigrants in the Southwest and at Latin Americans in general. Through a different kind of music African Americans such as Duke Ellington and Louis Armstrong also won the hearts of Latin Americans, many of whom—happily for hemispheric goodwill—could not have guessed at the magnitude of discrimination musicians of dark skin still endured among racist Americans enraptured by the music they created.

Despite all the blemishes and warning signals, these were heady times in the American hemisphere for those who believed the so-called New World might genuinely become new as it fostered a new culture and a new politics that derived from that culture. To pensadores on both sides of the border, mystical ties became discernible, ties that bound the Americas, North and South, together and set them apart from the decadence and corruption and overall fatigue and ennui of much of the Old World. Pensadores on both sides of the border came, for a moment, to believe in miracles, and in their power to accomplish those miracles.

Robert Hughes, whose skepticism about the power of art to alter material life I referred to in the preceding chapter, sounds a note of warning that seems applicable to those New World–culture apostles who succumbed to delusions of grandeur in the 1930s. "We know, in our hearts," writes Hughes, "that the idea that people are morally ennobled by contact with works of art is a pious fiction."[2] How true—especially if Hughes would change his sentence ever so slightly to read, "We know . . . that the idea that people are *permanently* ennobled morally by contact with works of art is a pious fiction."

In the Depression era, a great many Americans, north and south of the border, succumbed to the pious fiction that underlay the Krausist-Arielist-Marxist nonmaterial rewards aspect of good neighborliness. And yet, although perhaps I should know better, I cannot help wondering if much good cannot sometimes emerge from illusions, from pious fictions. Without the occasional seasoning of pious fictions, concocted by intellectuals who in their delusions of grandeur try to introduce elements of dream life into crude reality, might not the real world be a far more vicious jungle than it is?

## Sacco and Vanzetti and Shifting Attitudes on Americanism

Fragile innocents of the dream life, or hardened criminals of the world of crude reality: into which category do Sacco and Vanzetti fall? For the overwhelming majority of America's discontented intelligentsia in the 1920s and '30s, Sacco and Vanzetti were idealistic, perhaps even dreamy pursuers of a better life for humanity. For more conventional Americans, pleased with the basic features of national life, satisfied that its traditional capitalist and individualistic values would see the country out of whatever temporary crisis might afflict it, Sacco and Vanzetti were militant advocates of dangerous, exotic delusions, and quite willing to resort to dynamite and assassination in order to serve those delusions. As it happened, the conventionally minded Americans in this instance were quite correct.[3] However, they allowed their imaginations to get the better of them in assuming a natural connection between the two Italians and the worrisome Mexican revolutionaries just across the border.

Italian immigrants Nicola Sacco and Bartolomeo Vanzetti after a short residence left the United States in 1917 to avoid draft registration. Moving to Mexico, they lived communally in Monterrey, along with other anarchist Italian immigrants. Later, when Sacco and Vanzetti got into trouble in the United States, Justice Department investigators surmised they had gone to Mexico to receive instruction in the use of explosives. American nativists were not surprised: those wild-eyed Latin terrorists, whether Italian or Mexican, were all the same! Especially with Mexico in the throes of a revolution that struck them as Bolshevik- and/or anarchist-inspired, self-styled decent and patriotic Americans had to be ever more on guard against subversion. But this is getting ahead of the story.

When word came by late 1917 that draft avoidance was easy, the Italian anarchists gradually left their Monterrey refuge and filtered back into the United States. When Sacco and Vanzetti left, they made their way to Massachusetts. Not far from where they settled a paymaster and his guard were shot to death (on April 15, 1920) during the robbery of a shoe factory in South Braintree. Three weeks later Sacco, a shoe worker at the time, and Vanzetti, then a fish peddler, were arrested as suspects. The following year they came to trial. Sacco was charged with murdering at least the guard, Vanzetti with being an accomplice, if not necessarily an actual murderer. Paul Avrich, one of the most objective among the dozens, even hundreds, of authors who have written on the case, observes that "the evidence against them was contradictory."[4] However that may be, and the matter has been endlessly debated through the decades, the two Italians were found guilty as charged and executed in August of 1927, after a lengthy process of appeals had run its course.

Boston's Irish working classes, striving to gain acceptance in their new

Albert James Webb, *Cafe Strategists,* between 1935 and 1943, drypoint, image: 7$^{15}$/₁₆ × 9¼ in. Gift of Dr. and Mrs. Corbin S. Carnell, in memory of E. Muriel Adams. Collection of the Harn Museum of Art, University of Florida. 1992.11.145 *With their foreign and "wild-eyed" appearance, the "Strategists" conform to the stereotyped conception that many Americans had of immigrants, both in the 1920s and the '30s.*

homeland by being more American than old-line Americans, tended to applaud the execution. And they held not just the alleged murders against the Italian duo. Beyond this, they assailed the Italians for their un-American beliefs. They were Reds! "That's bad enough," wrote a novelist attuned to the attitudes of Irish workers straining to prove their Americanism, "but that ain't all, not by a Damn sight." Worse even than this, Sacco and Vanzetti were "a couple o' God damned dagos; Now me, I'm an American, I am."⁵ To many marginal citizens, new and old, anxious to assert their Americanism, it helped to condemn not only "God damn dagos" but other exotics as well, including Jews and Mexicans and "spicks" of all provenance. Many Americans of old and eminently respectable lineage felt essentially the same way, though they expressed their prejudices with greater gentility.

On the other hand, intellectuals, writers, the representatives of the world of culture and arts, tended to see things differently. Widely respected journalist Heywood Broun spoke for these and other Americans when he argued that the execution of the two Italians, whom he presumed innocent with less evidence than those who presumed them guilty, arose out of American hatred of the Other, of the person who was different, of the foreigner. "Why," he asked, "does America hate the foreigner so profoundly?" He provided his own answer: "I think it is because we have wronged him so much."[6]

Many a Depression-era American intellectual, convinced as to the inherently exploitive nature of capitalism, assumed that if the Latin Americans did not like us it was because we had wronged them, for years, through our economic imperialism, our dollar diplomacy. Latin Americans were victims; and now they deserved compensation—if not monetary compensation, then at least a friendly, neighborly pat on the back. One is curious as to whether those intellectuals who advanced the foreigner-as-victim thesis wondered why it was that foreigners in such overwhelming numbers had made their way to America, why they fretted when immigration barriers went up in the 1920s, and why Mexican farm workers in the Southwest regarded it a catastrophe when in the 1930s they were made to return to their native land so that unemployed Americans could replace them.

America's left—lyrical, ethereal, and sometimes down-to-earth in their gutter nastiness—tended to ignore the pretty well established facts that Sacco and Vanzetti were dangerous and violence-prone (even if not necessarily murderers). Instead, they saw them as benign individuals, victimized because of ideas, of ethnicity, language, and culture, that made them different. In a similar mood American leftists in their lyrical flights of fancy dismissed all the blemishes that their allegedly callow and xenophobic and nativist fellow citizens had habitually attributed to Latin Americans. These were slanderous, malicious lies, or at best misperceptions, inspired by nothing more than the fact that Latins were different.

Out of the hokum that the Other, always noble in himself or herself, was invariably victimized by American intolerance and prejudice emerged a part of the spirit that, in the attempt to make amends, ushered in the Good Neighbor era. At least the principal architect of that era, Franklin Roosevelt, was never taken in by such hokum. But he utilized it, took full advantage of it, as he pursued practical good neighbor objectives.

Defense of Sacco and Vanzetti may in many instances have been foolish and self-serving, amounting to little more than ideological breast-beating.

Often, though, it sprang from noble instincts. Defense of the Italian anarchists emerged, *to some degree,* out of one of the great virtues that Americans *sometimes* display: an inclusionary opening to the Other instead of the disdainful rebuff of exclusion.

The Sacco and Vanzetti case, lending itself to oversimplified stereotyping and generalization, highlighted a basic issue over which two diametrically opposed Americas, each with its own valid and persuasive claims to representing the public interest and the national spirit, have clashed through the years. For citizens of one America, the two Italian immigrants symbolized the nefariousness of foreign fanatics who simply could not function constructively in the city on the hill. Sacco and Vanzetti stood for, in some measure encapsulated, all the un-American threats that the unregenerate outsider posed to national ideas. Americans of this persuasion can be dubbed nativists or exclusionists.

Then, there was the other America. Its constituents, the inclusionists, stood constantly on the lookout for new and energizing forces from outside the mainstream; they criticized an ossified American civilization shot through, as they saw it, with moral, social, economic, and political imperfections. Frontier analogies sometimes colored their thinking, frontier analogies to which they gave a reverse spin; for inclusionists saw themselves not as conquerors of other frontiers, but as comprising in themselves, in their civilization, a frontier constantly in need of infusions of new ideas, of new blood, of new and different associates.

With America's physical frontier of virgin land at an end, together with the old dream of recurring national regeneration through territorial expansion, some Americans assumed they would have to turn more and more to the outsider for the ongoing rebirth that the West once provided, at least according to a revered national myth. This meant that Americans would have to welcome the Other in their midst or from across the ocean or the Rio Grande; at the very least, they would have to welcome the ideas from abroad that the Other happened to incarnate. They would have to place their faith in inclusion, in pluralism, even as their rivals in interpreting the American dream preached exclusion and the timeless superiority of the one American culture that embodied both truth and virtue—or at least during a golden age in the past had embodied truth and virtue, before alien outsiders had managed to besmirch them.

For the exclusionists, whose ideological ancestors prevailingly had doubted the beneficent effects of the frontier and regretted the way in which its settlement destroyed established, eastern refinement and morality, there was no need for redemption, for rebirth, as provided by outsiders. For the inclusionists, whose ideological forebears welcomed the way in which the settlement of new lands had chronically, periodically, shaken up a closed, depleted, sclerotic eastern establishment, the process of American rebirth must continue. For them, Sacco and Vanzetti symbolized a broad spectrum of new peoples, with new ideas, for whom a place must be made in the republic. Otherwise, that republic would lose its vitality, as its fountain of youth dried up. For inclusionists, there was no golden age in the past. Rather, Americans were engaged in a never-ending long march toward a better future; and they needed a constant influx of new recruits and fresh ideas to energize them on that march.

The tide of opinion on Sacco and Vanzetti changed in the 1930s, with those who believed in their innocence, even their nobility, gaining in numbers and vehemence. Especially among intellectuals, artists, and writers, Sacco and Vanzetti rode high. So did virtually anyone else with a claim to departing from traditional Yankee normalcy. And this provided an indication that Depression-era Americans stood ready to accept what became a defining Good Neighbor vision: a vision of a big-tent, inclusionist hemisphere capable of accommodating differences in culture, ethnicity, language, and religion. Like all visions, this one never achieved reality. But reality came closer to approximating the vision than it would have had the vision never existed.

Virtually throughout Latin America, from Argentina to Central America and Mexico, strikes and protests erupted upon the execution of Sacco and Vanzetti in 1927. In that prosperous year, a majority of Americans must have resented, keenly resented, the Latin American response to American justice. In the hard times of the 1930s, though, American intellectuals and writers and artists and those disaffected in general and for virtually any reason from the old standards and measures of Americanism could regard Latin American protesters as kindred souls. Against a background of depression, the politics of protest had enveloped the hemisphere.

However much they might have responded to Krausist-Arielist perceptions and thereby felt themselves linked to their Latin American counterparts, American intellectuals could hardly propagandize their cause through such esoteric philosophical concepts. However, by keeping the Sacco-Vanzetti flame alive they could indeed propagandize for the sort of inclusionist approach, for the sort of questioning of past assumptions and prejudices, that underlay the whole Good Neighbor era and made it possible.

# SECTION
# III

❖❖❖❖❖❖❖❖❖❖❖❖❖❖❖❖❖❖❖❖❖❖❖❖❖❖❖❖❖❖❖

*Ambivalence
of Mood:
North Americans
Contemplate
Latin Americans*

# 10. The Lure of the Primitive and the Acceptance of Cultural Diversity

❖ ❖ ❖ ❖ ❖ ❖ ❖ ❖ ❖ ❖ ❖ ❖ ❖ ❖ ❖ ❖ ❖ ❖ ❖ ❖ ❖ ❖ ❖ ❖ ❖ ❖ ❖ ❖ ❖ ❖ ❖ ❖ ❖ ❖ ❖

## The Quest for Alternatives to Civilization

The title of one of Sigmund Freud's books, published in 1930, seemed especially applicable to Depression-era Americans: *Civilization and Its Discontents*. Discontent with the plight into which the capitalist ethic, previously assumed to be the bedrock of true civilization, had cast them, Americans looked for alternatives to pouring all their energies into the competitive rush toward greater accumulation of money and goods. Perhaps all along the persons who could not accommodate to civilization, the misfits, the Wozzecks, were the only really sane persons. Perhaps civilization, at least as defined in capitalist, Protestant Ethic America, was insane.

Perhaps primitives who, romantics averred, had never succumbed to the compulsion to accumulate money and goods were onto a better approach to life. Rather than disparaging them, perhaps Americans should contemplate taking them as role models. Perhaps they would be richer, in the final analysis, if they lived by the primitive's supposed "religion of instinct," rather than civilization's religion of constraint and restriction. Expatriate author Henry Miller, living mostly in Paris in the early-to-mid 1930s, certainly thought so, and although most Americans could not read his books because they were banned in his native country, they came on their own, at least many did, to seek the religion of instinct and spontaneity.[1] And, rather than seeking sources of inspiration among far-out authors who had turned against civilization, they tended to turn, for role models, to genuine primitives fortunate enough never to have been corrupted by civilization, never to have experienced its curbs on instinct, its frustrations and discontents.

Claude Bowers, a staunch Jeffersonian Democrat, a journalist, historian, and future ambassador to Spain and Chile, found some genuine "primitives" when attending, at the beginning of the 1930s, one of Theodore Dreiser's Thursday evening soirees. In attendance that evening were a dozen or so "Congo Negroes, all but naked in costumes representing various animals and birds." Civilization, it seemed to Dreiser, an eminent author who had taken up a serious flirtation with communism, had gone wrong. It inculcated an obsessive yearning for economic success that left its victims no time for warm human relationships.[2] Here was a character flaw of which neither "Congo Negroes" nor Latin Americans, at least as traditionally stereotyped by Americans, could be accused.

Americans who had formed their impressions of their southern neighbors from the many nineteenth- and early-twentieth-century travel accounts that found a steady market in the United States could not doubt that although the Latins might be hopelessly backward in the ways of capitalism, they had mastered the art of forming warm human relationships, in part because they slighted money-grubbing pursuits so as to have more time for cultivating warm human relationships, even with Yankee strangers who had wandered into their midst. They might avoid work time but never shirked when it came to hospitality and conviviality time. To Americans of the 1930s who wondered more and more just how much they had benefited from all their work, it began to seem that "primitive" Latins, all along, might have been onto the secret of the good life.

The primitive way of life had advantages far exceeding mere hospitality and conviviality, or at least it seemed so to many Americans caught in a time of adversity. In this, Americans were by no means unusual. Throughout history, when civilization disappoints, men and women have turned for renewal to role models thought to embody the natural, the passionate, the authentic lifestyle. They have turned, in short, to primitives, or to their idealized visions of primitives. They have imagined that primitives are somehow free of the rampant, selfish individualism of "civilized" people. Not only this, but the primitives appear as whole beings, not alienated from, not constrained to repress, their instinctual drives. They live also, do these wonderful primitives, in symbiotic union with their environment, not at constant war with it as modern persons driven to wring ever more wealth out of nature.

When intellectuals have reached out to the primitive in their rejection of the times in which they live, they have stressed the other half of the Krausist-Arielist vision, generally left unstated. The Krausist-Arielist prescription enjoined intellectuals and culturally sensitive souls to penetrate among the masses in order to uplift the masses. The other half of the equation pertained to the renewal and rebirth, the quickening of energies and the overall fulfillment and wholeness that would come to sensitive cultural aesthetes as they absorbed the vitality and energies of the primitive masses.

Americans in quest of renewal (and the number included not just intellectuals and artists but seekers from all walks of life) found primitives in virtually all parts of the world to fulfill their psychic needs and longings. For some questers, Chinese peasants afforded the proper role models. These distant, all-wise, all-suffering, premodern men and women remained in touch with the good earth, absorbing wisdom and virtue from it. For a time, the peasants of China became the favorite far-distant primitives with whom Americans chose to identify. When Pearl Buck published her novel *The Good Earth* in 1931, the American reading public soon made it a best-seller, and critics awarded it the Pulitzer Prize. Later, audiences flocked to see the movie version. Readers or viewers, puzzled and perplexed by what had befallen urban existence in Depression-era America, could respond to protagonist Wang Lung when, feeling besmirched by city residence, he proclaims, "We must get back to the land." In quest of renewal (or perhaps just survival), many Americans did return to the land, in some instances encouraged by New Deal bureaucrats and financed by government programs. Without going so far as actually to return to the land, many Americans sought vicarious renewal by identifying with noble peasant types depicted in works of fiction, types who—like Wang Lung—knew enough to reject the wiles of a corrupt and enervating bourgeois civilization. Not surprisingly, given the perplexed mood of the early 1930s, China exerted "an extraordinary grip . . . on American opinion."[3]

Later, the image of the all-wise, all-suffering, noble and unalienated peasants of China, struggling against modernizing Japanese intruders, was transferred to Spain. Spanish peasants, locked in struggle with the forces of modernity symbolized by dive bombers supplied by fascist Italy and Germany to aid the Nationalists under Francisco Franco, became the preferred role model for Americans out of sorts with modern civilization. In between, for a brief moment before they succumbed to Italian invaders, Ethiopians had come to symbolize, especially for African Americans but for many Caucasians as well, the noble savage at war with a foul and corrupt civilization that instead of producing utopia had delivered dystopia.

All the while a fair sprinkling of Americans disposed to empathize with the Chinese, Spanish, or African peasants turned their attention to Russia. Perhaps the Soviet Union, barbaric and therefore pure, and underdeveloped and therefore undefiled, was onto the secret of how to stop civilization in its tracks and return humanity to the communalism that was natural to all undefiled peoples. Reborn by the communist experience, might not the Soviets be in the best position to guide the world toward utopia?

Perhaps natural, uncorrupted types in their own midst held forth the promise of redemption to Americans burdened by a civilization whose vitality had been sapped by materialism and greed. Perhaps American Negroes, with their rhythmic vitality, with their alleged instinctualness and childlike simplicity—with their all-consuming naturalness—held out to decadent Anglo Americans the promise of redemption. Such, at least, was one basis of the virtual adulation with which a small circle of largely New York–based literati had begun to regard black Americans during the late 1920s when the "Harlem Renaissance" flourished.

Before he discovered the life-renewing energies available from Latin Americans, Waldo Frank, the previously cited writer and mystic, turned to the African American as the symbol of renewal. In his novel *The Death and Birth of David Markand* (1934), Frank portrays a man who abandons a stultifying middle-class career, and also a less-than-satisfying marriage. Markand wants to embrace the grimy workers, whom he finds life-affirming, not life-denying. As his symbolic initiation rite into a new, liberated, whole, and fulfilling life, Markand has sex with a black woman. She "represents a joyful and uninhibited sexuality, in contrast with Markand's earlier guilty and uncertain gropings." When Frank switched his attention to Latin America, he retained this theme, using sex with a Brazilian mulatta as a symbol of civilized man's rebirth in the natural.[4]

Another Caucasian American who reached out to African Americans to help her transcend the emotionally stifling and repressive life of bourgeois America was the well-to-do Charlotte Mason, who maintained a lavish home on Park Avenue. She came to her interest in the "primitive" by way of her fascination with the occultism and nonconventional religious practices that she associated with Africa, and that she felt remained alive among African Americans. Overly civilized people had lost touch with their occult powers, and could renew these powers only through contact with people who had remained close to their primitive roots and therefore retained access to the magic of nature. At one time or another Mason befriended and financially supported Langston Hughes, Zora Neale Hurston, and Alain Locke, enormously talented black Americans who played important roles in the Harlem Renaissance. Invariably, though, she alienated her "primitive" wards by seeking to assume too dictatorial a control over their lives, supposedly in the interest of keeping them pure and uncontaminated by bourgeois aspirations.[5] This was also one of the traits John Collier demonstrated in his approach to American Indians, in whom he hoped that, together with his fellow Caucasians in general, he could find renewal.

Along with his New Deal brain-truster friend Adolf A. Berle, Jr., John Collier provides a perfect example of fulfillment of the pensador's dream: the intellectual transformed into the power wielder and policy-maker in government. The two men had formed a friendship in New Mexico during the 1920s when both engaged in an ultimately successful attempt to protect the Pueblo Indians from land-grabbing Anglo Americans and from the attempts of the Bureau of Indian Affairs to snuff out authentic Indian culture. Berle we have already encountered, and we come across him again at various later points in our story; for he became one of FDR's principal Latin America hands. For now, the focus is on Collier, the prime example of an American disillusioned with his country's modern business culture who turned for inspiration and wisdom, and even occult religious enlightenment, to the ways of the Native American. Within the United States, Collier led the sort of movement that, as shortly we shall see, was simultaneously gaining strength in Latin America, where it was referred to as *indigenismo*.

Collier, as it happened, would serve as commissioner of Indian affairs during the entire Roosevelt presidency. Thus, he was not just a thinker, but a doer. While his mysticism and readiness to see in Indian communalism a cure for the ills of American civilization horrified traditionally thinking Americans, Collier enjoyed the firm support of Interior Secretary Harold Ickes, touched in his own way—despite his notorious orneriness—by a bit of mystical worship of nature and the natural.

Born in 1884 into an Atlanta family of some social prominence but declining economic security, Collier had graduated from Columbia University, after which he traveled in Europe, where he discovered the writings of various utopian socialists. Back in America, he had become active in New York social work. Relaxation as well as intellectual stimulation he often found at the Mabel Dodge salon on lower Fifth Avenue.

More the social activist than the socialite, Buffalo-born Mabel Dodge had become active in modern art circles and in the radical, bohemian politics of New York City shortly before the First World War. At her famous salons, labor radicals, social reformers, intellectuals of various but predominantly leftist stripes, dancers, modern artists, occultists, and many other sorts as well mingled together. At one time the mistress of radical writer John Reed, who before going off to find a new life in revolutionary Russia had fallen under the spell of Pancho Villa in Mexico, Dodge in the midst of the First World War had married a Jewish artist named Maurice Sterne, and moved to New Mexico. There, she settled in Taos, divorced Sterne, and took up with the Indian Tony Lujan, whom eventually she married. Finding in the lifestyle and beliefs of the Pueblo Indians the spiritual fulfillment she had previously sought in vain from various seers and from Freudian psychoanalysis, Mabel Dodge Sterne Luhan (she preferred the Anglicized spelling for her new name) made of her Taos residence a mecca for artists, writers, and intellectuals—all of them seeking an alternative to capitalist, bourgeois modern times. In 1920 she renewed her friendship with John Collier.

Discouraged by the postwar tide of reaction that impeded social reform, Collier had departed New York and settled in California. There, too, he found frustration in his social work, and so decided to take off for Mexico, where the revolution then in progress might afford him the opportunity to become a part of a process intended to usher in a new, less materialistic culture based on the ancient wisdom of Indian society. On his way to Mexico, however, he received an invitation to visit Mabel in Taos. Once arrived there, Collier became as much taken up with the cause of American Indians as Mabel Dodge Luhan.

Before long Collier had decided that Anglo Americans could save their society from its besetting materialism and selfishness only by adopting the Indian value system—which he equated with Pueblo beliefs as he came to understand them. The Pueblos, he believed, had remained in touch with the vital, renewing, telluric forces of Mother Earth, at the same time that they absorbed the cosmic wisdom and supernatural forces of Father Sky. Not only this, but the Pueblos were onto another secret that involved the merging of opposites. They were onto a secret of life that all Americans must discover: how to be "both communists and individualists at the same time."[6]

Had he stayed in New York, Collier might have joined in a resurgent counterculture that viewed the Negro as the blessed primitive who could redeem a decadent, moribund civilization. But, because he had gone west, he found the redeeming Other in the Indian. Just barely, owing to Mabel's intervention, Collier had failed to find the redeemer in Mexico. Nevertheless, he would soon thrill to the Mexican revolution's indigenismo, to its purported attempt to forge a new society on the foundation of Indian communalism. Collier once remarked, in open-mouthed admiration of what was transpiring in Mexico in the 1930s: "Our duty of land-restoration [in the United States] affects perhaps only 200,000 Indians, while Mexico, a very poor country, has assumed as a moral obligation the restoration of land to more than 2,000,000 Indians."[7]

Just as Charlotte Mason, the patron of African American writers, wanted her wards to remain uncontaminated by mainstream American materialism and modernity, so Collier wanted Native Americans to retain what he regarded as their innate, communal, rooted-in-the-land qualities, together with their exalted spiritualism that altogether transcended mere worldly wisdom. Not surprisingly, Collier's endeavors to protect them were not appreciated by those American Indians who chose the assimilationist path. To these Indians, as well as to many non-Indian critics of New

Deal Indian policies, Collier's approach smacked of occultism at best, of communism at worst.

## Cross-Border Indigenismo: A Basis for U.S.–Latin American Rapport

By and large, Latin America's accommodated classes had through the years regarded their natives in largely the same light in which mainstream North Americans had seen their Indians: as benighted beings hopelessly refractory to modern times, as hapless humans perhaps forever doomed to marginal existence in advanced societies whose principles lay beyond their grasp. Early in the twentieth century, however, and with mounting intensity in the 1920s and '30s, mainly left-wing, non-Indian Latin American intellectuals had launched an *indigenista* movement that glorified Indian mysticism along with Indian socialism. The Latin American indigenista movement was especially strong in Mexico, where it inspired much of the rhetoric at least of the 1910 revolution, and in Peru. In the latter country it tinged the so-called communism of José Carlos Mariátegui and the non-Marxian socialism of Víctor Raúl Haya de la Torre's Alianza Popular Revolucionaria Americana. Especially for Haya, but for Mariátegui as well, their country's socialist future would derive from the institutions of preconquest Indian civilizations. In the United States, Indian Commissioner John Collier found inspiration in the same belief.

Even in Argentina, notoriously anti-Indian in its rapid ascent to becoming Latin America's most modern, most Europeanized country, indigenista movements took root and grew. Still more did they grow in Brazil, along with a vogue for Afro-Brazilian culture, of which America's Harlem Renaissance provided only a pale reflection.

To some considerable degree, then, intellectuals and artists, on both sides of the border, disillusioned and discontented in the 1930s with modern civilization (the sort of condition Freud had dealt with in his 1930 book), convinced along with Oswald Spengler as to *The Decline of the West,* converged in their belief that the New World's "primitives," those of African and aboriginal descent, held the secret to a better future. Without this convergence, the Good Neighbor approach would have lacked one vital ingredient: a millennialist vision and drive shared on both sides of the border by those who saw the future emerging out of a past in which "primitives" had continued to live and to which they could lead errant moderns back.

Sometimes I wonder if Franklin Roosevelt even knew about the vital indigenista-primitivist element that facilitated the establishment of the Good Neighbor policy. I rather doubt that he did. Sumner Welles, though, the Latin America specialist on whom the president so frequently relied, undoubtedly knew. As to Secretary of State Cordell Hull, I'd bet that he either did not know about the indigenista-primitivist phenomenon or, if he might have caught wind of it, dismissed it out of hand as irrelevant tomfoolery. However, many others—among them Henry Wallace, Harold Ickes, John Collier, and to some degree A. A. Berle, Jr., as well as brain-truster turned Latin America hand Rexford Tugwell—knew about the phenomenon and did not dismiss it as hokum.

## Some Americans Develop a Vogue for Things Mexican

For many Americans who found the Chinese too far distant to serve as a useful personification of the primitivism to which they yearned to revert, and who did not respond to the lure of the African American or the native Indian, Mexico and Mexicans provided the necessary source of the exotic and the premodern. Beginning in the 1920s, more and more Americans succumbed to what Helen Delpar, in the title she gives to her fine 1992 book, calls *The Enormous Vogue of Things Mexican.*

Perhaps the most influential American to fall under the spell of things Mexican was Dwight Morrow, the Wall Street executive appointed am-bassador to Mexico by President Coolidge in 1927. Coolidge wanted Morrow to improve relations with Mexico—relations that had grown alarmingly acrimonious as American business leaders accused the govern-ment of Plutarco Elías Calles of going communist, while Calles in turn lashed out against gringo imperialists. Not only did Morrow restore ci-vility to relations between the two countries as Coolidge intended; beyond this, he initiated an era of good feelings far exceeding anything anticipated by the Republican president. Indeed, Morrow paved the way for the ac-complishments of Josephus Daniels when Roosevelt appointed him am-bassador to Mexico at the official inception of the Good Neighbor era.

Dwight Morrow and his wife, Elizabeth Cutter Morrow, fell in love with Mexico, its history, its traditions, above all its pre-Columbian indige-nous art as well as its more recent folk art, so much of it deriving from Indian traditions. It was as if Morrow came to believe that far more than the sort of economic success he had enjoyed, it was letters and *arts* that conferred nobility. If indeed this perception did come to color Morrow's outlook, it may have contributed to his unhappy old age when, long after he had left Mexico to return to the typical life of the affluent American, he literally drank himself to death. Morrow's disillusionment with the life of affluence was already indicated at the outset of the Depression when he speculated that economic hard times might restore the "fiber of the people," weakened by too much prosperity. "The men and women that built this country, that founded it," he pointed out, "were people reared in adversity."[8] Certainly, Morrow and his wife responded warmly to Mexicans who lived in adversity, whether in the past or present, above all if those Mexicans had produced art.

To improve relations between the neighbor republics, Morrow arranged a tour by the era's entertainer superstar, Will Rogers; also he brought his future son-in-law Charles Lindbergh as a goodwill ambassador, shortly after he had become the first person to fly the Atlantic non-stop. Above all, though, Morrow and his wife, who very quickly overcame her originally condescending attitudes toward Mexicans, cemented good relations by growing as enthusiastic over Mexican folk art, and the Indians who had produced it, as the country's own artists and political leaders, caught up at the time in a romantic rediscovery and glorification of Indians and their culture.

To introduce other Americans to their newfound enthusiasm, the Morrows conceived the idea of arranging a major touring exhibition that would reveal various facets of Mexican art, especially folk art, ranging from the prehistoric to the modern. With principal funding coming from the Carnegie Corporation of New York, the Mexican art exhibition opened at the Metropolitan Museum in October of 1930. After four weeks in New York, the exhibition traveled to numerous other cities, large and not so large, including Boston, Pittsburgh, Washington, Louisville, and San Antonio. In all, the exhibition drew some 450,000 viewers. Americans, as one writer put it, awakened to the fact that "Mexico was not a backward country full of bandits, as so many had previously imagined; instead it was revealed now as a nation of culture."[9]

Although the most prestigious of American goodwill ambassadors to Mexico, the Morrows actually were only two among hundreds and even thousands of their compatriots who had gone south of the border, often disillusioned by life in their own country, and found a haven of tranquility that contrasted with what they regarded as the materialistic rat race of American civilization. Some stayed only a short time, some remained for years or settled permanently. Sharing in the "romantic primitivism" in vogue during the late 1920s and throughout the Depression era, the American "cultural pilgrims . . . sought a simpler, more harmonious culture than the machine-driven society they knew at home, which . . . seemed incapable even of providing material security."[10]

The American expatriates included a fair number of Jews, many of whom had socialist leanings—for this was an era when the lure of the primitive often went hand-in-hand with a belief in socialism; a few of them even had become Communist Party members. One of the expatriates, Bertram Wolfe, who for a time joined the party, wrote eloquently on the lure of Mexico. The country afforded an American, raised in a "highly developed pecuniary, mercantile, and industrial civilization," the chance to "double one's personality" by absorbing the ways of a local trade-and-barter, largely prepecuniary, basically subsistence society. It was in Mexico, Wolfe writes of himself and his wife, Ella, both of whom took up residence in the country in 1923, that they realized "something valuable and humane" had gone out of their lives in the United States.[11] They recaptured that something in Mexico. In the process, they manifested an important element of the isolationist mood that caused Americans to look suspiciously on modern, advanced, developed Europe, even as they warmed to and enthused over the redeeming simple gifts that lay to the south. To the south lived people resembling the romanticized "primitives" of Russia whom their leaders, ostensibly, were directing back to the future.

## The Negative Response to Primitivism

To many Americans, the 1930s vogue of primitivism that to some degree underlay the warming of attitudes toward Latin America was romantic nonsense, the sort of nonsense that, in their view, typified the New Deal's tendency to pamper ne'er-do-wells. To Americans who clung still to what they considered their country's formative values, primitives, whether American Negroes or Indians or the bulk of Latin Americans, were childlike and irrational troublemakers, strongly in need of the firm guiding hand if ever they were to take a responsible place among modern, civilized persons. Primitives, after all, as every right-thinking person knew, inclined to be sexually overactive. Unable to channel, through sublimation, their sexual drives into worthwhile, profit-yielding enterprise in the marketplace, they bred profligately and heedlessly—like the black woman depicted in a 1937 book who allegedly says of the children she produces, "They keep coming along like watermelons in the summertime."[12]

Self-styled defenders of authentic, traditional American civilization scoffed at the notion of pandering to primitives, whether in the United States, or to the south, or any place else in the world. Their clinching justification for this stance they often couched in racial terms. After all, wherever found, primitives were likely to be of darker skin color than the Anglo Saxon; and every right-thinking person knew that the white race was destined to control and dominate and perhaps in the process uplift dark primitives—to whatever small degree their natures permitted.[13]

The way to emerge from the Depression, in the view of upholders of traditional values, was to give encouragement to modern men and women, above all to America's capitalists; they had achieved the highest levels of material civilization the world had yet seen, and they could readily enough cure capitalism's temporary ills if given a little encouragement instead of the harassment allegedly meted out by New Dealers. Obviously the way out of present difficulties did not lie with fawning over primitives who on their own had scarcely known how to emerge from a stone age.

The antiprimitivists undoubtedly represented mainstream American thought, even during the Depression years. Franklin Roosevelt would have to be careful about going too far with a Good Neighbor policy, the tone of which was to some limited degree at least set by culturati infatuated with the romantic nonsense of primitivism.

Still, one did not have to go all the way toward romantic nonsense in order to conclude that people culturally different from establishment Anglo-Saxon Americans were not thereby inferior. Indeed, new and supposedly scientific investigations had reached this conclusion. The findings of the anthropologists who fathered the cultural relativism movement in the United States lent what appeared to be scientific confirmation to the thesis that people should not be judged inferior simply because they departed from the cultural norms embraced by those who judged them. More than the ascendancy of primitivism, the rising star of cultural relativism in the 1930s contributed to the tolerance of the Other that underlay the whole Good Neighbor approach to hemispheric relations. Cultural relativists did not assail Latin Americans or any other people for their "primitivism"; nor—except for extremists in their midst—did they censure acculturated, mainstream Americans for not being primitives.

### Cultural Relativism Challenges American Ethnocentrism

To the degree that Caucasian Americans were informed enough to know about them, new developments in biology and anthropology were bound to exercise at least a subtle influence on their attitudes toward Latin Americans, and toward peoples of different races and different cultures in general. Among biologists and anthropologists, and also psychiatrists, two movements were underway, beginning in the 1920s. One of them laid down the principle that culture, not race, is crucial in accounting for differences among people; the second movement inched tentatively toward the conclusion that no one culture can claim basic, fundamental superiority over another.

As early as 1907, sociologist-paleontologist Lester Frank Ward had argued "there was no reason to consider the lower classes as any less worthy genetically than the upper classes. Only the former's lack of educational and other opportunities, he insisted, had left them in that position." Here was a challenge to racist assumptions. At about the same time American pragmatists, headed by John Dewey and William James, asserted there "could be no set of fixed values because conduct determined values and conduct altered constantly."[14] Here was a challenge to notions about the inherent superiority of one culture over another.

Up through the 1920s, however, U.S. delegates at various inter-American conferences persisted, often with Cuban backing, in championing racist views of eugenics. Except for the lack of sensitivity it betrayed given the venue in which delegates voiced their views, the U.S. stance was hardly surprising. After all, the United States was at the time engaged in a genteel version of ethnic cleansing as it imposed quotas to block the immigration of people of "undesirable" race and culture, and as many states became more adamant than ever in prohibiting interracial marriage, and as the Ku Klux Klan with its doctrine of keeping racial and cultural inferiors in their place registered a dramatic resurgence. To Latin Americans informed about U.S. attitudes, it was perfectly clear that there could be no genuine neighborliness in the hemisphere until the Yankees began to reject the tenets of eugenics and ethnocentric culture biases.[15]

In Depression-era America, elites no longer seemed so prescient, so brilliant, so superior. Just a few years after they had brought about exclusion of ostensibly inferior immigrants, they had contrived to drive the country into its worst crisis since the Civil War. With more and more of their "ethnically right" and properly reared fellow citizens having fallen upon economic hardship, with more and more of them demonstrable failures, by all the old criteria at least, Americans grew more cautious about attributing economic backwardness to innate or to socially conditioned inferiority. Leftist political analyses swept through the social sciences in America and began to exert an influence also on the hard sciences; and the result was a mounting challenge to eugenics and to notions that suggested the desirability of ethnic or cultural cleansing. What the Depression began, Hitler helped to finish with his odious theories on race and culture. Understandably, then, during the 1930s "the popularity of eugenics declined precipitously, not only among social scientists and biologists but among the public."[16]

In many ways, the antiracist critique reflected "the expanding space created for nurture at the expense of nature."[17] And, to some considerable degree, this sort of change in opinion, scientific and public, was an essential foundation to the New Deal. After all, it made relatively little sense—except just possibly as a means of forestalling social violence—to try to aid down-on-their-luck citizens if their plight proceeded from race rather than from socioeconomic factors, or if they were hopelessly immersed in cultural aberrations that had brought about their plight in the first place. An interesting and fruitful symbiosis developed in which science was driven by social attitudes, and social attitudes in turn were influenced or justified by scientific theory.

So, already by the early 1930s the move against eugenics, against concepts of inferior and superior races, against belief in the racial determinants of behavior, was on the ascendant, although biologists for a time lagged behind social scientists. But if culture and not nature controlled conduct, then what about culture? Were there good cultures and bad cultures, some with values that in a rightly ordered world should command respect, others with criteria that should be rejected? Latin Americans, and all other peoples who were culturally distinct from American archetypes, could not earn full acceptance by the Yankees so long as they, the Yankees, continued to believe that cultures should be ranked in a moral hierarchy. Belief of this sort, given the way ethnocentrism operates, meant inevitably that Yankees would still have grounds for claiming superiority over their southern neighbors. And belief in the moral hierarchy of cultures would prevail until cultural relativism began to change scientific and popular assumptions.

In advancing the cause of cultural relativism, no man played a more significant role than anthropologist Franz Boas. However, he did not advance all the way toward acceptance of out-and-out relativism. That role was reserved for his students, for his disciples.

A Jewish immigrant from Germany, Boas (1858–1942) arrived in the United States in 1889. Ten years later he became Columbia University's first professor of anthropology, a position he held for thirty-seven years. Boas insisted that strengths and virtues inhered in all cultures, including those once dismissed by "civilized" men and women as backward, primitive, and savage. During the 1920s, his views began to overwhelm the opposition among social scientists. The cultural relativism that he proclaimed challenged the sort of American conventional wisdom that had inspired the immigration restriction legislation of the 1920s. According to this wisdom, virtue in its highest forms inhered only in the culture, in the lifestyle and values, developed by Anglo Saxons. Furthermore, conventional wisdom had taught that Anglo-Saxon virtue arose out of superior racial endowments developed through a Darwinian process of natural selection. In stark contrast, the new school of cultural anthropology as pioneered by Boas taught that culture developed not in response to determinants of race but rather to those of environment.

Anthropological relativism proclaimed that the cultural influences that operated on human beings, far more than genetic factors, determined behavior. Cultural influences were transmitted from generation to generation by exogenetic or nongenetic influences: by the totality of influences that parents, peer groups, schooling mechanisms, churches, the media, and society in general brought to bear through "socialization"—socialization being the process through which new generations acquired the codes of conduct that their society had developed through all its preceding generations in response to the various circumstances of environment, both physical and social. Above all, Boas stressed that "from an anatomical perspective a basic equality of mental capacity exists among all races."[18]

So, Boas stressed that differences in culture did not derive from differences in innate capacity. In line with this conviction, he urged the incorporation of Amerindians and African Americans into the general, mainstream American population—even though these minorities retained the major traditional features of their culture. This position helps explain why Boas, as mentioned in an earlier chapter, charged that treatment of blacks in the United States even during the New Deal was as shameful as Hitler's treatment of Jews.

Students who came from Latin America to study under Boas, especially the Brazilian Gilberto Freyre, particularly welcomed the Boas position on cultural and ethnic mixing, for it justified the typically Latin acceptance of miscegenation that traditionally had horrified the racial purists of North America. At Columbia, Freyre also welcomed the message propounded by one of Boas's colleagues, the biologist Leslie Dunn. More than any other major figure in his field, Dunn rejected the notion that race mixture caused degeneration and loss of vigor.[19]

From a point early in the twentieth century, Latin American social scientists and biologists had begun to move toward the belief that not genes but rather "racial poisons," such as alcohol and venereal disease, accounted for whatever degeneration might have affected portions of their populace. In consequence, they had seen the solution to what earlier generations had called "race problems" not in such programs as sterilization of the so-called unfit, but rather in welfare programs and health campaigns.[20] Not surprisingly, the Boas outlook that originally made slow progress against the pro-eugenicist bias in the United States found instantaneous support in Latin America, where by the 1920s his works were beginning to have major impact. Then, in the 1930s, as Boas became more of a recognized prophet in his own country, Americans and Latin Americans converged, at least some of them did to some degree, in their attitudes on nature and nurture.

Contrary to popular belief, Franz Boas—as already indicated—never went all the way toward cultural relativism. Refusing to recognize all cultures as equal, he continued to posit a hierarchy among them. In his mind, European culture ranked at the top of the hierarchy. Other cultures certainly had full potential to reach European levels, but many still had a long road to travel.[21] As is so often the case, though, many of Boas's students and disciples went further than the master; they advanced all the way toward cultural relativism, accepting the principle that one culture, even a primitive one, was as good as any other, whether judged on moral or aesthetic or any other grounds. Different most certainly the cultures were, but differences did not imply rank or gradation. Each culture had its own strengths and its peculiar weaknesses, but in their totality one was as good as another. Indeed, in some specific ways a "primitive" culture might enjoy the edge over advanced cultures.

Typical of Boas's students who advanced all the way to cultural relativism was fellow Jewish immigrant Edward Sapir. "Always uncomfortable with any ranking of cultures into developmental hierarchies," Sapir, who carved out a distinguished career in anthropology, was "unable to conceive of any single index" for establishing hierarchies among cultures.[22]

Two of Boas's women students, Ruth Benedict and Margaret Mead, also advanced well beyond the master in acceptance of thoroughgoing cultural relativism. Obviously stung as well they should have been by the "biology is destiny" school, they always stressed "the small scope of biologically transmitted behavior, and the enormous role of cultural process."[23] Beyond this, they argued that mainstream American culture, with its individualistic materialism, did not represent the one true and highest mode of human existence. It was only one among many approaches to life; and in altogether different approaches, one might very well find far more pleasing, benign, and beneficent features than in European and American culture.

At the very time when racial segregation intensified in more and more states of the American South, Boas had begun his virtual crusade to destroy the basis on which racial injustice had been predicated and rationalized. Finally, in the 1930s, the crusade began to yield a harvest, at least among scientifically literate Americans. Indeed, it may have gone too far in challenging beliefs about genetic determinants of individual destiny. If cultural relativism's attack on the influence of heredity did go too far, at least that attack during the Depression era yielded socially beneficent results: internally within the United States itself and externally in the nation's relations with the culturally and racially different peoples to the south.

Cultural relativism's influence should not be exaggerated. Even by the end of the 1930s, only a small segment of the educated public had changed its attitudes on matters of race and culture, and the change had come about more because of Hitler's aberrations than because of the teachings of anthropologists, sociologists, biologists, and psychiatrists.[24] Many of the scholars who took up the Boas cause were considered marginal types by the public at large: after all, the best-known among them tended to be women and Jews who, some detractors suggested, were twisting science to serve their own, minority interests. Later, the charge would arise that Ruth Benedict's *Patterns of Culture* (1934), which began to sell briskly in a new 1946 paperback edition, had been inspired only by her wish to undermine antilesbian prejudices. Not until the *Brown v. Board of Edu-*

*cation* decision in 1954 that struck down racial segregation in public schools did some of the spirit of the cultural relativists begin to influence the shaping of American social policy.

Still, Latin American impressions of the United States often derived not so much from man-and-woman-on-the-street conventional wisdom as from the ideas of scholars and social scientists; it was the men of letras, the pensadores, with whom opinion makers to the south were concerned. To them, the work of America's cultural relativists was genuinely significant, and they welcomed it with delight. All in all, then, even if unwittingly and tangentially, American men and women of science contributed enormously to making viable FDR's new approach to Latin America.

# 11. Single-Minded Bigots No Longer

❖ ❖ ❖ ❖ ❖ ❖ ❖ ❖ ❖ ❖ ❖ ❖ ❖ ❖ ❖ ❖ ❖ ❖ ❖ ❖ ❖ ❖ ❖ ❖ ❖ ❖ ❖ ❖ ❖ ❖ ❖

### North Americans and Strangers in Their Midst: Mexican Americans in the Southwest

Cultural relativism's principal message had been: culture matters, not blood. But, as of the 1930s, however much the message had influenced scientists, soft and hard, it had not been taken to heart by America's Everyman and Everywoman. Moreover, it scarcely mattered if he or she attributed the alleged inferiority of people other than native-born white Americans to racial or to cultural causes. Either would suffice to justify the stance of a bigot, though prejudice based on blood was apt to be harsher than that justified by culture.

A Texas farmer, late in the nineteenth century, is reported to have observed: "We feel toward the Mexicans just like toward the nigger, but not so much."[1] To a large extent this same attitude still prevailed in the 1930s and beyond, not only among old-stock Texans but among Southwesterners in general, and also among Floridians and Americans wherever they lived who had been exposed to any significant number of Mexican immigrants or seasonal laborers. The attitude was no secret to Mexicans and to Latin Americans in general, and certainly made it difficult for many of them to take Good Neighbor rhetoric seriously.

Mexicans were by no means unique among Latin-American-origin residents in the discrimination they encountered in the United States. If anything Cuban immigrants living in Ybor City just to the west of

Tampa experienced even harsher discrimination than Mexicans or Mexican Americans residing in the Southwest.[2] While Mexicans were not unique among Hispanics in being considered just one short cut above the Negro, there were more of them living in the United States than immigrants from any other Latin American country. And so, they bore the brunt of Anglo prejudice.

In the Southwest, Mexican Americans (often referred to as Hispanics in the pages that follow) clustered around the bottom rung of the socioeconomic ladder, as blacks did in other parts of the country. They lived in seedy neighborhoods or slums with unpaved streets. "Local whites considered them lazy, degenerate, and dirty." Where blacks and Hispanics lived in the same community, white residents tended to lump them together. In Los Angeles, for example, Mexicans and blacks could swim in city pools only on Wednesday; on Thursday, the water was changed. One factor that caused Anglos to lump Hispanics and African Americans together was the high incidence of marijuana use that prevailed among both groups. The common wisdom prevailing at the time among the *gente decente*—the decent, and therefore Anglo, Caucasian elements—had it that marijuana users were prone to the "wildest debauchery and sexual crimes," even to "thrill murders."[3]

A 1928 article by Kenneth L. Roberts published in the *Saturday Evening Post* took a dim view of Mexican immigrants in the Southwest. The "constantly increasing flow of chocolate-colored Mexican peons" into the United States might benefit employers; but their ignorance, filthy habits, and high fertility made them a burden on taxpayers. Among the so-called peons was the young César Chávez, who in later decades attained fame as one of the all-time great organizers of marginalized agricultural workers of the Southwest. In an interview with Studs Terkel, he related some of his experiences as a boy. He told, for example, of a trip he had taken with his family in California. "Along the highway there were signs in most of the small restaurants that said 'White Only.' My dad read English, but he didn't really know the meaning. He went in to get some coffee. . . . He asked us not to come in, but we followed him anyway. And this young waitress said, 'We don't serve Mexicans here. Get out of here.'" The father and children returned to the car, hit the road again, and, as César Chávez concludes, "we never got the coffee."[4]

Virtually everywhere in the Southwest evidence of discrimination abounded. In the 1920s and '30s, signs on bakeries and breweries, on oil company and other offices read "No Mexicans Hired," "No Mexicans Need Apply," "No Mexicans, for White Only," "No Chili, Mexicans Keep Out." Mexicans received "inferior wages for hard work that no one else would do for that or any other wage." Not surprisingly, a careful study made in 1936 revealed that in and around San Antonio Mexican wages amounted to "pure exploitation." Moreover, owing largely to discrimination, the school dropout rate for Hispanics living in El Paso was close to 100 percent. In the area of Houston and its environs, although virtually every barrio had a local "Mexican School," unwritten rules "discouraged promotion into the junior high schools." Outside the San Antonio barrio district (on the city's west side), Catholic schools maintained segregation through the 1930s and '40s; "Mexican and black children were often refused admission to them . . . because of color, race, or poverty."[5]

Robert A. Millikan, a University of Chicago Nobel Laureate in physics, had moved on to the California Institute of Technology by the onset of the Depression. Sounding very much like many Californians in the midst of their depression some sixty years later, Millikan stressed the negative consequences to his adopted state of providing social services and assistance to Mexicans during economic hard times. Even in good times, he alleged, the Mexicans just could not make a go of it in California, any more than they could in their native land. They were inclined to work one day and then loaf until their food supply ran out, whereupon they would work another day.[6]

Even the socially conscious writer Lorena Hickock, a friend of Franklin and especially of Eleanor Roosevelt who toured the country in 1933 in order to provide eyewitness accounts of conditions to the president and First Lady and also to Harry Hopkins (head of the Federal Emergency Relief Administration), did not always rise above stereotypes. Rather than seriously looking for work, Mexicans in the Southwest, she reported, were "coming on relief just as fast as they can get on."[7] In contrast to Americans who were ashamed to go onto relief, Hickock seemed to imply that Mexicans were *sin vergüenzas* (shameless).


How could it be that American residents of the Southwest who flocked to see exhibitions of Mexican art, who virtually swooned over Diego Rivera and other muralists, who showed utter fascination for so many things Mexican, at the same time displayed a sometimes savage intolerance toward Mexican migrants and toward Mexican Americans who were citizens of the United States? Fundamentally, the Depression provides the answer: it was easy enough to empathize with far-distant Latins, but not those close at hand and competing for jobs, when jobs had virtually disappeared. Two additional explanations come to mind. The first stems from an observation that Bernice Reagon, curator at the National Museum of American History, made in 1992: "It is possible," she noted, "to respond to cultural outpourings . . . without responding to the status of the community that created those cultural expressions. The expressions become products separated from the community that produced them."[8] A second explanation is even more to the point. Americans distinguished between the educated, "presentable" Mexicans who produced works of art and who did not compete with them for jobs, and the uneducated, unrefined, untrained laborers who, victimized by poverty in their own land, sought opportunities to survive in America.

Down-and-out Mexicans living in the United States were not surprised by their treatment. On the whole, it was as good as, probably even better than, they would have received from the accommodated classes in Mexico itself. And that was one of the reasons they had come to the United States, and why they did everything in their power to avoid being forced to return to their homeland during the Depression years. By 1937, though, nearly 500,000 Mexicans had been forced to leave the United States.[9] Overwhelmingly, they regarded the homeward trek as a tragedy, a true trail of tears.

In some ways, what was tragedy for the returnees represented good fortune for the Mexicans and Mexican Americans who remained behind. The deportations, coming on the heels of the immigration restriction legislation of the 1920s, relieved the anxiety of Anglo Americans that they were being swamped by waves of foreigners, and may well have made them feel a shade more tolerant of the foreign-born still in their midst. Awareness of this likelihood may have contributed to the general approbation with which Mexican Americans viewed the departure of the Mexicans. More directly involved in their approbation was the hope that now they would face less competition in the Depression-diminished job market. Parallels to this situation emerged in the early 1990s when Americans, feeling swamped by huge waves of immigration, grew more hostile toward the strangers in their midst. At the same time, immigrants already safely in the country joined in the clamor against admitting large numbers of new immigrants.

## Embourgeoisement of Mexican Americans in the Southwest

The "Okies" and the "Arkies" who had made their way to California, fleeing the Dust Bowl catastrophes that crippled their native states, received a reception from accommodated Californians no warmer than that accorded indigent Mexican immigrants. Yet, when some of the Dust Bowl migrants finally began to achieve a measure of economic success, they were welcomed by Californians and accepted as pillars of society. Many Mexican Americans decided they could follow the same road to acceptance, by rising to the middle-class status that accompanied economic success.

Booker T. Washington had urged his fellow American Negroes not to concern themselves unduly about disenfranchisement, about social restrictions and discrimination. Let them become economically responsible and productive; once they acquired economic status, political rights and social acceptance would come automatically in its wake. Washington was wrong. Prejudice against Negroes was too strong to permit their acceptance among whites even after they had learned to play the economic game by white middle-class rules. With Mexicans, though, it was often different. They were like the "nigger, but not so much." If they learned to play the game by American rules, and to succeed materially, they could eventually gain acceptance. At least, this is what many Mexican Americans thought in the 1920s and '30s as they dedicated themselves to attaining bourgeois security and social acceptance by practicing the so-called Protestant Ethic and the Horatio Alger formula thought to assure the economic success that led to social acceptance. Even against the unpromising backdrop of the Depression, many Mexican Americans did achieve some degree of middle-class security. Thereby they initiated the process that would gain them acceptance in the country in which they had chosen to live, or in which they had been born.

Already in 1930, according to that year's census, nearly 57 percent of Mexican-background residents had been born in the United States. Although they wanted to cling to some elements of their Hispanic culture, they were proud to be citizens of their new homeland, and anxious to succeed by American standards. And they believed that in the wake of economic upward mobility would come social upward mobility, the end result being not just second-class but first-class American citizenship. In the mid-1930s Mexican President Lázaro Cárdenas advised Mexican citizens living in the United States to become citizens of what had become their homeland and to demonstrate their loyalty to that new homeland. Thereupon the rush to U.S. citizenship intensified among the Southwest's Hispanics, speeding along the acculturation process.[10]

In this process no institution played a more important role than the League of United Latin American Citizens (LULAC), founded at a 1929 convention in Harlingen, Texas. Attended by representatives of numerous Mexican-American organizations, the convention has been compared to the American Constitutional Convention of 1789.[11] The Philadelphia convention was the culminating step in the Americanization of all those people who had come to their new homeland from overseas; and the Harlingen convention was the crucial first step that Mexican-origin citizens took toward truly integrating themselves into the country that had provided a haven from conditions in the old patria that for one reason or another they deemed unacceptable.

Historian Mario T. García points out that by 1933 LULAC chapters not only dotted Texas but from there had spread to New Mexico, Colorado, California, and even to the District of Columbia and several eastern states. Indeed, "wherever there was a Mexican middle-class community, LULAC was embraced."[12] A *Mexican-American middle-class community:* there is the essence of LULAC. It was an organization built around notions of inculcating among Mexican-origin Americans a middle-class set of values based on the need to achieve, on self-help and personal accountability, on the drive not only for security but for excellence in whatever calling people chose to earn their living.

Many years ago the Belgian Jesuit Roger Vekemans, who lived for an extended period in Chile, remarked that there was no hope for Latin America's development unless its overwhelmingly Catholic citizenry basically made some sort of an opening toward the Protestant Ethic, with its stress on individual initiative and probity in waging the struggle for economic security.[13] To some degree the Catholic Church beginning in the 1980s has done just that in Latin America, the transition often spearheaded by the Opus Dei, a lay order founded in 1928. When they have felt their traditional church has not gone far enough in this direction, many Latin Americans have converted to one denomination or another of Protestantism. The process has contributed to the "economic miracles" that some Latin American countries began to show signs of bringing off in the early 1990s.

All of this was anticipated in the American Southwest in the 1930s when, with the organizational support of LULAC, Mexican Americans— even in the midst of a depression that had caused many Americans to abandon hope in traditional middle-class, Protestant Ethic values—set out to achieve the American middle-class dream, happily shouldering all the personal responsibilities demanded of anyone who hopes to achieve that dream. Some of them, just like Latin Americans in general in the 1990s, found it possible to retain their traditional religion even as they adopted the historical guidelines of American Protestantism and of America's secular religion built on the middle-class success myth. Other Mexican Americans in the 1930s, even as Latin Americans in the 1990s, felt that only in Protestantism could they find religious reinforcement for the values they associated with embourgeoisement: meaning acculturation into the middle-class, bourgeois lifestyle. In a striking way, what began to take shape in the American Southwest provided a harbinger of what was to come in the hemisphere as a whole some sixty years later.

Much of the rhetoric of good neighborliness in the 1930s flowed out of concepts of cultural relativism, based on the noble but impossible dream that people would learn truly to live understandingly, even lovingly, with others who shared few if any of their values. But the seeds of genuine, not just rhetorical, good neighborliness were being planted in the Southwest. There, with LULAC offering support all along the way, Mexican Americans assimilated to the economic and social values traditionally dear to norteamericanos, even as they clung also to respect for many of the cultural riches of their Hispanic and Indian past.

Among the many Mexican Americans who began to succeed in professions and in middle-class occupations in general during the 1930s was Carlos Eduardo Castañeda (who, as mentioned in the preface, became my mentor and compadre in the early 1950s at the University of Texas). Not only as a LULAC guiding spirit, but later as a regional director for the Fair Employment Practices Committee (FEPC), through which the Roosevelt administration sought to extend just working conditions to American minorities and thereby guarantee their maximum contribution to wartime productivity, Carlos Castañeda extended the helping hand and the power of example to Hispanics who sought genuine acceptance in the land they had chosen as their home.

There were many Castañeda types in the Southwest of the 1930s, role models not only for their fellow Hispanics but for many Anglos as well. Far more than the much publicized cultural relativists sprouting at Columbia University, the Castañeda types energetically involved in LULAC and the FEPC, in addition to their full-time jobs and professions, pointed the way toward a hemisphere of better neighbors than anyone in Washington, from FDR on down, really believed possible.

LULAC and Hispanic acculturation to the values of American middle-class life, whose norms the Hispanics often observed more faithfully than old-line WASPs, were not the whole story of Latin life in the United States during the Depression and World War II. This story also included the deeds of the zoot suiters and pachucos (gang members), mainly teenage Hispanics in California and other parts of the Southwest, who defied the norms of respectable middle-class culture just as thoroughly as did the later Beats and hippies. These latter in many ways paid zoot suiters the compliment of imitation—not of their sartorial style but of their lifestyle.

The zoot suit, with its long tapered coat excessively padded in the shoulders and its flared trousers, was suitable for dancing and carousing but certainly not for work. With its emphasis on nonutility, the zoot suit "became a kind of ode to a leisure life, to effortlessness rather than effort," to diversion rather than application.[14] Those who wore the suit fairly shouted out to all about them that they did not wish to conform to American middle-class norms. Although some two-thirds of Mexican boys in Los Angeles in the early 1930s may have at least occasionally donned zoot suits, only some 5 percent were members of pachuco gangs that habitually engaged in criminal activity. But the mere desire of the zoot suiters not to conform sufficed to turn the bulk of Angelenos against them. White Los Angeles, then, looked on with approval or at least indifference when Anglo sailors went on a rampage in 1943 and beat up all the zoot suiters they could lay their hands or clubs on. The police did little to control the rampaging Anglo sailors. Indeed, they tended to justify the Anglo rioters by conjuring up old stereotypes about the worthlessness of most Mexicans.[15]

Perhaps more Americans tended by the mid-1940s to judge Mexicans, Hispanics, and even Latin Americans in general by the zoot suiters and pachucos in their midst than by the upwardly mobile, model-citizen types who flocked to LULAC meetings. And perhaps this is one reason why the reservoir of goodwill on which the Good Neighbor policy had floated began to dry up by the mid-1940's.

Nevertheless, something had changed, permanently; a little of the old animus directed against Latins had begun to diminish. Anglo Americans might not know a great deal about LULAC. But many of them did get to know Hispanics in their midst: Hispanics, for example, who distinguished themselves as U.S. soldiers in World War II. Men who had served with distinction, who had won medals of honor, who had commanded Anglo troops in battle no longer cringed before Anglos in civilian life. "Sergeants and captains and buck privates turned into professional men and entrepreneurs; the vets no longer felt like intruders in a strange country."[16] Nor were Anglos able any longer to treat them as intruders. Service in World War II, along with the rise of a middle-class culture among Hispanics who stayed at home, had converted stereotyped Mexican derelicts into respectable middle-class citizens.

From this time on it would be more difficult for Americans to discriminate against Latins in their midst on the basis of old stereotypes that assumed them incapable of assimilating to middle-class culture. Americans by and large had not become cultural relativists; but Latin Americans had proved they were fully capable of empathizing with and fitting into the sort of culture that gringos respected. The spontaneous Americanization of Hispanics within the United States, unplanned and unforeseen by gringos, opened up the possibility of a future good neighborliness of hemispheric proportions—once south-of-the-border Latins began, en masse, to accommodate to a culture they had once reviled because to a large extent they had never understood it.

Yankees might not understand Latin culture, either. At least, though, after World War II, they could hardly be taken in anymore by the sort of report that Dr. Roy L. Garis of Vanderbilt University prepared for Representative John Box of Texas in the early 1930s. According to this report, Mexicans thought mainly of animal functions: eating, sleeping, and sexual debauchery. By 1945, many Americans, especially those in the Southwest who could witness the rise of a Mexican-American middle class, knew better. They knew, too, Garis to the contrary notwithstanding, that Mexicans were not given exclusively to living in shacks infested by "idleness, hordes of hungry dogs, and filthy children with faces plastered with flies";

Betty Waldo Parish, *Portuguese Yard*, between 1935 and 1938, woodcut, image: 5⅝ × 8 in. Gift of Dr. and Mrs. Corbin S. Carnell, in memory of E. Muriel Adams. Collection of the Harn Museum of Art, University of Florida. 1992.11.109

*Whether immigrants came from south of the border and settled in the Southwest, or from Portugal and settled in Massachusetts (the likely locale that the artist depicts), status-quo-oriented native sons and daughters often regarded them as violence-prone predators.*

infested, too, by "disease, lice, human filth, stench, promiscuous fornication, bastardy," by "lounging, apathetic peons and lazy squaws, beans and dried chili, liquor, [and] general squalor"; infested, too, by "envy and hatred of the gringo," and, finally, by "people who slept by day and prowled by night, like coyotes, stealing anything they can get their hands on."[17]

By the end of the war, norteamericanos living in the Southwest, at least those among them inclined at all to be decent and fair-minded, understood that old stereotypes did not afford accurate and complete descriptions of Hispanics. They understood that Hispanics were a people far more complex than the stereotypes had suggested. This understanding, which would ultimately make possible better neighborliness between gringos and Latins living in the United States and also on opposite sides of international borders, came about quite independently of the made-in-Washington Good Neighbor policy.

## North Americans Discover the Complexity of Judging Latin Americans

Beginning early in the twentieth century, modern art, especially in its cubist stage, had stressed the need to view objects from many different perspectives, and to combine the different perspectives in the same painting. The governing principle here was one of relativity: there are different perspectives to all things, and each perspective is as accurate as another. In a way, North Americans as they viewed Latin Americans in the 1930s had become more and more like modern artists. They viewed the neighbor to the south from many different perspectives, some flattering, some decidedly unflattering. In assessing the Latin, Americans had lost the ability to be single-minded bigots. Complexity had diffused the focus of prejudice.

By the 1930s, every gringo was beginning to have his or her own Latin American, and—as often as not—to like that Latin. For some gringos, the elegant, Latin American Arielist, ostensibly steeped in cultural refinements that reached back to ancient Greece, became an enormously appealing figure. Other gringos focused on the pensador, the intellectual active in politics, and liked what they saw. Others looked southward and perceived Marxist or anarchist radicals, Sacco-and-Vanzetti types, and found them pleasing, possibly even worthy role models. Similarly pleasing to American leftists were the Latin economic nationalists who refused to pay the huge debts that unscrupulous Wall Street bankers had foisted on them during the roaring 1920s. Other norteamericanos looked approvingly on socially conscious artists in Mexico, convinced they could change society through their art. Still other Yankees looked south and discovered primitives, in touch with the soil, with their own instincts: beautiful innocents whose backwardness was a blessing. Blessed also were those Latin mystical thinkers, shaman types in touch with a body of higher knowledge inaccessible to ordinary folk. Then there were gringo movie addicts who, perhaps with Ramón Navarro in mind, saw Latin males as suave romantic lovers, or who, maybe with Dolores del Rio in mind, saw Latin women as enticing beauties, accessible only to the most resolute and persistent suitors, but worth dying for; or, perhaps with Carmen Miranda in mind, Yankee movie addicts might see Latinas as ideal partners with whom to shack up for a night. For some gringos, the Latins were the ideal people among whom to seek laid-back adventure and pleasure, of the sort Bing Crosby and Bob Hope experienced in their enormously popular escape movies that comprised the "Road" series.

For popular-music-loving Yankees, the Latins were masters of pleasing melody (the Jimmy Dorsey recording of "María Elena" backed by "Green Eyes" sold nearly a million copies in 1941); they were masters, too, of exotic rhythms that fairly commanded a person to take to the dance floor. If you could not take to the dance floor yourself, you could go to the local theater and see *Flying Down to Rio*, featuring Mexican-born Dolores del Rio as a sultry Brazilian beauty, and also highlighting Ginger Rogers and Fred Astaire as they danced the carioca in an exotic, sensuous setting. In the 1933–1934 winter, this movie was the second best box office draw, trailing only *Little Women,* which starred Katharine Hepburn.[18] Perhaps there was something condescending on the part of those Americans who in the Depression and war years found Latin Americans almost as diverting as Mickey Mouse.

The issue, however, is more complex than this. The plot line of *Flying Down to Rio* revolves around an unemployed American dance troupe that finds new opportunity in Rio. Perhaps, in a way, the movie symbolized the vast new economic ties Yankees began to envision between their country and the lands to the south. Moreover, the movie's real star was America's fledgling aviation industry. *Flying Down to Rio* left an "impression of irrepressible aeronautical enthusiasm and the limitless possibilities of love and international communication opened up by the new technology."[19] As of the 1930s, the nascent aviation industry seemed more likely to create U.S. ties with at least the northern reaches of Latin America than with distant Europe. In all, the 1933 movie suggested two attitudes toward Latin America: it was the land that inspired escapist fantasy, and that also portended vast new economic opportunities.

At the same time that some Americans sought frothy escapism through romantic depictions of the Latin ambient, New York tycoons could gaze expectantly at new fields for investment. Simultaneously, they could regard with approbation and envy stereotyped visions of Latin entrepreneurs, on to every trick of the trade when it came to exploiting labor, and

Mildred Rackley, *La Jota,* between 1935 and 1943, woodcut, image: 9¹⁄₁₆ ×
12¹⁄₁₆ in. Gift of Dr. and Mrs. Corbin S. Carnell, in memory of E. Muriel Adams.
Collection of the Harn Museum of Art, University of Florida. 1992.11.123
*Americans discontented with old conventions often saw Latin immigrants in their*
*midst as a source of vitality, ready to inject erotic and exotic new rhythms into a*
*tired and stuffy old civilization.*

ever adept at arranging sweetheart deals through the auspices of bought
politicians. And southern estate owners with romantic ideas about the benevolent master looked to rural Latin America and saw it as the sort of
place that all too much was "gone with the wind" in the United States:
a region where large-scale landowners dealt paternalistically with docile
serfs, perpetuating a lifestyle that might have a chance to reestablish itself
in the U.S. South, now that the masters of northern capital had made such
a mess of things. This was the sort of message that some viewers might
have derived from the sensationally popular 1939 film *Gone with the
Wind,* which could be taken in some of its moments to suggest that good-
hearted racist southern estate owners should be viewed in a favorable
light, just like good-hearted racist hacendados south of the border.

The soaring popularity of country music in the 1930s also tended to
rely on the sort of romantic agrarianism that might have encouraged

Americans to think kindly about Latin Americans who, supposedly, remained rooted in the land, uncorrupted by urban vice. Hollywood picked up on this theme, too, in movies such as the King Vidor–directed *Our Daily Bread* (1934), with its message of the blessings attendant upon exchanging the capitalist urban rat race for the rural, more communal existence. All the while the New Deal encouraged the same sort of romantic foolishness with its federally supported back-to-the-land movement.

Other Yankees didn't like at all what they observed, or thought they observed, across the border to the south. From their perspective, Latin Americans were clowns and buffoons at best, dirty, fornicating rural beasts and urban savages at worst. In between were business swindlers and cheats of every kind, the sort of people who reneged on their foreign debts, the sort of people in fact with whom you had best sit with your back to the wall lest they stick a knife in it. Viewed from this sort of perspective, the scene to the south abounded also in political demagogues and liars, bloodthirsty dictators or would-be dictators (like an animalistic Pancho Villa as portrayed on the screen by Wallace Beery), drunkards, immoral priests who traded on superstition and from the confessional solicited women all too eager to yield to them—women of the sort who were too ignorant even to take the measures that would prevent them from breeding like cows, whether they copulated with husbands, priests, or casual lovers. Even as the volatile Italians, these people required a dictator, a sort of animal trainer, like Mussolini, to crack the whip and keep them in order. If good and decent, God-fearing and law-abiding Americans had to deal with such people, let it be through the sort of gunboat diplomacy that FDR in his mushy, do-good liberalism had halted. Better still, just leave such people alone. They were refractory to civilization, no more upliftable than the domestic riff-raff that empty-headed social workers, taking their cue from the likes of Eleanor Roosevelt, Frances Perkins, and Harry Hopkins, wanted to uplift—at the expense of upright taxpayers.

To Americans with favorable perspectives of their Latin neighbors, virtually every measure that Roosevelt took to implement a Good Neighbor policy deserved support and exhibited the president's wisdom and decent instincts. To Americans with unfavorable perspectives, Roosevelt's sidling up to the greasers proved his own moral baseness, and furnished additional grounds for hating the president.

Ever attentive to the changing winds of public opinion, FDR on the whole discovered considerable public support for his opening toward Latin Americans. Support on such a scale would not have been forthcoming prior to the 1930s. In earlier times, gringos had tended to have only one Latin American occupying their fantasies, and that one had been by and large disreputable. Now they had many Latins, and more often than not during the Good Neighbor years they rather tended to like some of those Latins, at least to give them the benefit of the doubt.

South of the border, changes were underway that reflected those taking place among North Americans. Up through the 1920s, the words and phrases most commonly found in the works of Latin American intellectuals describing norteamericanos and their culture included: imperialistic, materialistic, utilitarian, cold, vulgar, immoral, contemptuous, barbarians, lustful, brutal, expansionist, lack of idealism, no soul, hostile to art, worship of money, sense of superiority, Octopus of the North, Colossus of the North, rude, coarse, crude, stupid, racist.[20] In the 1930s, many Latin American thinkers found it necessary to revise, to render more complex, their evaluations of the Yankee. Like gringos contemplating their neighbors in the hemisphere, Latin Americans recognized complexity and ceased, at least to some considerable degree, to be single-minded bigots. Like gringos themselves, Latins grew confused about what sort of person lived on the other side of the border. This was a step ahead, in some ways the biggest one taken during the entire Good Neighbor era.

# 12. Racial Bigotry and Hemispheric Relations

❖ ❖ ❖ ❖ ❖ ❖ ❖ ❖ ❖ ❖ ❖ ❖ ❖ ❖ ❖ ❖ ❖ ❖ ❖ ❖ ❖ ❖ ❖ ❖ ❖ ❖ ❖ ❖ ❖ ❖ ❖ ❖ ❖ ❖ ❖

### Racism North of the Border: A Source of Hemispheric Friction

Racist! That was one of the accusations Latin Americans hurled against gringos. They were right, of course, by and large, although their accusations issued from members of a society shot through with racism of a more subtle but no less pervasive type than that found in the United States. Complexities abound in issues of comparative racism in the American hemisphere, and this chapter focuses on some of them.

The nineteenth-century Ecuadoran pensador Juan Montalvo refused to set foot in the United States, although he admired many of the country's liberal values. A mestizo, Montalvo feared that in the United States he would be treated with the discourtesy he heard had been accorded a certain dark-skinned Brazilian diplomat. Criminals from Europe, he complained in an 1882 publication, are accepted in the United States if they have a white skin, whereas the most respectable persons from Ecuador suffer enormous affronts should their skin bear the slightest color. In Venezuela, Peru, and Ecuador, he added, persons of dark skin could aspire to rise, even to attain prominence, and could fulfill their ambitions; but in the United States it was necessary to have a white skin to gain acceptance as a human being.[1]

The sort of situation Montalvo described remained unchanged during the Good Neighbor era. Although FDR consulted occasionally with prominent African Americans, and although he occasionally heeded his wife's high-minded nagging that he do something about blatant discrimination, his heart was never really involved in issues of racial justice—beyond his genuine desire to provide jobs for black Americans through the WPA and other New Deal agencies. As it turned out, this was as far as he needed to go in order to win overwhelming majorities among black voters; and it was as far as he dared go lest he lose white votes. When a federal antilynching bill died at the hands of southern filibusterers in 1935, FDR, fearful lest he offend southern committee chairmen, lent the bill no public support. Later, in 1941, only under the threat of a massive march on Washington to be led by A. Philip Randolph, head of the Brotherhood of Sleeping Car Porters, did a foot-dragging president sign an Executive Order that created a Committee on Fair Employment Practices. The committee was empowered to receive and investigate complaints of discrimination in war industries and in government departments and agencies. But it was decidedly a half loaf for blacks, owing to the omission of any move to end segregation in the armed services, the goal that Randolph and other African-American leaders had hoped to achieve.[2]

Before the Depression finally began to yield to the economic upturn sparked by defense industries, the kitchen pot remained a more pressing issue for most blacks than even the most basic of civil rights. This is suggested by the "Ballad of Roosevelt" that African-American poet Langston Hughes wrote. In it a boy asks his father what's the matter, how come the cupboards are bare and the pot is empty. The father replies, "I'm waitin' on Roosevelt, son."[3] And on issues of the pot, and of jobs, Roosevelt came through often enough. This is suggested in the 1936 "W.P.A. Blues," written and recorded in 1936 by Casey Bill Weldon. The song tells of the black man who at least got a job with the WPA, even if that agency through inadvertence managed somehow to demolish his house. Then there was the multiverse song of uncertain authorship sung by many blacks in the Depression era that included this stanza:

> Oh, I'm for you, Mr. President,
> I'm for you all the way.
> You can take away the alphabet,
> But don't take away this WPA.[4]

Another song, this one of the early 1940s, suggested that Roosevelt was doing well enough among blacks not to have to take on divisive issues pertaining to political and social rights. The song tells of a black family that named its brand new boy "Franklin D. Roosevelt Jones." In the version recorded by black band leader Cab Calloway, the song gained considerable popularity—undoubtedly intensifying anti-Roosevelt sentiments among the country's more out-and-out white bigots.

With the black vote rendered secure through economic means, FDR continued to ignore civil rights issues. This was still the case as America entered World War II in December of 1941 following the Japanese attack on Pearl Harbor. Blacks could now find more and more employment opportunities in defense industries, and they could join segregated units in the armed forces. Was there need to do more for them? Most white Americans thought not, and FDR was not about to challenge their judgment. Justice for the Negro just wasn't a goal he could achieve, not at any time in his long administration; and FDR had enough on his hands trying to muster support on issues that were winnable.

So it was that the marvelous song Thomas (Fats) Waller wrote in 1929, with lyrics by Andy Razaf, continued to say it all. "What Did I Do to Be So Black and Blue," when "My only sin is in my skin?" Later immortalized by a glorious Louis Armstrong recording, "Black and Blue" has been described as America's first song of racial protest. Really, though, the tone is more of lament than protest, the latter not being tolerated from blacks at that time.

In many ways, a real Good Neighbor policy could take hold only after the United States had passed through the first stages of the civil rights movement that remains the glory of the 1960s, amidst all of that decade's aberrations. Thanks to the civil rights movement, it became possible for a dark-complected Latin American mestizo or for a mulatto, with just a bit of discretion, to move more or less freely in the United States without encountering overt discrimination.

By and large, though, issues arising out of the treatment of the dark of skin in the United States were not as harmful to FDR's attempt to fashion good neighborliness as might be thought—at least not among the top-level Latin Americans who shaped and conducted foreign policy. This was because Latin American society itself was shot through with deeply embedded racism, albeit of a strain considerably less vicious than the one that flourished to the north.

## The Racism of Latin Americans Tempers Their Outrage at U.S. Racism

Latin America's gente decente ensconced at the top of their pigmentocracies (societies white at the top but brown or black at the bottom) had little love for the dark-skinned masses below, although they were tolerant enough to take up unabashedly the policy of co-opting exceptional persons of color by accepting them, virtually as equals, in white society. Throughout much of the second third of the nineteenth century North Americans had themselves toyed half-heartedly with such a policy. Even

Southerners showed some inclination to tolerate partial integration of the lighter-skinned, most "civilized" mulattoes. Increasingly, the latter responded by identifying more with white than with black society.[5] Then, as racism grew more virulent in the post–Civil War South, whites abandoned their opening to the mulatto. Latin Americans tended to think Americans were ill-advised in this policy, one destined inevitably to build up race resentment that would someday explode. Their northern neighbors, they believed, would be better off in the long term if they emulated Latin habits of accepting and co-opting the more talented people of color, especially those least off-white in pigmentation.

By and large, though, North America's increasingly inflexible racial discrimination perturbed Latin America's ruling sectors only slightly: and the whiter they were the less it perturbed them. Those Latins who witnessed racism at first hand in the United States came generally from the exalted white social circles. Even if not lily-white, they could generally count on being able to "pass" in most parts of the United States. Latin American governments made it a point to "put their best foot forward" by sending diplomats to the United States who were white or could pass. Furthermore, within their own countries Latin upper classes clung to racist assumptions in assessing run-of-the-mill persons of color. They had managed to co-opt the generally lighter-skinned talented elites among the nonwhites; and they saw no need to extend their tolerance further down pigmentocracy's ladder.

When Martin Luther King, Jr., appeared on the U.S. scene just past the midpoint of the twentieth century, his idea of a mass human rights movement that did not distinguish among skin hues struck many Latin Americans as dangerous, but also as the predictable consequence of earlier Anglo-Saxon refusal to play the game of selective co-optation. Had American whites from an early point proved willing to incorporate the often relatively light-skinned "talented tenth" (the term by which African-American intellectual W. E. B. Du Bois described a black cultural elite in the United States), then they would not have incurred the disruptive challenge posed by a movement that demanded full-fledged civil rights for *all* persons of color.


Whether in the 1960s or in the 1930s, the nearly pure white Latin American directing classes harbored relatively little in the way of burning resentment against American racism as directed against African Americans—however much they tried to justify their anti-Yankeeism inspired by other causes on the grounds of Yankee racism. With Latin American mulattoes or mestizos, though, at least with those who were educated and accommodated, the case was different, as Juan Montalvo's quotation at the beginning of this chapter attests. They shared, along with Yankee mixed-bloods, a genuine resentment against racism as practiced in the United States. Consequently Mexican mulatto and mestizo men of letters who enjoyed virtually full acceptance in their country could sympathize with light-skinned mulatto Langston Hughes when he complained that he had to go south of the border to find a benign racial environment.

In his 1927 poem "Mulatto," Hughes depicts the U.S. white Everyman and Everywoman as they shout to all nonwhites, no matter how nearly white they may be: "Git back there in the night, You ain't white." In Mexico, no one commanded mulattoes or mestizos, at least not the educated ones, to "Git back there in the night." Little wonder, then, that Hughes, who incidentally found his light skin tone an impediment to gaining acceptance among African leaders when much later he visited their continent, regarded the times he spent in Mexico as among the best moments of his life.

By and large, America's talented tenth among blacks in the 1920s and '30s, prevailingly rather light-complected, probably desired not so much a universal civil rights movement as the Latin Americanization of race relations. They wanted the system to open its doors to them, but not necessarily to the darker masses below them. While there were exceptions, like Langston Hughes, who professed racial solidarity with all shades of African Americans, the bulk of America's talented tenth seems to have had reservations about a universal civil rights movement. Such a movement might have threatened their own distinctive place among black Americans. And if some of the talented tenth toyed with communism, it was—at least in part—because they perceived it as a movement that would grant special status to them, the choicest of black souls. Certainly the communist movement in America went out of its way to strengthen this perception, wooing with particular intensity the Negro intellectual and artist.

As the American Communist Party (CPUSA) forged ties with select black Americans, so also did Latin American leftist intellectuals. In some ways good neighborliness in the 1930s rested as much on the ties that Latin America's out-of-power intellectuals established with America's talented tenth among the Negro population as upon the bonds that Latin America's political leaders formed with their U.S. counterparts. In short, along with official good neighborliness, there developed an unofficial, intellectual private-sector good neighborliness; it grew out of the bonds developed between dusky and partially excluded Latin Americans of talent and well-nigh totally excluded off-white North Americans of talent. As the years went by, this private-sector, unofficial good neighborliness may have yielded as rich a harvest as the official kind cultivated by leaders in Washington and the capitals of Latin America. The intellectual, private-sector brand of good neighborliness that developed mainly outside the circles of power had not only a bountiful future. It had roots in the past, fecund roots that sent forth abundant new growth in the 1930s.

## The Culturati and Their Private-Sector Good Neighborliness

Latin America's literati and intellectuals, its culturally gifted elites who stood on the fringes of power rather than wielding it, were long accustomed (like Juan Montalvo) to taking American racism seriously. More than ever before, though, they began to take it seriously in the 1920s, at the time of the Harlem Renaissance—that remarkable, prodigious flowering of black talent, in prose, poetry, dance, music, painting, and, just simply, in stimulating cultural discourse. In spite of their obvious gifts, the guiding figures in the black cultural renaissance remained excluded from anything even remotely approximating full-fledged participation in U.S. social, cultural, economic, and political life. Here was a form of exclusion that Latin American cultural elites took note of and responded to with genuine indignation. Latin Americans by and large might not care in the least when black laborers suffered cruel discrimination in the United States. But the artists of Latin America, the literati, the intellectuals, many of whom themselves were not lily-white but whose talents had resulted in their "whitening" and their acceptance into "whitish" elite society, responded with outrage when their dark-skinned fellow literati and artists north of the border failed to gain meaningful access to society. Here was proof of what cultural barbarians white gringos truly were.

Never before had a North American colored talented tenth been so visible as during the Harlem Renaissance of the 1920s. Therefore, never before had United States racism been so starkly on display to Latin America's cultural elites. In general, they saw the ongoing exclusion of blacks, all blacks regardless of how light their skin color and how great their talent, as one glaring indication of Latin America's moral superiority over the United States. In their eyes, this superiority more than compensated for Latin America's mere economic inferiority.

The American talented tenth of color who congregated in and around Harlem in the 1920s and early '30s sometimes referred to themselves not as the literati but the "niggerati."[6] With the "niggerati," and also with discriminated-against U.S. Jewish intellectuals, Latin American pensadores tended to identify as they had never previously identified with any group of norteamericanos. And they felt personally violated by the discrimination to which North American society in general subjected talented Americans of the wrong skin color or religious creed.

Especially in Mexico and Cuba, and sometimes also in Jamaica or Haiti or other Caribbean areas, the "niggerati" and leading Latin American literati met. Frequently they established close personal bonds and shared their dreams about a coming age in which the message of *négritude*, proclaiming an eventual ideal union of colored and white cultures, would gain fulfillment. The rise of a colored talented tenth in America coincided with the negritude movement of the Caribbean and French colonial Africa; and Latin American pensadores responded enthusiastically to both phenomena.

The "niggerati" and representatives of Latin America's cultural elites met also in Depression-era America. Often their contact came about in consequence of the interaction of public and privately supported arts projects. Some of the New Deal artists' and writers' programs supported both black and white persons of cultural distinction. In consequence of the opportunities thus afforded them, some American black artists and writers enjoyed the opportunity to fraternize with some of the Latin American artists, especially the Mexican muralists, brought to the United States primarily through the support of private foundations and philanthropists and art patrons. Moreover, representatives of America's colored talented tenth won an occasional Guggenheim grant that took them on south-of-the-border projects. Above all, an emerging American Negro intelligentsia met with Latin American writers and artists of all color shades in Spain during its civil war. There, in Madrid or Barcelona or elsewhere on the fighting front, they strengthened their bonds as they joined in supporting the Republic against the allegedly fascistic Nationalists led by Francisco Franco. In Spain, black Americans and Latin Americans of all colors fought side by side, ten years before the U.S. Armed Forces were integrated (in 1948).

In Spain, Latin American intellectuals came not only to admire dark-skinned American intellectuals and artists, among them Langston Hughes and Paul Robeson, but also less educated American Negroes who joined the Abraham Lincoln Battalion to fight for a new order of socialist democracy in which color barriers were expected to disappear. By fighting together in Spain along with Latin American intellectuals and artists of all skin hues, North America's dark-skinned culture leaders and commoners hoped to sustain and nourish the kinds of freedom denied them at home. Simultaneously, American men of color, in league with their new allies, would help forge a new Spain in which "higher" values took precedence over merely material considerations and bourgeois values. Such, at least, was the often communist- or anarchist-inspired vision that motivated members of the Abraham Lincoln Battalion and their native Spanish-speaking comrades as they set about to redeem Spain: first Spain, then America, then the world. It goes without saying that less exalted and more self-serving ambitions and hopes also motivated the Americans, North and South, seeking the adventure of their lives in Spain.

Meanwhile, back in the New World hemisphere in the interim between world wars black North American musicians had been forging a new music that often drew upon Latin American sources of inspiration, both melodic and rhythmic. Clearly, the new music possessed what Jelly Roll Morton (who played a principal role in inventing jazz piano playing) called a "Latin tinge." Jazz, a hemispheric new music that in its origins also had ties to the African continent, won widespread admiration among Latin Americans from various walks of life. With good reason, some Latin Americans regarded jazz as the most significant contribution that their norteamericano neighbors had made to world culture. Jazz played a prominent role in tightening American–Latin American ties and in heightening Latin American distaste for the racism that led gringos to relegate cultural giants to underling status.

In an era when folk arts and "primitivism" were in vogue, and appreciated as much as anywhere in the world among Latin America's au courant culturati, American blacks—the creators of one of the great musical folk arts in all of history—were still denied acceptance in their native land. This fact fostered widespread resentment against American racism even in London and Paris and Copenhagen. But the resentment and incredulity closer to the home of jazz, in Havana and Mexico City, for example, were even stronger. At the same time, out of this resentment grew the sort of person-to-person hemispheric bonds that caused good neighborliness to bubble up spontaneously from below, altogether independent of a top-down, government-to-government Good Neighbor policy.

## Latin America's Selective Outrage over U.S. Racism

Many Latin Americans of the leading classes considered themselves men of practical *and* cultural affairs. Often such men operated effectively and successfully both in the realm of business and politics and diplomacy on the one hand and in the world of letters and arts on the other. Inclined to appreciate and admire the artistic, cultural attainments of a new generation of dark-skinned men and women of talent in the United States, they tended also to fret over the fact that, regardless of the size of their talents, these persons in their native land were denied status, dignity, and full-fledged citizenship. In the largely premodern, preembourgeoisement setting of early twentieth-century Latin America, social and political leaders liked at least to pretend that they took matters of art and aesthetics more seriously than the allegedly rank materialists to the north. In Latin America, cultural attainments on the part of the dark-skinned were often quite sufficient to provide the talented person access to some of the most prestigious circles. That this was not generally true in the United States proved, at least to many Latin American culturati, that gringo civilization was seriously flawed.

The Latin culturati might not fret unduly in the 1930s when eight laboring-class American Negroes, the so-called Scottsboro Boys, awaited execution on quite patently trumped-up charges that they had raped two white women. Throughout Latin America, after all, business, political, and cultural leaders agreed that a bit of terrorism was quite in order so as to keep the masses in their place. But when a Langston Hughes or a Paul Robeson or a Louis Armstrong or a Duke Ellington was denied seating and accommodations not just in the South but even in New York City when he tried to enter various restaurants or register in hotels, they, the Latin culturati, were outraged. This was not the way they treated their talented persons of color. In consequence, within their own countries, white-skinned cultural, political, and business leaders could count on the support of the talented dark of skin in enforcing a system of justice that meted out swift retribution to untalented, lower-class persons of color who stepped out of line.

### Issues of Race: Looking beyond the Good Neighbor Era

Not until the latter part of the twentieth century would North Americans awaken to the advantages of permitting some degree of Latin Americanization in race relations. When this occurred, a giant step was taken toward hemispheric convergence. When, at last, the American civil rights movement came into its own, U.S. hemispheric diplomacy at the highest level could finally capitalize on the gains made through the informal, unofficial networks of interpersonal and interracial diplomacy that had begun to flourish, largely out of public view, in the 1930s.

One must not exaggerate the beauties of down-below good neighborliness. On that level, sensitive egos bumped and collided all too often. Still, to a degree not often seen before in hemispheric dealings, gringo and Latin egos, often enclosed in less-than-white bodies, came harmoniously together. Official U.S. architects of the Good Neighbor policy took advantage of this fact when, during World War II, they enlisted the services of some of the country's black talented tenth, including jazz musicians, and sent them to Latin America on goodwill tours. These tours might have accomplished more had they not rested on pretense: the pretense that white norteamericanos were by and large beginning to do better by their dark compatriots. Still, the pretense probably had to precede the reality. That the U.S. establishment went at least so far as to give its imprimatur to the pretense of racial decency constitutes a Good Neighbor ploy not altogether to be despised. Before the wartime Good Neighbor era, would

Americans even have bothered to resort to ploys, would they even have cared what Latin Americans thought about their racism?

Even the willingness to resort to ploys may have come about under the duress of wartime exigencies. Still, that willingness held out some hope for the future.

# SECTION
# IV

❖❖❖❖❖❖❖❖❖❖❖❖❖❖❖❖❖❖❖❖❖❖❖❖❖❖❖❖❖❖

*The Roosevelt
Styles in
Latin American
Relations*

# 13. Sizing Up Latin America: The Young and the Mature Roosevelt

❖ ❖ ❖ ❖ ❖ ❖ ❖ ❖ ❖ ❖ ❖ ❖ ❖ ❖ ❖ ❖ ❖ ❖ ❖ ❖ ❖ ❖ ❖ ❖ ❖ ❖ ❖ ❖ ❖ ❖ ❖ ❖ ❖ ❖ ❖ ❖

### Roosevelt's Early Impressions of Latin America

Growing up, the young Roosevelt heard tales about the wealth his father, James, had amassed in the China trade. Perhaps this caused him to muse on the profit-making opportunities that awaited the resourceful Yankee investor in "backward" parts of the world—one did not speak in those days about the "underdeveloped" world. He also heard about his father's failure in 1893 in a Nicaraguan interoceanic canal-building project; and one wonders if this might have caused the youth to have doubts about the fiscal responsibility of Central Americans. In any event, his main interest in foreign countries while growing up focused on Europe; as a child and youth he visited Europe eight times, and—abetted by governesses—acquired some skills in speaking and reading German and French. There is no evidence he developed any interest in Latin America, other than to applaud what his cousin Theodore Roosevelt had accomplished (as assistant secretary of the Navy) in helping drive the Spaniards out of Cuba and then (as president) in plundering Colombia of the Panamanian territory across which Yankees proposed to build an interoceanic canal.

Going on thirty years of age in April of 1912, Franklin Roosevelt viewed the not quite completed Panama Canal in the course of a cruise. In a letter to his mother he expressed awe at the engineering efficiency that was speeding the project along. He marveled also at the American quarters in the canal zone at Cristobal, contrasting "their air of absolute efficiency" with the chaotic native scene. At the same time, he expressed tempered admiration for Panama's Spanish background as he commented on the ruins of old Panama City. The ruins provided some indication of "what a centre of Spanish power and riches existed here when the Pilgrims and Puritans had only a precarious foothold in New England."[1] Might he have wondered what had subsequently gone wrong with Latin civilization on the isthmus?

Some three years later, after he had become assistant secretary of the Navy in the Woodrow Wilson administration (the post from which cousin Theodore had launched his career in national politics), FDR from Washington wrote to Eleanor at the Roosevelt Campobello compound in New Brunswick, noting a lunch he had had with the Brazilian minister to Mexico. The Brazilian, a certain "Senhor Cardoso," was handling U.S. interests in Mexico after the withdrawal of the American ambassador in the wake of the diplomatic difficulties that had accompanied the landing of U.S. Marines at Veracruz—an event precipitated by Wilson's obsession with ridding the republic of its dictator Victoriano Huerta. FDR praised Senhor Cardoso as a "gentleman" who "knows how to treat Ambassadors and Ministers from other civilized nations"—clearly implying that Mexicans lacked this badge of civilized diplomatic intercourse. Roosevelt repeated his praise for Cardoso the following day in a letter to his mother, noting how efficiently the Brazilian was handling U.S. interests. Did he reveal a touch of racial condescension when he described the Brazilian diplomat as "a dusky gentleman" who had a duskier still wife and daughter? Is it significant he did not allude to duskiness in his letter to Eleanor, perhaps in deference to her "peculiar" obsession with racial equality?[2]

At this time the young assistant secretary was deeply involved in helping oversee the U.S. occupation of Veracruz, all the while giving off blustering statements to the effect that perhaps it heralded a war in which the wayward Mexicans would be disciplined by a civilized country. At this time, too, the young man engaged privately and even publicly in chiding Josephus Daniels, his immediate superior as secretary of the Navy, for his spineless pacifism in the face of alleged Mexican provocation. Perhaps the young assistant secretary hoped a good war with backward peoples would do for his reputation what the Spanish American War had done for his illustrious cousin's. "Sooner or later," FDR declared in 1914, "the United States must go down there and clean up the Mexican mess. I believe that the best time is right now."[3]

Some three to four years later, in June of 1918, FDR became involved in the U.S. military occupation of Panamanian territory in an endeavor to force the government to hold elections. Lasting until August of 1920, the occupation "left a residue of bitterness among all Panamanians." This did not concern Roosevelt, who applauded the operation and apparently agreed with its commander, Gen. Richard Blatchford, in assessing its significance. According to Blatchford, the American troops carried out "a moralistic and (for the Panamanians) humiliating campaign to clean up vice in the terminal cities [of the Canal]." The general noted that prior to Yankee intervention, these cities "were worse than Sodom and Gomorrah." Much to the general's satisfaction, and undoubtedly to the disgust of the U.S. soldiers on the scene, American intervention led to the deportation of some of Panama's prostitutes.[4] The moral uplift of natives was not all that recommended the venture to Roosevelt. If the canal's full potential for economic gain were to be realized, then Americans must let wayward people know that they would not be allowed to jeopardize its smooth and uninterrupted operation.

Meantime the assistant secretary, militantly inclined toward cleaning up messes wherever they appeared in the Caribbean area, thereby smoothing the way for trade and commerce, had played a role in the occupation of Haiti in 1915 and of the Dominican Republic the following year. Again he had found occasion to criticize his superior, Josephus Daniels, for his reluctance to carry out the Caribbean adventure. A pacifist by nature, Daniels regarded the occupations as a "bitter pill" rather than an opportunity to discipline dark-skinned neighbors while blocking whatever inclinations they might have had to welcome German economic penetration. One biographer hits the nail squarely in concluding that as a young man (and just how immature does one expect a person in his early thirties to be?) "Roosevelt supported the march of the flag into foreign lands not only to protect American interests but also to civilize supposedly backward peoples." On one occasion he alleged that Haitians had been " 'little more than primitive savages' before the uplifting experience of armed American intervention." Not only Haiti and the Dominican Republic but to a lesser degree Latin America in general impressed Roosevelt as "something to be acted upon rather than an actor in its own right."[5]

On a tour of Haiti in 1917, Roosevelt expressed warm admiration for Marine Major Smedley Butler, who led the occupation troops. Although he would later repent of his heavy-handed methods employed in the interest of U.S. capital, Butler at the time had no concern for the rights of Haitians or natives of the Caribbean region in general, dismissing them as "niggers" and "coons." Certainly he made no effort to hide his disdain for Haitians, putting the peons to work as forced laborers on road-building projects. Once he forced the refined head of government to sleep on the floor while he, the major, occupied the only bed in the room at the quarters where they put up during a tour of the country. Yet when Roosevelt returned from Haiti, he had only the highest praise for Butler and his occupation troops; and many of the favorite stories he related, though not we can assume in Eleanor's presence, revolved about the color of the island's occupants—which, given the pervasiveness of U.S. prejudices at the time, was not remarkable. Later, in 1918, when Haitians rebelled against the harsh occupation, Roosevelt applauded the brutal suppression effected by the Marines that resulted in the death of some fifteen hundred of the ill-mannered natives.[6]

While in Haiti in 1917, FDR showed a keen eye for the economic opportunities that awaited Yankee investors once the natives were whipped into line. He thought even about investing some of his own money in a resort. Later, he looked into the possibility of starting a chain of variety stores across Haiti. Clearly he believed that despite their present low levels of achievement, Haitians up to a point were civilizable. In 1922 he wrote a friend, "I cannot agree that just because the Haytian native population does not use knives, forks, cups, etc., that they will never use them. As a matter of fact, I feel convinced that during the next generation the Haytian population will adopt the standards more generally in vogue."[7] This assumed, of course, that Americans would continue to shoulder the white man's burden.

Not all Latin Americans were trouble-makers. A few of them, like the dusky Brazilian ambassador, were people of some distinction. Badly hung over one morning in Cuba in 1917, the assistant secretary called on that country's chief executive and found him "distinctly the gentleman-businessman," committed to "orderly progress . . . and not . . . radicalism."[8] In spite of his later preaching against economic royalists, FDR always had a certain fondness for hustling businessmen, whether they were Cubans or swashbuckling Irish predators like Joseph Kennedy.

Still, FDR at this stage of life showed a prevailingly contemptuous attitude toward natives of the Caribbean republics. And this fact got him into trouble when campaigning as the Democratic vice-presidential candidate in 1920. On a campaign swing through Montana, FDR delivered a speech on August 18 in which he claimed that Cuba, Haiti, Santo Domingo, Panama, Nicaragua, and the other Central American states would cast their votes in the proposed League of Nations Assembly as their Yankee big brother instructed them. "I have something to do with the running of a couple of these little Republics," he added. "Until last week I had two of these votes in my pocket. One of them was Haiti. I know, for I wrote Haiti's Constitution myself, and if I do say it, I think it was a pretty good Constitution." The claim to have written the Haitian constitution was a bald-faced lie, and when Republicans leapt to take advantage of the gaffe, shedding crocodile tears over what they referred to as the "rape of Haiti," FDR falsely claimed he had been misquoted.[9]

Beginning his recovery from poliomyelitis in 1921, FDR set to work on writing a history of the United States. He never advanced beyond the first few pages, but in them he reverted to a point he had made in the cited

1912 letter to his mother. Spanish civilization had made a strong and laudable start in establishing itself in Central and South America. Indeed, the Spaniards had constructed notable cathedrals and launched a flourishing commerce "before ever Jamestown or Plymouth were conceived." However, it had all proved to be a "false glory." How did Roosevelt account for the rapid decline? It began from almost the first moment, when the conquerors left their wives behind in Spain. As a result, they had created a hybrid race, "part cavalier, part Indian, later on in part negro." Even pure-blooded Spaniards, moreover, had "staked all on the great adventure," on "glorious riches to be gained for little labor. . . . Nothing in the method of these Spanish cavaliers made for a sound and permanent colonization. Their whole object from King to soldier was exploitation— to get as much out in as short a time as possible."[10] At the time, Roosevelt did not see the irony lying in the fact that Latin Americans had begun to accuse Yankees of exactly the same traits. By the time he became president, though, and began to grapple with U.S. "economic royalists," one suspects he could have seen the irony.

It remains a moot point, though, as to whether Roosevelt by the time he became president had mitigated even slightly the racism that underlay his comments on "a hybrid" race. He had attested all the more to an abhorrence for race-mixture, well-nigh universal at the time among U.S. Caucasians, in a 1923 article wherein he observed: "Californians have properly objected [to Japanese immigration] on the sound basic grounds that . . . the mingling of Asiatic blood with European or American blood produces, in nine cases out of ten, the most unfortunate results."[11]

Also in 1923 FDR expressed anew his harsh appraisal of Haitians when referring to their primitive religions that existed beneath a thin facade of Christianity. True to the African origins of their religious outlook, Haitians even indulged in "well-known forms of human sacrifice." What is more, Roosevelt declared in a valid but not very sensitive assessment, Haiti prior to the American occupation was no more "a Republic in our accepted sense of the term, than were the principalities of India, before the advent of the British." While it was true that Marines had found themselves forced to kill several hundred among the "tens of thousands" of bandits infesting the countryside, they had also protected the more decent people from bandits, had built roads and hospitals, and ensured honest collection of taxes, while cleaning up disease-ridden ports and establishing "peace throughout the island for the first time in a century and a quarter."[12] Although at an earlier time FDR had gone along with the Frederick Jackson Turner thesis that the frontier had ceased to exist in America, he obviously thought that in parts of Latin America the Wild West persisted, and that it was up to Yankee agents of civilization to tame this last frontier.

Given what is known about FDR's attitudes toward Latin Americans from the years 1912 to 1923, how could this man have launched in 1933 his Good Neighbor policy? One answer, certainly with good claims to validity, is that duplicity was never a stranger to FDR. Still, one wonders if he could have been sincere when, rather condescendingly, he observed that "Latin Americans think they are just as good as we are and many of them are." [13] I suspect he could have been partially sincere; he could, after all, have had the whiter elements among Latin Americans in mind when he made this statement. And in this case, he would not have been far removed in attitude from Latin America's ruling classes who were, outside of some of the Caribbean republics, prevailingly light of skin.

Certainly the light-skinned ruling classes in Latin America's leading republics, among them Argentina, Colombia, Chile, and Uruguay, tended to regard as racially inferior the dark-skinned inhabitants of their own countries; nor did they waste any love on the generality of inhabitants in what they disparagingly dubbed the "tropical, turbulent" republics of Central America and the Caribbean. Furthermore, there was a biting edge of condescension when South American elites referred to Mexico as the "Aztec Republic." So long as FDR accepted them, the white Latin Americans, as among "some" of the Latin Americans who were as good as North Americans, they, the Latin Americans, would not quibble with the gringo president.

In the mid-1930s Henry Stimson, who had served Herbert Hoover as secretary of state and later would serve the Democratic administration as secretary of war, addressed a telling question to Roosevelt. Apropos of the withdrawal of Marines from Haiti early in the Good Neighbor era, Stimson asked if Haiti "would permanently stay put." Did the president, he further inquired, know of any self-governing Negro community that had stayed put? FDR, as Stimson reported to his diary, "could not suggest any." Well, neither I suspect could the Latin American ruling classes. Even in Haiti, mulattoes doubted the ability of Negroes to rule. And in the prevailingly mulatto Dominican Republic the ruling classes looked down disdainfully on the dark republic that shared a border with them. Dominicans, moreover, were downright obsessive about preserving their relative whiteness "against a possible Haitian migrant onslaught." [14]

Still, it is possible that as Franz Boas's theories on cultural relativism began to spread in Latin America, some of that region's ruling classes may have discarded a bit of the pessimism, of the fatalism, with which they regarded the future of their countries because of their large admixture of colored blood. In this case, informed Latin Americans would have resented Roosevelt's racist pronouncements of the 1920s. In all probability, though, the great majority knew nothing about these pronouncements. Furthermore, it is easily possible that FDR himself, under the tutelage of his wife and under the influence of the new teachings of cultural relativism, could have revised his earlier attitudes by the time he came to the White House. A man or woman can, after all, undergo profound change in ten years; indeed, almost any intelligent person, alive to fresh ideas and to widely publicized new research findings, will inevitably change in ten years. All the more might a person of reason change if living in a country that itself had undergone dramatic transition from the spirited "dance of the millions," as some commentators described the booming 1920s, to the dispirited shuffle that accompanied the loss of the millions in the 1930s.

If Smedley Butler, whose heavy-handed militaristic approach to Haitians Franklin Roosevelt had so admired, could change his opinion on issues of hemispheric relations, why could not an assistant secretary of the Navy suddenly become president undergo a similar change of heart? For most of his career, Butler took pride in disciplining the sort of people whom President William Howard Taft, speaking of Filipinos, once referred to as "little brown brothers." When serving Yankee interests throughout much of the Caribbean region, whether in Central America or in Haiti, Butler had not felt very brotherly toward brown-skinned, or darker, natives. His heart lay with the civilized capitalists of the North, whose agent he happily and proudly regarded himself. Then came a change as Butler, acquiring new perspectives in the Depression era along with countless other Americans, took on attitudes more in line with the values of his Quaker background. In 1931 Butler confessed: "I helped in the rape of half a dozen Central American republics for the benefit of Wall Street." [15]

Roosevelt's apparent change of heart as he presided over the Good Neighbor policy was far less dramatic, far less the "Road to Damascus" sort of conversion than occurred with Butler. Still, the change may have been genuine. In any event, FDR had the ability to make it *seem* genuine; and in politics, perhaps in most human relationships, appearances are often as important as reality.

### Perspectives of Latin America from the White House: The Mature Roosevelt as Good Neighbor

Even if he did no more than indulge his passion for watching opinion survey results, Roosevelt would have changed, or at least gone out of his way to present the appearance of having changed, in his attitudes toward Latin America. A 1940 opinion poll indicated that Americans by and large took Latin Americans seriously. Some 84 percent of the sample queried wanted to know more about Latin America; 75 percent "called for more articles on the Americas and favored closer contacts, even at the cost of greater governmental expenditures. Over 50 percent advocated loans for Latin American industrial development, railroads and defense," and were willing to pay higher taxes to support such projects. These sentiments among a people only just barely beginning to emerge from a devastating depression are little short of startling. Moreover, with many European vacation resorts closed, more and more American tourists visited the republics to the south, often developing avid interest in them. Accompanying this trend was a dramatic rise in enrollment in Spanish- and Portuguese-language classes. In 1941 *Reader's Digest* and *Time* inaugurated Spanish editions, "and the two largest United States radio networks started weekly broadcasts to and from Latin America. The Copacabana and Latin Quarter opened in New York City, where performers like Carmen Miranda from Brazil popularized songs such as 'South of the Border' and 'The South American Way.'" As the Depression finally began to ease, Americans flocked to night clubs, where more and more often they danced to Latin American rhythms.[16]

Here were signs that, along with many other developments described in preceding chapters, suggested a new opening to Latin America among North Americans. Clearly, good neighborliness had become a political asset. So, whether he had undergone a change of heart or not, FDR could not have avoided the conclusion that blustering racism directed against Latin Americans no longer played well to the home audiences, though racism directed against America's internal people of color still was politically de rigueur. Moreover, quite apart from issues of race, good neighborliness played well with the American electorate, especially when it might be perceived in terms of clipping the wings of discredited Yankee capitalists involved in clashes with Latin American governments.

Writing in 1933 to William H. Woodin, his first secretary of the treasury, FDR noted: "You and I understand this national situation and wish our banking and economist friends would realize the seriousness of the situation from the point of view of the debtor classes—i.e., 90 percent of the human beings in the country—and think less from the point of view of the 10 percent who constitute the creditor classes."[17] Even when it came to Latin America, FDR was prepared now to think more of the native masses than of the tiny percentage of American citizens with south-of-the-border investments. Even if his heart had not necessarily pulled him in that direction, the mood of the Depression-era U.S. electorate would have.

If FDR had once been an old-fashioned imperialist, he no longer was. In the 1920s being an old-fashioned imperialist brought a political payoff. It no longer did by the time he entered the White House.

## FDR as Good Neighbor: Inconsistent or Insincere?

In his March 4, 1933, inaugural address, Roosevelt proclaimed he would dedicate America to the policy of "the good-neighbor—the neighbor who resolutely respects himself and, because he does so, respects the rights of others." From that point on the president went out of his way, at least occasionally, to create the impression that Latin America counted. With White House encouragement, Pan American Day was celebrated widely in American schools. Moreover, "ministries were raised to the embassy level," while "Latin American leaders were treated more or less as equals and accorded prestigious treatment during their visits to Washington." In perhaps the most satisfying single volume devoted to the Good Neighbor era, Irwin F. Gellman concludes that FDR "brought Latin America to the limelight as no chief executive before him had. If any period can be labeled the golden age of Pan American cooperation, the Roosevelt presidency deserves to be so labeled."[18]

Given the isolationist mood of Depression-era Americans, Roosevelt would not have found it expedient to reveal any keen interest in affairs of Europe or the Far East, even had his heart led him in that direction. Apparently, though, FDR himself shared in the isolationist mood of his fellow citizens until late in the '30s. Soured on relations with Europe, the president turned to the endeavor to create a more economically self-sufficient American hemisphere. So far as foreign relations were concerned, Latin America was practically the only show in town, at least the only show the public might be expected to applaud.[19] Then, by the late 1930s, security considerations added their input to hemispheric diplomacy: Latin Americans must be wooed more assiduously away from attachment to Old World powers that could pose not just an economic but a military challenge to the United States. So, toward the end of a troubled decade, security considerations had joined with domestic political expediency and with hemispheric trade-and-investment incentives in driving FDR to become a better neighbor than in his heart he really wanted to be.

Perhaps British historian D. Cameron Watt is not wide of the mark when he observes: "Roosevelt's disdain for small nations was almost Stalinist." Perhaps, too, FDR saw Latin American states in the same light in which William Bullitt saw the minor states of Europe. Until a definitive falling out at the beginning of the 1940s, Bullitt was one of FDR's most trusted foreign policy advisers; and he had no time for what he referred to as "those dinky little European states."[20] There is good reason to believe that FDR, most of the time at least, located the "dinky little states" to the south.

Out of the pursuit of economic opportunities, out of security interests, and out of the quest for domestic political gain in an era of good neighborliness driven by forces that bubbled up from below rather than descending from Washington, FDR would play the role of Good Neighbor. Always, though, what most concerned him was to maintain, in line with the spirit of the Monroe Doctrine as built upon by nineteenth-century statesmen and more recently by his cousin Teddy, a Latin America basically confined to the Yankee sphere of influence. Given the demands of realpolitik, was there anything reprehensible in this?

Through the decades, though, Latin American political leaders and intellectuals alike—quite understandably from their perspective—had aspired to emerge from the shadow of Monroeism, which they equated with Yankee hegemony. How was it, then, that FDR became among a broad social spectrum of Latin Americans—political and economic leaders, intellectuals, and masses—the most popular president ever to lead the Yankee nation? The answer lies partly, among many other factors, in the economic concessions Washington began to make to various Latin American countries, and in the more subtle methods it adopted to pursue its goals: methods that did not cause Latin leaders to lose face. Here, in this last consideration, we are dealing with FDR's style, than which there was no more important ingredient in the whole Good Neighbor mix.

To the Latins, FDR seemed one of them: here was a gringo in the Latin mold, a man they could understand and empathize with as a projection of their own political and social style. North America at the top seemed to have undergone Latin Americanization. So strong was this perception that Latin American leaders and to some considerable degree the masses as well tended, when at all possible, to ignore evidence suggesting FDR really might not be so very much interested in them after all. The man was so simpático: and that papered over a multitude of sins.

Perhaps another element was at work here. Through the years many North American and even a few Latin American writers have suggested that in many instances at least some of the bombast with which the Americans to the south attacked the spirit of Monroeism was empty bombast. Many Latin Americans, the interpretation goes, have not really minded a hemispheric caudillo headquartered in Washington so long as that caudillo did not threaten their macho image, so long as he was discreet and diplomatic and went out of his way never to flaunt the fact that, when push really came to shove, he was the person ultimately in charge—and so long as he, the caudillo, was not niggardly in dispensing some of the favors that it lay in his power to dispense.

Perhaps FDR's supreme manifestation of political genius was his unrivaled ability to deal commandingly, even peremptorily, with others without diminishing their sense of *dignidad*. Somehow, altogether fortuitously, he had been supremely endowed with what for Latin Americans, perhaps for persons in general, is the consummate gift in human relations.

# 14. Hyde Park Patrician in the Latin Style

❖ ❖ ❖ ❖ ❖ ❖ ❖ ❖ ❖ ❖ ❖ ❖ ❖ ❖ ❖ ❖ ❖ ❖ ❖ ❖ ❖ ❖ ❖ ❖ ❖ ❖ ❖ ❖ ❖ ❖ ❖ ❖

### Roosevelt Traits as Latin American Traits

For the sake of argument, let us assume that people of any nationality or culture feel more at home with the person from outside their own immediate milieu who seems to share with them the traits that they commonly attribute to their own culture. Beyond this, let us assume that Franklin Roosevelt often revealed a personality attuned to the traits that not only gringos attributed to Latin Americans but that even the Latins tended to attribute to themselves. If this seems plausible, then it is certainly possible, even likely, that the Roosevelt personality contributed significantly toward the creation of a hemispheric good neighbor ambience.

Proceeding on this assumption, I shall briefly allude to some of the characteristics, widely perceived by FDR watchers born north and south of the border, that seemed to suggest the president had some propensity to operate *a la Latina*. Whether or not Roosevelt actually had this propensity may be beside the point. What mattered is that the chameleonlike president (Herbert Hoover in an inspired moment described him as a "chameleon on plaid") managed, at least much of the time, to project the sort of public persona that just might have encouraged Latins to feel that in dealing with him they were dealing with one of their own.

*Fun Loving*   Roosevelt's mother once remarked, "I do not believe I have ever seen a little boy who seemed always to be so consistently enjoying himself." What was true of Roosevelt the boy continued to be true of Roosevelt the man. As a young law clerk, his associates remembered him as a laid-back individual who liked long, chatty, gossip- and anecdote-spiced lunches, perhaps of "*arroz con pollo* at any one of several Spanish restaurants along Water and Pearl Streets."[1]

In contrast to the dour Coolidge, or the serious Hoover, a fun-loving prankster, perhaps even something of a hedonist, took over the White House in March 1933. The famous, radiant, and somewhat mischievous Roosevelt grin was a tipoff to his personality. Warren Harding, of course, had been something of a mischievous hedonist. But, as Alice Roosevelt Longworth once remarked of Harding, he "wasn't a bad man. He was just a slob." Latin Americans, at least of the upper sectors, have an aversion to slobs. No one could have taken Roosevelt for a slob: a bit of a dandy, perhaps, but definitely not a slob. And, on the surface, he seemed utterly without the agonizing, introspective soul-searching that many a Latin found a mite put-offish in the Lincoln image. Nor did he present the stiff, unbending, corseted demeanor of Woodrow Wilson, who seemed to exude smug confidence in the morality of his every thought and deed and came across as the typical holier-than-thou gringo that Latins could not abide.

Franklin's cousin Theodore Roosevelt had also projected the image of a fun-loving little boy. At the same time he could appear an ethnocentric, hectoring, bullying moralist. There was little of the moralist in the younger Roosevelt. Tired of Yankee presidents who acted as if—as one observer said of TR—they had discovered the Ten Commandments, Latin Americans on the whole heaved a sigh of relief over the new president's live-and-let-live demeanor. Moreover, Latins liked dealing with a Roosevelt who was not always intent, as TR had been, on proving he was more macho than they.

On the other hand, Latin American men, so the stereotypes tell us, insist on wives who are morally upright if not indeed uptight, wives who can be just a touch boring in their righteousness, in their purity. In her public persona, Eleanor seemed admirably to fulfill Latin expectations of the ideal wife. In still another way she was the sort of woman coveted as wife by well-born Latin men, notoriously disinclined to be punctilious about fulfilling the moral precepts laid down by the Catholic Church. Eleanor Roosevelt seemed the sort of woman who possessed enough virtue (in theological terms, enough grace) to assure salvation not only for herself but for her errant husband, and sons, as well. In many ways, the Roosevelt pair seemed the ideal couple when judged from the Latin American perspective. With highly derogatory implications, one American observer had described an early nineteenth-century political alliance in his country as the union of the puritan and the blackleg. Well, Latin American males, perhaps like males in general, can rather fancy being blacklegs if they have puritan wives who will save them from the consequences, both temporal and eternal, of being creatures of easy virtue.

Moreover, Eleanor fulfilled the social-reform functions that well-positioned Latin males seemed, since colonial times, to expect of their wives. She was the devout woman (*beata*) whose terribly sincere devoutness led her to take an active role in charitable work that would placate the lower classes so that males could safely continue to pursue, should they choose, heedless and hedonistic lifestyles. First Lady ER in her social work was, as already noted, in line with Latin American–style supermadres. In a way, in a sincere and honest and terribly serious manner, she did what many Argentine males a few years later would admire Eva Perón for flamboyantly pretending to do.

*Machiavellian-Jesuitical* Elegant, smooth-talking, but seldom constrained to abide by the letter of what he had verbally committed himself to, FDR could impress Latin American elites as a Machiavellian prince. Historian Richard M. Morse has argued, convincingly, that Latin American mores from colonial times have been profoundly influenced by Machiavelli. If so, then those Latin Americans who dealt with FDR would not have been put off by the fact that he seemed so often to follow the advice once rendered by Machiavelli: "A prudent ruler ought not to keep faith when by doing so it would be against his interests, and when the reasons which made him bind himself no longer exist." If men were all good, Machiavelli added, "this precept would not be a good one; but as they are bad, and would not observe their faith with you, so you are not bound to keep faith with them."[2] Here were principles on which FDR, who entertained few illusions about human nature, operated—principles, too, on which the worldly and often cynical men who conducted Latin America's affairs expected him to operate. If Latins went back on their word, the pious and self-righteous (but refreshingly profane) secretary of state Cordell Hull could be expected to lambaste them; but not necessarily the president. He took such things in stride. Turnabout, after all, was fair play.

An observer of one-time assistant for national security affairs and Secretary of State Henry Kissinger has written: "Henry does not lie because it is in his interest. He lies because it is in his nature."[3] But did Kissinger, or did Roosevelt, really have a mania for lying? It all depends on definitions. According to an old Jesuit maxim, a lie can be defined as information contrary to the truth that is *due* one. It becomes possible, then, if one wants to be Jesuitical, to decide that a particular person is not due a particular truth, in which case it becomes quite all right to tell that person virtually whatever one finds it expedient to tell.

Huey Long, the wily Louisiana "Kingfish," recognized the kind of man he was dealing with when he had a conference with Roosevelt. With a touch of complaint, but also I suspect of admiration, Long had this to say about the president: "When I talk to him he says, 'Fine! Fine! Fine!' Maybe he says 'Fine!' to everybody."[4]

When living in lands to the south I was impressed by the fact that a Latin American virtually never said no to requests I might place. More likely, the response would be "Fine!" To a Latin gentleman, saying no seemed brusque, in bad form. So, one should always say yes, fine, and then allow unforeseen and terribly regretted circumstances totally beyond one's control to render it impossible to do what one had agreed to do. Always say yes, then allow circumstances to provide the no, if indeed it becomes suitable to negate the original yes. This is not lying, it's simply conforming to the protocol of gracious manners. In this sense, Roosevelt seemed born not just to a so-called Jesuitical style but to the style of gracious manners.

*Aristocratic, Patronalistic*　In its vaunted paternalism, America's "Old South" seemed—in various fictional accounts and sometimes in reality as well—to embody traditional, precommercial attitudes that posit social hierarchy as part of the natural order of things. Roosevelt, the Hyde Park patrician who often enough gave off hints of a sense of superiority vis-à-vis mere businessmen, stood more in an agrarian-aristocratic tradition of the sort attributed to Southerner Thomas Jefferson than in the capitalist-ethic mold attributed to Alexander Hamilton—by character if not by birth an archetypal Northerner. Beyond this, as historian Page Smith observes, Roosevelt "was amply endowed with that expansive charm common to Southern politicians":[5] common not only to southern but to South American politicians. These latter, with the obvious exception of the overtly barbarian types who occasionally managed to grab power, prided themselves on their charm, graciousness, warmth, good form, and manners.

Henry Stimson once observed that in order to win the friendship of Filipinos one needed to display a certain degree of "Latin warmth."[6] One needed the same warmth, always manifested in a refined, tasteful way, to win the friendship of Latin Americans. Even his enemies conceded that FDR possessed this warmth. And the warmth of the gentleman had a bearing on matters of truthfulness as well. The gentleman raised in the aristocratic-patronalist style did not like to give the offense that often issues from the lips of persons fanatically devoted to truth telling.

Lyndon B. Johnson, president from 1963 to 1968, has come down in history as a man who, in addition to whatever virtues he possessed, was infuriatingly insensitive, cruel, even brutal. With an instinct for the jugular whether dealing with friends or foes, he did not hesitate to inflict humiliation on those with whom he came in contact. In his aristocratic-patronalist approach, the Hyde Park scion to the manor born was the exact opposite of the self-made man from the hills of Texas. Even though in matters of substance the Texan might treat them as equitably as the Hyde Parker, Latin Americans tended to find Johnson insufferable. They could not forgive him his manner. With FDR, they could sometimes forgive the end results of his conduct because they so fancied his manner.

Detractors might say that FDR simply lacked Johnson's courage to be forthright. But does courage impart the right to be insensitive to the feelings of others? In general, Latin America's ruling classes thought not. And this is one reason why they found FDR their kind of man. In their concept, not only letters and arts but also even the externals of aristocratic behavior conferred nobility.

For the aristocrat, it was de rigueur that he be a patronalist: willing to assume some obligation for the material security of those dependent upon him. As power wielders within a patronalist society, Latin America's leaders liked to pay at least lip service to the obligations of the *patrón* to his serfs. And by the 1920s the ruling classes had discovered the usefulness of forging nationwide social programs that extended the paternal, patronal hand to social and economic underlings. Indeed, Latin Americans had discovered the political usefulness of government-administered patronalist programs long before FDR began to employ them in the Depression-wracked early days of the New Deal. To the Latins, it seemed that, in shouldering at the national level the duties and obligations of the well-born patrón, FDR had begun to pay them the compliment of imitation. No longer could the Latin Americans, at least not so long as Roosevelt was at America's helm, accuse the Yankees of having snuffed out all sense of noblesse oblige in their vulgar bourgeois individualism.

One thing Roosevelt learned from Endicott Peabody, his headmaster at Groton, "was the Christian gentleman's ideal of service to the less fortunate." School confirmed what Roosevelt had already learned at home: the duty of the well-born to succor society's less fortunate elements. On entering the White House, FDR brought with him the lessons of school and home. Not surprisingly, then, he presided over the creation of a new policy "toward labor that was basically paternalistic."[7] Many Americans grumbled that such an approach was not in the national grain, and they were at least partially right. But it was in the Latin American grain. Once more, Latin Americans could feel flattered by what they might choose to regard as virtual imitation by the new American president.

*Populist*   One of the many distinguishing traits of the populist politician is the ability to establish rapport with commoners. Often the populist accomplishes this by ostentatiously moving to curb real and alleged abuses perpetrated by persons who take advantage of privileged status in order to exploit the masses. Both in the United States and in Latin America, populism in its modern guise emerged as a major political force in the late nineteenth century, only to recede a bit when signs of prosperity burgeoned early in the next century—more, of course, to the north than to the south of the border. Then, in the Depression era, populism reemerged, stronger than ever, throughout the Americas. A number of Latin American presidents in the '30s owed their elections to recent laws that had vastly extended voting rights; and their success in office depended in no small part on their skill in attributing hard times to the exploitive ways of the privileged few, especially to the men of new wealth whose economic success could be depicted as a consequence of their thumbing their noses at the old mores of patronalist obligations. None of Latin America's populist presidents, however, exceeded the skills of FDR in mobilizing mass support by blaming the plight of the many on the selfishness and greed of the few. None exceeded Roosevelt's virtuosity in preaching the populist creed of redirecting governmental priorities so as to provide security and dignity for ordinary people, even if this meant diminishing the status of people who considered themselves extraordinary.

The populist's stock-in-trade is to praise the masses for their virtue, while pointing to the vices of the privileged sectors who exploit them. Roosevelt resorted to this approach in much of his oratory. Moreover, he showed the instincts of the populist in assessing the situation in Haiti as that country prepared in 1934 for the departure of the U.S. army of occupation—an important event in launching the Good Neighbor policy. In a letter to his wife dated July 5, 1934, FDR noted the impending event and indicated concern lest the Haitians "start revolting as soon as we withdraw the last marines on August 15th." He hoped "the Haitians will recognize the vast amount of good things we have done for them in these eighteen years." He had no doubt that "*the people*" recognized and appreciated these good things; "but," he added, "the ruling mulatto class doesn't, I fear."[8] Just as much as in the case of Haiti, FDR throughout his presidency hoped that the people, the people of the United States, would recognize what he, their leader, had done and was doing in their behalf, even though the privileged sectors might thoroughly hate him for his good-hearted instincts.

Playing the populist role to the hilt in his January 3, 1936, state of the union address, FDR declared: "We have earned the hatred of entrenched greed." Although successfully challenged during his presidency, men of entrenched greed, the president warned, were scheming to bring about "the restoration of their selfish power." They wanted a return to what for them had been the good old days when they could, with impunity, "steal the livery of great national constitutional ideals to serve discredited special interests." The guardians and trustees of vested wealth, Roosevelt continued, "wrongfully seek to carry the property and interests entrusted to them into the arena of partisan politics. They seek—this minority in business and industry—to control and often do control and use for their own purposes legitimate and highly honored business associations; they engage in vast propaganda to spread fear and discord among the people."[9] In Mexico, Brazil, Argentina, Chile, Peru, Colombia, Uruguay, even in Bolivia and Paraguay, as well as in Central America and much of the Caribbean, one could have heard similar messages, but none delivered more effectively than by the wily populist in Washington.

Masters of privilege, the "economic royalists" against whom Roosevelt loved to target his rhetorical guns, grumbled that the president was descending to the cheap demagoguery allegedly prevalent in tropical, turbulent, half-baked republics to the south. Actually, Roosevelt had begun to pull out all the populist stops because for a time he had felt threatened by a fellow citizen not in the mold of respectable populism, whether in America or Latin America, but rather in the pattern of the cheap and tawdry rabble-rousing that unfortunately flourished at various times on both sides of the border. FDR's nemesis, until his assassination in 1935, was Huey P. Long, once the governor of Louisiana, more recently its senator (and still *de facto* governor)—and the man who, as already noted, had quickly grasped the president's inclination to say "Fine!" to anyone and everyone. Even after Long's assassination, his spirit remained alive in the country; and FDR had somehow to contain or co-opt it.

Preaching a doctrine of "Share Our Wealth," Long had advocated a thirty-hour work week, a month's paid vacation for all workers, forgiveness of all personal debt, free education through college, and a cash grant to every family of $5,000 (the equivalent of $50,000 in terms of 1990 purchasing power). All of this was to be financed by soak-the-rich taxes. By the spring of 1935, some 7.7 million people belonged to the more than twenty-five thousand Share Our Wealth clubs throughout the country.[10] Truly, Long threatened to turn America into a banana republic; but, according to many a conservative, so did Roosevelt himself.

To fight Long's fire, and that of such heirs apparent as Detroit's radio priest Father Charles Coughlin, Roosevelt intensified his own populist fire. And this led his foes all the more to perceive a hateful Latin Americanization process at work in the president. On the other hand, viewers from across the border tended to applaud what was going on in Washington. In effect, they applauded because they recognized themselves and their political ways in the president's personalist approach to politics. In their time of doubt and failed expectations, gringos were responding as Latins traditionally reacted to their chronically threatening circumstances.

*Personalism*  At the heart of the Latin American political style, it is often assumed both by outside observers and Latins themselves, lies not only populism but another closely related trait: personalism. In the politics of personalism legitimacy derives from the larger-than-life persona of the leader. Thus, legitimacy is a personalized rather than an institutionalized thing; it prescinds altogether from deep-rooted historical precedent, from the accumulation of decades of respect accorded institutions or constitutions. To hear his detractors tell it, FDR sought to rule in the Latin style of personalism, ignoring, bending, subverting the institutional, constitutional underpinnings of democracy. Rather than encouraging voters to respect institutional procedures as they had evolved since the time of the founding fathers, he tempted them to focus on him personally, and his purportedly unique personal ability to deliver to them what they most desired. Furthermore, he thought nothing of flouting hallowed precedent as when, for example, he attempted to pack the Supreme Court in 1937–1938 and then ran for a third term in 1940. Like the allegedly typical Latin ruler, Roosevelt placed personal whim above time-honored traditions.

Actually, the circumstances of the Depression era rather than the conscious desire of FDR to minimize the importance of government's institutional structures encouraged the rise of a personalist style in U.S. governance. The system seemed to have failed; so, the system's basic institutions could no longer be relied upon. More than at any time at least since the Civil War, Americans felt tempted to grant unquestioning faith and devotion to a leader who exuded supreme confidence in his ability to solve overwhelming problems. The Latin style of politics came to the United States in the 1930s because America faced the sort of monumental crisis that seemed chronically to confront Latin American countries, perennially tempting their citizens to place their faith in the man who could persuasively argue that he had solutions.

Roosevelt did not pin himself down as to the specifics of solutions. He would try one thing and if it did not work, he told voters, then he would try something else. In the final analysis, it was the power of his personality that led voters to trust Roosevelt's ability, one way or another, to come up with a solution. All of this was very much in the Latin American style, wherein ideological conviction or rigidity is more often the badge of failed than of successful caudillos.

Generally the most successful caudillos have specialized in avoiding specificity as to their programs while inspiring the masses to trust in their personal gifts and above all in their ability to reach truth not only through trial and error experimentation but through intuition. For the successful Latin caudillo, the most essential talent was the ability to convince his people as to his superior, unique powers of *intuición*. Among the gifts of intuición was the ability to divine just what it was the masses most desired, to decipher their inchoate, inarticulate longings, and then to articulate those longings, and having done that, to fulfill them.

Roosevelt fell as naturally as Latin American caudillos into the politics of intuición, time and again relying on this faculty rather than advice from so-called experts in shaping policy. Like so many Latin American leaders, he had a deep suspicion of "scientific" government. The consummate politician, he would not share credit with the so-called scientists of politics and economics. And the times were right for this a la Latina approach. For decades Americans had heard about the wonders of scientific management, and they had entrusted the presidential office in 1928 to an engineer. In 1929 they began to taste the bitter fruits harvested by scientific managers and an engineer president. So, they were not resentful when FDR, again operating a la Latina, turned to intellectual humanists to help him sharpen his powers of intuition.

Negative aspects undoubtedly attached to the style of Latin American personalism as practiced by FDR. Any leadership cult that rests on unquestioning devotion of masses to a leader should ring alarm bells among U.S. citizens; and the FDR phenomenon was not without its cult aspects. Personally, I've always felt uneasy about the 1941 hit song "How about You?" Its lyrics include the line that, just like New York in June or a Gershwin tune, "Franklin Roosevelt's looks give me a thrill."[11] This is more the approach an ego-driven Latin caudillo might revel in than, say, an Abraham Lincoln. It was also what a later practitioner of Latin-style personalism, John Kennedy, might have relished, and might have accepted as confirmation that he stood above the rules that applied to ordinary mortals. Similarly, I feel uneasy about a line in the 1943 film *Action in the North Atlantic:* "I believe in God, President Roosevelt, and the Brooklyn Dodgers." Nor can I enthuse over efforts to enhance the Roosevelt charisma by depicting him as just another American Everyman. In the 1943 film *The Princess O'Rourke* a Roosevelt impersonator witnesses the marriage of Joe O'Rourke (Robert Cummings) and Princess Maria (Olivia de Haviland). Joe mistakes the president for one of the White House servants and tips him.[12] Latin American propagandists also engaged in phony public relations ploys intended to show the exalted leader as really just a man of the masses.

One of FDR's detractors who thought his head had been turned by the sycophancy he invited and received was *Baltimore Sun* pundit H. L. Mencken. Writing in the November 10, 1940, edition, Mencken charged: "In the popularity of Roosevelt there has always been something false and meretricious; it is the popularity of a radio crooner or movie actor." Not so many years later, a few brave Argentine pundits rendered the same sort of judgment on the popularity of Juan and Evita Perón. The great strength of FDR was that although he might toy with the meretricious style of popularity cultivated by crooners, movie stars, and Latin caudillos, something in his own personality, to say nothing of the political culture of his country, prevented him from going totally overboard, the prejudiced Mencken to the contrary notwithstanding. Nevertheless, at times he came pretty close to going overboard, and never more so than when he returned at the beginning of 1937 from a triumphal visit to Latin America.

### Roosevelt in Latin America: The Apogee of Personalist Delusions

There is always the danger that the leader who inspires a cult of personality, who inclines to base his legitimacy on personalism rather than institutionalism, will become the victim of an inflated ego that inspires delusions of grandeur. Certainly the pages of Latin American history abound in tales of caudillos who have fallen into this pattern. Perhaps, then, it was appropriate that personal experiences in Latin America helped foster dangerous delusions in Roosevelt.

Already in 1934 Roosevelt's head was turned by the cheering masses he encountered "all along the way" when visiting Puerto Rico. These cheering throngs, FDR wrote to ER, showed a "really pathetic *faith* in what we are trying to do."[13] There is no doubt that FDR relished this outpouring of "pathetic *faith*." The Puerto Rican response, though, was nothing compared to that afforded him two and a half years later in South America, in the course of his trip to Brazil, Argentina, and Uruguay in late 1936, following his landslide reelection to a second term.

Stopping first in Brazil on the cruise that would take him to Buenos Aires to address the special Inter-American Conference for the Maintenance of Peace, FDR received an exuberant welcome as his motorcade passed along rain-slicked streets. "Never," reported an American military attaché in Rio, "has a national guest been received with so much enthusiasm." All along the way, school children by the thousands waved little American flags. In a letter to his wife, Roosevelt exulted: "There was real enthusiasm in the streets. I really begin to think the moral effect of the Good Neighbor Policy is making itself definitely felt."[14] Was it the moral effect of the Good Neighbor policy or the testimony to his own powers of personalism that delighted the president?

In Buenos Aires, capital of the country that typically had posed the greatest stumbling block to U.S. ambitions to lead the hemisphere, Roosevelt received a still more tumultuous and adoring reception—at least from the masses, if not necessarily from the country's political leaders, some of whom remained almost as immune to personal charm as Republicans back home. Buenos Aires produced an outpouring of people numbering in the hundreds of thousands, their presence encouraged by an officially declared national holiday. An ecstatic president reported to his wife on the flower-throwing multitudes that lined the streets, a vast, surging, cheering throng pressed together beneath balconies filled by more cheering, flower-throwing throngs. Similar adulation greeted Roosevelt in Montevideo as he commenced his homeward voyage.[15]

Back in Washington, Roosevelt wrote of the Latin American experience to his ambassador in Berlin, William E. Dodd. He stressed the manner in which the cheering masses of Buenos Aires had raised the chant "Viva la democracia."[16] Like many before him accorded such a reception, and especially like Woodrow Wilson, whose head had been turned by the tumultuous reception the European multitudes accorded him at the end of World War I, Roosevelt succumbed to delusions of grandeur. The forces of populism, incarnate in the armies of American voters who in November had ignored hate-mongering critics and overwhelmingly cast their ballots for him, incarnate also in December's delirious South American crowds, nourished and sated Roosevelt's personalism. For a moment, a sense of grandiosity overcame his usual Machiavellian political shrewdness, the process helped along by the recent death of Louis Howe, the inseparable friend and shrewd adviser who above all others had always reinforced Roosevelt's own sense of reality. For a moment, remembering the chant "Viva la democracia," Roosevelt believed he was democracy. For a moment, the worst of the Latin American caudillo had come to life in him— or so I find it tempting to think.

### Don Quijote Roosevelt Cured of His Madness

Utilizing the power base and the moral example of what he assumed was the established fact of a unified hemispheric power bloc, created by a Good Neighbor approach assumed to be unique in the dealings of a powerful nation with impotent neighbors, FDR dreamed of staring Hitler and Mussolini down and ending the crisis in Europe that Old World powers had not known how to resolve. Delusions of grandeur on the international front were matched by those on the domestic scene. FDR believed that now he could ride roughshod over such impediments to New Deal justice as the Supreme Court and his more intransigent foes in Congress. Not long back in Washington, Roosevelt sprang the court-packing scheme on the public. Then, in 1938, he waged a no-holds-barred midterm election campaign to defeat congressional leaders who blocked his programs: programs that, like the true populist-personalist, he identified with the will of the people.

Dreams and delusions came to nought. Hitler and Mussolini scorned finger-wagging from America; nor did Britain and France heed advice from a supposedly united-in-harmony New World. On the domestic front, grandiose schemes fared little better. The court-packing plan elicited an overwhelmingly negative response from the American electorate, economic indicators took a downward turn in 1938, and voters returned to Congress the politicians FDR had sought to purge. Finally, in spite of all the cheers the masses had lofted at the circus occasioned by FDR's visit, many a Latin American government, especially Argentina's, remained indifferent to what Washington considered hemispheric security obligations as war clouds gathered abroad.

By 1939, FDR had reacquired a great deal of his reality principle; he was back home in the realms of practical domestic politics and realistic foreign policy.[17] Cured like Don Quijote of his madness, ready to live once again by his customary pragmatism, he would hesitate henceforth to equate the will of the people, whether at home or abroad, with his own mercurial flights of fancy.

One trait, though, that many North Americans tended to equate with Latin America's alleged preference for the magical over the real, FDR never discarded. He remained fascinated by, irresistibly drawn toward, the ways of the trickster. And the trickster, regardless of the provenance of the "primitive" mythology that lent him credence, scoffed at the restraints of what the practical-minded regarded as not-to-be-tampered-with reality. FDR as trickster is a matter explored in the next chapter, but only after consideration of another allegedly Latin American trait that FDR exhibited: fascination with corporatism. Like trickster mythology, corporatism dealt in the reconciliation of opposites perceived in the light of mere reason as irreconcilable.

# 15. *The Roosevelt Style: Corporatism and Tricksterism*

❖ ❖ ❖ ❖ ❖ ❖ ❖ ❖ ❖ ❖ ❖ ❖ ❖ ❖ ❖ ❖ ❖ ❖ ❖ ❖ ❖ ❖ ❖ ❖ ❖ ❖ ❖ ❖ ❖ ❖ ❖ ❖ ❖

### *FDR in the Latin Mold: Depression-Era Corporatism South and North of the Border*

In the latter part of the nineteenth century, as a few republics began to enjoy somewhat longer-than-usual moments of political stability, a fair number of Latin American leaders developed a mania for economic progress. In some instances inclined to emulate U.S. social and economic models, progress-oriented Latin Americans looked upon classical liberalism and the bourgeois, individualistic, profit ethic as the keys to success. Traditional paternalistic devices were repudiated in the interest of converting all members of society capable of the transformation—considerable doubt prevailing as to whether those of dark skin hue were on the whole capable—into competitive, individualistic capitalists. Their individual success in attaining economic self-reliance would, so it was assumed, produce the composite effect of overall national development.

The attempt to transform the masses, heretofore encouraged to remain inert in an ostensibly paternalistic system, into individualistic and self-reliant citizens ready to compete with others on a basis of liberty and equality and without a government-guaranteed social safety net, ended more in catastrophe than in progress—as already suggested in Chapter 6. It left the masses isolated and impotent before privileged men who knew how to take advantage of the opportunities afforded by untrammeled individualism. In fact, the new processes intended to bring about development invited a form of social and economic exploitation more ruthless than in the past—anticipating in a way some of the abuses Russia encountered when, upon the collapse of the Soviet Union, it attempted to create a privatized, market economy.

In turn-of-the-century Latin America, ongoing urbanization exacerbated a burgeoning social problem. Arrived in mushrooming cities at a time when laissez-faire principles underlay incipient industrialization, emigrants from the countryside discovered none of the paternalistic safeguards that had at least guaranteed them subsistence in a manorial setting.

Out of the worsening social problems that appeared in most Latin American republics as the twentieth century began there emerged a full-fledged challenge to the legitimacy of the nascent capitalist order. Alarmed by signs of rebelliousness and fearful of the sort of leveling social revolutions that anarchists and other radicals began to preach among urban workers, elements within the ruling classes longed for a return to an idealized past in which, as they viewed it, harmony had prevailed within and among the body politic's various components.

Within the colonial era's corporate structure, its theoretical framework established by Catholic Scholasticism and Thomistic theories of social justice, the objective had been to divide all society into semiautonomous local, regional, and functional associations. More important than the compartmentalization of society in maintaining social peace and solidarity had been the dichotomized nature of each and every compartment or corporation. Within each corporation was a patrón sector, made up of those who gave the orders, who planned and managed, who were to some degree independent and self-reliant and individualistic. Within each corporation there was also a sector comprising those who depended for subsistence upon the benevolence of the responsibility-bearing patrones. Should social responsibility and benevolence prove in short supply, then church and state, acting together, would demand that patrones fulfill their obligations to their wards and thereby to society's common good. The power through which church and state harmonized relations between the two components in each compartment, whether local, regional, or functional, was termed the "moderating power." Through its exercise, the interrelated bureaucracies of church and state assured the mutually advantageous interaction of opposed interests. At least that was the theory.[1]

As social tensions mounted at the turn of the century with the rise of the typically predatory practices of incipient capitalism, Latin American leaders, desperate to relieve revolutionary pressures, began to reexamine the theory. In it, or at least in modern-day adaptations of it that frequently omitted a role for the church in the exercise of the moderating power, they professed to find a panacea for modern problems. They turned all the more urgently toward corporatist theory as the Great Depression tightened its grip in the 1930s, intensifying the suffering of the masses and, in the view of frightened elites, raising still higher their revolutionary potential.

In response to the threat of revolutionary change, there emerged a group of resourceful Latin American leaders who presided over the reinvention of corporatism. The new corporatists included elected chief executives such as Arturo Alessandri in Chile, Alfonso López Pumarejo in Colombia, and Lázaro Cárdenas in Mexico, as well as dictators such as Getulio Vargas in Brazil, Oscar Benavides in Peru, and Germán Busch in Bolivia. Before any of these men, José Batlle y Ordóñez in early twentieth-century Uruguay had anticipated the move toward social-justice corporatism. Under his leadership Uruguayans ushered in many trends that later found their way into sister republics and even into Roosevelt's New Deal, undoubtedly unbeknownst to New Dealers blissfully unaware that some of their ideas had been anticipated in a tiny South American republic.

The goal of the new corporatists was to compartmentalize society into functional corporations or guilds. Each corporate entity would include a labor component as well as a management-capital-employer sector. Within each corporate entity, representatives of government would mediate between the two components or sectors, exercising the moderating power intended to replace raw struggle with bureaucratically conceived harmony—and intended also to render the less powerful, labor sector within each corporation grateful to and dependent upon government.

While bureaucratic wielders of the moderating power within the newly assembled corporate structures did not always manage to increase the economic well-being of the dependent, laboring sectors, they at least contrived, in many instances, to impart to them the belief that government cared about them, was concerned for their welfare, would do all that could be done to protect their interests, and would not leave them to the mercies of private capitalists. Seldom knowledgeable about efficient production practices, moderating-power bureaucrats often intervened in ways little calculated to enhance productivity. Sometimes only through bribery of bureaucrats could the management-capital-employer sectors assure their own survival. But this dark side of a beautiful theory did not fully reveal itself in the 1930s. For a while it seemed that Latin Americans, by reverting to colonial traditions, had discovered what a later generation of their politicians and intellectuals would call a Third Way: a way between market capitalism and socialism.

Ultimately, the new experiments with corporatism led to populist extremes and to financial finagling that benefited the friends of presidents and dictators more directly and consistently than the masses. On the negative side, the experiments could also grow over into neofascist schemes as in Argentina under Perón, or into crypto-Marxist experiments in a number of countries including Chile under Salvador Allende, or into out-and-out Marxism under Fidel Castro in Cuba. Nevertheless, in the gloomiest moments of the Depression when few if any observers of the Latin scene foresaw the dark potential, corporatism seemed a reasonable, pragmatic way to go.

Up north, across the border, Depression-era Americans under Roosevelt also began to experiment with their own version of corporatism. For most Americans, though, from the president on down, corporatist tendencies owed far more to trans-Atlantic influences than to those from across the border. Whatever their origins, these tendencies unquestionably helped improve hemispheric relations by making it possible for Latin Americans and norteamericanos to recognize something of themselves in their neighbors.

Influenced by intellectual trends of the time that reflected the ideas of British economics guru John Maynard Keynes (with whom he conferred in the White House in 1934), FDR believed that modern capitalism was essentially chaotic, and that government action was required to impose some measure of order on its chaos. At the same time, he questioned—as Keynes also did—the omniscience of persons, including Marx, who pontificated in behalf of all-encompassing, imposed-from-above economic "rationality." FDR seemed to sense that out of too concerted an attempt to quell chaos could come the stifling of innovation and the withering of the prevailingly vulnerable and fragile economic order.

The Roosevelt approach, very much a product of his time, made it possible for him both to admire the freewheeling spirit of U.S. entrepreneurial capitalism *and* the spirit associated not just with the newly evolving Keynesian school but also, although FDR may not quite have liked to admit it (if indeed he knew it), with Iberian corporatism. Without a sort of unplanned, grudgingly conceded, and only hazily perceived White House–encouraged U.S. drift toward the values of corporatism, FDR's Good Neighbor policy might never have flourished, not even briefly.

Inevitably, though, convergence was doomed to a short life. For all its inherent pitfalls, corporatism in Latin America was at least a natural phenomenon, arising out of deeply ingrained traditions. In reverting to corporatism during troubled economic times, Latin Americans were coming home. For norteamericanos, however, corporatism was something of an aberration, a departure from traditions. Perhaps it was acceptable if it could be given an Anglo-Saxon connotation and referred to as Keynesianism. But, as openly acknowledged and frankly named corporatism, and therefore suggestive of a Latin connection, it passed out of vogue even before the Depression ended.

Still, there had been a brief moment of hemispheric convergence built around almost openly acknowledged gringo tolerance of Latin-tinged corporatism. A comparable moment of convergence would not return in hemispheric relations until nearly the end of the century when the Latins began what seemed, here and there at least, a genuine attempt to abandon old traditions in favor of more market-oriented capitalism. Convergence in its end-of-the-century manifestation would rest on Latins acting a la Yankee, rather than on Yankees acting a la Latina. But this is jumping way ahead of the story. For now, in dealing with the hemispheric convergence of the 1930s that underlay good neighborliness, a word about the U.S. flirtation with corporatism is in order.

At the beginning of the 1930s, corporatism may indeed, as *Fortune* magazine suggested, have been "less well known in [North] America than the geography of Tibet."[2] This changed rapidly. During the early days of the New Deal Roosevelt and his brain-trusters placed high hopes in the ability of the National Recovery Administration (NRA) to mediate between the interests of labor and capital in virtually every functional component, every economic sector, within the country. In the president's view, at least at the outset of his administration, private enterprise was much too vital to national interests to be left to private enterprisers. In whatever niche they found themselves, in whatever economic activity they pursued, private enterprisers must be checked and balanced by organized labor. And between the two interests, government would have to exercise a moderating power, balancing and harmonizing opposite forces.

Details of the National Recovery Administration's utter failure to achieve harmony between the capital and labor moieties in America's various producing sectors need not detain us. Suffice it to say that the NRA's failure came about under the leadership of Hugh Johnson, a flamboyant, drunken, retired army general who deserves pity more than blame. With his many faults, and his relatively few redeeming features, Johnson provided all too clear a preview of the sort of leaders who captured control of the new corporatism in Latin America and eventually—within half a century or so—managed largely to discredit it there.

In the United States, NRA corporatism was already discredited when the Supreme Court mercifully found the whole experiment unconstitutional in 1935. Many New Dealers heaved a sigh of relief. Even the president seemed in some ways relieved by the Court's death sentence on an experiment that already in its brief life-span had "disintegrated in an acid bath of acrimonious self-interest, administrative ineptitude, and political vacillation."[3]

Even if the overt attempt to recast America's economy into a corporatist mold had not worked out as hoped, FDR remained committed to the idea of active government intervention to achieve equitable balances between the interests of capital and labor. Upon this commitment, or at least the appearance of such a commitment, rested the solid labor support that Roosevelt counted on to assure a second, a third, and then a fourth term.

Riva Helfond, *Waiting for the Doctor*, around 1941, color lithograph, image: 17¹⁄₁₆ × 12 in. Gift of Dr. and Mrs. Corbin S. Carnell, in memory of E. Muriel Adams. Collection of the Harn Museum of Art, University of Florida. 1992.11.54 *Accepting the need for corporatist intervention in society, the Roosevelt administration fell into line with Latin traditions in expanding state health services to the needy. Perhaps more in line with U.S. traditions were the notorious Tuskegee experiments, carried out during New Deal days, in which black Americans, used as a control group, were denied treatment for syphilis.*

Upon this commitment rested, too, the approval of liberal intellectuals (both in America and Latin America), convinced that individual liberty could not survive without an interventionist state with power to control corporate organizations that, if left unchecked, posed a far greater threat to liberty than expansion of government power.

Although it struck many Americans as tantamount to an attempt to square the circle, FDR remained convinced, even as Latin American corporatists, that somehow it was possible to reconcile the opposite interests of capital and labor, to synthesize them into mutually beneficial symbiosis, to bring to life the oxymoron of "state-regulated market capitalism." To Roosevelt's enraged business-community opponents, this was a foolhardy endeavor, one that placed odious statism, whether smacking of communism or fascism, on a par with free enterprise. The endeavor demonstrated moral equivalency—the equating of good with evil—of the most pernicious sort. Let the Latin Americans indulge in this sort of devious chicanery. It was to be expected from them. But seal the border off against the spread of their nefarious ideas.

A considerable number of Americans in the 1930s saw no need to seal their borders against penetration of ideas from the south. They perceived the potential evils of corporatist regulation as no worse than the actual evils of unregulated capitalism. They saw government bureaucrats, of whom they had known few, as less to be feared than predatory private-sector capitalists, of whom they likely had experienced many. Above all, a fair number of Americans stood ready to try to square the circle by combining two opposite approaches; they were ready to start out in quest of state-regulated market capitalism. In these predispositions, Americans inclined toward good neighborliness, toward open-mindedness in assessing Latin ways.

In still another way, Americans, many of them at least, showed they could be open-minded about politics a la Latina. They seemed to delight in having a president in the stereotyped Latin American mold, a president who was a trickster.

### In the Latin Mold? FDR as Trickster

Did the FDR who emerged after the devastating attack of poliomyelitis in 1921 differ in character from the young and physically robust Roosevelt? Biographer Geoffrey C. Ward convincingly challenges the conventional wisdom that there were two Roosevelts, pre- and postpolio. As Ward sees them, both Roosevelts, the one who could walk and the one who could not, were spoiled and self-absorbed and also compassionate. Both Roosevelts, moreover, displayed an abundance of easy charm, extravagant ebullience, and above all, perhaps, a "gift for breezy duplicity."[4] If Ward is right, and I suspect he is, then, in consequence of his unchanging and constant duplicity, there were always at least two Roosevelts, whether before or after the onslaught of polio. Certainly this was what the man's enemies assumed—and many admirers, too, who expressed concern over Roosevelt's inclination toward deception, both before and after his polio affliction. In this respect, foes and friends alike saw Roosevelt in the Latin mold: for North American stereotypes invariably attached the word duplicity to Latins, whether they came from Italy or Portugal or Spain or from below the border.

Another biographer, James MacGregor Burns, also sees two Roosevelts, both before and after the devastating sickness: the Lion and the Fox. An undersecretary of state who served the president found more than just two Roosevelts. He referred to the "three or four personalities" Roosevelt could turn on and off, with "such speed that you often never knew where you were or to which personality you were talking." Finally, here is FDR speaking about himself to his treasury secretary and old friend Henry Morgenthau, Jr., in 1942: "I am a juggler, and I never let my right hand know what my left hand does. . . . I may have one policy for Europe and one diametrically opposite for North and South America. I may be entirely inconsistent, and furthermore I am perfectly willing to mislead and tell untruths if it will help win the war."[5] This was the Roosevelt approach not only when it came to winning World War II but to winning whatever skirmish happened at any moment to concern him.

To give the man the benefit of the doubt, it is conceivable that his duplicity sprang not so much from the conscious desire to deceive as from an ingrained ability to see opposite sides to any issue, both of which might be valid depending on the particular perspective from which the issue was confronted. A consummate political artist, Roosevelt found his style in cubism's perspectivism. Out of his perspectivism issued Roosevelt's fascination with corporatism, with exercising a moderating power that would reconcile the opposite interests, the opposing perspectives, of capital and labor, management and workers, owners and hired hands, estate owners and peons. Indeed, in his approach to life in general FDR sought to harmonize, to unify contrary interests, to play the role of master broker in a world of diversity and conflict, to bring together in one great painting perspectives from numerous vantage points.

Because of his talent to entertain two or more contrary and clashing perspectives, to accept that one thing could be valid and also its opposite, FDR seemed always to chase after the time-honored objective of mystics and shamans, and sometimes of poets and artists: the objective of reconciling opposites, the left and the right, the yin and the yang, the feminine and the masculine. In this, FDR reflected the worldview not necessarily of the stereotyped cunning and conniving and guile-ridden Latin, or of the

Hindu wise man or the Taoist, but of one of America's greatest and most archetypal poets of realism *and* mysticism, Walt Whitman: a man who exulted in his refusal to look on the world through either/or blinders, who suspected all consistency and all system and anything that hardened the person into any one type, who insisted on being—like Ralph Waldo Emerson, whom he revered—"all-inclosing."[6]

A close Roosevelt watcher, Rexford G. Tugwell, a one-time brain-truster who helped preside over the Depression era's back-to-the-land movement and later governed America's Puerto Rican colonial outpost, had this to say about the president: "Roosevelt was certainly an exaggerated example of nonrational decision-making." Precisely: rational decision generally rests on an assumption that one position basically is right, its opposite basically wrong. FDR resisted this assumption. He inclined consistently toward the belief that it was possible to reconcile opposites (neither of which was necessarily, inherently right or wrong, good or bad) in harmony. This trait in Roosevelt suggested to Tugwell a penchant for "holistic thinking." In his "holistic thinking," FDR seems linked to a premodern worldview that eschews linear logic. It was this, I think, not necessarily just sheer out-and-out duplicity, that placed Roosevelt in a Latin American mold. So did his reliance on what one author, writing before the late twentieth century's long overdue smashing of old stereotypes, called the president's "almost feminine intuition."[7]

From Franciscan millennialism to Masonic occultism to popular-religion beliefs of folk Catholicism to African spiritism to survivals of pre-Columbian shamanism, in which a place of honor was assigned the berdache or hermaphrodite personage who combined both sexes (in some ways like the spiritually, sacramentally desexed and feminized Catholic priest), Latin America has been the land par excellence of the extra-rational, mystical, magical, combining-of-opposites approach to life. Its greatest twentieth-century literary movement has been described as magical realism, a genre in which authors weave together magical realms with the domains of reality, assuming always that the magical is no less real than "reality." In all of this, one detects the living presence of the preconquest Aztec belief that the purpose of life was to sleep so as to dream so as to find reality—a conviction in some ways no less appealing to Spanish dramatist Pedro Calderón de la Barca (who tells us "Life is a Dream"), or to Sigmund Freud and Carl Jung, than to Latin American novelists.

In Latin America it is not just novelists who feel at home in domains of the magical and the real and who encounter difficulty in distinguishing between them. Indeed, I suspect that here is a case in which literature reflects and finds its inspiration in and takes its point of departure from a political world where extrasensory realms of magic interfuse with sentient reality. Political leaders who have found it altogether natural to conflate the realm of the spirits, of the mystical and the supernatural, with the hard realities of mean and grubby and very much down-to-earth life range from Hipólito Irigoyen to Isabel Perón in Argentina, from Arnulfo Arias to Manuel Noriega in Panama. Leaders of this type include, too (among ever so many others), the so-called witch doctor Maximiliano Hernández Martínez, who dabbled both in theosophy and atrocity in El Salvador, as well as Augusto César Sandino in Nicaragua, Víctor Raúl Haya de la Torre in Peru, and José María Velasco Ibarra in Ecuador, all of them under the spell in one way or another of spiritualist beliefs. Nor can one overlook the mystical Marxist Ernesto (Che) Guevara in Argentina and Cuba, or Haitian leaders too numerous to mention, or—if rumors are to be credited—Brazil's president Fernando Collor de Mello, impeached in 1993 in spite of recourse to spirit helpers. Any semipro Latin America watcher worth his or her salt could add to the list of practitioners of spiritualist politics.

If there is anything to the old stereotype so common among Yankee observers of scenes to the south, Latin American rulers tend all too often to rest their legitimacy on their charisma. So, obviously, did FDR. But charisma is a far loftier and transcendent quality than is assumed in the common understanding of the term. Charisma, for many a Latin American ruler and for Roosevelt alike, involves more than just charm and graciousness, a hail-fellow-well-met magnetism and a disarming or even overwhelming smile. Whether in the case of Roosevelt or of a fair number of Latin American presidents and caudillos, charisma seems to correspond to the original meaning of the word: "the quality which attaches to men [and women] and things by virtue of their relations with the 'supernatural,' that is, with the nonempirical aspects of reality."[8] Alike for FDR and for many of Latin America's most successful, larger-than-life super caudillos, charisma rested on some sense, vaguely intuited or imputed by supporters and true believers even though scoffed at by doubters and haters, of connectedness to something transcending mere mundane reality.

Like Loge in Wagner's "Ring" operas, FDR, along with many a Latin American ruler, has been a trickster, and by this I do not mean a common deceiver or prankster: I mean a person who operates in the realm of reality and of magic, who combines opposites, even as a medieval wizard, or, going back earlier, to the legendary King Arthur's Merlin, or earlier still to Heraclitus, who saw no trick at all in resolving thesis and antithesis into synthesis and thereby laid the foundation for a modern-day trickster, Karl Marx. Roosevelt's charisma, like that of many south-of-the-border counterparts, tapped into the old, premodern myths, some of them deriving from pre-Columbian mysticism of the sort that fascinated Latin

American indigenistas in the 1920s and '30s and that also fascinated FDR's commissioner of Indian affairs John Collier as well as his secretary of agriculture Henry Wallace.

Trickster mythology, whether deriving from the Teutonic legends that fascinated Wagner as well as some of psychiatry's father figures including Freud and Jung, or issuing from the pre-Columbian myths that intrigued Americans both north and south of the Rio Grande, has at least this one constant: it envisions the managed and constructive schizophrenia achieved by the simultaneously rational and extrarational being who juggles happily at life's *center,* where all opposites converge.

The trickster defied the Aristotelian principle of contradiction, according to which a thing cannot be what it is and something else altogether at the same time. The trickster knew, and his or her power derived from this knowledge, that something could be what it was and also something completely different at the same time. From this faith sprang the power to achieve what ordinary, convention-bound individuals could not aspire to. Latin American caudillos, the most fascinating of them at least, had this faith, this confidence that they could be Heraclitus rather than merely Aristotle. So did Franklin Roosevelt. This is why so many Latin Americans felt that in looking at Roosevelt they were looking at one of their own. FDR, I suspect, felt at times the same way about leaders to the south, some of them at least.

As much as to Winston Churchill at the far end of an Atlantic Alliance, Roosevelt—though he might have hated to concede the fact—was akin to Simón Bolívar at the other end of a North-South axis: Bolívar the aesthetic vulgarian, the ethereal sensualist, the mystical realist, the believing skeptic, the austere hedonist, the stoic bon vivant, the wizard with his head in the white, fleecy clouds and his feet on the dark, grubby earth. Roosevelt and Bolívar bestride their respective worlds like colossi and render their two worlds one world. They may have been a century or so and a continent apart, but spiritually, as flawed and noble souls, as earthbound explorers of the realms of fancy, they breathe the same air.

In the Depression era, norteamericanos craved a man who promised change, however sweeping it might be, in order to retain or restore the same old traditional system to which they and their ancestors were accustomed. A century or so earlier, Latin Americans had expected the same of Bolívar. Here indeed were tasks for tricksters.

During the crisis years of their struggle for liberation from the Old World, Latin Americans had turned hopefully to the White House and found it occupied by what appeared to them to be cold and calculating gringos. In the blight of the Depression, they gazed northward once again. This time, in a new hour of need, they found more what they wanted.

Rather than a one-dimensional gringo, typically intent upon recasting the Latin American in his own image, they found a multidimensional man of limitless perspectives willing to assimilate the Latin American temperament and personality in his own "all-inclosing" psyche. At least they found a man, and this is what mattered, who appeared willing to attempt to do that.

Delighted by the Roosevelt persona and psyche, Peruvian political leader and self-perceived guru Víctor Raúl Haya de la Torre detected in the American president a kindred soul. Satisfied as to his own well-nigh supernatural powers to reconcile opposites in the manner of the larger-than-life trickster who descended out of a long tradition going back to ancient Egypt, Haya de la Torre credited Roosevelt with an ability to synthesize the "vertical traits of masculine individualism and nationalism with the horizontal characteristics of feminine collectivism and internationalism." Up to now, most of the western world, with the United States in the forefront, had exaggerated the claims of individualism. Under Roosevelt, however, the United States had taken up the quest to harmonize the vertical and the horizontal, the individual and the collective, the masculine and the feminine.[9] Out of Roosevelt's rare, mystical capacity issued the Good Neighbor policy that, according to Haya, would transform the American hemisphere by reconciling previously contentious opposites. Other Latin American self-perceived mystics expected similar prodigies from the president in a wheelchair who relied on spiritual power rather than brute strength.

Meanwhile, those of a more practical bent expected rewards more material and economic from the American president; and, as we shall see, they were not altogether disappointed. The "chameleon on plaid" truly could seem different things to different observers from below the border.

By now readers may have detected some tricksterism in the author of these lines. In earlier chapters I argued (by implication, at least) in favor of impersonal circumstances, of economic and social conditions, of trends among artists, writers, and intellectuals, as the main shapers of the Good Neighbor policy. In this chapter I've emphasized the primacy of the great or at the very least the highly unusual man. Maybe I can't have it both ways. Still, even if in defiance of the principle of contradiction, I'm willing to argue that in creating the Good Neighbor era both the man and the circumstances were most important.

The circumstances of the 1930s presented a unique opportunity for forging the Good Neighbor policy. But, unless there had been an adequate personality to capitalize on those circumstances, the opportunity would have been wasted. This is why it makes *some* sense to insist that the Good Neighbor policy was FDR's policy, that it owed its life to him.

## In the U.S. Mold as Well? FDR as Trickster

In his 1994 book *Diplomacy,* former Secretary of State and assistant for national security affairs Henry Kissinger contends that Americans will extend wholehearted support to a particular foreign policy only when persuaded that the policy ultimately issues out of, or at least can be reconciled with, U.S. morality and exceptionalism. And Kissinger draws on the example of Woodrow Wilson, especially as he drew the country into his era's World War, to support his thesis.

Part of FDR's success in gaining domestic support for his Good Neighbor policy rested on his ability to justify it on the altogether Wilsonian grounds that the United States could be counted on to deal with Latin Americans on a more equitable basis than could be expected of Old World powers. Consequently, Americans should feel themselves morally driven to establish a special sphere of influence in the New World hemisphere.

For all their fits-and-starts obsession with morality, Americans surely possess also a strong aversion to any form of idealism that leaves them open to being played for the sucker by those who ostensibly are less high-minded than they. They tend, too, Americans do, to admire the shrewd trader, the sharp bargainer, the wheeler-dealer—all those types whose conduct comes tantalizingly close to crossing the line that separates ethical pursuit of the common good from morally dubious, self-serving, self-enriching conduct. Indeed, a dark secret of many Americans has always tended to be their admiration for the confidence man.

As implementer and sometimes as architect of hemispheric diplomacy, FDR's tricksterism manifested itself in an uncanny ability to combine American high-mindedness with the W. C. Fields admonition never to give a sucker (or a weaker partner in a relationship) an even break. Out of this rare ability to combine the Wilson and the Fields personas issued FDR's success: if not necessarily as founder then at least as chief executive officer of the Good Neighbor policy. On both sides of the border, the Roosevelt presence was essential to that policy.

❖ ❖ ❖ ❖ ❖ ❖ ❖ ❖ ❖ ❖ ❖ ❖ ❖ ❖ ❖ ❖ ❖ ❖ ❖ ❖ ❖ ❖ ❖ ❖ ❖ ❖ ❖

*Launching and
Targeting the
Good Neighbor
Policy*

# 16. Discarding the Burdens of Interventionism

❖ ❖ ❖ ❖ ❖ ❖ ❖ ❖ ❖ ❖ ❖ ❖ ❖ ❖ ❖ ❖ ❖ ❖ ❖ ❖ ❖ ❖ ❖ ❖ ❖ ❖ ❖ ❖ ❖ ❖ ❖ ❖ ❖ ❖ ❖

### Roosevelt and Nonintervention: The Trickster in His Element

In constructing a Good Neighbor policy, nonintervention was a key building block. Through his personal touch Franklin Roosevelt shaped and
polished that building block. As a refined gentleman who prided himself
on elegant manners, he was loathe to give overt offense. And in the 1930s,
Latin Americans professed to find virtually no facet of Yankee behavior
more offensive than overt intervention in their internal affairs. But far
more than reluctance to give offense lay behind FDR's espousal of nonintervention in hemispheric affairs. Roosevelt was also looking for positive, tangible payoffs—tantamount to the payoffs he garnered from voters
in the American South by refusing to intervene in what they regarded exclusively as internal affairs.

Roosevelt helped strengthen the Democratic hold on the "Solid South"
through his willingness to allow the area's white electorate a free hand in
establishing the parameters of race relations. Similarly, he helped bring
about a more harmonious hemisphere through his willingness to allow
Latin Americans greater freedom than previous Washington administrations had accorded them in setting the terms of their relationship to Yankee capitalists. With his highly developed sense of reciprocity, of the nice-
ties of tit-for-tat relationships, Roosevelt expected Latin Americans to
respond to concessions he extended them as generously as white voters in
the American South had responded. He expected Latin Americans to

indicate their appreciation for favors extended by keeping the door open to American capitalists, at least to those good-mannered capitalists willing to conduct themselves according to the more demanding code about to be prescribed by New Dealers.

As much as the president's expectations of gentlemanly reciprocity on the part of Latin Americans to Yankee gentlemanliness, it was Depression-era circumstances that shaped America's noninterventionist demeanor. During the Coolidge administration and the first few months of Hoover's presidency when all had been well on Wall Street, a fair number of Americans would have endorsed a judgment rendered by Chandler Anderson, a prominent international lawyer and lobbyist for various U.S. firms with substantial Latin American investments. Anderson insisted that whether in Mexico or in Central America, or indeed in any part of the "uncivilized" world, the native peoples depended well-nigh exclusively for whatever prosperity they might hope to attain "upon the continued and successful operation of the foreign owned oil wells and mines and agricultural properties."[1] By the early 1930s, only a tiny minority of Americans could still pretend that their nation's capitalists were uniquely knowledgeable in the ways of bringing about sustained economic development, whether in the "uncivilized" world or in the United States itself. In consequence, only a tiny minority of Americans would have countenanced overt intervention in Latin America aimed at protecting the interests of Yankee investors.

People who make a habit of intervening in the affairs of foreign countries, in order to improve and develop and uplift those countries, must have supreme confidence in their own political, social, and economic wisdom and virtue. By 1930, the Great Depression had delivered a staggering blow to American self-confidence, and thereby ended the mood out of which crusades to uplift benighted foreigners had issued. Moreover, the Depression rendered Americans unwilling and unable to assume the economic burdens of intervention. Just as they had found high principles with which to justify intervention that sometimes sprang mainly from hopes of economic gain, so now they found rationales to justify discarding interventionist policies that cost too much.

As Americans began to lose confidence in their own culture (economic, political, and even moral), the sort of relativism associated with Franz Boas (as described in Chapter 10) acquired a widening sphere of influence. Already in the 1920s, viewing the failure of armed intervention to achieve the announced goals of social, political, economic, and moral uplift in the Philippines as well as in the Caribbean and Central America, U.S. statesmen had begun to conclude that uplift or cultural change *could* not be imposed on others. Now, in the 1930s, a growing number of intellectuals—both ivory tower types and Washington power brokers—as well as informed citizens decided that change *should* not be imposed on others.

Together, the two convictions made possible widespread public acceptance of nonintervention, that key element in the Good Neighbor policy.

Perhaps what most appealed to FDR about nonintervention was the undefinability of the term. It was a slippery term that designated an amorphous policy that was different to the eye of each beholder. It was, in short, exactly the sort of term, the sort of policy, that a trickster liked to deal with. Charles Talleyrand, an eminent trickster in his own right who helped shape French foreign policy around the turn of the nineteenth century, once described nonintervention as a policy meaning very much the same thing as intervention. This is the sort of policy that appealed to FDR. About as far as he chose to advance in giving meaning to the term was to associate it with reciprocity. If, he and his advisers decided, they agreed not to intervene in Latin American affairs, whatever that might specifically mean at any specific moment, then Latins would reciprocate by doing what Americans most wanted them to do, whatever that might be at a given moment.

When the Democrats took over in 1933, most State Department officials tended to give the narrowest possible meaning to nonintervention in hemispheric affairs. To them it meant simply not using military force in persuading Latin Americans to do what Americans desired them to do. To Latin Americans, however, nonintervention meant Americans should not use any means to push them into doing what they really did not want to do. To policy-makers in Washington, it seemed that what the Latins demanded was not just nonintervention but *noninterference*. At first, Americans insisted upon the Good Neighbor's right to "interfere" through diplomatic or economic pressures in order to persuade Latins to follow policies not inimical to perceived U.S. interests. But then security issues, arising out of troubling developments in the Old World that seemed likely to insinuate themselves in the New World, brought a new urgency to Washington's desire to forge hemispheric solidarity against un-American meddling. When this occurred, Roosevelt and his advisers decided the United States must become a much better neighbor than originally intended, and concede that nonintervention was really tantamount to noninterference. The most dramatic instance of the transition from nonintervention to noninterference occurred in the case of the 1938 Mexican expropriation of foreign oil interests that is described in Chapter 18.

Still, the situation remained fluid. What Washington defined one day when dealing with a particular Latin American country as interference and therefore perfectly legitimate might be defined the next day when dealing with another, perhaps more powerful and crucial, country as intervention and therefore not permissible. In this sort of game the trickster could come up with constantly shifting concepts of just what the Yankee nation could and could not do; in this sort of game, he could play off "dinky little republics," some dinkier than others, against each other.

## The Luck of the Good Neighbor: FDR Inherits a Nonintervention Policy

Whatever nonintervention might mean, it did pertain to actions that the Colossus through the years had deemed perfectly licit in hemispheric relations, and which Latin American states had deemed illicit. So far as Latin Americans were concerned, the most egregious manifestation of intervention was the use of force, whether through gunboat diplomacy or armed occupation of territory, so as to bend Latin Americans to Yankee will. It was Roosevelt's extreme good luck that already by the time he came to office the two preceding Republican administrations had moved to withdraw from intervention, defined as the use of armed force. Had Republicans not already moved to end intervention as narrowly defined (i.e., military action), Roosevelt would have found it far more difficult to persuade the southern republics that the Colossus was capable of becoming a good neighbor.

Along with Mexico, State Department officials as of the mid-1920s had considered Nicaragua a beachhead of communist penetration. However, the general public failed to buy this line. Increasingly they lined up with columnist Walter Lippmann, who maintained that difficulties with the two republics stemmed not from communism but rather from the desire of Mexicans and Nicaraguans to assert national dignity and independence. What is more, Lippmann could claim the support of a good number of U.S. congressmen and senators, and even of financiers with south-of-the-border investments who wanted to avoid needless offense to countries in which they had placed substantial assets.[2]

As public opinion increasingly rejected the notion that communism was rife in lands to the south or that it lay at the heart of Republican concern with disciplining Mexico and Nicaragua, President Calvin Coolidge sought to abate the foreign relations tempest by dispatching Dwight Morrow as ambassador to Mexico (see Chapter 10) and Col. Henry L. Stimson as special trouble-shooter to Nicaragua. The latter arrived in the factious republic, occupied off and on since 1912 by U.S. Marines, in 1927. His presence there bore testimony to the fact that like a great many Republicans, Coolidge had decided "that policing Central America was not as easy as it had seemed and that it prompted nationalistic hatred of the United States."[3]

Like FDR, with whom he had a great deal in common and whom he would serve as secretary of war beginning in 1940, Henry Stimson had once entertained disparaging attitudes not only toward Filipinos but also toward Central Americans. In fact, he regarded them as little if at all better than the allegedly dirty, savage Indians that Americans had managed to quell along their frontier only toward the end of the nineteenth century.[4] Later on, though, when he fulfilled his Nicaraguan assignment and served as governor-general of the Philippines (1927–1928), he came to acquire respect, even empathy, for many of the people among whom he represented his country. Understandably, not all Filipinos or Nicaraguans caught Stimson's fancy. In Nicaragua he could not abide Augusto César Sandino, a man he regarded as socially uncouth (good manners and breeding counted just a bit too much with Stimson, and perhaps also with Franklin Roosevelt). Stimson also regarded Sandino, who had taken up arms against the American army of occupation, as demented in his socialist ideas. On the other hand, the colonel developed a certain admiration for the smooth-talking (whether in Spanish or in English) and smooth-dancing Anastasio (Tacho) Somoza García. Here was a man who had the requisite social graces and who also seemed to appreciate the essential role of free-enterprise capitalism in accomplishing economic development.

No more than the Democratic president he would later serve did Stimson extend his blessings to all American practitioners of free-enterprise capitalism. Much like Roosevelt's idol Woodrow Wilson, Stimson believed there were pirates among the species who must be shackled, as well as honest and even idealistic types concerned with the overall common good not only of their own country but of those foreign republics in which they invested. Undeveloped countries, he believed, could fulfill their potential by entrusting government to honest men who in turn would encourage the good type of foreign investors. Like FDR himself, Stimson did not necessarily object when presidents of small and relatively powerless republics delivered spankings to Yankee capitalist buccaneers operating in their lands. The sooner the buccaneers were spanked, both in the United States itself and in undeveloped banana republics, the sooner the socially conscious capitalists would encounter the proper circumstances in which to exercise their nation-building expertise—an expertise about which Stimson quite possibly was overconfident.

Above all, as of 1927, Henry Stimson was convinced that the continuing presence of U.S. Marines in Nicaragua played into the hands of demagogues and dangerous ideologues, and delayed the day when the country could, under responsible leadership and with the collaboration of the nation-building variety of Yankee capitalists, begin the march toward progress. His diplomacy set in motion the process that led to the withdrawal of American Marines from Nicaragua. This withdrawal made it possible "for the incoming administration of Franklin D. Roosevelt to enter upon its Good Neighbor Policy with one embarrassment less." Meantime another embarrassment had been removed when President Herbert Hoover, alert to the need to curtail foreign policy expenses in a depression era, accepted the recommendations of the Cameron Forbes commission that the United States move to end its occupation of Haiti.[5]

So, it might seem that the Roosevelt luck was never more in evidence than when circumstances contrived to cast Morrow and Stimson and Cameron Forbes, along with Presidents Coolidge and Hoover, in the roles of precursors of nonintervention. Trouble loomed immediately ahead, though, in Nicaragua.

Stimson-initiated policies led to the final withdrawal of Marines in 1933 and to relatively honest elections that brought Juan B. Sacasa to the presidency, but left Anastasio Somoza, commander of the U.S.-created and U.S.-trained Guardia Nacional, as the real power broker. The year after the Marines departed Nicaragua Sandino, who now had laid down his arms and begun the pursuit of power through democratic means, was assassinated—a deed undoubtedly perpetrated by Somoza's henchmen. One branch, at least, of Nicaraguan nationalists have mourned Sandino's death ever since, depicting him in the final analysis as the victim of Yankee machinations. As a martyr, Sandino was worth more to anti-Yankee Nicaraguan nationalists and leftist ideologues than as a living guerrilla warrior.

Looking at the end results of the handiwork that he had initiated in Nicaragua, Stimson as of the early 1930s could only have concluded that as often as not there were no good alternatives in Latin America, or that if there were, gringo outsiders were incapable of discerning what they were. That being the case, overt intervention should be abandoned. At the beginning of his presidency, Franklin Roosevelt stood to benefit from the knowledge Stimson had acquired the hard way.

The beneficiary of Stimson's loss of innocence, FDR also inherited the consequences of the Republican statesman's Nicaraguan diplomacy. The most noteworthy of these was the entrenched power of Stimson favorite Anastasio Somoza. No longer content to rule behind the scenes as the commander of the Guardia Nacional, Somoza seized the presidency in 1937. Sorely pressed in his attempt to shore up democracy and market capitalism in the Depression-ravaged United States, FDR was hardly inclined to lecture Somoza, or any other Latin American ruler for that matter, on civics and economics. He would simply make the best of the legacy bequeathed him by the Stimson-initiated policy.

From hindsight we know now that although "Tacho" Somoza García himself was no paragon of disinterested, nation-building virtue, neither was he the destructive, kleptocratic sort of ruler that a son or two of his later became. What we do not know is what the alternative might have been had the Stimson-initiated policy not helped block Sandino's access to power. Unquestionably brave, patriotic, and charismatic, Sandino was also volatile and erratic, and a foggy-minded dabbler in esoteric communist millennialism.[6] Conceivably, he could have wrought far greater havoc in Nicaragua than did the pragmatic "Tacho" Somoza. In any event, neither Stimson nor FDR, sincerely hopeful that their policies would ultimately pave the way for democracy in Nicaragua, can be held accountable for failing to foresee that Somoza would be succeeded by offspring who included men virtually without redeeming feature.

FDR came to power enlightened by the obvious failure of past interventionist policies to achieve desired results. He came to power, too, against a background of a loss of American nerve and confidence occasioned by the devastating impact of the Depression. These circumstances led the president to surprise Latin Americans by yielding more quickly and more thoroughly than ever they had anticipated to their persistently voiced demands for nonintervention—and beyond this even to accede in some instances to their demands for abandonment of Yankee interference in internal affairs. Most Latin American leaders publicly applauded the new stance. Behind the scene, though, many grumbled and complained; for they had grown accustomed to seeking Yankee interference, whether overt or covert, to help them achieve goals, whether political or economic, that they could not accomplish on their own. Indeed, the Good Neighbor policy was still in its infancy when Víctor Raúl Haya de la Torre in Peru and Juan Andreu Almazán in Mexico addressed pleas to Washington to help install them as presidents of their respective republics by ousting allegedly fascistic chief executives who, so they charged, had come to power through electoral fraud.[7]

The real quarrel of Latin Americans with intervention and interference had often originated in their feeling that they had not been the beneficiaries of Yankee meddling. It was by no means an altogether appealing prospect for many a Latin American politician and businessman to contemplate a new hemispheric system in which they could no longer manipulate a naive Uncle Sam into doing for them what they could not do themselves. As Roosevelt and those persons who helped plan and execute the Good Neighbor policy discovered, colonialism often lives on among colonials even after the colonialists have tried to call it off. In consequence, Yankee withdrawal from intervention, and partial withdrawal from interference, did not prove a cure-all for hemispheric ill will.

Still, for all their apprehension and misgivings about possible undesirable consequences, Latin Americans on balance, on the whole, approved the Good Neighbor's move toward nonintervention. If in private that approval might be hedged with reservations and doubt, in public it tended to be unstinting. While not exactly the essence of good neighborism, the rhetoric at least provided an impressive facade.

## FDR and the Democrats on Their Own as Noninterventionists

Having inherited a Republican policy that leaned toward nonintervention, FDR almost immediately after his inauguration faced the challenge to define his own approach. The challenge originated in Cuba, where Gerardo Machado, a notoriously venal and brutal ruler who had enjoyed warm support from Republican colonial headquarters in Washington, faced a major uprising sparked by university students and supported by a broad array of the populace. To the troubled island, FDR sent as ambassador his top Latin America hand and close personal friend, Sumner Welles.

Arriving in Havana in May of 1933, Welles withdrew the American support that Machado previously had counted on. By mid-August, the dictator had fled the island, and shortly Carlos Manuel de Céspedes succeeded to the presidency. A one-time ambassador to the United States (1914–1922), Céspedes had left behind a favorable impression. Now, as Cuban president, he proved amenable to advice from Welles on cabinet appointments and other matters. All in all, he impressed the ambassador as a man of proper manners and genteel social background, as a person whose outlook on island politics and economics was shaped by proper respect for advice from Washington and by solicitude for American investors accustomed to regard the island as their fief. Welles could take satisfaction in the way Cuban affairs were going—but not for long.

Unfortunately for Welles, less socially polished, less white, and less status-quo-oriented elements, including a strong sprinkling of socialist- and communist-leaning university students and labor groups, seemed to be getting the upper hand in the revolution they shortly unleashed against Céspedes. The insurgents by and large supported the cause of Ramón Grau San Martín, a man who struck Welles as a dangerous intellectual imbued with hostility toward the foreign owners of the island's basic industries and toward the old order in general. Moreover, so far as Welles was concerned, Grau did not represent the island's best social classes. Here, Welles followed down the trail that Stimson had blazed in Nicaragua when he objected to Sandino in part because of his radical ideas, in part because of his lack of proper social background.

Above all, though, so far as the ambassador was concerned, Grau was unacceptable because the sort of socioeconomic changes he had in mind altogether exceeded acceptable New Deal parameters. So, when the "Sergeants' Revolt" in which Fulgencio Batista played a leading part overthrew Céspedes and placed Grau in the presidency, Sumner Welles pulled a page out of the past as he requested that U.S. Marines be landed—

ostensibly to protect American lives and property, but actually to shore up the island's colonial status quo.[8]

President Roosevelt found the request awkward in the extreme. Here it was September and preparations were underway in Washington for the inter-American conference to be held the next month in Montevideo, at which Secretary of State Cordell Hull would head the U.S. delegation. It was no secret that Latin Americans, urged on by the traditionally Yankee-baiting Argentina, would press the new administration to prove it was indeed a good neighbor by renouncing the right to intervene in the internal affairs of Latin American republics. If Hull had to attend the Montevideo conference on the heels of a Yankee reversion to gunboat diplomacy in Cuba, he might find Latin Americans united as never before against the Colossus and ready to dismiss the whole Good Neighbor policy as empty rhetoric that actually disguised a retreat from the noninterventionist stance that Presidents Coolidge and Hoover had, somewhat unsteadily, assumed. Moreover, compliance with the Welles request could only have embarrassed the president during a projected 10,000-mile "Pan American Cruise" that would include stops in Haiti, Puerto Rico, the Virgin Islands, Colombia, Panama, and Hawaii.

Moving to save his nascent Latin American policy, FDR denied Ambassador Welles's request. Although beginning already to waver in his support of Roosevelt, H. L. Mencken responded warmly to this development. In his view, American capitalists displayed an "eerie inability" to do anything honest or even intelligent, whether in Cuba or Haiti, or in Nicaragua.[9] The public mood, which FDR had gauged accurately, generally reflected the Mencken view. Most definitely, the electorate would have condemned a reversion to gunboat diplomacy. The generality of North American citizens were not interested in pulling the chestnuts of U.S. capitalists out of Latin American fires.

By late September Welles was back in Washington, enjoying what actually was a promotion to the post of assistant secretary of state for Latin American affairs: the trickster had given more with one hand than he had taken away with the other. Clearly, though, Welles had gotten the message that the president was not going to risk the impression of retreating on the nonintervention front. In short order Welles had the opportunity to reverse the meddling policies initiated by Woodrow Wilson and continued by Presidents Coolidge and Hoover that had denied diplomatic recognition to Central American regimes that came to power by extraconstitutional means. Latin Americans, it was hoped, would appreciate this withdrawal from old-time nonrecognition interventionism, and many of them did. Others, though, recognized the new policy for what to some extent it was: an adaptation of traditional British attitudes toward empire based on assumptions that natives in backward republics simply were not up to democratic practices and no purpose was to be served by pretending otherwise.

Meantime, Cordell Hull, freed from the sort of embarrassments that could have made his mission to Montevideo a disaster, turned on his Tennessee charm, curbed his famous irascibility, and managed almost to charm even the Argentine delegation to the inter-American conference. Furthermore, he added substance to his personal triumph by committing the United States henceforth to a policy of nonintervention (meaning no use of military force to advance U.S. policy), except in those instances in which use of force was clearly countenanced by international law as most commonly understood and interpreted by the major powers. Three years later in Buenos Aires, at a meeting that FDR personally attended (garnering the tumultuously warm reception previously described), the United States committed itself to nonintervention, without reservations.

From the very beginning, however, the new U.S. president demonstrated that when it came to nonintervention he would pursue a Talleyrand-like course of tricksterism; he would show that nonintervention was a policy meaning fundamentally very much the same thing as intervention. Owing to the president's insistence on nonintervention, Grau San Martín occupied the Cuban presidency as Sumner Welles returned to Washington; but Roosevelt thought no more highly of the man than did his ambassador now promoted to assistant secretary of state. Although rejecting the intervention of gunboat diplomacy, FDR saw nothing wrong with the interference of nonrecognition, or with encouraging the Cuban military to overturn a suspect government. With his sensitive antennae Batista perceived what was up, turned against Grau in January of 1934, and installed Carlos Mendieta in the presidency. Within five days, Washington extended recognition to the new government. Before long, the new ambassador to Cuba, Jefferson Caffery, had assumed the customary role of helping shape internal policy.[10] At least in private, Cuba's accommodated beneficiaries of the status quo applauded the preservation of normalcy. Frustrated revolutionaries, meanwhile, grumbled impotently. In the 1950s, though, some of them would remember and be ready to act out of their old frustrations when Fidel Castro appeared upon the scene.

In other instances as well, the Roosevelt administration demonstrated that nonintervention was a policy meaning very much the same thing as intervention. Roosevelt fulfilled his pledge to Cubans of never again landing troops to restore order; but he stationed warships in Cuban waters to lend substance to suggestions tendered by the American ambassador in Havana. Moreover, the Good Neighbor president retained military forces at Guantánamo Bay, Cuba, and in the Panama Canal Zone. He did at least promise certain concessions regarding special American perquisites in the Canal Zone. However, he failed fully to deliver on the promise—in effect withdrawing with one hand that responded to War Department advice what the other hand had granted in response to State Department counsel. Meantime, in the Dominican Republic U.S. diplomats showed they did not need the presence of troops in order to set economic policy that guaranteed security to American investors. In short, the Good Neighbor surrendered powers that had become obsolete while retaining those it considered still vital to national interests. As Irwin F. Gellman concludes, "No intervention was never an absolute reality—only an illusion that was valuable in popularizing the Good Neighbor principle."[11]

Except when trying to inflame gullible voters, many Latin American leaders saw very little to complain about with Washington's ambiguous policy. At the very least double-edged, that policy proclaimed an end to the sort of overt intervention that Latin Americans found galling, while leaving open the possibility that Washington might resort to interference to remove leaders it deemed unfit. Invariably, such leaders were also regarded as objectionable by a good number of local political rivals. In short, Yankee intervention had ended but it still persisted; and Latin Americans understood they might very well derive advantages from two diametrically opposed policies if they played their cards right. They understood tricksterism as well as the affable American in the White House.

## Nonintervention, Security, and Conservation Principles

A debate has long raged among diplomatic historians as to whether U.S. policy in Latin America was motivated primarily by economic or by security objectives. The debate is largely void of content, because from the U.S. perspective there is no possibility of separating, of distinguishing between, the two objectives. Ultimately for the United States to be strong enough to defeat any and all potential enemies, it would have to develop its economic capacity to the fullest degree possible. It would have to develop that capacity not only within its own continental confines but also within the extracontinental reaches to the south. Assumptions based on principles of realpolitik and on their own reading of providence and destiny led Americans, from the 1820s onward, to regard the portion of the New World that lay to their south as their sphere of influence, a sphere whose economic potential to the degree that it benefited foreigners must benefit primarily the citizens of the United States. Inseparably intertwined, economic *and* security interests dictated this.

In settling their continental frontier, Americans naturally enough had always insisted on reserving the main yield for Americans, even though British and other foreign concerns were allowed an ancillary role in developing virgin resources. In terms of the hemisphere, Americans tended to regard Latin America primarily as their frontier: Europeans and Asiatics could help develop it, but the main profits should be reserved to norte-americanos. This would help assure North Americans ongoing security for their expand-or-perish capitalist way of life.

Initially, America's inseparably intertwined economic and security interests seemed to demand heavy-handed colonial policies dictated from Washington that guaranteed Yankee investors the right to operate south of the border in a way that best guaranteed immediate maximum profits. Before long, though, it became apparent that insistence on immediate maximum gain might, by inflaming the resentment of Latin Americans, imperil American prospects to derive sustained, long-term profits from "their" southern frontier. The principle of hemispheric nonintervention arose out of recognition of this fact, and it bore close resemblance to its domestic counterpart, the principle of conservation. Perhaps it is no accident that Franklin Roosevelt, who proved even more dedicated to conservation within the United States than his cousin Theodore, also advanced further than any of his predecessors—no matter how inconsistent his sense of direction—toward hemispheric nonintervention.

Conservation within the United States demanded the husbanding of resources so that they would deliver long-term yields even though short-term payoffs might decline. Similarly, conservation of resources below the border demanded tempering maximum short-term expectations in the interest of sustained, long-duration yields. Fixation on yields of the moment would exhaust both the resources of the American earth and the patience of Latin American governments that, not unreasonably, claimed sovereignty over their national domains. In both cases (both within the United States and within the hemisphere), long-term returns to U.S. investors, developers, or exploiters—call them what you will—would decline, thereby imperiling long-term U.S. security interests.

In the long run, did nonintervention help serve America's symbiotically joined security and economic interests? At least in some cases it appears that nonintervention did help. Consider the following item. A Venezuelan president commenting in 1993 on his country's willingness to extend generous terms to American oil investors explained his reasons for easing nationalistic restrictions on petroleum exploitation. "Remember," he said, "that in the past, warships even came to Venezuela to claim debts." Now times had changed, he pointed out, and Venezuelans had responded to the change.[12]

It took the seeds that the Good Neighbor planted in the 1930s a long time to sprout. Eventually, though, some of them did sprout. With the long-term view of the conservationist, FDR would have been satisfied had he been able to witness Latin America's increasing opening to Yankee capital that became apparent near century's end. This opening, described in the final section of this book, shows that a policy that curtailed con-

cern for the immediate profits of Yankee investors in Latin America and
thereby increased the patience of Latin regimes with those investors produced long-term benefits to the U.S. economy. And this is tantamount to
saying it produced long-term benefits to U.S. security.

Short-sighted U.S. businessmen in the '30s railed against both Roosevelt's conservation policies in the United States (of which vested capitalist
interests would turn out to be the main beneficiaries) and his insistence on
conserving Latin American goodwill so as to guarantee future economic
and security payoffs. As former president Hoover had observed, U.S. businessmen could be stupid. So, of course, could bureaucrats, and that's one
reason Roosevelt, whether in domestic or in foreign policy, sought so often to play off the traditional antagonists against each other. All the while
he viewed them both from the vantage point of the naval strategist that,
since his days as assistant secretary of the Navy, he had always fancied
himself.

# 17. Agrarian Myths and the Good Neighbor Policy

❖ ❖ ❖ ❖ ❖ ❖ ❖ ❖ ❖ ❖ ❖ ❖ ❖ ❖ ❖ ❖ ❖ ❖ ❖ ❖ ❖ ❖ ❖ ❖ ❖ ❖ ❖ ❖ ❖ ❖ ❖ ❖ ❖ ❖ ❖ ❖

## Roosevelt as Jeffersonian Conservationist

A key element in the vogue for primitivism (alluded to in Chapter 10) was the agrarian myth. That myth occupies center stage in the present chapter. Franklin Roosevelt himself was deeply influenced by agrarianism and its myth. In consequence, he believed in the redeeming, uplifting effect of proximity to, of intimacy with, the land. This belief enabled him to ride the wave of the vogue for things Mexican, which was one manifestation of America's Depression-era fling with primitivism. Riding that wave, he presided over a major breakthrough in relations with Mexico (described in the following chapter). Riding that wave, which came along at just the right moment to propel Good Neighbor approaches, the president led a breakthrough, though on a lesser scale, with much of the rest of Latin America as well. Romanticism and myth, almost as much as hard reality based on economic-security considerations, sometimes lay behind the Good Neighbor policy.

Reflecting the strong Jeffersonian influence that ran through the Democratic Party during the Depression era, Franklin Roosevelt in a 1931 article declared, "[L]and is not only the source of all wealth, it is also the source of all human happiness."[1] In Roosevelt's deep love of the land lies a major contributing factor to the principle of conservation that, as noted in the preceding chapter, he honored: both in domestic and in hemispheric policy.

In his 1931 article and in many other statements, written and verbal, both before and during his presidency, FDR gave voice to the agrarian myth, according to which not only happiness but human virtue spring from the land. The good people, therefore, is the people that remains in touch with the land. It followed that, to some degree, profit-driven exploiters of the land, insensitive to its mystique, should be seen not so much as contributors to American development and economic might as plunderers of the national bank of virtue.

Never more clearly than when he established one particular new national park in the mid-1930s did FDR demonstrate his conviction that, at times at least, the claims of nature should take precedence over the profit drive that motivated big industry; never did he demonstrate more clearly a prevailing, but certainly not consistent, preference for Jeffersonian over Hamiltonian mythology.

Traveling to the forests of the Olympia Peninsula in far western Washington state, FDR spent a long night assessing the debate between the timber industry that wanted to log the centuries-old cedars, Douglas firs, and spruce trees and the handful of rangers who favored converting the area into a national park. Had these been normal times in which the expansionist business ethic epitomized national values, the president undoubtedly would have decided in favor of the timber industry. But these were not normal times; the expansionist business ethic was on the defensive, in part because of natural disasters such as Dust Bowl erosion to which, in the minds of many Americans, that ethic had contributed. Under these circumstances, FDR knew he could count on public support when he arose after his restless night and announced in favor of a national park.

By the 1990s, Olympia National Park had become "one of the top five visitor attractions in the park system."[2] Had it not been for the eclipse of big business's reputation and the questioning of the whole concept of capitalist modernity, it might never have come into being. But for the unique circumstances of the 1930s FDR would not have dared to act on his conviction that the purity and virtue of American life derived from the unique opportunity of its citizens to remain rooted in the land or, if not that, then at least to visit as tourists the nation's great scenes of natural splendor where personal purity and virtue could be recharged. Similarly, had it not been for the unique circumstances of the 1930s, FDR would not have dared side with Latin American governments anxious to curtail, to slow down, the assault of Yankee firms on natural resources—or, failing that, at least to claim a higher cut of the profits deriving from the assault. Whether for the United States or for Latin America, Roosevelt seemed in accord with the spirit of Woody Guthrie's famous song: "This Land Is Your Land, This Land Is My Land." The land, in other words, belonged to the people, not to the conglomerates.

Once again, in 1936, when dedicating the Shenandoah National Park in Virginia, Roosevelt had occasion to proclaim his agrarian doctrines, his faith in agrarian mythology. In his prepared remarks the president extolled "the perspective that comes to men and women who every morning and night can lift up their eyes to Mother Nature." He closed his brief address "by recalling a favorite figure in Greek mythology, the giant Antaeus, invincible on the ground but crushed by Hercules when he lost contact with the earth. 'There is merit for all of us in that ancient tale,' he said."[3]

In the Depression era, Latin America remained more rural in its population dispersal than the United States, a sign of backwardness to traditional Yankee prophets of progress. The Roosevelt administration, however, to the degree it was politically feasible to do so, ignored those prophets and sought to transfer Americans back to the land, so that—by implication, at least—they could catch up with the advantages of rural, agrarian Latin America.

Rexford G. Tugwell, a brain-truster and undersecretary of agriculture who headed the Resettlement Administration (established in 1935, found unconstitutional the following year by the Supreme Court, and replaced by the Farm Security Administration), understood his president. Roosevelt, Tugwell explained, was a "child of the country" who saw cities as nothing "other than a perhaps necessary nuisance," who understood that—as Tugwell put the matter—"We shall solve the problems of the cities by leaving the city."[4]

FDR's contentious and often irascible secretary of the interior, Harold Ickes, also wanted Americans to have the chance to leave the cities—at least temporarily, in order to visit and find inspiration in national parks. During the first seven years in his post, Ickes saw to it that the National Park System "grew from 8.2 million acres to more than twenty million." Moreover, it was due to Ickes's insistence that John Collier became commissioner of Indian affairs. As previously noted, Collier believed in the superiority of the Indian way of life because it was rooted in the land. Ultimately, Collier believed, all Americans would begin to adopt the Indian set of values: premodern, antiurban, partially collectivist, and above all based on reverence for the land. To some degree, Ickes shared Collier's view, though not so vehemently as his first wife Anna, who found in the Indians of the Southwest the model for the good life that all Americans should aspire to.[5]

As initially conceived, the giant Tennessee Valley Authority (TVA) found its ideological inspiration in the agrarian myth, with its conviction as to the superiority of rural over urban life, with its faith that the future for America lay in a return to the land. Behind TVA lay Roosevelt's "overwhelming ambition to bring two unlike entities, the old and new, the shiny machine and the leafy bough, into close alignment along an extended valley." Perhaps in no other instance does FDR's obsessive quest for reconciling opposites show itself to such advantage: as exalted and morally pure and relatively free of self-interest and political expediency. At the same time, Roosevelt's quest to unite opposites in the Tennessee Valley was wildly utopian. In envisioning a valley where (as Roosevelt put it) "Men and Nature must walk hand in hand," where there would arise a community of farmers and engineers, rustics and intellectuals, FDR plugged into a prominent strain of American utopianism. No wonder a young man interviewed by Studs Terkel gave this appraisal of TVA: it was "sort of regeneration and so forth." Roosevelt himself had put the "sort of regeneration" issue this way in a 1937 Fireside Chat: "Year by year, we propose to add more valleys to take care of thousands of other families who need the same kind of a second chance in new green pastures."[6]

In some ways the Good Neighbor policy also had a visionary, utopian quality. It was a Tennessee Valley project writ large, one in which modernity and the premodern would combine throughout an entire hemisphere. In that hemisphere a people regenerated by a return to the land but still largely urban and oriented toward business and manufacturing would walk hand in hand with a people more pervasively rooted in the land.

### The Agrarian Myth in the Land at Large: Depression-Era Disillusionment with Urban, Industrial-Based Modernity

So long as twentieth-century Northerners in the United States had teemed with confidence about the present wonders and future potential of their modern industrial society, they looked disparagingly upon Southerners— whether they resided in the American South or south of the border. The southern, agrarian way of life ostensibly produced persons indifferent if not hostile to the sort of self-improvement that translated into national progress. Northerners of this persuasion often felt they had an obligation to force reform, and with it modernity, upon Southerners who if left to their own devices would remain refractory to civilization.

In some ways the noninterventionist vogue in hemispheric relations grew out of American doubts and disillusionment about industrial-based modernity. Losing faith in their own predestined progress toward a utopian future of economic development, many Americans—even urban-based northern entrepreneurs—began to look nostalgically toward a golden age in the past of small towns and agrarian tranquility. To many of those caught up in nostalgia for the past as the present turned sour, it seemed that Latin Americans, far more than the hustling, enterprising, always-on-the-go Yankees, understood the secrets of the good life. They had clung to the ways of sleepy villages and relaxed, humanely inefficient agrarianism.

What had been taken for the Latin American curse turned out to be a blessing.

John Collier, Jr., son of the commissioner of Indian affairs and employed by the Resettlement Administration that sought to return Americans to the good life of small communities and family farms, joined many other thinkers of his era in condemning the industrialized progress that had obliterated an earlier sense of community. All too often American modernity, young Collier alleged, was an "American Tragedy." At about the same time, novelist John Dos Passos extolled the advantages that earlier generations of Americans had enjoyed, growing up "with only the sky over their heads," rather than in the cramped and blighted urban environment out of which modernity had sprung. Architect extraordinaire and self-imagined seer Frank Lloyd Wright hailed "the true life" that was lived "close to the soil" in those small settlements that he deemed infinitely preferable to large urban centers. Harold Ickes agreed with Wright, noting that when it came to fashioning good persons nature was "preeminently the master artist," whereas urban industrialization fashioned warped human products.[7]

A new generation of American composers, some of them Jewish like Aaron Copland, and some of them descendants of Nordic immigrants, like Roy Harris, extolled through their music the agrarian roots of American life. At the same time, country music enjoyed a revival as it featured a plethora of back-to-nature songs: songs such as "Carry Me Back to the Lone Prairie" (1933) and "Take Me Back to My Boots and Saddle" (1935), as well as "Carry Me Back to the Mountains," "My Blue Ridge Mountain Home," "Little Green Valley," and "I'm Going Back to Whur I Came From." Even sophisticated Cole Porter joined the trend in 1944, pleading for land, lots of land, under starry skies above, in his song (actually, he bought it from a relatively unknown composer) "Don't Fence Me In." All in all, a rising number of composers and performers in America "saw country music as an antidote for a society—and a music—that had become urban, overcivilized, and false."[8]

Hollywood caught the trend, and so in 1934 the "Singing Cowboy" Gene Autry made his debut on the silver screen, appearing in the movie *In Old Santa Fe*. The movie cast disparaging glances at the city with its odious business ethic, while praising at least inferentially the purity of rural America. Any aficionado of the western genre can provide numerous other examples of Depression-era films that extolled the virtues of simple living under the big sky.

A group of southern thinkers who called themselves Agrarians just happened to congregate around Vanderbilt University; but they gave voice to beliefs that flourished throughout the South during the Depression years. The Agrarians issued "a rebuke of materialism, a corrective to the worship of progress, and a reaffirmation of man's spiritual and aesthetic needs." Humane values, they alleged, withered away in a technocratic, urban-industrial society "organized on a mass basis around a cash nexus." Above all, the leisurely approach to labor enshrined in the southern aristocratic tradition assured abundance of time for the development of the higher human gifts of intellect and spirit.[9]

Southerners of aristocratic circumstances or pretensions could almost welcome the Great Depression as providence's just punishment for industrial-financial capitalism and urban-based modernity run amuck. They could welcome it, too, because it seemed to promise relief from the northern attempt to impose its way of life on the South, initiated with a vengeance during the Reconstruction era. They could even applaud the likelihood that Northerners would now ease up in their attempt to penetrate Latin America and convert that area to the leveling mores of the Industrial Revolution and the Calvinist work ethic.

Southerners in this frame of mind welcomed Roosevelt's Good Neighbor approach, just as they welcomed what seemed his empathy for the southern aristocratic way of life during the times he spent at Warm Springs, Georgia, seeking relief in the medicinal waters from his crippling affliction. Meantime, Southerners relished the new power they enjoyed, owing to Roosevelt's political dependence on their support, to shield their culture against northern intrusions. Latin Americans, benefiting from the Good Neighbor's withdrawal from intervention, relished a similar power.

Perhaps the finest creative mind the South nourished in the Depression era belonged to William Faulkner. Something of a maverick, he had little time for the myth that southern traditionalism yielded cultural, aesthetic, and humane values superior to those spawned by the North's urban, capitalist, industrial milieu. Faulkner's unforgettable character Thomas Sutpen in *Absalom, Absalom!* (1936) personifies the rapacious sort of conqueror who tamed a wild domain so as to create a civilization in which protestations of concern for culture served to mask a lifestyle that was cruel, harsh, and inherently exploitive. Sutpen, who (like a Spanish conquistador) "contrived somehow to swagger even on a horse," wasn't a gentleman. Culture never interested him. He took his land "from a tribe of ignorant Indians,"[10] cleared it and developed it through the labor of Negroes whom he brutalized and cheated and whose women he raped; he left behind progeny, legitimate and illegitimate, white and mulatto, permanently scarred by the traditions he bequeathed them.

Faulkner's depiction of the South could just as well have applied to South America. In the 1930s, though, dismayed by the apparent failures of Calvinist, urban, capitalist, individualistic modernity, Americans were in a mood to romanticize almost any culture that seemed the antithesis of one that, so it seemed, had failed them. This is one reason why they rallied behind the Good Neighbor policy, picturing its beneficiaries in the lands to the south as living relatively uncontaminated lives in countries that despite some large cities were overwhelmingly agrarian in values and in population deployment.

## The Myth of the Happy Peasant, of the Contented Yeoman Farmer

To the degree that they addressed race issues at all, southern Agrarians, socially conservative by and large in their outlook, liked to assume that their region's blacks were a well-off, happy, and contented lot (at least when compared to northern industrial laborers) because they remained rooted in the land. On the left of the political spectrum, American social-ists and Communists were sometimes sympathetic to this appraisal. Often they advocated an independent homeland in the American South where Negroes could lead happy agrarian lives in socialist equality. Yet, when given the chance to vote with their feet, southern blacks responded to defense-plant employment opportunities by staging a massive migration to the North and the West. For them, the promised land was a city, with factories.[11] So much for the myth of the happy peasant! Moreover, once urban economic life resumed its vitality, white farmers embarked upon a massive exodus from their supposedly idyllic existence in daily commu-nion with the land. In the forefront of the exodus were those persons whom various New Deal programs had resettled on farms during the worst days of the Depression. Sixty years after New Dealers embarked on their back-to-the-land movement, America's farm population had fallen from approximately thirty to about five million.

For more and more Americans from the Depression era onward, a visit to a national park brought them quite close enough and for long enough to nature. Nor did they envy or particularly admire those who made their living out of day-to-day communion with the land. What is more, many Native Americans, perhaps even a majority, resented John Collier's efforts to keep them on the land as communal farmers. To many Indian spokes-men, Collier's approach smacked of un-Americanism, of communism, and they wanted nothing to do with it. In all of these respects utopianist New Dealers, beginning with the usually eminently realistic FDR, were quite out of touch with what proved to be the enduring essence of the American spirit—perhaps indeed of the human spirit.

The temporary, Depression-spawned revitalization of America's agrar-ian myth, positing the moral superiority of the rural way of life, more often than not originated with city-bred intellectuals. Of course, there are exceptions to this pattern, many exceptions. Prevailingly, though, the New Deal's back-to-the-land movement, insofar as it arose out of wholeness and regeneration myths and not just out of a desperate grasping at expedients to alleviate urban poverty, originated with people who were not way-of-life farmers and who knew little about those who were. Sometimes the less they knew about men and women of the soil, the more the agrarian mythologists thought they knew what those people surely must believe and want. Be that as it may, the agrarian myth helped shape the attitudes with which many U.S. government officials and a good slice of the general public regarded Latin America as a whole and Mexico in particular. Among those influenced by the myth was the president himself.

Rexford Tugwell, who, it will be recalled, described his president as a "child of the country" who regarded cities as no more than "a perhaps necessary nuisance," for a time carried out Roosevelt's policy of returning Americans to the land. Discouraged in 1936 when the Supreme Court declared unconstitutional the Resettlement Administration that he had headed, Rexford Tugwell briefly found solace in Mexico, then in the midst of a sweeping agrarian reform movement, the centerpiece of which was to be resumption on a massive scale of the sort of communal farming attributed to indigenous traditions. About a decade earlier Tugwell had thought he might be seeing the future at work while inspecting the Soviet Union's collectivized farming; now he thought he might be seeing it in Mexico. Tugwell was not alone among the shapers of the Good Neighbor policy in grasping at this delusion.

# 18. The Good Neighbor's Romance with Mexico

❖ ❖ ❖ ❖ ❖ ❖ ❖ ❖ ❖ ❖ ❖ ❖ ❖ ❖ ❖ ❖ ❖ ❖ ❖ ❖ ❖ ❖ ❖ ❖ ❖ ❖ ❖ ❖ ❖ ❖ ❖ ❖ ❖

### What Morrow Begins, Daniels Continues

"South of the Border, Down Mexico Way," went the refrain of a popular song at the end of the 1930s, "That's where I fell in love where stars at night come out to play." [1] At the end of the 1920s and the beginning of the '30s, Ambassador Dwight Morrow and his wife had fallen in love with Mexico, as had a host of tourists and expatriates who visited and settled there. By the time the Depression fastened its grip on their own country, Americans discomfited by their culture's traditional capitalist credo had turned Mexico into a kind of downscale version of what Left Bank Paris had been for the "Lost Generation" at the end of the First World War. Into this environment stepped a new American ambassador who, together with his wife, soon acquired the same degree of affection for Mexico that the Morrows had displayed. And Mexicans reciprocated the affection.

In the Woodrow Wilson administration Josephus Daniels, from North Carolina, had served as secretary of the Navy, which meant he was boss to young Franklin Roosevelt, beginning his career in national politics as assistant secretary of the Navy. It required all of Daniels's forbearance and charity to maintain warm relations with his young assistant; for Roosevelt chafed at his boss's perceived pacifism and actually seems to have schemed to discredit Daniels, hoping to claim for himself his superior's post. This was an especially sordid interlude in FDR's early career, but Josephus

Daniels remained endlessly forgiving. Still, he must have felt his one-time subordinate owed him something.

Ever since his stint at the helm of the Navy Department, when reluctantly he had helped preside over the occupation of Veracruz ordered by Wilson, Daniels had developed a deep interest in Mexico. When he requested appointment as ambassador to that country, the new president could scarcely have turned him down. Nor would he have wanted to. Despite the rocky beginning in their relationship, Roosevelt by the end of his stint in the Navy Department had developed genuine affection and respect, albeit still tinged with just a smidgen of condescension, for his endlessly patient and forbearing superior. Daniels was a man he knew he could rely on to initiate the Good Neighbor policy in a country where success was absolutely essential. Sumner Welles was nothing short of prophetic when, in writing Daniels about the appointment, he predicted that it would "be productive of the greatest benefit in promoting a good feeling toward the United States," not only in Mexico but in her sister republics as well.[2]

In the letter of resignation he had sent Daniels in 1920 after receiving the Democratic vice-presidential nomination, Roosevelt wrote: "You have taught me so wisely and kept my feet on the ground when I was about to skyrocket—and in all there has never been a real dispute or antagonism or distrust."[3] FDR may have exaggerated in claiming total lack of dispute or antagonism, but there can be no doubt that he appreciated his boss's stabilizing influence. If disputes arose with Mexico, the president understood that Daniels could be counted on to help Washington remain calm and collected.

In different times, the election of change-oriented Lázaro Cárdenas as president of Mexico in 1934 could have served warning of coming crises with the United States. Prior to the Depression, the sweeping land reform that he hoped to make the centerpiece of his administration would have prompted misgivings and even outrage in Washington; for that program's key element was a return to the collectivized agriculture of the pre-Columbian ejidal system—a move that threatened the private-ownership latifundia system with extinction. In 1934, though, FDR saw in Cárdenas a kindred soul in his desire, at a time of crisis, to return Mexicans to the land, and to improve the lot of peasants already on the land.

Every bit as much as his president, Ambassador Daniels also sympathized with the Mexican leader's agrarian reform visions. In the spirit of the Nashville Agrarians, Daniels believed that Mexicans, even as American Southerners, needed to strengthen their roots in the land in order to domesticate industrialism and assimilate it, under certain checks and balances, into their traditional culture. Just as the American South, so Mexico and the rest of Latin America required, so far as Daniels was concerned, a program that would preserve the essence of a traditional way of life against the intrusion of industrialism and obsessive individualism. If the privately owned estate seemed most suitable to the needs of his native South, Daniels conceded that Mexicans, with their different heritage and traditions, might be best served by agrarian communalism. Apparently he had not been untouched by the spirit of cultural relativism.

## Agrarianism North of the Border Resonates with Agrarianism South of the Border

In the Roosevelt administration, interest in, indeed passionate concern for, encouraging a return to the land, for decentralizing industrial production by moving plants to rural areas so that employees could keep their hands in the soil, originated at the very top. Roosevelt himself, during a 1931 University of Virginia address, speculated on the possibility of creating through cooperative effort "some new form of living which will combine industry and agriculture." Even more than her husband, Eleanor Roosevelt hoped to see government launch an attack on runaway urbanization by establishing rural-industrial communes that would simultaneously provide escape from crowded cities and from rural poverty. Thereby the Jeffersonian agrarian dream might be adapted to modern times. Even the usually hard-bitten Louis Howe began to enthuse over visions of resettlement programs, of industrial decentralization, and of small-scale factories in fields; and so did industrialist Henry Ford. So, too, more predictably, did Frank Lloyd Wright and Lewis Mumford, among other prophets of a revitalized and reborn America referred to in the preceding chapter.[4]

North Americans, then, many of them at least, were in a mood to celebrate when Lázaro Cárdenas initiated the greatest program of land redistribution ever witnessed in the Spanish New World since the time of conquest. With Cárdenas at the helm, and with an approving U.S. president and ambassador urging him on, Americans could hope that the dreams which economist Stuart Chase and journalist Carleton Beals had shared with a broad reading public in the early 1930s were approaching realization.

Harvard- and Massachusetts Institute of Technology–trained economist Stuart Chase presented a typical example of a Depression-era North American intellectual who fell out of love with Yankee capitalism and in love with the alternative lifestyle he discovered in Mexico. He provided the particulars of his south-of-the-border love affair in his book *Mexico: A Study of Two Americas,* written in collaboration with Marian Tyler and published in mid-1931. For all its vogue during the Depression era, one of the few things about the book that does not strike a 1990s reader as absurd are the illustrations by Diego Rivera.

The product of a five-month stay in Mexico in 1930, Chase's book enjoyed best-seller status for half a year after its publication. Chase employed as his major thematic device a comparison of Middletown, as depicted by sociologists Helen Lynd and Robert Lynd and actually a description of Muncie, Indiana, with the village of Tepoztlán, which Chase found to be living still in the leisurely patterns of the handicraft age.

"Mexico," Chase enthused, "takes no back talk from clocks." Addressing the occupants of Middletown, U.S.A., he admonished, "It is an art which you too some day must learn; for it is the art of living." In Tepoztlán, the people "take their fun as they take their food, part and parcel of the organic life." In contrast to Middletowners, "they are not driven to play by boredom; they are not organized into recreation by strenuous young men and women with badges on their arms and community chests behind them." To the Mexicans, play comes naturally; it bubbles up out of lives that are unalienated. Unlike Middletown, where the gospel is work, "the gospel of Tepoztlán is play," Chase enthused. Reversing the sanctimonious condemnations with which typical nineteenth-century gringo travelers had responded to time wasted on religious fiestas, Chase enthused: "One day in three, the year around, the southern community is celebrating a major or minor fiesta." Moreover, "flowers are more important to Mexicans than are motor cars, radios, and bathrooms combined, to Americans."[5] Chase's romanticism appealed to many Americans perhaps hoping themselves, in the throes of their economic hard times, to learn how to derive satisfaction from flowers now that automobiles, and even indoor plumbing, increasingly seemed beyond their reach.

Shaping his ideas against the backdrop of the Great Depression, Chase believed that mass industrialism was not inevitable for Mexico, and that it could be reversed even in the United States. "The future for industrialism in the sense of mass production is not rosy, for which we can thank whatever gods there be. As a result Mexico has an unparalleled opportunity to evolve a master plan whereby the machine is admitted only on good behavior."[6] What a heady picture for Americans disillusioned by their country's civilization: the machine on good behavior, not threatening nature with oblivion, or men and women with dehumanization.

Predictably, given the nature of American millennialist thought through the decades and particularly as it reemerged in the revitalized agrarian myth of the 1930s, Chase urged a combination, a synthesis, a fusion of the ways of Tepoztlán and Middletown. Let the Mexican village preserve "all that is rich, beautiful and useful" in its Indian traditions but at the same time absorb "all that can be used of the new and modern in science" and medicine. Meantime, let Middletowners cling to modern inventions but learn to cherish their soil, nourish their group life, and warm to the beauty of arts and crafts rather than coveting surfeits of mass-produced goods.[7]

In *Mexican Maize,* published just before Chase's book, journalist and long-time Mexico hand Carleton Beals presented a similar message. Mexican peasants, he argued, were happier than New York City laborers. The New Yorkers, like most Americans, led disjointed, compartmentalized lives, seeking pleasure in pursuits that had nothing to do with their labor. Mexicans, on the other hand, led lives that were whole. Finding pleasure in their work, they led unalienated lives—lives marked by a completeness in which opposites merged.[8]

Both Chase and Beals envisioned a hemispheric future in which Mexicans, and by implication other Latin Americans, would absorb some of the drives of industrial life without relinquishing the basic wisdom of the rooted-in-the-soil peasant; at the same time, norteamericanos would shed the compulsiveness of city-based capitalism as they took part in processes of deurbanization and industrial decentralization that would move factories to rural towns and fields, allowing workers to feel at home in two disparate realms.

When Josephus Daniels arrived on the Mexican scene to represent his country, and especially when Lázaro Cárdenas became president and launched his sweeping agrarian reforms in 1934, it seemed that Mexico was well on the way toward implementing the sort of reforms that Americans at home could only dream about, thwarted as they were by powerful entrenched interests that not even the New Deal could dislodge. Daniels knew not only the Chase and Beals books on Mexico; shortly he would know also, and warmly approve, University of North Carolina professor Eyler N. Simpson's 1937 book *The Ejido, Mexico's Way Out.* In this influential study (produced in Daniels's home state), Simpson argued that collective farming together with decentralized manufacturing carried out through factories in the field held the solution to Mexico's ills. Daniels appeared, like Simpson, to believe that by returning to preconquest, aboriginal agricultural practices based on communal ownership and labor, Mexicans could establish a new era of social justice in which human rights took precedence over property rights.

As a mentor on Mexican history and destiny, Daniels also had Frank Tannenbaum, a Columbia University Latin Americanist with a background in radical labor movements that some years before had earned him a prison sentence. In 1931 Tannenbaum had published his influential *Peace by Revolution: An Interpretation of Mexico.* In it, he hailed the Mexican revolution, erupting in 1910, as a death-and-regeneration process whereby Mexico would undo the effects of Spanish conquest and liberate the energies of the true sons and daughters of the soil. "Mexico is returning to the children of the Indian mother, and will be colored largely by her blood and her patterns," Tannenbaum wrote,[9] sounding a great deal like D. H. Lawrence in his novel *The Plumed Serpent.* When Cárdenas became president in 1934, Tannenbaum hailed him as the embodiment of Mexico's most exalted revolutionary goals. Establishing a friendship with Daniels, Tannenbaum reinforced the favorable impression that Daniels and his wife had already formed of this apparently incorruptible leader.

Regarded suspiciously by the State Department in the 1920s as leagued with an allegedly Jewish-Bolshevik clique of American expatriates in Mexico who plotted against U.S. national interests, Tannenbaum less than a decade later was the close personal friend of President Cárdenas and a trusted confidant and adviser of the U.S. ambassador. He symbolized, moreover, the enthusiasm with which many Jewish intellectuals, from their homes in the United States, followed events in Mexico. In the ejido they tended to find a New World replica of the kibbutz. Some of them may even have accepted the theories, bandied about since the time of Spanish conquest, that New World Indians were really descendants of the Lost Tribes of Israel. If this were the case, little wonder that the reforms to which an Indian-blooded president of Mexico had turned resembled the social experiments underway in Palestine.

Another adviser on whose wisdom Daniels drew at least briefly was U.S. Commissioner of Indian Affairs John Collier. On one occasion when visiting Mexico and bolstering the ambassador's favorable impression of the Cárdenas program, Collier had declared (as quoted in an earlier chapter): "Our duty of land-restoration affects perhaps 200,000 Indians, while Mexico, a very poor country, has assumed as a moral obligation the restoration of land to more than 2,000,000 Indians."[10]

Some cynics may see in the Daniels approval of Mexican land reform, coming on top of his affiliation with some of the basically conservative Nashville Agrarians, who urged the need to keep southern traditions alive, simply an endeavor to keep peasants on ice—the approach that so many Southerners hoped to employ in dealing with their region's semipeasant class of African Americans. But this appraisal, I think, is not fair to the ambassador. Like Roosevelt himself, Daniels responded to deeply ingrained American regeneration mythology.

Toward the end of World War II Franklin Roosevelt still responded to this mythology, and that is one reason why, for a time, he went along with the notions of his secretary of the treasury Henry Morgenthau, Jr., about what should be done with Germany once the Allies had won the war.

Morgenthau advocated the dismantling of German industry and a massive return of Germans to the land. "What better way," writes one of Roosevelt's most persuasive biographers, "to remake a people than to dismember their political institutions, and simultaneously move them out of the industrial age and into contact with their honest, peaceful, Jeffersonian agrarian roots."[11] Roosevelt was thwarted in his visionary plans to return countless Americans to their roots. He was thwarted, too, in the scheme to remake Germans by sending them back to the land; for his advisers led him ultimately to reject the Morgenthau plan. But in Mexico, regeneration might remain possible. This hope, I suspect, at least tinged the Roosevelt and the Daniels approach to Mexico. It was a hope that arose in part out of America's frontier mythology.

Whatever its origins, the Roosevelt-Daniels approach to Mexico delighted New Deal left-wingers and perhaps helped distract them once in a while from the degree to which the administration was abandoning utopian schemes for reshaping the United States itself. If Roosevelt helped cover his flank against attacks from the left by going along with Mexican radicalism, he incurred the consistent objections of Secretary of State Cordell Hull. Genuine good neighborliness, so far as Hull was concerned, consisted in helping Latin Americans move away from statism, whether in agriculture or any other field of endeavor, toward a private, free-enterprise, market economy. In no instance was Hull so perturbed over Roosevelt-Daniels policy toward Mexico as when the administration went along, supinely in his opinion, with Lázaro Cárdenas's expropriation of foreign oil holdings in 1938.

Looking at the Mexican situation from the vantage point of the mid-1990s, as the "Aztec republic" moves inexorably toward global, privatized agribusiness and begins even to toy with notions of allowing foreign investors back into its troubled, inefficient petroleum industry, Hull emerges as a prescient if hard-nosed and irascible friend of Mexico; and endlessly forgiving, turn-the-other-cheek Americans from the president and his ambassador on down seem misguided and overly indulgent friends. Still, it is possible to be right for the times even if wrong for the ages. Given the immediate Depression-era setting, when cultural relativism of every sort beguiled the intelligentsia, when all things primitive held out promises of redemption to afflicted moderns, and when considerations of hemispheric security pushed even some hard-headed realists toward indulgence of "un-American" habits among neighbors and among Americans themselves, the Roosevelt-Daniels policies were right. Any approach other than theirs would have alienated not only Mexicans but Latin Americans in general, to say nothing of the reform wing of the Democratic Party as well.

## Good Neighborliness Survives the Petroleum Issue

A story is told to the effect that when Roosevelt learned in May of 1938 that Germany might soon be obliged to cease payment of the interest on American loans, he ignored his secretary of state's outrage, slapped his thigh, and exclaimed with a laugh: "Serves the Wall Street bankers right." [12] The story may or may not be apocryphal. In any event a different crisis had erupted the previous March, one that had already evoked sharply contrasting responses from the president and his secretary of state.

In March of 1938 Lázaro Cárdenas responded in fury to what he considered an affront to his honor by representatives of foreign oil concerns. These latter demanded written confirmation after Cárdenas had reached an oral agreement that would have permitted them to continue their operations in Mexico under a more generous profit-sharing arrangement with the government. Taking to the airwaves in high dudgeon, Cárdenas announced the expropriation of foreign oil holdings. FDR, who considered Cárdenas "one of the tiny group of Latin leaders who was actually preaching and trying to practice democracy," [13] may not have slapped his thigh on hearing the news; but he did show some sympathy toward the Mexican president's startling action. Just possibly the American president saw a chance to duplicate the populist successes Huey Long and Father Coughlin had scored by badgering Standard Oil and American petroleum conglomerates in general. Beyond this, Roosevelt by this time seethed with anger against the "economic royalists" who had so far in his second term contrived to block much of the New Deal's reformist thrust. In his pique, he welcomed the opportunity to watch some of those economic royalists squirm, specifically the oil interests among them, as Mexico applied the heat.

Like the president he served and with whom he retained a warm friendship, Treasury Secretary Morgenthau, more and more concerned about the menace of Nazi Germany and anxious to achieve hemispheric solidarity in the face of possible security threats from the Old World, saw no reason to throw down the gauntlet to Cárdenas. However, Cordell Hull worked himself into a tantrum and fired off a communique to the Mexican foreign office threatening dire consequences if expropriation were not called off.

At this juncture, Ambassador Daniels conferred with Mexico's foreign minister, a close personal friend, and persuaded him to consider Hull's communique as not having been received. Perhaps the former secretary of the Navy figured that his president owed him a favor for the patience he had shown an insubordinate assistant during the Wilson administration. However that may be, Roosevelt did indeed back his ambassador's unprecedented act of diplomatic insubordination. This left Hull to fume that he had "to deal with those communists down there" without administration backing as he sought to enforce principles of international law.[14]

Hull continued to fume, but to no avail. On April 1 President Roosevelt told reporters that the Good Neighbor policy would not be sacrificed so as to save the oil men. Ever alert to the public mood, FDR sensed he was taking no political risk in moving to save the Good Neighbor policy. Some time later an opinion poll showed the American public evenly divided in their response to the question: Should the United States use force to protect American property if Mexico or any other Latin American nation seized it? Approximately 39 percent each responded for and against, with the remainder undecided.[15] Obviously the majority of those responding affirmatively were Republicans, whose backing Roosevelt did not expect. Among those who mattered to him, the Democratic electorate, he had bolstered his political stock.

Apparently the Mexican president was no more surprised than his North American counterpart by the mildness of U.S. public response to expropriation. In his book *Waldo Frank: Prophet of Hispanic Regeneration* (1994), historian Michael Ogorzaly sheds light on the matter. Going on Frank's testimony, he describes a 1939 meeting in which Cárdenas bared his soul to the North American self-styled prophet. The Mexican leader confessed to his American Jewish friend how, in his concern about U.S. reprisals, he had agonized over nationalizing foreign oil holdings. Only when he thought back on the message contained in Frank's book *The Re-Discovery of America* (published both in English and in a Spanish translation in 1929 and prophesying that U.S. spiritual regeneration was at hand) had he found the courage to proceed with nationalization. Construing the Good Neighbor policy as a harbinger of the fulfillment of Frank's prophecy, he assumed he could count on understanding from norteamericanos, already beginning to shed their contumely and greed as they rediscovered how to be more fully human. This, at least, was the gist of the tête-à-tête with the Mexican president as described by Waldo Frank.

While Cárdenas was not without a mystical bent, one can doubt that he was led by Frank's visionary verbiage to count on a new kind of spiritual—or spiritualist—politics from the gringos. Probably he simply accepted Frank as a credible witness to the degree to which Depression-era North Americans were disinclined to rally to the cause of big business.

Predictably, unregenerate American oil interests launched a vicious propaganda assault against their adversary, trading in traditional stereotypes to depict Mexicans in general as less than fully human, as lazy Indians, as naughty children, and as a people that had undergone "racial degeneration." The old epithets and stereotypes tumbled out in an article published in the July 1938 edition of *Atlantic Monthly*. Its author aimed at whipping up popular indignation against Mexicans and forcing the

State Department into a stronger response to the nationalization, depicted as a criminal expropriation.[16] Rather than mobilizing Americans, the *Atlantic Monthly* article seemed to embarrass them and even to arouse their ire against anti-Mexican militancy.

By now Adolf A. Berle, Jr., had been appointed assistant secretary of state, and one of his duties was to contain and hopefully mollify Hull. Berle, who desired a basic restructuring of U.S. business so as to provide greater scope for government supervision in the alleged interest of fair play and the common good, had little sympathy with his country's oil interests. In 1938 and again in 1945, when he served as ambassador to Brazil, Berle believed that the life of a U.S. diplomat was "incomplete without a scrimmage with the international oil people."[17]

President Roosevelt, meantime, took security considerations more and more to heart as he sought crisis-containment policies for dealing with Mexico. He agreed completely with Josephus Daniels when the ambassador argued that oil "ought not to smear" the sort of hemispheric solidarity that might ultimately be essential to save democracy "in a mad world."[18] More than pique against what he regarded as blindly selfish U.S. oil profiteers, it was security considerations that induced Roosevelt to go along with the soft policy toward Mexico that his ambassador recommended— security considerations tinged, however, with a romantic sympathy for the Cárdenas land policy.

It was the security card that FDR played on the last day of January 1939, when the entire Senate Military Affairs Committee assembled for a White House briefing. The predominantly conservative members of that committee sharply criticized what they considered the president's pusillanimous stance on the Mexican issue. Roosevelt defended his administration's position by pointing to a security threat that extended all the way from Mexico to Argentina. If the United States unduly provoked Mexicans on the petroleum issue, it would provoke Brazilians and Argentines as well and thereby exacerbate the Nazi menace in Latin America, all the way from the Rio Grande down to the Straits of Magellan.[19]

Already, in defending lenience with Mexico, FDR had begun to stress hemispheric security. Increasingly, from 1938 on, he would rely on security arguments to combat isolationist sentiments typical of American conservatives—sentiments dramatically in evidence among key members of the Senate Military Affairs Committee. As the later section of this book that deals specifically with security matters makes clear, Roosevelt argued, essentially, that if the United States did not become involved in the defense of Europe, soon it would have to defend itself in its own hemisphere. He first resorted seriously to this strategy when dealing with the Mexican oil crisis of 1938. Confronting it, he argued that security factors forced the United States to contemporize, more than ever it would in an ideal world, with Mexico and indeed with all of Latin America. Among his conservative, isolationist critics, he sought to plant the notion that the way for Americans to gain the freedom they needed to deal with recalcitrant Latin Americans as they might deserve to be dealt with was to take on security commitments in Europe. With their outer lines of defense intact, Americans would not have to be so solicitous of their unreliable neighbors. In toying with this approach FDR was, in effect, conceding that his hemispheric policies had not transformed Latin Americans into genuinely good neighbors.

Let us imagine for the moment that Roosevelt as juggler dealt with Latin America with his left and Europe with his right hand. In effect, the performer told one audience (of Good Neighbor enthusiasts) to watch the marvelous dexterity of the left hand (as it kept the Latin American balls safely in the air); and he told another audience (of Good Neighbor critics) to focus on the precariousness of the left hand's juggling, and to wait with bated breath for the right hand's prodigies to restore equilibrium to the whole act.

For a moment in 1940 it seemed that the juggler's left hand might not be able to control all the balls that were aloft. During that moment's brief duration it appeared that the Good Neighbor policy's equilibrium might be in jeopardy. Against the background of Manuel Avila Camacho's election to the presidency at the end of Cárdenas's term, rumors circulated about a plot hatched by foreign oil companies to overthrow the new leader and replace him with one more sympathetic to their interests. Getting wind of the plot just after his reelection to a third term, FDR showed his support for the new Mexican president by sending Vice President Henry Wallace to represent the United States at his inauguration. It was the first official vice-presidential trip to any Latin American nation; and it conveyed enormous symbolical meaning.[20] Among New Dealers, Henry Wallace was one of the least kindly disposed toward the free-enterprise philosophy (in 1948 he would run on a basically socialist platform with the backing of the Communist Party of the United States). His cross-border mission sent the message that Mexicans need not concern themselves about pleasing U.S. oil barons. Watching these events, Diego Rivera may have felt avenged for the destruction of his Rockefeller Center murals as ordered by John D. Rockefeller, Jr., son of the founder of Standard Oil. Meanwhile, conservative U.S. tycoons grumbled anew over the dexterity of their White House adversary's left hand.

With war clouds darkening over Europe and with the need for hemispheric solidarity becoming ever more urgent, FDR and Berle and Sumner Welles played leading roles in Washington, always with the collaboration of Josephus Daniels in Mexico City, in moving the State Department toward a comprehensive agreement on compensation for the expropriated oil holdings. Finally in November of 1941 came announcement of an agreement that called for creation of a joint commission to decide what the oil companies should receive. Mexico pledged $40 million in advance to help cover what might be agreed to by way of satisfaction for American claims. In turn, the United States extended a $95 million economic aid package. This prompted the *New York Times,* seldom friendly to Cárdenas in its reporting, to observe that Washington in effect "furnished Mexico with the funds to pay for the properties . . . [Mexico] had expropriated." "Wall Street winced and the companies shrieked betrayal," as one American historian observes.[21] But the Good Neighbor policy survived. Not only did it survive, but under wartime security exigencies it evolved into a policy that committed the United States to being a far better neighbor than originally intended—a development Bryce Wood repeatedly draws attention to in a splendid study of the Good Neighbor era.[22]

In 1992 Mexican writer, leftist critic, all-around savant, and perennial Yankee-baiter Carlos Fuentes praised "President Franklin Roosevelt for his 'Good Neighbor' policy."[23] Arguably, his praise grows out of the great petroleum controversy when his country scored a dramatic victory over Yankee oil interests. The victory, of course, may have saddled Mexicans with an inefficient, overstaffed, underfinanced, and underproducing national oil industry; but then the ideological thrust that characterized the Good Neighbor era as it developed on both sides of the border rested on the assumption that men and women did not live by oil and oil profits alone. In looking at these issues, one must not lose track of the Depression era's often romantic mindset.

By 1941, with the signing of the comprehensive agreement, Mexicans and North Americans had managed to patch up their differences. But it had been a close call. In part this was because of the superheated atmosphere in which the two countries carried on their relationship. With all of the romantic, millennialist expectations that flourished on both sides of the border about creating new cultures and persons and somehow overcoming the pitfalls and shortcomings of modern life by fusing the traits of individualistic modernity with those of communalism, whether primitive and indigenous or Marxist and imported, diplomats had a hard time conducting their customary business. It is a tribute to officials both in Washington and Mexico City that they managed to avoid disaster.

## George Messersmith in Mexico:
## The Good Neighbor Policy as a Beginning

While the historian's attention generally focuses on Cárdenas and Daniels, on revolutionary challenge and diplomatic response, President Avila Camacho (1940–1946) and George Messersmith, who—with the United States now having entered World War II—succeeded Daniels in the embassy post in Mexico City in 1942, contributed as much as their more charismatic predecessors to establishing a Good Neighbor relationship. When Cordell Hull and Sumner Welles tried to initiate policies that would pressure Mexico to begin to readmit foreign capital into the petroleum industry, Messersmith contrived to veto the plan. In his mind, Hull and Welles simply did not grasp the depth of Mexican feelings; nor did they understand the symbolic importance of the expropriation. Having asserted at last their independence from the Yankees, Mexicans were now prepared to settle into routinized normalcy in their diplomacy with the United States. But, threaten the Mexicans in their great symbolic victory over their old antagonist, and they would respond with fury. FDR recognized the validity of the ambassador's analysis and rejected State Department advice.[24]

Along with his new ambassador to Mexico, FDR appreciated the importance of symbolism. The president demonstrated his attentiveness to the symbolic gesture when he traveled to the Buenos Aires conference in 1936. He demonstrated it again when he dispatched Henry Wallace to represent the United States at Avila Camacho's inauguration. He demonstrated it once more when consulting in Washington with Ambassador Messersmith about a forthcoming meeting between the presidents of the United States and Mexico. "George," said Roosevelt to his ambassador, "the big boy will have to go see the smaller boy first." Roosevelt appreciated the importance of initiating his contact with his Mexican counterpart on Mexican soil. Monterrey, "site of a new American-assisted industrial complex," was chosen as the location for the meeting; and this choice was not without its own symbolism, signaling the importance Roosevelt attached to improving the south-of-the-border climate for American investment. The meeting went smoothly, although "Mrs. Roosevelt created a small stir by holding forth on the touchy subject of racial injustice in America and its impact upon Mexicans there."[25] In its way, though, Eleanor's little speech was as fraught with meaning as her husband's insistence upon meeting his Mexican counterpart at Monterrey. Together, Franklin and Eleanor conveyed the message that investments *and* justice concerned Americans.

Ambassador Messersmith rejoiced that the meeting had gone so smoothly, serving practical purposes while symbolizing the new era of Yankee-Latin relations. But he fully realized a great deal of work remained to be accomplished in strengthening good relations. The Good Neighbor policy had made only a beginning.

As of the mid-1940s, Messersmith recognized that Mexicans by and large remained dubious about gringo neighbors and their ways. In a letter to Hull, Messersmith noted that despite the friendly overtures of Avila Camacho and many in his administration, despite their relative opening (compared to Cárdenas and his administration) toward the culture of modernity, "there remains the historical background, particularly among the masses," wherein there was "no love for us." Nor did Messersmith think this remarkable. He understood that, as biographer Jesse H. Stiller puts it, "A century of rancor could not be expunged overnight."[26]

The hit tune "Frenesi" backed a fabulously successful Artie Shaw recording of Cole Porter's "Begin the Beguine," a recording released (in that era's 78-revolutions-per-minute format) about the time the United States entered World War II. "Frenesi" tells the tale of a gringo who looked in on a south-of-the-border fiesta, fell in love with a señorita, married her, and blissfully lived ever after with her in "a bungalow in Mexico."[27] On the other hand, the 1939 song "South of the Border, Down Mexico Way," referred to at the beginning of this chapter, relates a different outcome. When eventually the gringo returns to Mexico to claim the woman he had fallen in love with at a fiesta, he discovers she has taken the veil. Mexican culture had clashed with and thwarted the ways of the gringo. There was no happy ending, even if both partners to the onetime romance continued to pine just a bit for each other.

In a way, this was the story of the Good Neighbor policy. In 1938, thanks in large part to Josephus Daniels and an understanding FDR, there had been a real fiesta; stars had come out to play (as "South of the Border" lyrics put it) and to bless the cross-border romance. As World War II ended, though, the bloom was off the romance. And the Mexican experience, whether in the song or in diplomatic reality, symbolizes in microcosm the thwarted romance with Latin America as a whole, once normalcy returned to the United States after the Depression and after the war. But a great deal of material remains to traverse before arriving at that downer of a conclusion.

# 19.
# Good Neighbor Policies: Soft, Hard, and Indeterminate

❖ ❖ ❖ ❖ ❖ ❖ ❖ ❖ ❖ ❖ ❖ ❖ ❖ ❖ ❖ ❖ ❖ ❖ ❖ ❖ ❖ ❖ ❖ ❖ ❖ ❖ ❖ ❖ ❖ ❖ ❖ ❖ ❖ ❖ ❖ ❖ ❖

### Targeting the Good Neighbor Policy

A great number of North Americans, whether in an official capacity or simply among the general public, were never romantically inclined to begin with toward Latin Americans. Throughout the Roosevelt years, various interest groups and various individuals representing disparate philosophical, economic, and social positions, some of which were downright hostile toward Latin Americans, struggled with each other to gain control over the Good Neighbor policy's targeting mechanism. As a result of the ongoing struggle, a consistent, clear-cut policy toward Latin America never emerged. The Good Neighbor policy was born anew virtually each day, its targeting determined by the results of that day's bureaucratic and interest-group infighting. In this regard, relations with Latin America simply reflected the way in which foreign policy generally is shaped, not only in the United States but in every democratic state.

Two broadly based coalitions emerged as the principal contestants over how to target Good Neighbor policy. The advocates of what I choose to call the soft approach to Latin America focused far less on encouraging the spread of free-enterprise, individualistic, market capitalism south of the border than did champions of the hard approach. More often than not the soft-school advocates inclined toward statist or even socialist expedients. Suspecting, and sometimes convinced, that untrammeled free enterprise produced unjust social consequences, they welcomed restraints on the business sector. They did not see red whenever Latin American governments interfered with free-enterprising Yankee profit-seekers. What they wanted was capitalism with a soft and gentle demeanor, with a restrained and cushioned hand. In contrast, the hard-school proponents believed that only out of competition waged in relatively unregulated markets would come the economic development that might, at some point far down the line, make possible the alleviation of social problems by, in effect, turning every competent, capable individual into a capitalist, whether a penny-capitalist or a millionaire. Hard-schoolers wanted capitalism with a tough demeanor; some did not shy away from capitalism with an uninhibited, bare-knuckle hand. They tended to see red whenever government bureaucracies, whether in Latin America or in the United States or any part of the world, interfered with and tried to soften market operations. Such bureaucracies were if not communist red at least a socialist pink.

Proponents of hard-school good neighborliness assumed that, in spite of the Depression, nothing of fundamental significance ailed the U.S. socioeconomic system. That system had only a bad case of the sniffles. In their altogether different diagnosis, soft-school good neighbors found their country's system seriously ailing; and they did not want to see Latin Americans fall into the kinds of habits that had brought on the North American illness.

One cannot draw clear, neat, and consistent lines between the two camps of hard and soft good neighbors. In addition to contending against each other, the two camps included elements that sometimes merged and coalesced with members of the opposite camp. Neither side could produce at any precise moment a clear, consistent, well-defined consensus as to just what objectives it hoped to target in individual Latin American republics. In trying to sketch the two camps I must settle for broad brush strokes that slight details, that do no more than suggest basic appearances. Furthermore, readers should keep in mind that by 1940, neither hard nor soft side was in a position to determine just what the Good Neighbor policy would be. By that time security considerations overrode philosophical disputes about what sort of socioeconomic and political system was best for the United States and best for the hemisphere. By that time, Good Neighbor targeting mechanisms had to be thoroughly readjusted. The topic of security, though, I leave for the next section's opening chapter.

For now, what intrigues me is the sometimes ill-defined bifurcation that characterized the Good Neighbor policy at the time when FDR operated as Dr. New Deal, not—as he later described himself—as Dr. Win-the-War. In the early years, Roosevelt sought not only lasting cures for domestic malaise but permanent remedies for the ills that beset relations between great and minor powers in the hemisphere—remedies of the sort that might ultimately be shipped overseas where they could heal Old World maladies spawned by the power disparities of colonialism.

The president found himself in his element as he strove to synthesize divergent elements, hard and soft, into his hemispheric policy. This was precisely the sort of situation that delighted him. Juggler and trickster that he was, had he not found divergence among those trying to target the Good Neighbor policy, he would have somehow contrived to create it.

Within the domestic context FDR trusted neither businessmen nor politicians, pragmatists nor dreamers, bottom-line watchers nor utopianists. Nor did he disdain them. All camps could be useful. He would use them all. Similarly, he welcomed the chance to use and manipulate diverse camps when targeting his Latin American policy.

## Soft Good Neighbor Policies: Some Perspectives

It is time to reiterate one of this book's central theses: The Depression years stimulated a utopian strain of American thought present, at one time or another, in one degree or another, since the creation of the republic. New utopian thinkers, picking up on some very old national refrains, proclaimed that out of catastrophe would emerge a reborn republic peopled by reborn citizens—cleansed of long accumulations of materialism and selfishness, newly awakened to the wonders of sharing and cooperation and community. Sometimes Marxism tinged Depression-era utopianism. Just as often, though, that utopianism reflected indigenous ideologies with a long historical lineage—among them progressivism, with its antipathy to giant corporations and to the whole spirit of greed and untrammeled economic liberalism that, allegedly, fostered heartless cartels and conglomerates.

In the 1930s, radicalized progressivism, absorbing new influences that ranged from Social Gospel and corporatism to more exotic ideological imports including not only Marxism but Zionism, won recruits even in the highest political echelons. The First Lady herself looked forward to a day when bloated individual incomes would be reduced to more modest proportions as a result of wide-ranging, government-administered social reforms, a day in which preoccupation with individual material aggrandizement would yield to social consciousness, to the sharing of wealth in the interest of the common good. Little wonder that defenders of an Americanism oriented more toward individualism and free enterprise, including FBI director J. Edgar Hoover, fretted that Eleanor Roosevelt exemplified those deluded souls who had succumbed to alien ideologies. Had Hoover and persons of his ilk been better grounded in American history, they might have understood that ER and "starry-eyed" reformers like her derived their ideology far more from traditional American utopianism and mainline religions than from communism—not that this would have made them any less dangerous in the eyes of defenders of uninhibited free-market capitalism.

To Hoover and other defenders of what they considered genuine U.S. traditions, the list of enemies included Jewish utopianists such as Waldo Frank, who hoped to transform American capitalism through an infusion of the socialism allegedly more congenial, more natural, to the Latin American historical tradition, both Iberian and Indian. For Waldo Frank and for some of his enthusiasts both in the United States and Latin America, this is what the Good Neighbor policy was all about: it provided the protective umbrella under which socialism would flourish from Maine and Washington and Minnesota all the way down to Uruguay and Argentina and Chile. And this is why Hoover and like-minded defenders of what they deemed traditional Americanism had their doubts about the Good Neighbor policy. In all too many instances, it seemed to have been taken over by un-American radicals.

Hoover fretted when Vice President Wallace phoned Frank in 1942 on the eve of the latter's departure for a Latin American lecture tour. In effect, the vice president extended his blessings to Frank's crusade to bring about an amalgam of Latin American statism and North American individualism. Hoover and like-thinking Americans worried also when Wallace himself went to Peru in 1943 and heaped unstinting praise on the preconquest socialist civilization that the Incas had fashioned, implying that reversion to Inca traditions—even as Cárdenas had reverted to indigenous traditions in Mexico—represented the best hope not only for Peruvians but for all Americans, from far south to far north.[1]

At the time of Wallace's Andean visit Hoover grew especially concerned that the vice president had fallen under the influence of "Bolivian Communists."[2] In truth, though, what Hoover perceived as a menace extended far beyond Bolivia. Latin America's Marxist- and Indianist-tinged socialism that delighted Depression-era U.S. liberals and radicals while dismaying Hoover and American conservatives as well as centrists had sunk deep roots all the way from Chile on up through Mexico and the Caribbean. The Cárdenas flirtation with socialism, apparently condoned even by the U.S. ambassador, was a particular cause of concern to Americans girding against the spread of socialism and international communism.

To North Americans worried that the thrust of the Good Neighbor policy issued from un-American ideology, it came as a shock to realize that Waldo Frank's 1942 lecture tour had been conducted under the auspices of the State Department. This might have shocked J. Edgar Hoover, but it did not surprise him. Already he had concluded that Sumner Welles, Franklin and Eleanor's dear friend in the department who allegedly had a good deal more influence in shaping Latin American policy than Cordell

Hull, was himself soft on communism. Nor was that the extent of the security risk posed by Welles; for his well-known alcoholism and his homosexuality, in which he demonstrated a preference for "the coarser and swarthier" type of young man, purportedly left him open to blackmail.[3] Under these conditions, it hardly surprised Hoover and a host of other critics that the Good Neighbor policy had become hopelessly "soft" on, hopelessly accommodating to, Latin American statism that was tantamount to disguised communism. Small wonder, then, that some elements within the State Department seemed insufficiently inclined, at least as perceived from the far right with its anticipatory McCarthyism, to protect the interests of U.S. investors who had placed their money south of the border.

All that seemed most "un-American" about Latin America's approach to politics and economics found summation in words that Juan D. Perón, the Argentine politico steadily on the rise since the early 1940s, pronounced after becoming president of his republic. "Give to the people," admonished Perón, "especially to the workers, all that is possible." Even when it seems "that you are giving them too much, give them more. You will see the results. Everyone will try to scare you," proclaimed Perón, "with the spectre of an economic collapse." Fear not, though, he advised, for "all of this is a lie. There is nothing more elastic than the economy which everyone fears so much because no one understands it."[4]

Here precisely was the sort of approach to government that his critics accused FDR of pursuing. No wonder such a man, they fumed, would choose to pursue a soft, permissive approach to congenitally statist-leaning, wildly impractical Latin Americans: a people who practiced the social-economic policies dearest to New Deal hearts, dearest to the hearts not only of Jewish radicals like Waldo Frank but of socialist-populist extremists like Henry Wallace and Rexford Tugwell and John Collier and Harold Ickes and Frances Perkins and Harry Hopkins and Eleanor Roosevelt and other vapid dreamers and dangerous utopianists likely to applaud any anticapitalist policy—dearest to the heart, finally, of the president himself.

Detractors of the New Deal and the Good Neighbor policy were scarcely surprised when Sumner Welles in a book published in 1946, three years after a homosexual scandal had forced a reluctant FDR to dismiss him from the State Department, praised Perón's policies—in part because he was still carrying on his State Department feud with Hull, who detested Perón. According to Welles, Perón had "the inherent capacity and the chance to make of his promised 'social revolution' a New Deal for the Argentine people."[5] Precisely, thought FDR's detractors. By trying to foist a Latin American–style revolution on North Americans through the New Deal, FDR had betrayed national traditions. No wonder such a person would preside over a policy that was altogether too soft on Latin Americans, altogether too forgiving, too encouraging, in fact, of their traditional aberrations as fortified by the new ideologies of communism and fascism. The New Deal and the Good Neighbor policy were part and parcel of the same opening toward statism that, so his critics never tired of contending, FDR aimed to encourage not just in the nation but in the entire hemisphere.

To FDR's detractors, it seemed only too logical that the president would appoint a man as duplicitous as himself to mastermind the Good Neighbor policy. Welles, the man whom anti–New Dealers assumed not altogether correctly to be primarily if not almost exclusively in charge of shaping Latin American policy, epitomized the two-facedness, the duplicity of the entire administration. Well-born, aristocratic in demeanor, carrying himself with such "dignified hauteur" that a British diplomat complained he seemed to have "swallowed a ramrod in his youth,"[6] Welles was in fact—allegedly—a lowlife. How appropriate for a roguish president to feel affinity with such a man and to entrust to him a hemispheric policy at odds, allegedly, with all that America, the real, the capitalist and free-enterprise, and also the smugly racist and ethnocentric and antiprimitive and homophobic America, stood for.

The real sin of those who were soft on Latin America was that they were soft on otherness in general. What some of its detractors could not forgive the Good Neighbor policy for was the fact that the men who shaped it, beginning with Sumner Welles himself, often showed a genuine empathy for the Latin American Other and a deep-seated sympathy for the tenets of cultural relativism.

One did not have to be a cultural bigot, though, to have not just occasional but frequent doubts about the Good Neighbor policy. That policy did have its soft, naive, mystical, mythical aspect. At least in the hands of some of its shapers and enthusiasts, it did betray a romantic, antimodern, primitivist mythology about new beginnings and the forging of new persons, about the almost miraculous powers of untried social and economic systems to create utopia. This was one side of the soft approach to hemispheric good neighborliness; and another side was a readiness to write off market capitalism and American traditions in general as proven failures, to extol whatever was different from established traditions for the mere fact that it was different, to reject the known in order to chase after chimeras.

As he helped shape the Good Neighbor policy, Sumner Welles most decidedly did not subscribe to those extreme features of the soft approach as sketched above; nor did the president consistently pursue this sort of soft approach. But they could not afford to dismiss out of hand those who did. These latter, in the troubled and turbulent times of the '30s, were simply too numerous to be ignored. They had, occasionally at least, to be courted and finessed.

By 1943, though, as the United States revved up the engines of capitalism to produce the materiel on which victory in World War II depended, fewer Americans looked romantically toward Latin Americans as the providentially supplied partners, as the significant others, who would help crusty, materialistic Yankees re-create themselves and their culture. The departure of Welles in that year did not cause, but it did serve in a way to mark, the end of Pan American solidarity based on North American romanticization of the Latin Other. Romanticization had served its purpose; but now it was time—past the time, perhaps—to focus on the reality principle in hemispheric relations.

## Hard Good Neighbor Policies: Some Perspectives

Seeking recovery from the devastation wrought by the Civil War, a good number of Americans, with artists such as Albert Bierstadt figuring prominently among them, cast their eyes on the western frontier as a source of both spiritual and economic revival. This was in line with the frontier myth, or with one of the many frontier myths, of improving character, of doing God's work, by conquering the wilderness, and in the process energizing the soul and enhancing the bank account. In the midst of a new crisis of national spirit occasioned by the Depression, some Americans at least thought of Latin America as a new West, as a new frontier, that—depending on the point of view and the objectives of the viewer—would provide renewal of soul and/or pocketbook.

But what of those people already occupying the lands of Latin America? How would their rights be attended to by Americans responding one final time to the lure of frontier mythology? Would the new American frontiersman deal any more equitably with Latin Americans than their predecessors had with Indians—any more equitably with those who crossed them than Clint Eastwood did in that western classic cited in Chapter 5, *The Unforgiven?* At least a few of the norteamericanos who developed quickened interest in the frontier to the south cared little more for the rights of the area's natives than their forebears had cared for the rights of the Native Americans. And these Americans gave an extremely hard edge to the Good Neighbor's concern with economic expansion into Latin America. But the hard edge was only one among many that would-be new frontiersmen of the Depression era brought to their hopes and their actions in confronting the lands to the south.

The hard edge of frontier mythology appeared to influence Henry Morgenthau when he recommended to FDR in 1939 "a financial Monroe Doctrine which I hope will be called the Roosevelt Doctrine."[7] The Roosevelt administration never publicly articulated a financial Monroe Doctrine, the underlying principle of which involved setting Latin America apart as a preserve for U.S. investments, a preserve largely closed to trans-Atlantic and trans-Pacific powers. Still, the essence of the Morgenthau suggestion did become one of many Good Neighbor objectives. But, just how hard-edged was Morgenthau? There can be little doubt, I think, that, unlike many nineteenth-century frontiersmen, Morgenthau conceived a new frontier strategy based on symbiosis, in which Latin American natives and gringo newcomers would share mutually in the benefits of development. He did not cast Latin Americans in the role of American Indians. Furthermore, he assumed that North American capitalists, under the New Deal's watchful eye, would behave more equitably with Latin Americans than would European or Japanese investors.

Brain-truster and State Department official and all-around economic guru Adolf A. Berle, Jr., already encountered more than once in these pages, also saw symbiosis as the objective for Americans in Latin American frontier development. Perhaps even more than Morgenthau, the rabidly isolationist Berle wanted to exclude Europeans and Asiatics from the pioneering task of developing Latin American resources. It was his country's destiny, he believed, to develop the full potential of the vast reaches to the south.[8] However, it was ethnocentric moralism more than covetousness that motivated Berle. In order to contribute toward economic and social justice, Berle believed (even as Morgenthau) that the southern continent's potential must be developed by a "rationalized," state-supervised form of capitalism—the same type of capitalism that he wanted to see replace the ways of the robber barons in the United States. Rationalized development, under the aegis of reformed U.S. capitalism, would ostensibly guarantee benefits to private investors, both American and Latin American, while also resulting in maximum wages for labor and optimum all-around social development. In rather more tentative manner, Woodrow Wilson had once toyed with similar ideas.

Arguably, the Berle approach was more soft- than hard-edged. But many students of the Good Neighbor era have their doubts about this, just as they have their doubts about the intended purposes of domestic New Deal programs carried out in rural, underdeveloped parts of the United States. The analogy they draw between domestic and Latin American development programs deserves a moment's attention.

Whatever the announced New Deal intentions, what actually happened in North America's remaining frontiers of relative underdevelopment was this: mammoth projects carried out in the Tennessee Valley and many a far-western river valley bestowed their rewards primarily on large private corporate interests while leaving the common men and women trapped in marginal existences. In short, state socialism was manipulated in such a way as to privilege already privileged persons. Critics of the Good Neighbor policy's economic thrust contend the Roosevelt administration had similar objectives in mind for Latin America. The critics assume, without ever being able to prove their assumption (any more than their adversaries can totally disprove it), that the result of state-sponsored development in the Tennessee River basin and in the West was foreseen and consciously pursued from the very beginning; and they maintain that pursuit of analogous results inspired the Good Neighbor's economic approach to Latin America. Allegedly, the intended beneficiaries in both instances were capitalist conglomerates, owned exclusively by U.S. economic giants within their country's domestic confines, and, to the south, owned jointly by U.S. and Latin American economic titans.

Perhaps, though, as is generally the case in human events, the ultimate consequences of policies were not foreseen by those who formulated them. Perhaps the showering of principal benefits on the powerful and the well-connected in once underdeveloped regions of the United States came about fortuitously and at cross-purposes to the intentions of those who designed the development programs. Perhaps, too, Berle and the many officials who supported his approach to Latin America really sought not the aggrandizement of persons already powerful, but the kind of broad-based social development that they said they sought. So, were Berle and his fellow Good Neighbor planners really hard-edged, bottom-line-watching economic manipulators out to serve their country's predatory capitalists? Or, however naive, were they would-be humanitarians and champions of the common men and women, on either side of the border? After the many books and dozens of articles that have been written on the matter, the case remains open.

Fundamentally, perhaps all that is involved is the tendency for government controls whenever imposed to wind up enhancing the perquisites of the very types of persons the controls were designed to whittle down to lesser dimensions. Bureaucratic intentions invariably are thwarted and reversed by private-enterprise cunning and/or deviousness. But this does not mean that the public sector's announced intentions are disingenuous to begin with.

British historian Godfrey Hodgson has sketched the rise, beginning early in the twentieth century, of a group of well-to-do U.S. international lawyers who often won appointment to important policy-making posts in government and who regarded mere economic pursuits as somehow sordid, wasting little sympathy on persons seemingly driven purely by motives of economic aggrandizement.[9] Could he be right when he suggests that persons of this sort played an important role in shaping the intentions of New Deal, and by implication, of Good Neighbor policies? I would assume he *could* be right, however much historians of the old or the new left regard such an assumption as, at best, naive.

What are we to conclude about Roosevelt's secretary of state? Does Cordell Hull exemplify some of the "soft" features that Hodgson attributes to a new breed of statesmen in America? Or, does he fit in the category of hard-nosed economic imperialists, of the sort that many observers on the left deem typical of the whole Good Neighbor approach to Latin America? The issue is important because Hull is coming to be recognized as having played a genuinely important role in shaping the Good Neighbor policy.

Once it was fashionable to dismiss Hull as little more than a foul-tempered bungler, incompetent to run the State Department, and almost always eclipsed in the formulation of Latin American policy by Sumner Welles—a man Hull detested, in part because of his allegedly "socialist" ideas. By the 1980s, however, historians had begun to regard Hull not as a mediocrity but as a genuine policy-making heavyweight, as a person whose advice was sought and sometimes followed by his president, as a statesman whose influence on Latin American policy was just as great as Sumner Welles's.[10] What, then, can be said about this possibly influential shaper of hemispheric policy?

There's no doubt about Hull's obsessive conviction that the world could solve its economic problems by embracing free trade. Hull's great accomplishment as secretary of state was to rebuild the world trading system from the ruins inherited from President Hoover's high-tariff administration. In all, he negotiated twenty-seven trade treaties, many of them with Latin American republics. These treaties became the basis, "after World War II, for the General Agreement on Tariffs and Trade (GATT)" and for what one observer describes as "the greatest economic boom in history."[11] Yet Hull's critics, and they include virtually all liberal and left-leaning analysts, insist that the secretary of state's passion for free trade with Latin America exemplified the crassest sort of "free-trade imperialism," motivated by the desire to gain economic suzerainty over less developed countries through trade arrangements that opened their markets to American manufactures while discouraging the development of their own national industries.

Hull's detractors have a point. So do his defenders. The latter, while sometimes conceding that free-trade policies tended generally to benefit the U.S. economy more than the economies of Latin America, see another side to the issue. They contend that Hull relied upon New Deal reforms to enhance the likelihood that Yankee firms in Latin America would be forced to operate in fair and statesmanlike ways that would confer as many benefits on local governments and laborers as upon the foreign investors. He sincerely believed, say his defenders, that U.S. firms, under the watchful eye of New Dealers, were likely to pay higher wages and higher taxes, while settling for lower profit margins, than local Latin American enterprises. Out of the approach pursued by American firms, he believed, would issue maximum economic development below the border, especially as this approach began to exercise a demonstrator effect and to influence Latin Americans in their own economic practices. In short, he, like Franklin Roosevelt himself and like Berle, pursued the old ideals of Woodrow Wilson in seeking to reform American business before unleashing it on Latin America. And, like Wilson and Roosevelt and Berle, Hull honestly believed, whether naively or not, that American firms, as supervised by a reform-minded Democratic administration, would deal more equitably with Latin Americans than business enterprises based in Europe or Japan—possibly, even more equitably than Latin American firms, at least until they had been influenced by the example of U.S. enterprise at its best.

To some limited degree at least Hull's expectations were not altogether visionary. Indeed, some Latin American economic nationalists during the 1930s had to tone down the rhetoric they directed against foreign enterprise precisely because local workers had developed a strong preference for employment by Yankee-owned rather than national firms. Moreover, Latin governments came to relish the higher taxes they could generally extract from Yankee than from locally owned firms.

On the other hand, there is the undeniable fact that Hull in general supported the hemispheric views of Spruille Braden, a man who served as ambassador to Colombia, Cuba, and eventually Argentina during the Good Neighbor era. Braden proved admirably capable of serving U.S. security interests and performed yeoman service (1937–1938) in mediating the Chaco War between Paraguay and Bolivia. Still, he often incited Latin American ill will by his readiness to brandish the big stick in defense of any and all American investors in Latin America, whether of the reformed and socially conscious variety or of the Neanderthal type. Indeed, Braden himself, who later in life became a member of the archconservative John Birch Society, was what I would consider a Neanderthal type of capitalist. Persuaded that in all places and in all times only unrestrained and unencumbered free-enterprise capitalism could accomplish worthwhile human objectives, Braden gloried in the fact—as he saw it—that Americans above all other people of the world had learned to apply free enterprise in its purest form. Any endeavor to curb them in their free-enterprise pursuits smacked of perversity, perhaps even of communism or fascism. Like international lawyer Chandler Anderson, cited near the beginning of Chapter 16, Braden seemed to believe that natives of the entire "uncivilized" world depended for whatever prosperity they might hope to attain "upon the continued and successful operation of the foreign owned oil wells and mines and agricultural properties."[12]

In part, but only in part, the Good Neighbor policy was carried out by Braden and men of his ilk. For them, natives of the lands to the south were indeed like the Indians of the American frontier: they must be made to take to the ways of civilization even if it killed them—killed, that is, the culture that had shaped them.

So, the Good Neighbor policy did have its hard edge. In most instances, though, it is extremely difficult to build a convincing case that the policy responded primarily to the urge to help private U.S. enterprise suck maximum amounts of economic blood out of Latin America.

As to the man at the top, how stood FDR on some of those issues that determine whether he was a hard or a soft Good Neighbor?

# 20.

## FDR: What Kind of a Good Neighbor?

❖ ❖ ❖ ❖ ❖ ❖ ❖ ❖ ❖ ❖ ❖ ❖ ❖ ❖ ❖ ❖ ❖ ❖ ❖ ❖ ❖ ❖ ❖ ❖ ❖ ❖ ❖ ❖ ❖ ❖ ❖ ❖ ❖ ❖ ❖ ❖

### The Hard and the Soft Edges of a Good Neighbor

Behind the soft approach that some Americans adopted toward Latin America in the 1930s lay the lingering appeal of what historian Arthur P. Whitaker in a classic 1954 study called "the Western Hemisphere Idea." In essence, the Western Hemisphere Idea rests on the conviction that mystical affinities create unique bonds among the peoples of the American hemisphere, all the way from the northernmost reaches of Canada down to the Straits of Magellan.[1] It is an idea that pertains to the power of a unique place—its telluric influences, if you will—to take precedence over genetic inheritance and historical-cultural backgrounds in determining, over time, the nature of the people who occupy it. It is a belief in nurture over nature, of environment over heredity; and it may even smack of the subsequently rejected Lamarckian notion of the inheritability of acquired characteristics that flourished in the nineteenth century—and even on into the twentieth century, especially among Marxists.

Enjoying some considerable vogue at the time of the Latin American independence movement early in the nineteenth century, by century's end the Western Hemisphere Idea had passed decidedly out of style in the increasingly ethnocentric United States. During the Depression era, though, it enjoyed a bit of a renaissance, nourished by the pervasive isolation-from-Europe mood and the ability of more Americans than usual, in an era of shattered self-confidence, to look upon Latin Americans almost as equals.

During those times of adversity, University of California scholar Herbert Eugene Bolton (briefly alluded to in Chapter 2) contributed a new variation to the theme of Western Hemisphere unity: a variation that in its own way buttressed the Western Hemisphere Idea. In his 1932 presidential address to the American Historical Association Bolton, who had done perhaps more than any single figure in the United States to popularize the university-level teaching of Latin American history, suggested that Americans, North and South, were bound together by reason of having forged a common history in responding to their shared New World experience.[2]

Insofar as a "soft" approach to Latin America was shaped by the idea of a common history or of mystical bonds that united, distinguished, and set apart all occupants of the New World, there was nothing soft about Franklin Roosevelt's approach to hemispheric relations. As I argue at the conclusion of this chapter and in the following chapter, Roosevelt was far more European- than hemispheric-oriented in his values and concepts. Above all, there was nothing in him to suggest the starry-eyed glorification of the purportedly more spiritual, less materialistic "primitive" Other, nothing to indicate a longing to join with that Other so as to be reborn—nothing, in short, of the distinguishing traits of some of the mystic and mythopoeic American thinkers alluded to earlier in this text.

Nevertheless, the cult of primitivism, the resuscitation of the Western Hemisphere Idea, and the advent of the Bolton thesis all contributed to a new and more accepting way, among many North Americans, of looking on Latin Americans. And FDR was able to take advantage of these new intellectual trends in garnering support for his hemispheric policy, which he was shrewd enough occasionally to depict as rather more romantic, mystical, and soft-edged than in reality it was.

As for FDR personally, though, there was more of a leaning toward a "black legend" than a common-history-of-the-Americas or Western Hemisphere Idea approach. His already quoted letter to his mother describing his initial response to Panama indicates a belief that something had gone wrong in Latin America, perhaps from the moment that backward natives were conquered by and began to interbreed with cruel Iberians. At the same time, he was quite capable of believing that Latin Americans, with the helping hand of North Americans, could overcome flaws of origin and eventually create and enjoy the fruits of advanced civilization. If there was a valid Western Hemisphere Idea or a common history of the Americas, that idea, that history would, so far as FDR was concerned, find fulfillment in the future. One would look vainly to the past, though, for signs of hemispheric cultural unity.

Insofar as FDR may personally have been in any way "soft" in his approach to Latin America, that softness arose simply out of his desire—like George Messersmith's and Adolf Berle's and Sumner Welles's and arguably like Cordell Hull's—to create situations in which Yankee capital at work in Latin America produced results beneficial not only to Yankees but to Latin Americans as well, thereby helping slowly to elevate the latter to the levels of civilization long since achieved by norteamericanos. Reciprocity was as far as FDR's softness extended: the hope that Americans and Latin Americans could derive reciprocal advantages from the operations of North American capitalists, whom the president saw not just as money-creating creatures but as agents of uplift, once they were properly leashed and domesticated. In all of this there was, of course, a considerable element of ethnocentrism; in all of it, too, there was a good dose of Wilsonian thought. Like his Democratic predecessor in the White House, Roosevelt believed cross-border U.S. economic operations need not be a zero-sum game in which there were winners and losers. If properly controlled, those operations could evolve into a non-zero-sum game, in which there were winners and winners. For this to come about, however, both North Americans and Latin Americans, and especially the latter, had a great deal of shaping up to do.

With Latin America in mind, FDR (as noted earlier) once admonished his fellow citizens: "Give them a share." Left to their own devices, North Americans might not be willing to cut Latin Americans in on an adequate share. FDR, taking up where Wilson had left off, wanted to make sure that henceforth his compatriots would extend Latins a better share—but without imposing on his countrymen the sort of excessive restraints that would unduly have hindered them from making large enough bundles of profits to make sharing worthwhile.

When asked on one occasion to identify his greatest accomplishment, FDR replied it had been to save American capitalism, "that combination of free enterprise and individual rights that, to him, characterized the society." However much he criticized some of his fellow Americans for their frequent failure to pay sufficient heed to broader social concerns, Roosevelt consistently argued for personal initiative and responsibility.[3] Still, to the abiding dismay of his domestic foes, the president assumed that government had to play a role in making sure that personal initiative did not suffocate social responsibility. Roosevelt's acceptance of the need for government intervention so as to harness individual initiative to the common good placed him very much within the already mentioned Iberian corporatist grain. As much as anything else the Roosevelt concern for balancing the realms of individual initiative and state controls accounted for his success in winning personal admiration and support for his Good Neighbor policy from Latin Americans. Appropriately, Puerto Rico—occupying an intermediate position between North Americans and Latin Americans—figured in Roosevelt's initiation of the quest to balance individual initiative with concern for the commonweal.

Brain-truster Charles W. Taussig, who played an important role in shaping American policy toward the Puerto Rican commonwealth (part U.S. colony, part self-governing entity), persuaded the Roosevelt administration that economic intervention in the form of job-creation and housing programs would actually help save market capitalism by taking the wind out of radicalism's sails. FDR went along with this analysis, and encouraged the sort of reforms Taussig had in mind for Puerto Rico.[4] Similarly, he condoned the economic and social interventionist policies to which many Latin American governments resorted in the 1930s. His enemies grumbled that FDR thereby was helping to finish off the tender seeds of capitalism that American investors had planted south of the border. The president thought otherwise.

### FDR and the American Hemisphere Cartel Idea: Security Concerns Begin to Transform Hemispheric Policy

In some ways President Roosevelt's major direct and hands-on foray into forging hemispheric policy, prior to U.S. entry into the World War, came in 1940 in connection with his spirited but ultimately unsuccessful advocacy of a so-called inter-American cartel (in bureaucratic infighting, even the president sometimes lost). The cartel idea—conceived largely by Adolf A. Berle, Jr., even though he hated the cartel designation that others attached to his plan—arose in response to massive accumulation of surplus commodities that glutted Latin American countries cut off from their usual European customers by wartime conditions. The cartel plan called for American financing of a huge trading corporation that would assume responsibility for marketing New World exports.

Predictably, the cartel concept provoked spirited attack both from right and left in Washington. Attacks from the right focused on the charge that the cartel signified intrusion of epic proportions into a sphere best left to market mechanisms. In fact, conservative critics (many of them Democrats) saw the cartel as an attempt to introduce on a hemispheric scale the sort of massive government intervention and economic "rationalization" that the Supreme Court and "right-thinking" congressmen and senators had managed to prevent New Deal zealots from introducing within the United States. Then, there were the critics from the left. Some of them saw—and have continued through the years to see—the cartel scheme as a callow attempt to gain monopolistic U.S. control over the entire Latin American economy and to eliminate the presence of foreign business rivals. Freed from foreign competition south of the border, American capitalists could henceforth write their own ticket in dealing with a southern continent rendered totally dependent on the north. Such, at least, was the argument with which many leftists denounced the cartel plan and castigated the president for supporting it.[5]

Looking back nostalgically on the aborted cartel, its advocates have seen it as a high-minded, statesmanlike project by means of which Roosevelt hoped to banish from the hemisphere the sort of free-trade imperialism through which Britain controlled and, in their view and the president's, economically exploited her colonies. "Rationalization" of the hemisphere's economies, cartel apologists contend, could have served as a model for postwar Britain and perhaps for France as well, demonstrating to them how to transform old colonial structures into commonwealths cleansed of the inequities of imperialism. This may or may not be reading too much into Roosevelt's position, although there is no question that FDR did hope the Good Neighbor policy ultimately would yield a model for equitable relations between great and minor countries that Old World powers would emulate. At the time, though, in 1940, his primary concern lay with security.

The president's hope for hemispheric commercial policies that were hammered out by all the countries of the Americas originated in the desire to forestall economic control over any Latin American country that a potential enemy of the United States (Germany, Italy, or Japan) might have acquired through bilateral trade agreements. However, even for ordinary and relatively risk-free times, Roosevelt and his advisers coveted circumstances in which the United States and Latin America would grow strong together, through mutually agreed upon terms of economic intercourse; this they deemed infinitely preferable to a situation in which Latin economies were integrated into those of trans-Atlantic or trans-Pacific powers. In part this preference arose out of the ethnocentric, chauvinistic conviction most clearly evident in Woodrow Wilson, but fully shared by Roosevelt since his youth, that the United States, once cleansed in its economic institutions by Democratic-inspired, made-in-Washington reforms, would operate more beneficently in Latin America than European or Asiatic powers. Even for normal times, the Wilson-Roosevelt hemispheric perception revealed a suspiciousness toward large-scale economic ties between Latin America and the Old World—at least until the Old World had been cured of its alleged proclivities to make of overseas trade and investment a zero-sum game.

In 1940, times were far from normal, and security considerations lay primarily behind Roosevelt's backing of the cartel scheme. Already as 1940 began Roosevelt had fretted for months over the possibility of an actual invasion of South America or Mexico by a foreign power that might become a military adversary of the United States. Even more he worried about the indirect and therefore more difficult to counteract threat that would arise should a potential foreign foe gain control over the economy of a Latin American country, and subsequently establish creeping political control. This was a concern that any responsible American statesman had to address as of 1940. Economic determinists who see behind the Good Neighbor policy only bottom-line financial motivation—focused on assuring maximum profits for private U.S. firms—consistently misread that policy, insofar as Roosevelt personally had anything to do with it, even as it evolved between 1933 and 1940; but they misread it most egregiously from 1940 onward. Not in 1940, not in 1933, not in the years in between did Roosevelt concern himself just or even primarily with a hard policy in hemispheric affairs, with a policy calculated exclusively or even primarily to result in maximum immediate profits for American capitalists at the expense of the just interests of Latin Americans.

By the early 1990s, many (perhaps even the majority) of Latin America's leaders seemed (at least for the moment) to have come around to the conclusion that their best hopes for economic development lay in adopting and adapting many of the practices of U.S.-style market capitalism: a style broad enough to include Roosevelt's concept of state-supervised market capitalism. For having perceived this possibility and dared occasionally to act upon it in the 1930s, FDR continues to be tarred by America's anticapitalist intelligentsia and the free marketeers as well. Both sides reject the combination of opposites implied by state-supervised market capitalism or, as the envisaged system was more commonly designated in the 1990s, social capitalism.

### FDR *and the* E Pluribus Unum *Concept*

In his conceptualization of the hemisphere's future and America's role in helping shape it, Roosevelt departed from the Wilsonian framework within which so many of his foreign policy ideas had been formed. Wilson had seen unity emerging out of an eventual conversion of Latin America to the political and economic culture of North Americans. The avid Presbyterian was very much the missionary at heart, out to convert Latin America not to his Protestant faith, necessarily, but to the American civil religion. Less religiously driven than Wilson, more tolerant of diversity, Roosevelt did not envision a hemispheric harmony based on an all-inclusive conversion of Latin Americans to North America's civil religion. Though he believed that Latin Americans eventually would come around to political democracy, and to state-mediated market capitalism that might gradually shift away a bit from the state and toward the market (depending on how well private capitalists were domesticated), he also believed that cultural differences between North and South would remain; and he did not see in these differences a cause of concern for the dominant member in the hemispheric partnership.

If the United States could demonstrate that within its own hemisphere it could forge an international system less exploitive and less given to producing the sort of friction that brought on wars, then the Old World might begin to attend to the New World; then its leaders might emulate American ways and reconcile themselves to the destiny of surrendering the mantle of international leadership to the country that had originated in thirteen rebellious colonies. Here was a heady dream indeed. But then Roosevelt liked to dream on the grand scale.

Even from the inception of the Good Neighbor policy, something far more compelling and also far more grandiose than mere national economic self-interest drove Roosevelt in his approach to Latin America. So far as he was concerned, hemispheric policy above all else provided the means, the springboard, whereby the United States ultimately could assume a role of paramount significance among those countries that truly interested him: the countries of the Old World, both Atlantic and Pacific. For Roosevelt, Latin America was the minor league wherein he and his compatriots could develop the skills needed to become dominant players in the major leagues of diplomacy's great game.

Latin America mattered to Roosevelt because if he could begin to accomplish his intentions within the hemisphere, then there might be some hope of accomplishing them in the world. A grandiose and conceited concept? Of course; but one at least marked by the cultural relativism of the era and by Whitman's "all-inclosing" spirit rather than by Wilson's culturally monistic approach to the hemisphere and the world.

Roosevelt's lifelong obsession with accommodating opposites, his tendency to tell his assistants to blend together utterly divergent policies, and his expectation that somehow they could actually do so resonate not just with opportunism and fuzzy-mindedness but also with the mystical and utopian elements that have often entered into the American dream. His obsession also reflects the sort of naivete that for a time led him to believe that even democracy and communism could peacefully and fruitfully cohabit, at least in concubinage if not in sanctified matrimony.

Definitely not a Boltonian who believed in a common history, Roosevelt saw vast differences in the American and Latin American pasts, differences that so far as he was concerned reflected unfavorably on Latin Americans. At the same time he was too hard-headed and practical and perhaps also too ethnocentric to succumb to the tenets of the Western Hemisphere Idea and to imagine a future in which cultural differences among Americans, North and South, would disappear. In his own way, though, he was even more visionary than true believers in the Western Hemisphere Idea; for he believed that out of diversity could come unity, a unity in which diversity still existed. Within his own country, FDR sought to revitalize the great American myth of e pluribus unum; beyond that, he hoped to bring the e pluribus unum principle to life on a hemispheric scale.

Roosevelt toyed with the belief that under Washington's inspiration and benign leadership Americans, North and South, could establish bonds of amity that would quite transcend differences of culture, of religious, social, political, and economic values (even if not for the moment differences of race). And the dream did not end there. Once it was fulfilled in the New World, why could it not come to life in virtually the whole world? First America, then the world.

# 21. *First the Hemisphere, Then the World*

❖ ❖ ❖ ❖ ❖ ❖ ❖ ❖ ❖ ❖ ❖ ❖ ❖ ❖ ❖ ❖ ❖ ❖ ❖ ❖ ❖ ❖ ❖ ❖ ❖ ❖ ❖ ❖ ❖ ❖ ❖ ❖ ❖

## *Isolationism and the Origins of the Hemispheric System: A Quick Review*

Never able to speak Spanish, Roosevelt as a youth was reasonably comfortable in the French and German languages, and (as already indicated in Chapter 13) by age fifteen a veteran of eight trips to Europe, where he had been introduced to social elites and members of the governing classes. A number of foreign periodicals arrived each month at the Hyde Park home in which he grew up, but none from Latin America, Spain, or Portugal. Roosevelt's lack of concern for Latin America as a young man, a lack of concern bordering on contempt, is beyond doubt and has been referred to in earlier pages. In this Roosevelt was by no means unusual; he merely reflected the attitudes of typical East Coast products of well-to-do families educated at exclusive boarding schools and at Harvard or Yale or other Ivy League universities. These attitudes created a predisposition to look eastward across the Atlantic when thinking about foreign relations of consequence. One looked southward only at those times when it seemed imperative to discipline wayward, recalcitrant republics.

In the 1930s, though, Roosevelt along with the majority of Americans of all classes settled into isolationist attitudes that caused their transAtlantic interests to wither. They were disillusioned by Europe's petty squabbling and trade wars, by its clinging to the old ways of imperialism that had already contributed once to plunging much of the world into war. Europeans, in Roosevelt's view and in that of most other Americans, whether privileged East Coasters or heartland commoners, seemed to have learned little from the great war and persisted still in the policies that had brought it on. Moreover, European powers had developed a reluctance to settle foreign debts that was approaching Latin American proportions.

If Roosevelt had one fixed idea on foreign relations when he entered the White House it was that "an open world trading system would do more than anything else to remove . . . occasions for conflict."[1] But Europe was in no mood to consider sweeping reforms of its trade system, or even to mitigate the old imperialism that presented the most flagrant example of restricted trade. Certainly at the London Economic Conference, held shortly after FDR's inauguration, Old World powers showed no disposition to mend their ways; and from that time on until the late 1930s (some historians say until 1940) FDR joined the general electorate in disillusionment about Europe, in preferring—most of the time, at least—to steer clear of involvement in its affairs, while expanding attentiveness to Latin America. One historian sums the situation up this way: "Shut out of European deliberations by its governments and domestic opposition, and frustrated by Japanese ambitions in the Far East, the president moved toward internationalism through the only available opening."[2]

Quite by historical accident Latin America began to intrigue the president, even if he never did abandon his contempt for small or undeveloped nations in general. At least by refining and perfecting relations with those weak nations to the south it might be possible for him to enhance America's diplomatic prestige and rebuild its economic strength so that at some future time the Old World would begin to take seriously the New World as Roosevelt had remade it.

### Delusions of Grandeur and Roosevelt's Attempt to Move from the Hemispheric to the International Arena

By the beginning of 1937, following his personal triumph at the Buenos Aires Special Inter-American Conference for the Preservation of Peace, it seemed to Roosevelt that the U.S.-led New World deserved as never before to be taken seriously in the capitals of Europe, where war clouds were gathering ominously and general disarray and bewilderment prevailed. At Buenos Aires in December of 1936 the American states had committed themselves to consultation in case of a threat to the peace of any one of them. Thereby, so it seemed, the Monroe Doctrine had undergone transformation from a unilateral declaration into a multilateral pact. By this time, moreover, the United States, aided by the patient and effective diplomacy waged by that paladin of free-enterprise capitalism Spruille Braden, was steering Paraguay and Bolivia toward the 1938 treaty that officially ended their bloody and protracted struggle over the Gran Chaco. By this time, too, the bilateral tariff agreements masterminded by Cordell Hull had begun to erode traditional barriers to commercial exchange.

What is more, whether in Rio or in Buenos Aires or in Montevideo, FDR had received demonstrations of public adulation, apparently arising out of the perception of him as an emissary of a new hemispheric order. Could impartial observers doubt, then, that America was well on the way to establishing a showcase system wherein the mighty and the relatively impotent could deal in harmony, wherein all partners could trade without serious impediment, wherein multilateral mechanisms assured the maintenance of peace? Did not these accomplishments indicate that the New World, led by Washington, had pioneered the development of a model for international order that could be expanded to worldwide dimensions? Was it not time for the Old World to heed what the Americas had accomplished, and to follow suit? With a bundle of triumphs in American-hemisphere diplomacy to point to, was it not time for the American president to turn his attention to Europe so as to point its fractious, antediluvian components toward the new world order that they had been unable, on their own, even to conceive?

In 1826 British Foreign Minister George Canning, referring to the assistance his country had rendered Latin Americans in their independence struggle and at the same time minimizing whatever contributions the United States might have made, declared: "I called the New World into existence to redress the balance of the Old."[3] In 1937, back in Washington from his Latin American triumphs, Roosevelt could well believe that *he* had called a New World into existence, a New World that could by its power of example lead the Old World to redress its imbalances and enter into a new day of open markets and prosperity and peace.

In the aftermath of his overwhelming reelection victory and of his South American triumphs at the end of 1936, Roosevelt succumbed for a time (as I have previously suggested), on both domestic and international fronts, to delusions of grandeur. Political setbacks at home soon showed him that he had to deal more cautiously and respectfully with entrenched interests hostile to New Deal reforms. And the trans-Atlantic rebuffs Roosevelt received in 1937 and 1938 as he sought to move America from the edge to the center of the world and to show European powers how to solve their problems proved just as stinging as those inflicted by the Supreme Court, by entrenched conservative enclaves throughout the country, and by the electorate in the 1938 midterm elections.

Hitler and Mussolini were downright mocking in their rejection of Roosevelt's bid to resolve European problems by following recently devised New World expedients. Although not openly so scathing as Hitler and Mussolini in rejecting Roosevelt's offers to be helpful, Winston Churchill seethed inwardly. His anger came in no small part from Roosevelt's insistence that Britain abandon its imperialism in favor of worldwide free markets. Churchill believed he detected here simply Roosevelt's desire to open new fields to American capital. In France, statesmen and writers also rejected American meddling. Some of them wondered how a country that had (allegedly) made such a mess of its Puerto Rican colony could deign to raise with Europeans issues that touched on imperialism.[4]

## World War II and America's Return to the International Arena

Ultimately, after the military calamities that led to the Dunkirk evacuation in 1940, Churchill did tend to look to the United States to save Europe, but by the power of its military machine rather than through the lessons in political science and international economics it had learned from dealing with Latin America. Following the Dunkirk debacle Churchill summoned the full and awesome powers of his oratory and delivered one of the great speeches of history. "We shall not flag or fail," he declared. "We shall go on to the end, we shall fight in France, we shall fight on the seas and oceans . . . whatever the cost may be, we shall fight on the beaches, we shall fight on the landing grounds, we shall fight in the hills, we shall never surrender." Even though the island homeland itself might be subjugated and starving, the fight would go on; for Britain would draw on its empire beyond the seas, "armed and guarded by the British Fleet." Britain would fight on "until, in God's good time, the New World, with all its power and might, steps forth to the rescue and the liberation of the old."[5] In ways never foreseen by Canning, Churchill looked to the New World to redress the balance of the Old.

Ultimately, the United States did rescue the Old World, not by the example of its new hemispheric system but by the tangible might that issued out of its factories. These were the factories that some Americans in deepest Depression days had assumed would never hum again, or would hum so softly as scarcely to disturb the bucolic serenity of the rural fields in which they had been relocated by a people turned sensitive to the wonders of nature and of nonmaterial rewards—like those wonderful peasants in Mexico laboring in their communal fields and occasionally taking time out to produce a few items in factories where machines were admitted, as Stuart Chase had put it, "only on good behavior."

The war ended a good deal of romantic nonsense that had flourished in the early Good Neighbor era. But throughout the war Roosevelt continued to believe in his own brand of romanticism: he continued to believe that the American hemisphere, under the guidance of those who had fashioned the Good Neighbor policy, had indeed pioneered the sort of international system that would guide Europe to serenity and economic development in the postwar world.

In the heroic British struggle and in the inspired rhetoric of Churchill, Americans began to find a grandeur that they had never found in Latin America, even in the palmiest days of gushing good neighborliness. Latin America might have provided comic, primitive relief to worried and harassed Americans, but Britain was now demonstrating the sort of heroism that reawakened pride in the mother country, its heritage, and its grandeur. As isolationism waned, so also did the interest in Latin America that to some degree had grown out of isolationism. All of a sudden the Latin American republics once more seemed pretty small beer. From this time on, Americans would judge Latins only by the enthusiasm of the support they lent the struggle that really mattered, the one going on in Europe and in the Pacific.

## World War II and American Aspirations for International Leadership

The war, not the breakthroughs in international relations the United States had wrought in its dealings with lesser neighbors to the south, fulfilled Roosevelt's hope to assume an honored place among the powers of the Old World. He persisted, however, in his conviction that what he had wrought in the American hemisphere through the Good Neighbor policy should serve as the foundation on which Europe and Asia would reconstruct themselves once Hitler and Mussolini and Hirohito had been crushed. Old-school imperialist blocs should disappear, free trade should replace closed markets, and disputes should be resolved through an international system modeled on the formulas that the Good Neighbor had developed for dealing with the once troublesome republics to the south: formulas that while paying lip service to equality realistically accorded *de facto* primacy to the mighty.

Throughout the war, Roosevelt periodically repeated the message he had first proclaimed in his April 14, 1939, Pan American Day address: let the European nations prepare, once peace returned, to adopt pledges against aggression similar to those that the twenty-one American republics had adopted. Such pledges, along with the "open door of trade and intercourse," would make dreams of conquest appear as "ridiculous and criminal" to Europeans as they had already begun to appear to Americans.[6] Repeatedly after 1939, Roosevelt continued to cite the American-hemisphere formulas that he had called into being as an example to Old World nations of how to achieve peaceful coexistence. Especially at the 1943 Tehran conference that brought him together with Churchill and Stalin, President Roosevelt held forth on this topic.

At Tehran, Roosevelt conducted for the leader of the USSR what one historian describes as a "seminar on the Good Neighbor Policy." He concluded the seminar with an observation that might cast some doubt on the sincerity of his Good Neighbor embrace of Latin Americans. The president suggested that Stalin would find it comparatively easy to become a good neighbor because he would be dealing with the Slavic nations that adjoined Russia: nations that "were 'nearer in blood' to the Russians than were Latin Americans to the United States."[7] Differences in blood might not mean anything to Eleanor Roosevelt, but I suspect they still did mean something to her husband—as they did to the overwhelming majority of Americans.

The following year Assistant Secretary of State Adolf Berle reflected Roosevelt's thinking in advocating a Soviet "sphere of influence" in Eastern Europe "modeled on America's role in Mexico and the Caribbean." While insisting on economic openness in that area and in the rest of Latin America as well, Roosevelt also envisioned (according to Berle) assumption by the United States of the role of "policeman," so as to guarantee that its citizens would not be unfairly limited in their commercial intercourse.[8] Apparently Roosevelt, in this unusually hard-edged stance vis-à-vis Latin Americans as explicated by Berle, saw nothing wrong with Stalin's assuming in his sphere of particular interest the role of policeman. In Latin America, Roosevelt had demonstrated to his own satisfaction that a powerful country could play this role with even-handed fairness when dealing with the relatively powerless. That the objects of police-imposed good order might have felt differently hardly mattered.

Undoubtedly, Roosevelt was far too ready to extrapolate from the imagined successes of the Good Neighbor policy when anticipating the ways in which Stalin would deal with "minor" countries in his postwar Soviet sphere of influence. A plain old-fashioned Machiavellian simply did not know how to deal with a psychopath nourished by the new ideology of Marxism-Leninism.

Even great world leaders tend all too often to make the mistake of ordinary mortals: they tend to judge others by themselves. At least Roosevelt did not live long enough to discover how much many Latin Americans, whom he had thought converted to the Good Neighbor system, would in the postwar world respond less to the Machiavellian credo than to the Marxist political philosophy of the psychopath from Soviet Georgia. Perhaps their post–World War II response was not altogether surprising in view of the fact that throughout the war many Latin Americans had been philosophically attracted by the political-social doctrines of Hitler and Mussolini and Hirohito, despite the Good Neighbor's attempts to make it worth their while to pretend otherwise. People accustomed, as Latin

Americans had been, to enduring chronically hard times turn often to messianic promises of deliverance.

## From Regionalism to Internationalism: The United States in the Major Leagues

In a September 1943 letter to George W. Norris, the Nebraska representative in the lower chamber who fathered the bills that established the Tennessee Valley Authority, Roosevelt advanced the modest argument that beginning in 1933 the United States had planted the seeds in the American hemisphere of an ideal international relationship that replaced distrust with trust, and that provided a model for establishment of future peaceful and mutually beneficial relations among European powers. Immediate European prospects, he conceded, might not appear promising, because of "the very divisive nationalities and national egos of a vast number of separate people who, for one reason or another over a thousand years, have divided themselves into a hundred different forms of hate." But, the president continued, neither had the situation appeared promising when the United States at the outset of the Good Neighbor era had embarked on its mission to create a different kind of American hemisphere. In 1933, Roosevelt observed, "there were many times twenty-one different kinds of hate. They [the Latin Americans] disliked each other; they sought territorial expansion and material gain at the expense of their neighbors; and all of them united in common fear of the United States." But, beginning with the refusal to intervene in the Cuban crisis of 1933, North Americans had demonstrated they would leave the Latins alone to work out their own internal, domestic affairs, so long as they kept discord within their own territorial limits.

It took ten years, Roosevelt continued in his letter to Norris, to "sell the idea of peace and security among the American Republics. But today, there is substantial accord." With the hemispheric experience behind him, Roosevelt looked forward to achieving the same sort of success in future relations with Europe. That success, he thought, might come even more quickly than it had in the American hemisphere.[9]

In reminiscing to the Nebraskan about the origins and development of the Good Neighbor policy, Roosevelt clearly revealed that he regarded it primarily as a sort of dress rehearsal for the role the United States eventually would play in the area that really mattered: the Old World. He was concerned with making it in the major leagues; and to a large extent by the time he wrote Norris he had relatively little concern for the minor leagues where he had tried out some of the approaches that would, so he modestly hoped, change the way in which the game was played at the highest levels.

If not from the very outset, at least from the late 1930s Roosevelt had targeted the Good Neighbor policy as much toward Europe as toward Latin America, hoping that by hitting the desired target in the latter area he would prepare himself to score a bull's-eye in the former. As the war in Europe wound down in early 1945 Roosevelt—who died in April of that year—had lost interest in those republics that circumstances had forced him initially to accept as his only international relations laboratory. To the degree he still thought about those republics, he probably assumed that they would vote in the United Nations as Washington expected them to—just as he had boasted when campaigning for the vice presidency in 1920 that he had the votes of several Latin American republics in his pocket when it came to League of Nations issues. Inclined by 1945 to take Latin America for granted, Roosevelt was not even concerned about preserving for the inter-American regional system, forged through a number of meetings in the 1930s and early '40s, a place within the international organization that now commanded his attention: the United Nations.

Ultimately, only the insistence of the Latin American republics upon preserving the fruits of Good Neighbor diplomacy led to the inclusion in the United Nations charter of Article 52, which reserved a place for regional associations within the world organization. Had it not been for Latin American insistence, the United Nations, with its USSR veto, would have been, *de jure,* a principal arbiter of New World affairs.[10] Only by luck did the United States escape this outcome. Still, luck would never have played its role had not FDR, in the first place, helped allay Latin American suspiciousness of its northern neighbor through the Good Neighbor policy.

Roosevelt's indifference to the hemispheric system he had helped father may suggest that he never abandoned the disdain that as a young man he felt for Latin American republics and for small and relatively impotent countries in general. Disdain, though, is often fostered primarily by the objects of disdain. Perhaps in the case of Franklin Roosevelt, and many other Americans, disdain fed on wartime indications that not all Latin American republics lived up to the pretense, in which only Argentina did not join, of sharing full-heartedly in the struggle to defeat the Axis powers and their political ideology.

Actually, the fault—if fault there was—lay not so much with World War II–era Latin Americans as with historical circumstances that had immersed them in a political culture, in a civil religion, with little regard for one-person, one-vote democracy, for religious pluralism, and free-enterprise economic individualism.

# SECTION VI

❖❖❖❖❖❖❖❖❖❖❖❖❖❖❖❖❖❖❖❖❖❖❖❖❖❖❖❖❖❖❖❖❖❖❖

*Security Issues
and Good
Neighbor Tensions*

# 22. The Hemisphere in Danger

✧ ✧ ✧ ✧ ✧ ✧ ✧ ✧ ✧ ✧ ✧ ✧ ✧ ✧ ✧ ✧ ✧ ✧ ✧ ✧ ✧ ✧ ✧ ✧ ✧ ✧ ✧ ✧ ✧ ✧ ✧ ✧ ✧ ✧ ✧ ✧

### American Perceptions of Security Threats in Latin America, 1936–1939

As suggested in Chapter 18, one tries in vain to separate security from economic objectives in determining just what it was that drove the Good Neighbor policy. For the years between 1933 and 1937 economic determinists seem able to make a fairly convincing case, superficially at least, in explaining the Good Neighbor policy. In those years, the policy did seem economically motivated. From the president down, the persons who designed hemispheric policy concerned themselves primarily with figuring out how to cast the New World off from the economic doldrums in Europe and to summon a rising hemispheric tide that would lift all American boats. But, security was also a factor: security defined in terms of protecting established U.S. institutions against destruction threatened by internal economic collapse. By 1937, though, many a Good Neighbor policymaker, from the president on down, faced a different sort of security threat, one that originated across the seas.

Frances Perkins, Roosevelt's secretary of labor, once noted: "The President began to bring up the serious threats to peace in the Cabinet regularly in 1935; in 1936 he began nagging us about it; in 1937 he nagged on the subject all the time. . . . Yes, 1937 was the year he decided we really could not afford to bury our heads in the sand any longer." One distinguished diplomatic historian goes so far as to argue that already by 1935 FDR was convinced of the inevitability of U.S.-German confrontation.[1] If so, already by 1935 the president had to take very seriously the need for Latin America to contribute to, rather than detract from, U.S. security. At the same time, he had to assimilate Latin America into the U.S. effort to shore up its internal economy so that the United States would better be able to defend itself against external threats.

In 1936, witnessing Italy's successful absorption of Ethiopia, followed in March by Hitler's brazen repudiation of earlier nonaggression commitments, followed in the summer by the outbreak of the civil war in Spain, Roosevelt grew increasingly pessimistic about prospects for maintaining peace in Europe. In 1937, after the collapse of his fatuous dreams of acting as world peacemaker (dreams inspired by his triumph at the Buenos Aires Conference for the Maintenance of Peace), he grew more pessimistic still. In what came to be known as his "quarantine speech," delivered in Chicago in October 1937, the president remarked: "When an epidemic of physical disease starts to spread, the community approves and joins in a quarantine of the patients in order to protect the health of the community. . . . War is contagious. . . . There must be positive endeavors to preserve peace."

At an earlier point in the quarantine speech, FDR had directly linked the American hemisphere to the threat of war in Europe. If another major war erupted in Europe, he warned, "let no one imagine that America will escape, that America may expect mercy, that this Western Hemisphere will not be attacked and that it will continue tranquilly and peacefully to carry on the ethics and the arts of civilization."[2]

Some contemporary commentators as well as historians writing long after the event depict Roosevelt's quarantine speech as the opening salvo in a campaign to undermine the isolationist mood and prepare Americans for European intervention by inventing a threat to hemispheric security. If so, the ploy did not work. U.S. citizens remained solidly isolationist vis-à-vis the Old World. In any event, Roosevelt in 1938 returned to the argument that the American hemisphere was directly threatened by events in Europe. Not only must his fellow citizens awaken to the likelihood that Germany might seek economic control over Latin American republics; beyond that they must confront the possibility that a foreign foe would seek to secure military bases from which to launch operations against the United States.

At the beginning of 1939, as previously indicated in discussion of the Mexican petroleum nationalization crisis, FDR (when briefing the Senate Military Affairs Committee) stressed the creeping Nazi-fascist menace in Latin America. Indeed, he very likely exaggerated that menace, as he would justifiably continue to do during the next two to three years, in order to induce isolationist-minded policy-makers to wake up to the need to defend America's interests where they truly mattered: in Europe. Increasingly from that time on, Roosevelt pushed the idea that America's return to Europe, through the sending of military supplies, was the only sure way to avoid eventually having to defend democracy in the hemisphere itself.

On September 1, 1939, Roosevelt had scheduled a meeting with Sumner Welles to lay plans for a special Pan American conference to be held in the event of war in Europe. Some hours before Welles arrived, Ambassador to France William Bullitt had awakened Roosevelt with a call from Paris. His news was momentous but not unexpected. Hitler had invaded Poland, and France and England had decided to honor commitments to Poland. So, as Bullitt informed the president, a general European war was underway. Latin America now assumed a new urgency to American foreign policy planners. Therefore, the meeting with Welles proved of greater moment than either he or the president had anticipated.

Colonel Frank Knox, soon to become secretary of the Navy, began openly now to call for acquisition of Caribbean bases. "Certainly," he declared, "for the safety of the approaches to the Canal, we must make the Caribbean an American lake." A number of military authorities concurred wholeheartedly, arguing that for the first time in its history the United States might actually have to defend the hemisphere and that defense would be impossible without additional bases, "all the way from Labrador and Newfoundland, southward through Bermuda to Trinidad, the Guianas and Brazil."[3]

"The beauty of Social Darwinism," is has been observed, "was its devastating simplicity. The strong competed for domination of the weak."[4] Well, by 1940 it had come to this in the New World—or at least many Americans, the president included, thought it had. The strong, meaning the United States and the fascist powers, would compete for domination over the weak, meaning the Latin Americans. Rather than relying on brute force in the struggle, the United States would continue and indeed dramatically intensify the more subtle means it had been refining since 1933— some of them involving economic inducements that cynics saw as out-and-out bribery—to assure control over Latin Americans in vital matters of security.

### Europe at War and the Hemisphere (Allegedly) in Graver Danger: 1939–1941

During the dark days of late May and early June of 1940 as a steady stream of information poured in suggesting British vulnerability and German invincibility, a consensus began to emerge within the Roosevelt administration: in a struggle for its life, England might not win. Soon the United States might be "fighting the battle of its life in Latin America." The public mood reflected the administration's. In the summer of 1940 *Fortune* magazine published the results of an opinion poll. About 40 percent of Americans queried felt certain of an Axis victory, while only 30 percent believed Britain would win. Furthermore, 70 percent of those polled believed that Germany would try to gain control of South America, and that in order to prevent this the United States would have to fight Germany.[5]

In a Fireside Chat of December 1940, President Roosevelt shared his perspectives with the American public. "There are those who say that the Axis powers would never have any desire to attack the Western Hemisphere. That is the same dangerous form of wishful thinking which has destroyed the powers of resistance of so many conquered peoples." The vast resources of Latin America, Roosevelt assured his listeners, "constitute the most tempting loot in all of the round world." The president left the impression he did not expect the Axis powers to resist the temptation to grab at the loot. The following May in another Fireside Chat, the president declared: "The unity of the American republics is of supreme importance to each and every one of us and to the cause of freedom throughout the world. Our future, our future independence, is bound up with the future independence of all our sister republics." At the same time FDR maintained that Hitler had never considered the domination of Europe an end in itself. For Hitler, conquest of Europe was simply "a step toward ultimate goals in all the other continents."[6]

In September in yet another Fireside Chat the president returned to the Americas-in-peril theme. The ongoing Nazi endeavor to gain control of the seas constituted part of the larger project to gain mastery over the Western Hemisphere. Already Nazi plots to capture control of Uruguay and Argentina had been thwarted, as had a scheme to take over Bolivia, while "within the past few weeks" had come the discovery "of secret landing fields in Colombia, within easy range of the Panama Canal." The president added: "No tender whisperings of appeasers that Hitler is not interested in the Western Hemisphere, no soporific lullabies that a wide ocean protects us from him, can long have any effect on the hard-headed, farsighted, and realistic American people." At the same time, the president announced he possessed documents, including maps, that proved German and Italian intentions to establish a colonial empire in Latin America. Some years later it was proved that the German documents and maps FDR relied on to support his charge were forgeries—although the president very likely did not know this and some uncertainty still prevails as to the provenance of the forgeries, although most investigators point the finger at Britain.[7] However that may be, Roosevelt by 1940 apparently did not scruple over exaggerating the threat in Latin America in order to persuade Americans that Europe was the New World's first line of defense and that soon the moment might be at hand to defend the hemisphere by entering the war overseas.

Historians including Ronald C. Newton, Robert Dallek, and Irwin F. Gellman (among many others) have convincingly demonstrated that in fact Germany and Italy did not have designs to establish colonial outposts in Latin America from which to wage war on the United States. And it may indeed be true that, as a close observer of hemispheric relations contended early in 1940, "North Americans were as attracted to worst-case scenarios as lizards to sun-baked rocks."[8] Still, if the war against Britain had gone as Hitler hoped and if the German forces had not ultimately become bogged down in the Soviet Union, there is no telling what Hitler might have aspired to. Roosevelt and his advisers had to entertain worst-case scenarios. Prudent leaders in those times could not have helped but perceive possible security threats to the United States; nor could they have failed to construct policy based on such perceptions.[9]

President Roosevelt certainly had little difficulty persuading most of his fellow citizens as to the reality of Nazi plots to take over Latin America. From all walks of life and from all age groups, Americans tended to credit the existence of such plots; and they demonstrated an insatiable appetite for books and articles that exposed alleged Nazi intentions in the hemisphere. John Gunther, encouraged by Sumner Welles, fed this appetite with his briskly selling 1941 book *Inside Latin America*. So did journalist and old Latin America hand Carleton Beals, both in his *Coming Struggle for Latin America* (1938) that went through six printings and in his adventure novel (a Literary Guild selection) *Dawn over the Amazon* (1943), built around an imagined German-Japanese invasion of the southern continent. Indeed, exposés of German-Italian-Japanese designs on Latin America proved a bonanza to publishers. Readers in the United States apparently could not get enough books on the subject. Even in the early 1950s with the war some years behind them, graduate students in Latin American studies (judging from my own experiences) still read these books, under the friendly persuasion of their professors, and heatedly debated their validity.

Visiting Mexico in 1940, Vice President Wallace marveled "at the 'whale of a lot of fifth column activity'" in the country. And in Cuba Ernest Hemingway, convinced a German invasion was imminent, gained the backing of Ambassador Spruille Braden for a hare-brained scheme to organize a counterinsurgency corps. Headed by Hemingway, the counterinsurgents comprised a motley collection of individuals, some of them supplied with weapons by the U.S. government. Although gullibly helping Hemingway make a fool of himself, Braden before assuming his post in Havana had served with distinction as the first U.S. ambassador to Colombia (raised to embassy status in 1938). In Colombia he had calmed many a diplomatic squall while rendering yeoman service in liquidating German control over that country's commercial air system—a control that, it was logically enough assumed, might pose a serious threat to the Panama Canal in the event of war.[10]

Almost as influential as the president himself among Washington power wielders concerned about the security threat in Latin America was FBI Director J. Edgar Hoover. He sent the first cadres of his Special Intelligence Service (SIS) personnel to Central and South America in July of 1940. Their initial task was to gather intelligence, especially in countries with heavy concentrations of German and Italian emigrés and sympathizers. Relying on information provided by local informers, these agents, like Hoover himself, often proved exceptionally gullible. All too often they accepted as truth ingeniously concocted lies through which Latin American informers sought to ruin their political and personal foes by fabricating evidence of their fascist ties. All too often a later generation of U.S. historians looking back on these events judged gullibility a more heinous sin than mendaciousness. And these historians failed, by and large, to understand that Latin Americans took advantage of wartime conditions to lure the United States back into the practice of selective intervention that, despite their public protestations, they had never really wanted to see the Yankee nation abandon altogether.

SIS agents soon after their arrival played active roles in rounding up alleged "Axis agents, saboteurs and smugglers of strategic war materials." Moreover, once America entered the war at the end of 1941, Hoover brought a number of South and Central American police officers to the FBI academy for training.[11] Thereby he helped call into being an externally trained Latin American internal security apparatus that would prove as useful, and also as indiscriminately ruthless, when directed against suspected Cold War Communists as it had when ferreting out World War II fascists or suspected fascists. Indeed, left-leaning American writers in the 1960s and beyond tended to place ultimate responsibility on Hoover for many post–World War II south-of-the-border instances of torture and civil rights violations; but this appraisal slights the native talent and penchant of Latin Americans for waging dirty wars.

While he might enjoy the opportunity to train some of their "right-thinking" citizens at the FBI academy, J. Edgar Hoover held the generality of Latin Americans in disdain, seeing them in much the same light that Texans had traditionally cast on "greasers." If allowed to follow their natural inclinations Latin Americans all too often would, in Hoover's estimation, yield to un-American, totalitarian temptations, whether of right or left. Furthermore, they tended to be a sneaky, shifty, unreliable lot, ever on the prowl for American handouts. What had all the Good Neighbor pampering of Latin Americans accomplished? Very little, in Hoover's estimation. If given half a chance, if not kept under effective surveillance from Bureau headquarters in Washington, Latin Americans were as likely as not to throw in their lot with enemies of the United States.

In many ways Hoover's attitudes mirrored the suspicions that a growing number of North Americans by the early 1940s had begun to entertain about their "good neighbors." The mere fact that so many Americans believed in the reality of a security threat in the southern continent attested, in some ways, to the belief that Latin Americans were not reliable friends. The perceived threat in the South seemed to arise from internal as much as external factors; it originated, in fact, in the flawed nature of Latin Americans. Such at least was the gnawing suspicion to which many Americans succumbed as their country appeared to edge toward war. Republican politicians especially did all in their power to encourage doubts about the reliability of Latin Americans, hoping thereby to establish the futility of the entire Good Neighbor policy and the gullibility of those who had concocted it.

Watching the inter-American conferences held at the end of the 1930s and in 1940, more than a few Americans, both Republicans and Democrats, found grounds for disillusionment with their supposedly good neighbors. Washington intended these conferences to address the issue of achieving hemispheric solidarity in the face of security threats from abroad. But, rather than the security that was uppermost in North American minds, Latin Americans seemed to want only to discuss economic issues that involved loans and grants and economic concessions of any and every sort from the United States. While North Americans perceived themselves as girding to defend civilization, they saw Latin Americans as interested mainly in extracting more and more economic concessions out of Uncle Sam, and quite indifferent to defense of the civilization that North Americans had created.

The norteamericanos were hardly justified in their conclusion. What, after all, was more in accordance with the civilization developed and refined in their own country than going for the top dollar? Only yesterday North Americans in trying to assess blame for the Depression had censured many of their own citizens for their obsessive and devious pursuit of profit. Now, as the Depression began to lift, American hustlers, including those itching for the inflated profits of defense contracts, were splendid fellows while the Latin Americans showed their true colors as on-the-make opportunists.

## Changing American Perspectives on Latin Americans

As the 1930s gave way to the '40s, the hemispheric isolationist underpinning on which the Good Neighbor apparatus rested began to give way. Rather than with the charmingly feckless, light-hearted, let's-live-for-the-moment Latins with their dances and rhythms and their partying proclivities, Americans began to empathize with the gallant, stoic, and resolute men and women of Britain. Rather than surrendering emotionally to a culture that in hoary stereotypes embodied distraction and diversion, dissoluteness and dissipation, should not Americans concern themselves with their beleaguered overseas cousins living out what Churchill justifiably called their finest hour?

More and more Americans found that newscaster par excellence Edward R. Murrow provided them a window onto the world of edifying role models through his broadcasts from the embattled isle that always began with the words "This is London." When Murrow returned briefly to the United States in late 1941 his employer, the Columbia Broadcasting System (CBS), held a dinner in his honor. In rendering tribute to Murrow on this occasion, poet and Library of Congress director Archibald MacLeish had this to say: "You burned the city of London in our houses and we felt the flames that burned it. You laid the dead at our doors and we knew the dead were our dead—were all men's dead—were mankind's dead—and ours." [12]

A few years earlier MacLeish had burned with Good Neighbor enthusiasm for Latin Americans. And he had penned a poem that honored the heroic conquistador Hernán Cortés as well as the heroic Indians who had resisted him. Now, in 1941, Latin America was far from MacLeish's thoughts. Instead, those thoughts lay with the heroism of the moment, as it displayed itself in Britain. Countless other Americans felt the same way. Not only in economic and political criteria but in measurements of grandeur, Latin Americans struck many norteamericanos as strictly minor league, maybe even bush league. Already on the eve of American entry into war, the driving emotional force behind the Good Neighbor policy was waning.

# 23. Two in One Flesh: Economic and Security Issues

❖ ❖ ❖ ❖ ❖ ❖ ❖ ❖ ❖ ❖ ❖ ❖ ❖ ❖ ❖ ❖ ❖ ❖ ❖ ❖ ❖ ❖ ❖ ❖ ❖ ❖ ❖ ❖ ❖ ❖ ❖ ❖ ❖ ❖

### The 1938 Lima Conference

Reflecting the concerns of the president he served, Secretary of State Cordell Hull had security issues on his mind as he traveled to Lima, Peru, in December of 1938 at the head of the U.S. delegation to a regularly scheduled inter-American conference. The last such conference had been in 1933 at Montevideo, Uruguay. There, as previously noted, the United States agreed, with certain reservations, to the principle of nonintervention. Subsequently, at the December 1936 special conference held in Buenos Aires (where Roosevelt had scored a personal triumph), the United States bound itself without reservations to nonintervention, although not resolving differences with Latins over how to define the term.

Beyond the intervention issue, delegates assembled in Buenos Aires had agreed that "every act susceptible of disturbing the peace of the Americas" affected each and every one of them and would automatically activate the consultation procedures outlined in the principal document the conference produced: the Convention for the Maintenance, Preservation and Reestablishment of Peace. However, that convention did not specify precisely how consultation should be initiated; and it was hopelessly vague as to just what sort of menace to the peace of one republic should be considered a menace to all. Delegates to the Lima conference would, it was hoped, forge agreement on specifics. In actuality, a good part of these matters still remained unresolved after the Lima sessions and had to be settled at a subsequent conference held in Havana (and discussed in the following chapter).

Hull did not face an easy task in Lima, especially when dealing with Argentina, traditionally bound to Europe, especially Britain, by trade and foreign investments. Beyond this Argentina had strong ethnic ties to the Old World. The huge influx of Italian and, to a much lesser extent, German immigrants from the middle of the nineteenth century on through the 1920s was, in proportion to the original, early-nineteenth-century population, four times greater than immigration into the United States over a comparable period. Feeling in some ways more an Old than a New World republic, Argentina had steadfastly resisted U.S. attempts, beginning with the Monroe Doctrine, to isolate the American republics from Europe. What is more, Argentina had not yet surrendered aspirations to assume what it regarded as its rightful place at the head of a European-oriented coalition of Spanish American states. Through such a coalition Argentina could both checkmate Yankee aspirations to hemispheric suzerainty and isolate its Luso-American rival, Brazil. In 1938 at Lima, Argentine statesmen remained anxious to fulfill old dreams of national destiny by stiffening the resistance of lesser hemispheric republics—for most of which they felt disdain easily matching that of the most ethnocentric North Americans—to Yankee purposes.

The exigencies of good neighborliness had forced Hull since 1933 to pretend to an amicable predisposition toward Argentine statesmen. Actually, though, he detested most of them for what he saw as their efforts to lead Latin America away from all that he held dear: U.S.-style democracy, free-enterprise capitalism, and free trade. The destiny that Hull foresaw for Latin America was convergence with the political and social and economic culture of the United States.

By the time he arrived in Lima, Hull had already had more than ample time to nourish his resentment over the fact that Argentines cherished their Old World culture, with its aristocratic standards that held democratic, individualistic capitalism in suspicion if not disdain. Already Hull had grasped that the Argentine statesmen with whom he dueled saw themselves as the sentinels for Latin America, standing guard against Yankee intrusions, whether cultural or political. Nor, as Hull correctly perceived, did the Argentines welcome Yankee economic penetration into the hemisphere through the sort of free-trade arrangements that he sincerely believed would redound to the advantage of North and South America. Perhaps, though, Hull tended too much to slight and disparage the eminently practical grounds on which Argentines based their economic stance. How, after all, could Argentines benefit economically by looking northward? Argentina's rural-based economy was competitive with that of the United States—where the Great Plains produced the sort of crops and cattle that flourished on the deep, rich topsoil of the pampas. On the other hand, Argentina's economy was ideally complementary with Britain's.

Still, for all the economic factors that contributed to Yankee-Argentine animosity, the issue really lay deeper than economics. Since the inter-American system had first begun tentatively to emerge in the 1880s, its periodic conferences had chronically provided the occasion for U.S.-Argentine confrontations arising over disagreement as to which was the better, more virtuous, more cultured country, and which was most clearly destined for ultimate greatness and New World paramountcy. Undercurrents of animosity at Lima showed the old debate was still very much alive.

All in all, Hull regarded the ten days spent in Lima as "among the most difficult of my career." The Argentines, he complained, balked at agreeing "to anything that meant anything." In the end, he had to settle for the nonbinding Declaration of Lima (without the teeth of a treaty) by which the American republics reaffirmed their continental solidarity, "whatever that might mean," and agreed that in the event of a threat to the peace of the hemisphere the foreign ministers of the twenty-one republics would meet to deliberate on what measures to take.[1]

Some observers dismissed the Declaration of Lima as "extravagantly loopholed," as "another Argentine triumph for inocuity." A U.S. Treasury Department assessment showed the Argentines did not have a monopoly on the rhetoric of inocuity. According to this assessment, the declaration "indicated to the totalitarian powers that aggression in Latin America would meet more resistance than it has in the past."[2]

Unflappable as always, FDR early in 1939 resorted to the ploy he had used after the 1936 Buenos Aires conference: he appealed to the European powers to follow down the paths blazed by the Good Neighbor policy and adopt "pledges against aggression similar to those that bound the twenty-one American republics." Pledges of this sort, combined with the "open door of trade and intercourse" would make dreams of aggression and conquest seem as "ridiculous and criminal" to Europeans as they now did to Americans.[3] Needless to say, Europeans were no more impressed by the Pan American model in 1939 than they had been in 1937. Nor, I suppose, did Roosevelt expect them to be. In his utterances about the "success" of Pan Americanism, he was playing to a hemispheric audience.

### Economic Factors as Security Factors in Hemispheric Relations

Hull's difficulties at Lima, where some Latin American republics showed themselves more disposed to align with Argentina than with the United States, showed the need for diplomatic fence mending, which really meant economic fence mending. It became obvious that if the United States hoped to line up Latin Americans in the sort of hemispheric security system it desired, then it would have to become a better neighbor, specifically an economically more generous neighbor, than ever it had intended to be. Nor can Latin Americans necessarily be blamed for casting about for methods to extract economic concessions from North America. In some of their republics the Depression had hit even harder than in the United States. Now, with the trade disruptions resulting from the war in Europe, the Latins faced still bleaker times. Surely Uncle Sam, with an economy that Latin Americans tended to believe had entered a recovery mode, could be of assistance.

Perceptions from south of the border were not necessarily accurate. So convinced were Latin Americans of Uncle Sam's endlessly deep pockets that they failed to heed the indications of deepening depression that appeared in the United States in 1937–1938, signs suggesting to many North Americans that the New Deal simply was not working. Ignoring these signs, Latin Americans, many of them at least, continued to think that the United States could provide a deus-ex-machina solution to their woes if only it made a serious effort. By 1940, with the North American economy finally showing glimmers of recovery as the country began to arm itself and to supply Britain with vitally needed goods, Latin American leaders refused to believe that the United States could not take an effective role in ameliorating their economic woes. There was a way, they insisted, if only the Yankees had the will.

Despite its own economic woes in 1939, the Roosevelt administration found some trade and credit concessions with which to reward Brazil's foreign minister Oswaldo Aranha when he visited Washington in February and hit it off beautifully with the president and even the secretary of state. Since early in the twentieth century, the United States had cultivated a special relationship with Brazil that amounted, according to some observers, to an unofficial alliance. Now it was time to revitalize that alliance, to make it just a bit more official. The eastern hump of Brazil, after all, was closer to Europe than any other part of the American hemisphere; conceivably, it might lure Europe's expansionist Nazis and fascists. Moreover, large concentrations of Germans and Italians especially in the south raised Washington's fears of fifth column activity within Brazil. What is more, the Brazilian dictator Getulio Vargas, though a relatively mild-mannered caudillo, had adopted in his so-called Estado Novo (New State) some of the trappings of fascism and had held out the threat of entering into bilateral trade agreements with Germany in order to find an adequate market for his country's coffee. There was no question, though, that Vargas and Aranha far and away preferred doing business with the United States, if only the United States could make it sufficiently worth their while.[4]

By the time Aranha left Washington it seemed the Americans had come up with some of the economic inducements to good neighborliness that the Brazilians coveted. So far so good; but trouble loomed ahead.

## The United States in the Cockpit of Inter–Latin American Rivalry

Agreements hammered out in Washington sent Aranha home happy, and already thinking about a shopping list for future occasions. But the concessions to Brazil aroused the suspicions of that country's neighbors and plunged Washington into the jungle of inter–Latin American rivalries. Although having begun seriously to seek a rapprochement with Argentina, Brazil found that its long history of enmity with that country undermined the endeavor. Suspicious of overtures from Brazil as that country sought to launch its own version of a Good Neighbor policy in the southern hemisphere, Argentines resented Aranha's success at wresting economic concessions from Washington, while at the same time waxing resentful against the United States for having offered those concessions.

Leaders of other South American countries also remained suspicious of Brazil's recent friendly overtures. They interpreted these overtures as proof of Brazil's intention to gain recognition from sister republics as the area's benevolent superstate and therefore to some degree entitled to mediate between them and the United States—a role, of course, that Argentina wished to claim for itself. Brazil in past decades had expanded its boundaries at the expense of adjoining republics, and these republics remained unconvinced that their neighbor had mended its ways. Suspicious leaders in those countries tended to frown on U.S. policies that might unduly strengthen their old adversary. Indeed, whatever the way in which the United States treated Brazil, it was bound to stir up trouble for itself in Latin America.

What Washington did to succor Brazil delighted Chileans, chronically at odds and sometimes even on the verge of war with Argentina; but concessions to Brazil dismayed Peru, a country that had lost considerable territory to Chile in a late-nineteenth-century war and still looked suspiciously on its southern neighbor. Playing the game of checkerboard diplomacy that transformed inter–Latin American relations into an always treacherous cockpit, Peru sought a special relationship with Chile's major enemy, Argentina.

Meantime Ecuadorans worried about new territorial grabs by Peruvians. For Ecuadorans, Peru was a menacing colossus of the south. Nor could Ecuadorans trust the colossus to its northwest, Colombia. What is more, Bolivians and Paraguayans, tucked in among factious neighbors who had in the past despoiled both their republics of national domain, licked the wounds incurred in their recently concluded Chaco War; and leaders of each country schemed how to extract better concessions from Washington than those extended to the hated neighbor republic.[5]

In the months following Aranha's visit Adolf Berle and other State Department officials performed yeoman duty in trying to extend to additional republics some of the economic inducements toward good neighborliness already proffered Brazil—without unduly stirring up the Latin American hornet's nest. In the process, they encountered additional rancors that Washington had to be on guard against exacerbating. Venezuela and Colombia were traditional rivals and occasionally out-and-out military foes. Leaders of neither republic could abide the thought that Washington might treat them less generously than their cross-border rivals. Moving northward, Guatemalans sulked over any indication of Washington's preferential treatment of their great rival Mexico; and citizens of the smaller, less powerful Central American republics, especially Nicaraguans, resented any American policy that might unduly benefit their old imperialist nemesis, Guatemala. All the while Costa Ricans lived in fear of Nicaragua and anything the United States might do to bolster that country's dictator, Anastasio Somoza. Panama also entered into the game of inter–Central American rivalry and beyond this sought to parlay its vital strategic importance into special economic concessions and rewards from Washington by subtle and sometimes not so subtle signs of approbation for Nazism and fascism. As a relatively innocent would-be Good Neighbor, the United States had wandered into a seething cauldron of national hatreds, and would pay a price for its innocence and typically American conviction that other countries could easily discard history's cumbersome baggage.

Given Latin America's Balkans-like nineteenth- and early-twentieth-century history, the Good Neighbor in Washington had done remarkably well in contriving to get on better than usual with most of the republics to the south and in forging a peace-maintenance machinery that for all its failings represented a dramatic advance over anything achieved in the past. In a way, Roosevelt's hubris in seeing the Good Neighbor's accomplishments with its balkanized neighbors as a possible model for Europe is almost understandable. In some ways, though, Washington's main challenge was still ahead as it scrambled to bolster hemispheric security by addressing some of its neighbors' most pressing economic needs and expectations. And the challenge came from within.

## The Washington Cockpit Complicates Hemispheric Economic-Security Policy

The complexity of the U.S. quest for hemispheric security was compounded by internal divisiveness among statesmen and bureaucrats in

Washington. Often they differed not only over how but even whether their government should help Latin Americans solve their economic and financial problems. Some sought, while others argued against, a major role for the Export-Import Bank (established in 1934) in distributing U.S. funds to help Latin American republics bolster their economies.[6] This disagreement reflected the fact that statesmen and bureaucrats, financiers and bankers, business and labor spokesmen, farm and industry executives, differed profoundly over whether to give precedence to public or private finance in tackling Latin American problems; they disagreed also over whether assistance should be rendered governments in default on loans to U.S. banks or even to private firms in countries whose governments were in default.

Even if Hull and Welles at the State Department had been able to resolve their personal differences (the one preferring a private-enterprise, free-trade approach, the other more tolerant toward the disbursement of public funds), they would have found themselves in frequent stand-offs, among others: with chronically irascible Jesse Jones, the secretary of commerce who favored a strictly private-sector approach, regarded the Export-Import Bank as a dangerously radical, even socialist, institution, and felt Washington should impose an economic boycott on countries like Mexico (and later Bolivia and Ecuador) that seized or threatened to seize subsoil holdings from foreign concessionaires; with terrible-tempered Harold Ickes, the secretary of the interior, who seldom saw a private, free-enterprise capitalist he trusted; with Henry Morgenthau, secretary of the treasury, who sought to contemporize and thereby only contrived to antagonize extremists; with the FBI's J. Edgar Hoover, and sometimes with the secretaries of defense (Henry Stimson) and the Navy (Frank Knox), who wanted to use economic threats and rewards to pressure governments into adopting not necessarily correct financial policies but proper security measures; with Secretary of Labor Frances Perkins, who thought more about fair wages for Latin American workers employed by U.S. firms than about earnings for their owners; with Henry Wallace, the secretary of agriculture until Roosevelt's third term when he became vice president, who had to consider programs in terms not only of how they might affect Latin Americans, whom he sincerely wanted to help, but also of how they would affect the U.S. farming sector, whose interests his position committed him to serve.

That long paragraph only begins to hint at the barest beginning of a list of a few of the disparate influences that shaped North America's crucial and intertwined and coalesced economic and security policies toward Latin America. Even that notorious juggler FDR had more balls in the air than he could handle.

Largely because of bureaucratic infighting, plans for an Inter-American Bank had to be abandoned in 1940, even as the previously discussed Latin American cartel died stillborn; and because of incessant scrapping between Wallace and Jones the president in 1943 disbanded the Board of Economic Warfare (BEW), conceived with the purpose of coordinating wartime hemispheric economic policies. Dismemberment of BEW "meant more than just the end of another wartime agency; it also showed how fragile inter-American economic planning was," both before and during the war.[7]

The more grandiose designs of hemispheric economic cooperation seldom got beyond the drawing board. And the reason lies not just in bureaucratic infighting but in the flagging interest of Roosevelt himself in Latin American matters as Europe and Japan commanded more and more of his attention. Moreover, the president in his notorious willingness to settle for the half loaf rather than to risk undue divisiveness by insisting on the whole loaf sometimes wound up with little more than a slice or two.

## Latin American Diversity Results in Diverse Good Neighbor Policies

The failure to establish an overall blueprint for using economic concessions to advance Good Neighbor purposes lies, beyond already discussed factors, in the fact that from the president on down American statesmen often concluded that U.S. economic generosity was justified in some instances, and not in others. In the case of Mexico, administration figures by and large (with the notable exception of Hull and his immediate coterie) did not begrudge generous economic concessions even when that country expropriated foreign oil interests. And the reason for this was not exclusively one of security considerations. The reason also stemmed from the perception shared by Roosevelt and Welles and Ambassador Daniels that American generosity with Mexico ultimately would redound to the social and economic advantage of the Mexican people, given the apparent reformist aspirations and social-justice goals of the Mexican government.

Whether or not those who devised the U.S. policy with Mexico were naive or not, their predisposition toward generosity sprang from the best of intentions. In the case of Cuba, however, generosity in enhancing its share of American funds, whether public or private, did not make sense. This at least was the conclusion reached by Ambassador Jefferson Caffery and also George Messersmith, who succeeded him briefly in 1940. Along with first secretary of the legation Willard Beaulac, they shrewdly read the island's strongman Fulgencio Batista as a person on the make, concerned more with his power and with buying the continued support of his collaborators than with socioeconomic reforms. They were reluctant, therefore, to go along with Batista's attempts to extract more economic concessions out of Washington.[8]

Unlike Cuba, Venezuela seemed to be heading down the sort of trails blazed by Cárdenas in Mexico. Longtime tyrant Juan Vicente Gómez died in 1934, and by 1940 apparently honest and democratically inclined reformers seemed to have ushered in a new day. Under these conditions the State Department pressured Standard Oil to accept a new contract that increased Venezuela's share of petroleum profits. Thereby the State Department reversed the results traditionally associated with so-called dollar diplomacy—diplomacy in which Washington asserted its power in such a way as to advance the immediate interests of U.S. capitalists.

The Mexico-Cuba-Venezuela contrasts point to the kinds of decisions that embassy staffs throughout Latin America as well as Washington personnel were called upon to make during the Good Neighbor era as they sought to decide whether local rulers lined up with the Cárdenas or the Batista model. By and large, the contrasting approaches that U.S. diplomats followed in Mexico and Cuba and Venezuela were justified. Perhaps the precedents these disparate approaches established should have been encapsulated into formally declared policy. On the other hand, given the rarity and the difficulties of recognizing sincere and relatively honest reformers any time, any place in the hemisphere (including Washington), such a policy might have proved meaningless.

# 24.
# Three in One Flesh: Economic, Security, and Cultural Issues

❖ ❖ ❖ ❖ ❖ ❖ ❖ ❖ ❖ ❖ ❖ ❖ ❖ ❖ ❖ ❖ ❖ ❖ ❖ ❖ ❖ ❖ ❖ ❖ ❖ ❖ ❖ ❖ ❖ ❖ ❖ ❖

## Security and Economics: The 1939 Panama Conference

The late September 1939 Panama special meeting of the American republics (with the customary omission of Canada) came about because of President Roosevelt's wish, following the eruption of war in Europe, to establish an American-hemisphere neutrality zone wherein all acts of warfare were proscribed. Because the Latin American republics were almost as anxious as the United States about the prospects of naval war being waged along their shores an environment of consensus prevailed in Panama City. Even Argentina refrained from its usual obstructionist policies. No more than her sister republics did Argentina welcome the prospect of its coastal waters becoming the scene of battle waged by European combatants. Moreover, Roberto M. Ortiz, installed as Argentine president in 1938, unlike his immediate predecessors and also unlike those who would follow him in office, was at heart a liberal democrat, far more attracted to U.S.-style democracy than to the politics of Catholic corporatist conservatism or National Socialism or fascism. The atmosphere of good feelings, on which Sumner Welles (who headed the U.S. delegation) commented frequently, attested also to the fact that Washington had begun to address Latin American economic concerns and seemed disposed to go considerably further in this regard.

The eleven-day conference yielded as its principal fruit the Declaration of Panama, establishing a neutrality zone ranging from three hundred to a thousand miles around the hemisphere's coastline (with the exception of Canada's). Within this zone, non-American belligerent powers were forbidden to commit hostile acts, "whether such hostile acts be attempted or made from land, sea, or air." Delegates approved the Declaration almost in the very terms in which the United States had proposed it. While European powers, Britain as well as Germany, soon flouted its terms (as when the German pocket battleship *Graf Spee* fought a spectacular battle against three British cruisers off the coast of Uruguay), the Declaration of Panama did lead to closer U.S.–Latin American collaboration in military matters. As their ships joined with those of the U.S. Navy in patrolling coastal waters, Latin American presidents and military officers (sometimes one and the same) began to appreciate the degree to which Washington, if properly finessed, might become a supplier of modern military materiel. These expectations only grew once the United States entered the war and began then to do all in its power to shore up Latin America's military prowess, not only by supplying weapons but by providing military training and officer-exchange programs. Functions that once had been performed by European countries now came virtually to be monopolized by the United States.

If military plums began to entice some Latin Americans, far more numerous were those who anticipated general economic rewards after their governments had demonstrated such good neighborliness in Panama City. While there Sumner Welles and the members of the U.S. delegation to the conference acted as if they would do all in their power to meet Latin hopes. They agreed, for example, to create an Inter-American Financial and Economic Advisory Committee that would support monetary stability and work to relieve the loss of European trade through expansion of hemispheric commerce. Back in Washington, however, self-styled defenders of economic probity soon voiced opposition to what they regarded as giveaway programs agreed to in Panama. The Foreign Bondholders Protection Council, for example, objected to financial aid for countries in default on existing debts and payments for expropriated U.S. property. The usual bureaucratic infighting broke out as Jesse Jones rallied allies who excoriated the allegedly socialist expedients agreed to in Panama. The opposition proved strong enough to thwart many of the economic inducements through which Welles, carefully limiting himself to vague generalities, had sought to entice the Latin American delegates in Panama.

Latin hopes for financial succor had soared at Panama, where delegates considered no fewer than twenty-seven economic projects. However, these hopes remained unfulfilled when delegates of the American republics assembled the following year in Havana for another special conference. By and large, representatives of the Latin republics still anticipated greater economic largesse from Washington. Often they could not understand that their hopes so far had been dashed not by premeditated White House or State Department decisions but rather by the unintended outcome of bureaucratic infighting. Nor, in many instances, could the presidents of the countries the delegates represented understand what was going on. In many instances they had come to regard Roosevelt as a fellow caudillo. A caudillo could do as he willed. The notion that the will of a caudillo could be defeated by bureaucratic infighting was largely beyond their comprehension. Under these circumstances some Latin American leaders began to wonder just how good a neighbor they actually had in Franklin Roosevelt.

## More Security and Economics: The 1940 Havana Conference

Faced in 1940 with the rapid advance of Hitler's armies across Europe, Roosevelt and his advisers began to concern themselves with the fate of New World possessions of such German-occupied countries as France and the Netherlands. Might Germany having conquered the motherlands move to occupy the colonies? The danger seemed grave, for the colonies in question were in the Caribbean region, virtually atop vital shipping routes and close to the Panama Canal. The previous year at the Panama Conference delegates had agreed on the need for consultation in the event that any area of the hemisphere faced the possibility of a change in colonial masters owing to the military conquest of its motherland. It was now time for Washington to act on that Panama agreement, and invitations were dispatched on June 17 to a consultative meeting in Havana.

Circumstances seemed far from auspicious as the State Department assembled a delegation to be headed by Cordell Hull himself. Hull's old bête noire, Argentina, showed signs of reverting to form. Roberto Ortiz, that country's pro–United States champion of liberal democracy, had been forced by bad health temporarily to entrust the exercise of presidential powers to his vice president, Ramón Castillo. And this strongly traditionalist military man made little secret of his contempt for liberal democracy, whose days he thought might in fact be numbered in much of the world, given Hitler's spectacular advances and Mussolini's ascendance in Italy.

Another European leader also attracted Castillo's admiration: Francisco Franco, whose Nationalist armies had crushed the Spanish Republicans the previous year. Already Franco was gearing up for his *hispanidad* crusade, a diplomatic and public relations New World blitz through which he hoped to rally Latin American republics around their old madre patria—with its conservative, Catholic traditions that stood forever opposed to the leveling one-person, one-vote variety of democracy as practiced and propagated by the United States.[1] Franco's hispanidad added to its Spanish Catholic traditionalism at least some elements of the new fascist ideology. Altogether, Castillo's attraction to hispanidad did not bode well for the prospects of Argentine cooperation at Havana. Nor did the increasing signs that broad segments in the Argentine military and intellectual community hoped to make their country a beachhead for spreading traditionalism cum fascism throughout the southern hemisphere, thereby delivering a death blow to made-in-Washington Pan Americanism.

Under Argentine prodding several Latin American countries, including Brazil and Chile, decided not to send their foreign ministers to Havana—ostensibly because they were needed at home, but actually so as to avoid offense to the surging Axis powers by attaching priority and urgency to the meeting. Hull foresaw a difficult time in Havana, and to smooth his way Roosevelt, on the eve of the secretary of state's departure, requested Congress to increase the lending power of the Export-Import Bank from $200 million to $700 million. According to the president, this increase would enable the bank to be "of greater assistance to our neighbors south of the Rio Grande, including the handling and orderly marketing of some of their surpluses."[2]

In spite of Roosevelt's attempt to smooth the way, Hull in Havana soon encountered circumstances that confirmed his apprehensions. Well removed from the Caribbean territories in question, Argentina did not incline to see any likelihood of their transfer to a different overseas owner, or any danger if they should be transferred. For a time at a loss as to how to break the impasse with Argentina, Hull thought of contacting his ideological ally, the ailing president of Argentina. Roberto Ortiz, although having relinquished his powers, still had considerable clout in Argentina. At that particular moment Castillo and his cronies had not consolidated their power, and Argentina was experiencing its own variety of bureaucratic infighting. The ailing Ortiz, who would die before ever reclaiming his office, rallied his supporters and brought pressure to bear that resulted in the issuing of new instructions to the Argentine delegation in Havana.

With Argentina softening its obstructionist tactics, and "with the carrot of financial aid dangling . . . tantalizingly before them,"[3] the delegates at Havana approved a Convention permitting any New World possession of a subjugated European state to be placed under provisional Pan American trusteeship. The Argentine delegation, however, now registered a victory for the Castillo faction by gaining conference approval of a stipulation that the Convention would not go into effect until ratified by two-thirds of the American states. Hull now rallied his supporters and won approval of a crucial supplementary measure, the so-called Act of Havana. It stipulated that in an emergency and pending ratification of the Convention any American republic—meaning to all effects and purposes the United States—could step in and establish a provisional regime, thereby preventing transfer of colonial ownership.

In some ways the most significant triumph for the United States at Havana was securing approval of the Declaration of Reciprocal Assistance and Cooperation for the Defense of the Nations of the Americas. The Declaration embodied the all-for-one and one-for-all principle (discussed at some length at the Lima Conference) as adapted from earlier Uruguayan proposals prompted by concern about aggression not from overseas but from next-door Argentina. In its principal section the Declaration stipulated that "any attempt on the part of a non-American State against the integrity or inviolability of the territory, the sovereignty or the political independence of an American State shall be considered an act of aggression" against all the signatory states. The Declaration meant that should the United States be attacked by any power, all of the American states would consider themselves under attack.[4] At least this is what the United States presumed, though Argentina (and, for a time, Chile) would regard the matter differently following the Japanese attack on Pearl Harbor.

Included in the Declaration of Reciprocal Assistance were provisions for the signatories to enter into mutual defense agreements. Increasingly apprehensive about involvement in the war that had been underway for nearly a year in Europe, U.S. statesmen moved quickly to sign conventions with Mexico (the way paved by the 1941 agreement on compensation for expropriated foreign oil properties) and with eight other republics, including Brazil but not Argentina or Chile.

All in all Hull had not done badly. Back in Buenos Aires, Ramón Castillo showed his pique by relaxing his government's efforts to suppress Nazi activities in Argentina while making "overtures to Berlin for economic support."[5]

What about those American republics not so much interested in security affairs as the "dangling carrot" of U.S. financial aid? They received one of the rewards they had in mind when Congress approved FDR's request to raise Export-Import Bank funding. But the massive economic assistance Roosevelt had envisaged for Latin America through purchase of that area's surplus commodities that no longer had buyers in Europe (or the means of transportation to potential buyers across the war-infested Atlantic) never came to pass. Financial, agricultural, and business leaders admonished the president that his projected program would cost the government hundreds of millions of dollars, while resulting in the accumulation of unneeded goods competitive with U.S. produce and the extension of intrusive agricultural controls to all the Americas. Many Latin Americans were themselves skeptical about the plans, fearing the Yankees were up to their customary tricks of economic imperialism and hoping to cut them off permanently from their old European markets. Faced with internal opposition and doubts among the people whose interests ostensibly he had at heart, Roosevelt (as already indicated in Chapter 20) abandoned the cartel plan.

On a country-by-country approach, however, many economic agreements were hammered out—agreements that as often as not failed to satisfy Latin expectations while at the same time calling forth denunciations from U.S. economic traditionalists. These included Democrats and Republicans alike, who disparaged "socialist" economic intervention and complained about the need to buy the support of people whose allegiance supposedly had been won through earlier Good Neighbor concessions. Even as FDR continued to try to persuade Europeans eventually, once the war was over, to emulate the New World system that he had called into being, more and more of his fellow citizens began to grumble that Roosevelt had sold them a bill of goods about the accomplishments of his Good Neighbor policy.

### Harbingers of American Disillusionment with Latin Americans and the Good Neighbor Policy

Not long after the conclusion of the 1940 conference, the Soviet Union's Foreign Commissar Vyacheslav Molotov, his country allied at that time with Hitler's Germany, sharply criticized the Havana proceedings. Their only purpose, he contended, was to subjugate the Western Hemisphere to the imperialist designs of American capitalists.[6] Molotov's charges presaged the sort of accusations that thundered out of Moscow once the Cold War had been joined shortly after the Allies triumphed in World War II.

Many of those American capitalists whom Molotov assumed to be setting hemispheric policy as of 1940 actually complained, sometimes bitterly and vociferously, over their lack of influence on policy-making. Management of hemispheric affairs, they charged, had been turned over to intellectuals and bureaucrats whose judgment was clouded by statist predilections. They were bent upon solving whatever problems they discovered by lavishing U.S. public funds on Latin American malingerers who had never been interested in the Good Neighbor policy except for their perceptions of it as a potential gravy train. Having failed to solve domestic problems by putting blacks and other alleged ne'er-do-wells on the dole, Washington now thought of putting Latin Americans on the dole, hoping thereby to elicit from them the same sort of political support it had elicited from domestic wastrels who, purportedly, sought solutions to problems in handouts rather than in self-effort. In a way, Latin Americans became a projection, for some of Roosevelt's conservative critics, of the blacks and Irish and other immigrant blocs living within the United States whom the New Deal had co-opted through allegedly devious, dubious, and un-American expedients.

"Walking-around money" was the term used since the nineteenth century to designate the cash payments that political machines delivered to city bosses, cash which they in turn passed around through phalanxes of ward-heelers in order to buy votes in predominantly poor precincts. American patricians often assailed the system not so much for the corruption it bespoke as for the undeserved rewards it conferred on alleged malingerers whose poverty resulted only from their failings of character and morality. Similarly, once their own country began to stir out of the Depression, many Americans imbued with the most traditional of national values assumed that Latin America's historical poverty sprang from character flaws. Perhaps when faced with the exigencies of war it was necessary to distribute walking-around money to Latin American leaders, thereby winning from them a loyalty of sorts by permitting them to strengthen their own political position by further debasing the character of their countries' dependent mobs. Once the war ended, though, many Americans, angered by what they perceived as lukewarm support at best from Latin America in the struggle with the Axis powers, looked forward to cutting Latin caudillos off from their walking-around money.

So Americans—many of them at least—bided their time until, with the end of the war, they could terminate the handouts through which, ostensibly, the Roosevelt administration had sought to mollify troublesome neighbors. Imagine the frustration of America's upholders of traditional values, though, when not long after World War II ended they would have to accept reversion to walking-around money to assure acceptable Latin American conduct in the Cold War.

## The Cultural Dimension of Hemispheric Security

Meeting domestic opposition to some of its more lavish schemes to strengthen security by economic means, the Good Neighbor administration mixed a cultural element into its formula for bolstering hemispheric ties. Strong endorsement for the idea came from FDR himself, who had followed with interest some preliminary moves in this direction initiated by Laurence Duggan and other Latin American specialists in the State Department. Already activity on the cultural front had resulted in treaties negotiated at the Buenos Aires conference in 1936 that provided for exchange of publications, students, and professors among all the American republics, as well as for the promotion of exhibitions of the arts of the Americas.[7]

When advised at the end of the Havana conference on the need to create a special agency to deal with researching the hemisphere's economic problems and devising practical solutions, the president at once accepted the proposal. At the same time he suggested the addition of cultural relations to the new agency's purview. Roosevelt recalled the success his administration had scored in the darkest days of the Depression by extending public support to artists and writers. Thereby, to some degree at least, the Democratic Party had managed to co-opt a broad sampling of the nation's intellectuals and culturati in general and to mitigate the more revolutionary demands for social change that some of them had begun to voice. Support of artists and intellectuals may have helped bolster U.S. internal security in an hour of dire need. Perhaps the same approach might serve the purposes of hemispheric security by co-opting some of Latin America's cultural figures, whose stock-in-trade had been denunciation of Yankee civilization.

In the late summer of 1940 came the executive order that created the Office for Coordination of Commercial and Cultural Relations between the American Republics. In charge of the new agency would be a coordinator of inter-American affairs (CIAA). To this new post Roosevelt named the liberally inclined New York Republican millionaire Nelson A. Rockefeller—the grandson of Standard Oil founder John D. Rockefeller. This appointment was in line with the new policy of bipartisanship FDR was pursuing as he sought to retain in the Democratic camp those moderate Republicans who had supported him in his first two presidential bids. With considerable public unease about the president's violation of the two-term precedent established by George Washington, and with growing public dubiousness about many of the New Deal's more innovative—or radical—approaches, Roosevelt had begun to pull out all the bipartisan stops. All-out bipartisanship seemed the way to counter the electoral threat posed by the popular Wendell Willkie, who represented the Republican Party's moderate wing and who waged a strong campaign against the president.

In some ways the process through which FDR appointed Rockefeller suggests that the president did not take Latin America very seriously, at least not so far as the coordinator's position was concerned. Actually, though, the process reveals FDR at his most typical, when facing issues both of little and of enormous moment.

About the time the coordinator's post was conceived, Roosevelt had appointed Wall Street investment banker James Forrestal (a partner in Dillon, Read & Co.) to an influential Washington position. This was in line with the president's attempt to mend fences with big business as his interests moved from domestic to international affairs and to military preparedness. As one of his first tasks in Washington, Forrestal was charged with preparing a list of suitable appointees for the position of coordinator of inter-American affairs. At the head of the list that Forrestal prepared appeared the name William L. (Will) Clayton. Founder of the agricultural conglomerate Anderson, Clayton & Co., which had many connections in

Latin America, Clayton eventually would rise (in 1946) to the post of undersecretary of state for economic affairs. In 1940, though, FDR did not want him as his coordinator. Instead he picked Rockefeller, whose name appeared far down the list.

When Forrestal expressed dismay, asserting that Rockefeller was too self-centered and erratic to meet the responsibilities of the post, FDR set forth the reasoning behind his choice. Clayton, the president explained, had contributed $25,000 to the Republican Party in the midst of the crucial election campaign then underway, while Rockefeller, though a Republican, had made a contribution of $25,000 to the Democratic Party. Not long afterward, in a typical move, the president appointed Clayton as Rockefeller's assistant.[8]

Like Roosevelt, Nelson Rockefeller hoped that out of cultural exchange programs and out of a relatively modest expenditure of funds to provide grants and support to various Latin American cultural figures might come a growth in goodwill toward the United States. To some limited degree at least, cultural investments might strengthen hemispheric security. At the same time Rockefeller, whom the president eventually named assistant secretary of state for Latin American affairs, hoped that better cultural relations would pave the way for a dramatic expansion of economic relations between Latin America and the United States, both while the war was in progress and afterward. Thereby Rockefeller incited the lasting enmity of American and Latin American leftists who have tended through the years to dismiss him as a kid-gloved economic imperialist. At the beginning of the 1940s he also aroused the fears of Adolf Berle, who fretted lest Rockefeller create the impression that better cultural relations were merely a means to the end of expanding Yankee economic penetration.[9] Be that as it may, by 1940 culture, security, and economics (to say nothing of domestic politics) were all bound inseparably together in the rapidly evolving Good Neighbor policy. Instead of two entities in one skin, now there were three.

In his approach to Latin America, Rockefeller had stumbled onto the notion that culture could serve as an invaluable public relations ploy in encouraging broad acceptance by Latin Americans of a North American economic presence. Culturally spawned goodwill might also facilitate the sort of military presence south-of-the-border that security considerations counseled. In pursuit of his endeavor to package cultural, economic, and security considerations together, Rockefeller managed to enlist some business support for cultural exchange programs, thereby delivering the message to Latins that Yankee men and women of affairs had a genuine interest in promoting the better things of life: they were not the cultural barbarians that Latin American pensadores so often assumed them to be.

As coordinator of inter-American affairs and in charge of considerable public funds, Rockefeller encouraged a fair amount of insignificant froth—Latin American tours, for example, by Hollywood stars and starlets. At the same time, from the coordinator's office came funds that supported significant cultural exchange (including art exhibitions and tours by symphony orchestras as well as jazz and swing bands) and financed establishment of binational centers in Latin American cities where citizens could study the English language and American institutions and enjoy musical and theatrical presentations. These and other programs unquestionably heightened mutual understanding between U.S. and Latin American cultural leaders and commoners as well—even though not necessarily verifying the premise of some persons associated with the programs that knowledge of the United States and its culture would well-nigh guarantee Latin love of the gringo.

The Good Neighbor cultural program that Rockefeller coordinated yielded larger, and sometimes more controversial, results than originally foreseen. The coordinator's programs either strengthened or presaged cultural approaches that proved fruitful in the Cold War era. These approaches included assignment of political officers to embassy staffs; they included, also, burgeoning activities undertaken by the State Department's under-appreciated cultural division, as well as by the United States Information Agency, and by student and scholar exchanges under the auspices of the Fulbright-Hays program, a genuine national treasure. Not only in Latin America but throughout the world these new and innovative approaches to foreign relations rendered yeoman service in promoting international understanding, despite the fact that their occasional dramatic failures and general inability to fulfill unrealistic hopes often left a more lasting impression on cynical Americans than their subtle, largely unsung and unquantifiable triumphs. Moreover, it was the misfortune of the U.S. cultural initiative to clash with newly awakened Latin American cultural nationalism.

### Argentina and the Latin American Cultural Identity Quest

Precisely at the time the United States entered upon its attempt, as it were, to export its culture to Latin America, many of the intended recipients were caught up in the quest to define precisely what constituted their own cultural heritage and to bolster and defend that heritage once they had agreed on its essential elements. In many ways Argentina had established itself at the forefront of this quest.

Especially since the influential University Reform movement that originated in 1918, Argentine intellectuals had sought to reaffirm the nonmaterialistic and humanistic core that, so they believed, comprised the essence of their culture. In this endeavor, they borrowed frequently from the

Arielist tradition (described in Chapter 9), with its stress on the need for social hierarchies in order to preserve hierarchies of values. Above all, in addition to their statist, antiindividualistic, antibourgeois persuasions, the pensadores agreed that *letras,* not money-making talents, bestowed *nobleza.* Influential in sparking an upsurge in nationalistic sentiment, the Argentine pensadores, and their allies throughout the continent, agreed that their sort of nationalism was unalterably opposed to liberalism, that its economic foundations rested on protectionism and the establishment of domestic industries, and that authoritarian approaches probably represented the best way of achieving nationalism's goals.[10]

Support for the University Reform movement and its goals attained vast proportions throughout much of Latin America in the 1920s and '30s. Along with this support came widespread recognition that Argentina was in the forefront of the battle to prevent norteamericanos from establishing cultural hegemony. So far as pensadores in Argentina and throughout the southern hemisphere were concerned the real fifth column in their midst was composed not of fascist sympathizers but ideological collaborators with the Colossus. Precisely, then, at the moment the United States launched coordinated efforts to spread its cultural influence southward in line with the overall quest for security, Latin Americans (some of them, at least), with Argentines in the lead, were in the process of resolving that whatever their identity was it had little to do with and was indeed inimical to Yankee culture. Even in Cuba, where North American economic penetration had been most spectacular, an attempt was underway in the 1930s and '40s to find formulas that would permit the retention of a political culture distinct from that of the Yankees.[11]

In the State Department, Cordell Hull really did not know that the cultural identity debate had been joined in Latin America and was bolstering endemic cultural anti-Americanism. Some U.S. diplomats in the field, though, were well aware of these developments; and they were sensitive to the fact that if the Latins did not culturally identify with the United States they did not, *ipso facto,* align with German National Socialism or Italian fascism or even Franco's hispanidad. These diplomats and their allies in Washington, who more often than not included Sumner Welles before his 1943 dismissal, did not necessarily and automatically see anything inherently wrong with those Latin statist proclivities that automatically made the secretary of state see red. They believed Hull was ill-advised in his intransigent hostility to Argentina that reached new heights once the United States entered World War II. Argentina's desire to be Argentina did not imply that the country wanted to remake itself in the image of Germany or Italy.

The United States itself in the 1940s was undergoing an identity debate, and State Department divisiveness—indeed bureaucratic divisiveness in general—reflected this fact. On one side in the debate stood traditional-ists, totally dedicated to the principles of free markets and free enterprise, which they regarded as the very foundation stones of Americanism and well-nigh as sacrosanct as religious principles. On the other side stood New Deal liberals, permanently affected by having experienced the Great Depression, which they regarded not as an easily mended snag but rather as an indication of fundamental flaws in America's social-economic fabric. Basically, the liberals believed in the need permanently to temper laissez-faire individualism with statism, while making the Social Gospel a permanent part of the nation's civil religion. Hull and his allies belonged, of course, to the first school. Welles and his backers, whether in Washington or in the field, belonged to the second school. In between stood FDR, playing his usual game of trying to reconcile opposites. How he aligned himself depended on the hour of the day, or upon the particular person he was speaking with.

In the twilight years of the Good Neighbor policy the two identity debates underway in the Americas, the one in the United States and the other in Latin America, interacted with each other in such a way as often to sour hemispheric relations. Moreover, the same dual debate would complicate relations once the Cold War began and socialism rather than fascism emerged in Latin America as the main ideological basis for opposing laissez-faire capitalism.

# 25.

## Old and New Hemispheric Tensions as One War Gives Way to Another

❖ ❖ ❖ ❖ ❖ ❖ ❖ ❖ ❖ ❖ ❖ ❖ ❖ ❖ ❖ ❖ ❖ ❖ ❖ ❖ ❖ ❖ ❖ ❖ ❖ ❖ ❖ ❖ ❖ ❖ ❖ ❖

### The 1942 Rio Conference Precipitates a Crisis in U.S.-Argentine Relations

On December 7, 1941, Japan launched its war against the United States with a devastating sneak attack on Pearl Harbor; and shortly Japan's allies, Germany and Italy, declared war on the United States. The supreme test of the inter-American system forged during the Good Neighbor era was at hand. Would Latin American republics honor the agreement reached at Havana that an attack against the territory or sovereignty of one of the Americas constituted an act of aggression against all?

The nine Central American and Caribbean republics responded to the Japanese attack in the manner the State Department and most Americans thought all Latin American republics should respond: by December 12, each had declared war on Japan. Very shortly thereafter Venezuela, Colombia, and Mexico severed diplomatic relations with the Axis. Adolf Berle expressed delight with the "virtually unanimous support from all the republics of this hemisphere. If ever," he observed, "a policy paid dividends, the Good Neighbor policy has."[1]

Throughout the war, in fact, Berle and also the president himself continued to stress the overwhelming support the United States received from the Latin American republics. They were not always truthful in their utterances. Instead, they sought to put the best face possible on hemispheric developments, trying to practice what a later generation would refer to as "spin control." To have been truthful would have forced the president and his subordinates to concede that the Good Neighbor policy fell far short of producing the successes that the administration sought to attribute to it, to admit that Latin America had not reciprocated U.S. Good Neighbor concessions to the degree anticipated.

In January of 1942, not long after Berle had expressed his satisfaction with neighbors to the south, the foreign ministers of the American republics assembled in Rio de Janeiro, in line with hemispheric security commitments agreed to at the 1940 Havana meeting and at previous assemblies. The secretary of state could not leave Washington in its moment of supreme crisis, so Sumner Welles headed the U.S. delegation.

At Rio, the Mexican, Colombian, and Venezuelan delegations favored a resolution making severance of relations with the Axis powers well-nigh mandatory. However, objections came from several countries headed by Argentina and Chile, the latter justifiably apprehensive as to its ability to defend its long coastline if it provoked Japan into aggression. In the face of Argentine and Chilean intransigence, the delegates could produce no more than an accord that recommended a break in relations with the Axis powers. Reluctantly, Sumner Welles agreed to the watered-down accord. When Hull learned of this through a radio broadcast, he phoned Welles in Rio and spoke to him "more sharply than I had ever spoken to anyone in the Department," as he later wrote. "I said I considered this a change in our policy, made without consulting me, and the equivalent of a surrender to Argentina." At that point the president came on the line and indicated he would accept "the judgment of the man on the spot." Hull then warned the president that their country would pay heavily in the future for this failure at Rio. Even Berle shared Hull's outrage, describing himself as "heart-broken" over the "pretty miserable compromise."[2]

Nevertheless, the United States did have considerable grounds for celebration as the Rio meeting came to an end during an oppressively hot summer. It was no small consideration that on the last day of the assembly—after President Vargas had finally wrested consent from his generals—Brazil's Oswaldo Aranha made his way to the speaker's lectern and dramatically announced his country's rupture of relations with the Axis coalition.[3] Before the sessions adjourned, Ecuador became the eighteenth republic to sever relations.

Still, Welles himself was not pleased about the concessions he had felt constrained to make at Rio. In fact, the following October he described the "sinister passiveness" of Argentina and Chile in the face of Axis aggression as a "stab in the back at sister republics engaged in a life-and-death struggle to preserve the liberties and integrity of the New World." Already President Roosevelt had used similar language when, in June of 1940, he denounced Italy's declaration of war on France as the plunging of a dagger "into the back of its neighbor."[4] Perhaps in their own minds many Americans lumped together the stereotyped knife-wielding Italians and Argentines—who, after all, had acquired such a large admixture of Italian blood.

Rather than a genuine indication of his sentiments, Welles's "stab-in-the-back" statement may have represented an attempt to mollify Washington hardliners—he was then engaged in a desperate and ultimately unsuccessful attempt to retain his State Department position—and to put pressure on Chile, whose president was shortly due in Washington on a goodwill visit, to break relations with U.S. foes. If this was Welles's intention, he had to wait until January of 1943 for Chile to become the next-to-last Latin American republic formally to sever diplomatic relations with Germany, Italy, and Japan.

The one remaining country, Argentina, held out against breaking relations until March of 1945, acting just in time to assure itself—in line with a compromise the State Department worked out—an invitation to the founding conference of the United Nations in San Francisco. At least after Chile fell into line at the beginning of 1943, it appeared that the Americas, as Samuel Flagg Bemis puts the matter, were "one for all and almost all for one."[5]

For Cordell Hull, this was not good enough. Throughout the war he nursed his anger against Argentina and allowed it to explode whenever his department colleagues or the heads and assistants of other departments suggested contemporizing with that republic. What is more, throughout the war Hull was often allowed to have his way with Argentina, in total contrast to the 1938 crisis with Mexico precipitated by the oil expropriation. One policy-maker "even suggested that President Roosevelt 'more or less gave Argentina to Mr. Hull to play with, to keep him out of his hair.'" Roosevelt, after all, "had larger purposes to serve in which Argentina played only a minor part."[6]

As noted in Chapter 4, Argentina had always opposed the Monroe Doctrine's spirit of America for the Americans. Conscious of its ties to Europe, Argentina had grandiloquently proclaimed "let America be for humanity." Now it appeared that Argentina included Hitler's Germany, Mussolini's Italy, and Hirohito's Japan within the family of humanity. North Americans engaged in a life-or-death struggle with these countries, and patently disinclined to treat the Japanese in their midst in California as full-fledged human beings, were hardly disposed to concur with the Argentine position. By and large they regarded Nazi barbarism, and the barbarism of Italian and Japanese fascism, as "the farthest retreat from civilization the world had known";[7] and they found it difficult to forgive Argentina for what appeared to be acceptance if not out-and-out approbation of barbarism and inhumanity.

Neither were Americans, from men and women on the streets to highly placed officials, disposed to quarrel with Cordell Hull's absurdly exaggerated pronouncements on the possibility, perhaps even the likelihood, of a German and/or Italian takeover of Argentina. Indeed, not until midway in 1944 did the Joint Chiefs of Staff manage to assert their independence from the State Department line and to concede that there was a "diminishing and unimportant danger of any military operations from enemy activities in Argentina." Still, it is possible, even likely, that FDR believed what he said when in January of 1944 he informed a dubious Winston Churchill that Argentina was "a base of operations for activities dangerous both to our common war effort and to the peace of the Americas."[8]

Most decidedly, Hull was not alone in his apprehension over the Argentine menace. A good sprinkling of Washington officials, perhaps even a majority (with the president included), tended to mistake a "nationalism that often came out as anti-American" for a predisposition in behalf of North America's overseas enemies. More than paranoia was involved, though; for Argentina *did* come "dangerously close to endorsing the Axis in 1944," even when it should have been clear that "they had practically lost the war." And Argentina *did* promote a successful rightist coup in Bolivia in 1943 that placed in power what initially seemed, at least to suspicious observers in Washington, an anti–United States and pro-Axis administration. At this point some administration figures were honestly concerned lest Argentina spearhead a movement that might spread throughout much of South America and become a genuine danger to the war effort. And they kept in mind an aborted attempt by Chile's National Socialist or Nazi party to seize power through a coup in 1938. The circumstances of this aborted coup initially worried Roosevelt friend and Hoosier journalist-historian Claude G. Bowers, whose hatred of fascists had burgeoned while he was ambassador to the Spanish Republic and who began his five-year stint as ambassador to Chile in 1939. Soon, however, Bowers was sending a steady stream of dispatches to Washington lauding Chile's friendship and commitment to democratic, even Jeffersonian, values. But no such reassurances were forthcoming from U.S. representatives in Buenos Aires.[9]


In the United States–Argentina clash, two myths of national grandeur collided. Sensing that perhaps "for the time being at least" the country's "great future [lay] behind it," Argentine political and intellectual figures grew hypersensitive, perhaps even paranoid, about maintaining national claims to grandeur and to some sort of vaguely perceived suzerainty over the southern hemisphere.[10] To North Americans there was little doubt that their country's greatest splendors lay ahead; and they inclined to be anticipatory in claiming the perquisites of superpower status, along with which went the right not to be thwarted by minor powers.

## A Resentful Good Neighbor Feuds with Argentina, 1942–1945

By late 1942 and early 1943 not only Argentina but Latin America in general occasioned concern among those North Americans who hoped to parlay what they perceived as Good Neighbor policy successes into a concerted hemispheric war effort. Assistant Secretary of State Breckinridge Long complained that Venezuela had turned querulous, that Brazil's Nazi party seemed resurgent, that Bolivia was beginning to renege on pledges to expel Nazi diplomats, and that Ecuador and Peru remained hesitant in according full support to the war effort. All of Latin America, Long concluded, was cynically assessing the military prospects of the Allied effort against the Nazis, waiting to sense the outcome of the war before weighing in full-heartedly on one side or the other.[11]

British ambassador to the United States Lord Halifax believed that the State Department and Americans in general overreacted to Latin American indications of less than full-hearted appreciation of Yankees and their cause. Perhaps, he speculated, various government agencies had been "bemused by their own propaganda and thought they had produced that degree of Pan-American brotherly love which they were so lavishly attempting to buy." Good-hearted, well-intentioned Americans, Halifax mused, were of all people on earth the most "surprised when their good intentions are not always appreciated and understood by others. Equally, they were prone to resentment when disillusionment comes."[12] As of the early 1940s, disillusionment assuredly had come. And it only deepened as some Americans viewed, in particular, developments in Argentina.

In June of 1943 Gen. Ramón Castillo, who from Buenos Aires had posed a major challenge to Hull's agenda at the Havana conference, was pushed from power by an army rebellion. After a period of infighting among the successful rebels, Gen. Pedro Ramírez was installed in the Casa Rosada, Argentina's equivalent of the White House. He resided there only until the following January, when he was replaced by Gen. Edelmiro J. Farrell following another army coup. By now, with Welles out of the State Department, Hull was free to pursue a hard line. And he decided, with some justification from the U.S. perspective at least, that Argentina was going from bad to worse; for Farrell was scarcely more than the creature of the person who had become the most powerful figure in Argentina, the war minister and vice president Col. Juan D. Perón.

Perón and his largely military- and labor-based supporters envisaged a new and powerful Argentina, its economy based on rigid central planning and forced industrialization, its politics based on the techniques of mass mobilization and frenzied, nationalistic propaganda. Judged by twentieth-century manifestations of Latin American nationalism, there really was nothing out of the ordinary in this approach, except for Perón's greater than ordinary demagogic-populist skills; but Hull, in his deep-seated dislike of Latin American nationalism, which he was not very good at distinguishing from fascism (in part because of their many shared features), found the Farrell-Perón approach altogether contemptible and unpardonable. Hull's pique, indeed his outrage, may be understandable in view of the fact that the Farrell-Perón clique definitely went out of its way to stress the connection between a nationalism based on Argentine traditions and a nationalism that turned for revitalization to the ideological inspiration of Hitler's Germany and Mussolini's Italy and Franco's Spain. There, in the supposedly resurgent Old World, were the models that would help Argentines forge a new patria that also incorporated the worthiest features of its historic past.

Meanwhile Hull and his State Department continued to be bombarded by reports fed them by Argentine citizens who for their own purposes, combining high-mindedness with sordid self-seeking, detested Perón and his cronies and wanted the United States somehow to engineer their downfall, thereby paving the way for the dissidents to come to power. As so often in the past, as with J. Edgar Hoover's FBI, for example (as indicated in an earlier chapter), U.S. officials showed some degree of gullibility as they sifted through the analyses provided them by power-seeking Latin Americans. In his deep-seated dislike, even hatred, of Argentina, Hull wanted to believe the worst that dissidents in that country had to say about their country's government. By now, moreover, by 1944, Hull had grown so disillusioned with Latin America as a whole that he studiously avoided even uttering the words Good Neighbor policy. One reason for this was that from all over their continent Latin Americans reported on the nefariousness of incumbent governments; and a credulous Hull nourished his prejudices on the pejorative reports that his prejudices predisposed him to believe.

Until a reluctant Roosevelt in 1943 bowed to pressure to remove him from office in the wake of the already mentioned homosexual scandal, Sumner Welles had managed to tone down Hull's anti-Argentine belligerence. After his departure, some of his allies remained in the department, most notably Laurence Duggan, chief of the Division of American Republics Affairs, and his deputy, Philip W. Bonsal. They and like-minded subordinates sought to mitigate Hull's belligerency toward Argentina; and Hull in turn sought to make life difficult for them in the State Department. His tactics paid off. Before the end of 1944 Hull happily witnessed the departure of Duggan and Bonsal, along with other department moderates. At last the secretary of state had control over his department; now he could bend it to his will, all the while as it were thumbing his nose at Sumner Welles, who had begun to write newspaper columns defending Argentine policies or at least trying to place them in perspective.

Able now to pursue an Argentine policy after his own heart, and goaded by Welles's journalism, Hull sometimes went to unfortunate extremes. For example, he issued unfounded accusations to the effect that Argentina supplied the Axis with information that led to the sinking of Allied shipping. Then, in June of 1944 he recalled Ambassador Norman Armour from Buenos Aires. For almost a year the United States had no ambassador in Argentina. But Hull had little time to savor his control over Argentine policy, for in November of 1944—just after Roosevelt had won election to a fourth term—bad health forced him into retirement.

What about President Roosevelt, during Hull's last year at the State Department and after his retirement? Where did he stand on Argentina? For a time, presidential attitudes and actions had grievously concerned Hull. In January of 1944, for example, FDR had opposed harsh measures aimed at forcing Argentina into compliance with U.S. intentions. These measures, the president confided to Treasury Secretary Morgenthau, "just won't do. . . . [they] would kill our whole Good Neighbor Policy"[13]—a policy that Hull believed was already dead.

Increasingly, though, the president swung over to Hull's point of view. In February he wrote Getulio Vargas in Rio that while he thought things on the whole went well in Latin America, for which fact he gratefully acknowledged Brazil's contributions, he did wish "that Argentina would behave itself." However, Vargas and Foreign Minister Aranha were not willing to help make Argentina behave, or to do anything that might result in isolating that country. Instead, they hoped to forge the sort of solid Latin American front of autonomous nations that might prove useful if eventually, in a postwar world, the United States discarded the Good Neighbor guise and reverted to interventionist policies.[14]

By July of 1944 Roosevelt seemed, to judge from a letter to Winston Churchill, to have joined Hull in advocating a hard line. "I hope . . . that you will in very firm, clear, disgruntled tones of voice let Argentina know beyond a doubt that we are all fed up with her pro-Axis sentiments and practices. She is the only nation of North, Central or South America acting thus."[15] Roosevelt's tone in this instance and on subsequent occasions led Hull to believe that, as he went into retirement, he could trust the president to endorse a hard line against Argentina.

As always, though, the president hedged. In appointing Nelson Rockefeller, formerly the coordinator of inter-American affairs, to the post of assistant secretary of state for Latin American affairs, he chose a nonideological pragmatist mainly anxious to do whatever was necessary to assure U.S. capital a welcome in Argentina once the war was over. Enticed by the prospect of massive American investment, Argentina's fascist-militarist-nationalists would, so Rockefeller believed, soon swing into line as acceptable neighbors. As a member of Rockefeller's staff remarked, "Don't worry, we'll buy these people." Indeed, Rockefeller believed that once Argentines and Latin Americans in general came to understand that U.S. capital could help make them rich, hemispheric friction would disappear as the Good Neighbor policy gave way to a "Rich Neighbor" policy.[16]

Apparently the Rockefeller approach appealed to Roosevelt, though it is difficult to be certain, for by this time the president largely ignored Latin American affairs. When the president died in April of 1945 Rockefeller lost the man who at least had seemed to be shaping up as a supporter. The very next month Spruille Braden arrived as the new American ambassador in Buenos Aires. Braden we have already encountered as a crusading, ideological devotee of market economics who believed that free enterprise and only free enterprise could transform underdeveloped countries into developed countries, and who preached that Yankee know-how was needed to direct retarded republics to better futures. He was not inclined to "buy these people" in Argentina. He would shape them up, and not by dangling before them the carrot of massive investment by Yankees indifferent to the political orientation of countries in which they invested.[17]

Harsh, abrasive, and dogmatic in his views, Braden may not be an easy man to admire. Conceivably, though, he genuinely desired a better life for Argentines, and not just for a few privileged ones who could become rich neighbors by collaborating with Yankee investors totally unconcerned about the ideological leanings of officials they dealt with. To give genuine U.S.-style democratic capitalism a chance to create and spread wealth in Argentina, Braden may have believed it would first be necessary for his government to take steps to deliver the country from on-the-make state capitalists, like Perón and his cronies, bent on creating an economy based on huge government monopolies. In such an approach Braden, somewhat presciently as it turned out, saw a road to disaster.

Priding himself on hard-headed pragmatism, Braden looked with contempt on Argentine nationalism as shaped by Peronist demagogues given to mendaciousness and to ideological flights of fancy; he looked with contempt also on contrived-from-above political mobilization that made a mockery of democratic procedures. Nor could he abide a nebulous pursuit of national "grandeur" that took precedence over the down-to-earth individual pursuit of profit. In all these attitudes Braden may very well have been justified. But the ideological and economic tides in Argentina and in much of Latin America at the time were running inexorably against him.

Almost as much as Argentina's crypto-fascist ideology, on which nationalism as shaped by Perón and his cronies was partly based, Braden detested the development-from-above model favored by Rockefeller. In conformity with this model, as Braden saw it, American capitalists would pour money into Latin America, collaborate more with the bureaucrats who ran state enterprises than with private capitalists, and try to bring about economic miracles without foundations, miracles that left dependent masses totally unchanged in their precapitalist lifestyles and values and an easy prey for caudillos more intent upon personal than national grandeur. Surely there is something compelling about this aspect, even if not about the entirety, of Braden's perspective on Latin America.

Ultimately, in Braden's perspective, any Latin American leader who departed from U.S.-style private enterprise models of the pre–New Deal variety was either a rogue or a fool or both. In the case of Perón he may well have been right in seeing the Argentine as a knave. But this did not imply his prescience in assaying Latin America as a whole. And it did not seem to bode well for the future of hemispheric relations that, as World War II neared its end, an increasing number of Americans adopted the Braden perspective, in toto, as their own. This was a perspective that viewed only one element within the national tradition as amounting to a hill of beans: the unregulated, free-enterprise variety of individualism out of which all blessings flowed, moral, economic, and political.

Soon these Americans would share with Braden a sense of outrage over the defeat he sustained in his contest with Perón. Outrage abated, though, as it became increasingly clear that defeat had been incurred in the interests of waging a new war: the Cold War.

## Argentina Triumphant in Its Duel with the United States, 1945–1947

In Buenos Aires Ambassador Braden's chief undertaking was to project himself into the electoral campaign beginning to heat up about the time of his arrival. Determined to block the election of Perón to the presidency, Braden did all in his power to convince Argentines that the dashing military leader, so ably abetted by his equally dashing blond wife Evita, was an unreconstructed fascist. Seeking to justify his intervention in the politics of the country to which he was accredited, Braden recklessly charged that Perón and his accomplices were engaged in a nefarious scheme to establish a "Fourth Reich" in Argentina.[18]

Back in Washington, Rockefeller was horrified by Braden's actions. He and many of his friends among corporate leaders felt the ambassador was "ruining the richest market in Latin America by forcing the country to the brink of civil war." Perón, they believed, might well be the only man capable of maintaining stability. Braden himself conceded that companies such as General Motors and ITT "completely disagreed with my view of Perón and my advising against investment there while Perón lasted."[19]

Assuming an interventionist stance that appeared a mite excessive to the new Harry Truman administration, Braden found himself back in Washington in September of 1945. Actually, his recall tied in with a promotion—just as in the case of Sumner Welles's recall from Cuba in 1933. Much to Rockefeller's dismay, Braden returned to Washington to replace him as assistant secretary of state in charge of Latin American affairs. In taking charge of hemispheric policy, Truman had wasted no time in showing that he, even as his predecessor, could withdraw with one hand what he gave with the other.

Back in Washington Braden compiled what came to be known as the *Blue Book,* designed mainly for consumption in Argentina, where the electoral campaign was in its late stage. Braden hoped the documents reproduced in the *Blue Book* would prove to Argentines the extent to which Perón and his cronies had championed the Nazi cause. Many scholars have subsequently dismissed the validity of most of Braden's charges. Nevertheless, the extent (beginning fully to come to light only in the early 1990s) to which Perón after Hitler's defeat helped facilitate entrance into Argentina of hundreds of Nazis, among them some "of the most horrendous butchers," makes it appear that Braden might not have been altogether off-target in some of his charges.[20] Of course, acting under principles of raison d'etat the United States itself provided safe haven to many Nazi war criminals who happened to possess scientific talents that might make them useful in waging the newly joined struggle with the USSR. Conceivably, Perón could have been as interested in recruiting nation-building skills as in providing refuge for ideologically congenial war criminals. The issue remains murky, but there are grounds to suspect that Perón and his henchmen showed an abnormal compulsion to provide a safe haven for luminaries of the defeated Axis cause. And this possibility suggests the need to see Braden's crusade in its context. The following three paragraphs may hint at the context.


In perceiving a Nazi menace to the south, FDR and Hull and other official Latin America watchers, as well as some scholars and some sectors of the public in general, may have been guided by intuition and perhaps gringo prejudices, as well as by self-serving motives, all of which were hitched to exaggerated and sometimes even fraudulent intelligence reports. Nevertheless, they also had some valid grounds to suspect strong fascistic currents not only in Argentina but in many sister republics as well.

Had it not been for the way in which, as it turned out, World War II ended, Nazism and other forms of fascism might have proved a virtually irresistible temptation to vast numbers of Latin Americans, all of them anxious to promote varieties of nationalism that left no room for the rights of those who were not true believers. Those who were true believers found no appeal whatsoever in the ideology of the open, pluralistic society.

Even in the United States itself, it was—in the final analysis—only the preparations for and the waging of a successful war that restored prosperity and with it well-nigh universal faith and confidence in the open society with its twin pillars of market capitalism and liberal, individualistic democracy. In Latin America, that sort of faith and confidence had never been even remotely so robust as in the United States. So long as the Depression had maintained its grip, many Latin American politicians and intellectuals, as well as the preponderance of leaders both clerical and lay within the Catholic Church, had found various varieties of fascism often more appealing than the economic free enterprise and the one-person, one-vote democracy associated with U.S. traditions. Not necessarily justifiably, but certainly understandably, many North Americans stood ready, by 1945, to punish Latin Americans for not having properly foreseen, as of 1930 or even 1940, what the world would look like in 1945.

Whatever the mix of hearsay and valid charges Braden crammed into the *Blue Book,* the campaign he had begun against Perón in Buenos Aires and then continued from Washington ultimately redounded to the advantage of the Argentine strongman. His followers, chanting "Perón or Braden," elected their man president by a comfortable though not overwhelming margin.

In due course George Messersmith, who most recently had distinguished himself in Mexico as Josephus Daniels's successor, arrived as U.S. ambassador to Perón-led Argentina. Convinced, as indeed Rockefeller had been convinced, that Braden was fighting yesterday's war against fascism while today's and tomorrow's war had to be waged against Marxian socialism, Messersmith sought to mend fences in Argentina. A new vision of reciprocity had captured his fancy, and soon would capture the fancy of State Department officials as well. The Good Neighbor policy had been conceived in the spirit that if the United States withdrew from intervention and refrained from other actions that Latin Americans found distasteful, they, the Latin Americans, would reciprocate: initially, by providing environments propitious to the operation of U.S. capital, as cleansed and reformed by the New Deal; and, subsequently, by joining in the struggle against the Axis powers. The new reciprocity rested on the assumption that if Washington turned a blind eye to Latin American practices that departed both from the guidelines of American-style democracy and American-style free-enterprise capitalism, then at least those worrisome neighbors to the south would reciprocate by lining up against the USSR.

In his State Department office, Assistant Secretary Braden fumed over the way Messersmith temporized with the Argentines. In 1947 he won a battle but lost the war. Messersmith was recalled as ambassador to Argentina, his mission declared successfully accomplished; simultaneously, Secretary of State George Marshall accepted the resignation that Braden had been asked to submit. In effect, the diplomatic shuffling signified that the new reciprocity had become the mainstay of Washington's Latin American policy.

About this time Sumner Welles—getting in a final dig at his old adversary Cordell Hull—published a book arguing, as mentioned in a previous chapter, that Perón had the inherent capacity and a good chance "to make of his promised 'social revolution' a New Deal for the Argentine people."[21] While Welles's wildly optimistic appraisal may have gone altogether too far for most State Department officials at the time, they were prepared to tolerate, if not necessarily bless, Perón's attempt to reform his Argentine patria. Perhaps a dash of crypto-fascism might even be useful in strengthening Latin American bulwarks against communism once the Cold War began in earnest.

As a matter of fact, fascism of the very worst sort once feared by FDR, by Cordell Hull, and by countless other concerned Americans, fascism that scorned political and economic freedom, fascism that paid no heed to human rights, fascism that justified uncurbed official violence against perceived "enemies of the state" *did* come to Argentina, but not until the 1970s. It grew out of the seeds that many U.S. officials and Argentine democrats had justifiably been wary of in the 1930s and early '40s. When these seeds matured into the so-called "dirty war" of the early 1970s, they produced a form of state terrorism that was directed ostensibly against a new menace about which many North Americans had grown paranoid as they surveyed their neighbors to the south: the menace of communism and of all varieties and shades of Marxism. This being the case, fascism when it did indeed appear in Argentina—producing certain ripple effects that spread to contiguous republics and all the way to Central America—caused relatively little concern to most of those U.S. leaders who at the time presided over their country's security interests.

If the Good Neighbor team had still been in office in the early 1970s, would it have been more alarmed than the new incumbents about the fascist specter to the south?

Ironically, Argentina's swing toward fascism in the early 1970s represented in some ways a response to a genuine challenge posed by leftists who now, in many instances, called themselves Peronistas and who used much of the old Peronista rhetoric to justify their ideological and political stance. Thereby they proved that Peronismo lent itself as readily to Marxist as to fascist purposes. Little wonder, then, that Good Neighbor diplomats in FDR's era had been confused as to the real nature of pristine Peronismo.

# 26.

## The Good Neighbor Policy in Transition as Its Presiding Officer Dies

❖ ❖ ❖ ❖ ❖ ❖ ❖ ❖ ❖ ❖ ❖ ❖ ❖ ❖ ❖ ❖ ❖ ❖ ❖ ❖ ❖ ❖ ❖ ❖ ❖ ❖ ❖ ❖ ❖ ❖ ❖ ❖ ❖ ❖ ❖ ❖

### New Yet Old Parameters of U.S. Policy with Latin America: 1945–1947

Whether engaged in lining Latin Americans up to combat fascism or Marxist-Leninist socialism, many U.S. policy-makers realized they were going against the grain of their putative allies by demanding that they adhere to free-market economic guidelines. Better to go along, then, in pursuit of strategic interests, with Latin American proclivities toward statism. Better, also, to design large-scale government-to-government assistance programs, of the sort Latin Americans coveted, than to rely on free enterprise south of the border to mitigate potentially destabilizing socioeconomic problems. So, to some degree the United States would use the same approaches in combating a possible communist menace that it had employed in negating the perceived fascist threat. And this made considerable sense in view of the fact that both hostile forces, Marxist-Leninist communism and fascism, were in many ways quite similar. At least they converged on their outer edges, one blending into the other. Joseph Stalin must have realized this fact himself. And he must have been goaded by the embarrassing truth to launch his intellectually feeble campaign to prove that fascism was really just last-stage capitalism.

Historian Alan Cassels once wrote that Marxian socialism began as and remained "quintessentially anticapitalist no matter how many maximalist and minimalist programs proliferate. Similarly, fascism everywhere in Europe . . . constituted a reaction against the dominant materialist culture" of market capitalism as enshrined by the bourgeoisie. So, Cassels concluded, all fascisms, just as much as all extremist varieties of socialism, were "sworn and consistent foes of bourgeois liberalism and materialism." Another historian, A. James Gregor, has argued persuasively that most twentieth-century utopianist quests for rapid, state-directed material and cultural development were really offshoots of "paradigmatic fascism"—no matter how stridently their spokespersons might profess ideological commitment to Marxism.[1] In the final analysis, the most telling differences between fascism and Marxism may consist of little more than the former's more openly displayed infatuation with nationalism, and its greater honesty in professing the need for permanent totalitarianism.

Not surprisingly many Latin Americans in the post–World War II era, clinging still to nationalisms built around condemnation of money-grubbing, individualistic free-enterprise capitalism, favoring still political mobilization from above over genuine participatory democracy, seemed occasionally tempted to jump from the fascist frying pan into the Marxist fire. And to some degree U.S. policy-makers felt constrained to go along with the Latin proclivities toward statism, hoping that thereby they could keep those proclivities from leading to the all-out jump into Marxism-Leninism. That jump might even lead (though not necessarily so) to acceptance of party-line directives from Moscow and therefore constitute a threat to U.S. security interests in the Cold War era.

Not until the early 1990s, to look ahead now for a moment, did Latin Americans begin to do what centrist, mainstream North Americans by and large had for half a century and more hoped they would do. Finally, in the wake of Free World victory in the Cold War, Latin Americans responded to new circumstances by doing, by and large, what such spokesmen of American free-enterprise capitalism as Cordell Hull and Spruille Braden had urged upon them back in the 1930s and '40s. They began to lower trade barriers and to take en masse to the ways of privatization—matters that I deal with at some length in my concluding section.

At an earlier point in this book I referred to Braden as a Neanderthal man. To imply this, however, necessitates looking at him from the perspective of 1930s- and early '40s-style progressives. From the perspective of the 1990s Braden and Hull, along with countless other Americans who remained steadfast in their preference for the main currents of their country's civil religion, appear totally up-to-date and even prophetic. From the perspective of the '90s, Braden and Hull and like-minded Americans were precursors of the neoconservatives, who certainly see themselves as thoroughly modern and even prescient, however much they claim roots in traditional national values.

In all probability, however, neither adherents to the Braden-Hull school nor the ideological heirs of that school in the 1990s reckoned with what turned out to be the consequences (short-term, at the very least) of their recommended policies; they did not reckon with the intensifying impoverishment of the masses combined with the stunning enrichment of the most privileged sectors that the privatization mania encouraged, both in their own country and in the underdeveloped lands to the south.

For FDR, it was never hard to foresee the regressive income distribution likely to ensue from altogether unbridled market capitalism. He warned against this in the early days of the New Deal when he assailed the economic royalists; and he warned against it again toward the end of his life, in his 1944 state of the union address. In the foresight that prompted these warnings lies much of Roosevelt's greatness as a national and as a hemispheric statesman. In this foresight lies part of the explanation for the fact that the chaos issuing from his Latin American policies was a gentler chaos than that spawned by some of his late-twentieth-century successors.

### Roosevelt Dies as the Good Neighbor Policy Winds Down

When Roosevelt died in April of 1945, Mexicans appreciated how grievous a loss they had suffered. The president's death, the embassy reported, "has caused greater grief in Mexico than that of the passing of any Mexican in generations." At once the Mexican government declared a three-day mourning period, unprecedented for a foreigner. When President Avila Camacho exchanged condolences with the wife of Ambassador George Messersmith, tears welled in his eyes. "The world," he murmured, "has lost the greatest man it has produced in centuries."[2]

In Argentina, relatively few signs of mourning greeted news of the president's death, confirming a fact of life Roosevelt had already learned. In dealing with Latin American republics, it's impossible to win them all, if for no other reason than their mutual suspicions, enmities, and hatreds. But actions by the United States itself contributed to the diplomatic success with Mexico, and the relative failure with Argentina.

Circumstances had favored the United States–Mexico rapprochement that took place in the 1930s. Lázaro Cárdenas proved a president after the heart of Josephus Daniels, after the heart of Roosevelt as well. At the time the United States had embarked on a sweeping reform program aimed at remedying the apparent collapse of traditional market capitalism by altering that system. The fundamental reforms that Cárdenas had set in motion, based often on massive government intervention, did not necessarily seem out of line to the president or to many a New Deal brain-truster, or to the innovative and overwhelmingly young persons who flocked to Washington to design and implement the programs that would, so they believed, project their country into a happy future by severing some of the ties to a malfunctioning traditional system. Moreover, at that time cultural relativism was in the intellectual air that policy-makers and the general public breathed. If Mexico wanted, in line with its time-honored way of life, to proceed further than the United States toward the corporatist economic and political system, so be it.

By the time U.S.-Argentine relations settled into an acrimonious standoff, North America's traditional private-enterprise economy had returned to life, in no small part because of wartime mobilization. Against a background of impending military victory and a return to prosperity, Americans were hardly disposed to doubt that their system was the only good, the only acceptable system. Certainly they were less inclined than only a few years ago to countenance, let alone endorse, sweeping statist reforms. Yet it was precisely such reforms that a new generation of Argentines, about to assume control of their country under their leader Perón, had determined to implement. Given the mood of the times that always affected the mood of this consummate politician, Franklin Roosevelt listened to Daniels and to the liberal wing of his advisers in shaping Mexican policy. In contrast, by the early 1940s he inclined more to listen to Hull and other relatively conservative advisers—during the increasingly rare moments he listened to anyone discoursing on Latin America. Yet precisely at this time in Argentina a new group of rulers emerged who in their enthusiasm for innovation resembled, in some ways, American policy-makers at the beginning, not the end, of the New Deal.

Without Roosevelt and his warm, ingratiating, and also devious personality, Latin Americans could never have been won to the extent many of them were by the early Good Neighbor policy. Yet, without the circumstances of the time in which he shaped that policy initially, FDR would never have been able to cast himself and his country in the guise of a Good Neighbor. By the 1940s, though, the times had changed. For one thing— and this was fundamental—the hemispheric isolationist perspective had forever (or at least for a very long time) disappeared from American foreign policy perspectives. Inevitably, with the changing times Roosevelt's perspective on the world had changed.

By 1945 FDR no longer even went through the motions of attending very seriously to his neighbors to the south. By then he was back, in thought, word, and deed, in the European world, back among the major powers. Reverting to my baseball analogy, Roosevelt had served his time in the minors, and had been called back to the major leagues where he felt he had always belonged. At least he could take satisfaction in arguing that he had constructively reshuffled the major league farm system while serving as its unofficial commissioner; but it remains uncertain as to how much in his heart of hearts he actually believed, at the end, that he had fundamentally reshuffled that farm system. As his life wound down his indifference to the hemisphere's minor league, its farm system, may have sprung at least in part from the realization he had not gotten very far after all in reshuffling it.

FDR had had a woman, Lucy Page Mercer: warm, understanding, exhilarating, sensuous, and at least for a time his mistress. He loved her during much of his adult life, and on her his gaze fell in his final seconds of life in Warm Springs, Georgia, as the massive heart attack his doctors (but not the president) knew was imminent delivered its fatal blow. FDR also had a wife, high-minded and compassionate if not passionate (at least not with him), a wife who was serious about humanitarian reforms to the point of being a dour nag. He was devoted to her, part of the time anyway. The wife, but not the other woman, emerged from the same social and cultural environment of wealth and position that shaped the man. Both women helped Roosevelt fulfill his potential, just as he helped them fulfill theirs.

Metaphorically, Roosevelt's private love life had a counterpart in his public life. Metaphorically, he had a trans-Atlantic wife shaped by the same influences that had molded his life; yet for some time he was estranged from her. Along the way, he acquired a Latin mistress, shaped in altogether a different mold. His interest in both the overseas wife and the south-of-the-border mistress helped him become a better and more complete statesman, just as his interest in them enhanced and benefited both of them. But the metaphorical loves of Roosevelt ended differently from his real-life loves. Metaphorically, in his twilight days Roosevelt fixed his loving gaze on his trans-Atlantic wife, ignoring the mistress with whom he had had a marvelous fling. The mistress in the southern hemisphere had been just a stepping stone toward reconciliation with the wife from whom life circumstances had temporarily estranged him.

### An Archetypal Gringo in the White House

There was never a thought that the man who succeeded FDR in the White House might have a mistress. Harry Truman was the very personification of American middle-class sexual rectitude (at a time when such rectitude may actually have existed or at least been cherished as a desideratum). For this and many other reasons as well, including the fact that the former haberdasher and machine politician was rather rough around the edges, Latin American diplomats priding themselves on their aristocratic manners and often on their genteel breeding as well, tended to have difficulty empathizing with Truman. They looked back longingly, nostalgically, to the FDR days.

While most assuredly possessing the potential to become a more-than-adequate, a better-than-average president (and some observers have praised him in far more generous terms), Truman decidedly was not in the Latin American grain. This fact may have endeared him to many Americans perhaps grown just a mite weary of the Machiavellian Hyde Park aristocrat. By and large, Americans were ready to return to normalcy. Relieved that the crises of poverty and war had been successfully surmounted, not foreseeing that a Cold War was about to confront them, Americans on the whole were ready to welcome a president of normal dimensions, one who was not larger than life. In their hour of extreme crisis, they may have needed a paternal figure, a patriarch with a sense of noblesse oblige. Now, with their system functioning smoothly again and their confidence restored, they were ready to make do with a man who seemed just one of them. But Latin Americans, by no means as yet out of the economic woods, were not sure about the new man. Many of them longed still for a patriarchal, paternalistic, relatively nonjudgmental figure in Washington.

The sort of typical Yankee whom all too many Latin Americans tended blindly to denigrate, even to sneer at, Truman was unsubtle and forthright, direct to the point of bluntness. Generally shunning deviousness (or at least managing to create the impression that he did), Truman blurted out what was on his mind, even if the thoughts he expressed were highly distasteful to those to whom he addressed them. The gentlemanly code of conduct that proscribed giving offense struck Truman as an excuse for the sort of hypocrisy he detested.

After having been spoiled for years by the Roosevelt presence, Latin Americans now encountered an archetypal gringo in Washington. Deviousness they could often understand, perhaps even empathize with, certainly forgive. It would take them a while to adjust to the new man, and many of them never did. Meantime, they were reluctant to face up to the fact that had he lived into the postwar era their aristocratic friend in the White House might not have shown more solicitude toward them than the man from Missouri. Like so many of his fellow citizens FDR, as the war approached its end, had the feeling that to some degree Latin Americans had let him and his country down.

# SECTION
# VII

❖❖❖❖❖❖❖❖❖❖❖❖❖❖❖❖❖❖❖❖❖❖❖❖❖❖❖❖❖❖

*Farewell and
Welcome Back
the Good
Neighbor Policy*

# 27. The "American Century" Begins

❖ ❖ ❖ ❖ ❖ ❖ ❖ ❖ ❖ ❖ ❖ ❖ ❖ ❖ ❖ ❖ ❖ ❖ ❖ ❖ ❖ ❖ ❖ ❖ ❖ ❖ ❖ ❖ ❖ ❖ ❖ ❖ ❖

## Hemispheric Reassessments:
## The Chapúltepec Conference of 1945

In order to cover the outcome of the U.S.-Argentina contretemps, I looked ahead in Chapter 25 to the year 1947. It was then that the burgeoning Cold War drove the United States to exchange if not an abrazo then at least a handshake with Juan Domingo Perón. Now it is necessary to backtrack slightly and address other events of hemispheric significance that occurred just before and just after World War II came to an end.

Hoping to put hemispheric relations on a more solid footing by repairing some of the damage inflicted by the ongoing feud between the United States and Argentina, Latin American governments began in 1944 to urge the summoning of another inter-American conference. Due largely to U.S. pique with Argentina, no such conference had been held since January of 1942. With palpably little enthusiasm, U.S. officials decided to humor their neighbors; and the conference they urged convened in February of 1945. The setting was picturesque Chapúltepec, on the outskirts of Mexico City. The physically depleted Franklin Roosevelt, with only a few weeks to live as it turned out, paid scant attention to the sessions.

Headed by newly appointed Secretary of State Edward Stettinius, the U.S. delegation included such luminaries as Assistant Secretary of State for Latin American Affairs Nelson Rockefeller, Assistant Secretary of State for Economic Affairs William L. (Will) Clayton (who, as mentioned in Chapter 24, had been named by FDR as Rockefeller's assistant when the latter held the post of coordinator of inter-American affairs), and Adolf Berle. A longtime molder of hemispheric policy, Berle was about to take up his duties as newly appointed ambassador to Brazil. In that post, Berle would work to unseat the generally kid-gloved long-term dictator Getulio Vargas, thereby signaling that the Good Neighbor's reluctance to interfere in the internal affairs of Latin American republics was at an end. Meanwhile at Chapúltepec it became clear that other aspects of the wartime Good Neighbor policy were about to expire.

On February 27 "Will" Clayton delivered an address that reflected not only his thought but that of, among many other U.S. policy-makers, Spruille Braden, also on hand as a U.S. delegate to the conference. Clayton's address would have caused Cordell Hull, had he been present, to beam, just as it would have delighted hardliner free-enterprise advocate Jesse Jones, the former secretary of commerce for whom Clayton had served as chief procurement official after leaving the coordinator's office. Embracing the ideological approach of market liberalism (dubbed neoconservatism some forty years later), Clayton extolled the nation-building wonders of free enterprise, attacked all manifestations of economic nationalism and statist intervention, advised Latin Americans to resuscitate their economies through resumed sales of primary goods to their traditional European markets, and admonished them at least temporarily to postpone whatever plans they might have for industrialization. Behind the last piece of advice suspicious Latin Americans detected the desire of American manufacturers to avoid the competition of locally produced goods.

Nor did Clayton sweeten his message when—reasonably enough—he informed the delegates that they could expect little if anything in the way of economic succor from the government of the United States. In the immediate future that government would have to concentrate all of its resources on rebuilding European economies. Henceforth, the delegates inferred, there would be no more "walking-around" money distributed in Latin America, at least not if Clayton spoke for his government.[1]

In a way Clayton enunciated a policy that smacked of the "termination" approach that the U.S. government adopted in the postwar era in its relations with Native Americans. Under Commissioner of Indian Affairs John Collier, the government had embarked on a program to protect traditional indigenous life patterns, which Collier was convinced were based on communalism rather than individualism. In contrast, the termination policy sought to administer shock therapy to Native Americans. It rested on abandonment of government "handouts" and subsidization of traditional tribal ways. Shapers of the termination policy called on Indians to abandon their communal approaches and learn to enter into the competitive and individualistic American economic mainstream. In short, termination represented a new beginning in the long-sustained crusade to "Americanize the American Indians."[2] Similarly, North Americans now resumed their old crusade to Americanize the Latin Americans. At least for those who engaged in the crusade, the cultural relativism that had facilitated the emergence of a Good Neighbor policy was consigned to the dustbin of history.

While Spruille Braden enthusiastically applauded the Clayton address at Chapúltepec, Latin American delegates by and large sat on their hands. Indeed, one Latin American commentator swiftly suggested that Clayton had plagiarized a speech made by Theodore Roosevelt around the turn of the century. Just conceivably, though, the formulas laid down by Clayton would have provided the best models for Latin Americans—at least for privileged and well-to-do Latin Americans—to follow in their quest of development. As it turned out, though, Latin American leaders would instead experiment, disastrously on the whole, with old and new models of statism and government intervention in seeking to stimulate their economies, only to come (some of them, at least), by the beginning of the 1990s, to the sort of privatization policies Clayton had urged upon them.

Listening with general but reserved approbation to Clayton's address at Chapúltepec was another U.S. delegate, George Messersmith, the admirable ambassador to Mexico and shortly to become an admirable ambassador to Argentina. Could either man have foreseen that the sort of approaches Clayton urged would *not* necessarily lead to the kind of capitalism with a humane countenance that Messersmith (and long before him Adam Smith) expected to issue out of economic liberalism? This is a matter on which students of hemispheric affairs on both sides of the border strongly disagree. I suspect that if they were alive to see in the 1990s the social results issuing in some Latin American republics out of the sort of economic policies they urged in the 1940s, certainly Messersmith and perhaps Clayton would be sorely disturbed.


In the United States itself, with the Depression now behind it, there were no longer the starving people lurking in the shadows that a prescient Debussy had depicted in *Pelléas et Mélisande*—as described in this book's first section. Nor were there the sort of threatening social confrontations that Verdi had depicted in *Simon Boccanegra*. Nor was there loss of hope in the established order of the sort that had led Alban Berg to glorify the outcast, the social misfit, in his opera *Wozzeck*. Nor was there a widely perceived connection between violence and capitalism of the sort that Clint Eastwood would posit in his film *The Unforgiven*. In the United States, God was back in His heaven and all was well with the divinity's favorite country.

In Latin America, though, the circumstances of economic precariousness that had afflicted Depression-era North America continued to prevail. And to deal with those circumstances, Latin Americans felt they had to have recourse not only to their statist traditions, but to the sort of expedients adopted even by gringos in the initial stages of the New Deal, and perhaps also to some of the measures the USSR continued to resort to in the attempt to address the problems of late-developing nations. They might even want to tap into the ostensibly indigenous varieties of socialism that Africa's new nations would shortly begin to experiment with—to their everlasting misfortune.

The Latin American delegates at Chapúltepec soon discovered there were Yankee delegates who shared their aversion to the Clayton recommendations. With the assistance of those delegates, among them Adolf Berle, the Latin Americans managed to tone down the thrust of the Clayton formulas in the official documents that emerged from the conference. At the same time the Latin delegates (as indicated at the conclusion of Chapter 21) convinced their northern counterparts as to the advisability of retaining the regional hemispheric system painstakingly constructed between 1933 and 1942, and incorporating that system into the about-to-emerge United Nations. They also prevailed upon the North American delegates to collaborate with them in working out a formula whereby Argentina might be readmitted into the good graces of the inter-American system and ultimately invited to the San Francisco conference that would forge the United Nations charter. Fearing what appeared to be the new U.S. thrust in hemispheric policy, Latin Americans wanted to be able to present a solid front in dealing with Yankees who had reverted to pre–Good Neighbor form. And a solid front meant one that included Argentina.

For a time following the Chapúltepec conference, what began to concern Latin Americans even more than Washington's reversion to policies calculated to facilitate entry of Yankee investors was the specter of neglect. The isolationism vis-à-vis trans-Atlantic countries that had nourished the Good Neighbor policy had given way in the United States to a European-oriented worldview; and until the Cold War came along and with it the possibility of playing once more to U.S. security fears, Latin Americans found it increasingly difficult to capture the attention of a Colossus grown more colossal than ever and itching for the chance to throw its weight around among the great powers. North Americans now bestrode the center of the world; and they retained little interest in the Latin American periphery.

## The Depression Gives Way to Visions of the "American Century"

With the Depression well behind them in 1945, North Americans by and large banished from memory the revolution in values that the economic crisis had inspired. They no longer had to adjust to being poor. They no longer had to settle for nonmaterial gratifications that included friendly fraternization with once disparaged neighbors, whether next door or across the border. In the depths of the Depression, songwriters Harry Warren and Al Dubin had encouraged fantasy and escapism in their composition "We're in the Money." Ginger Rogers had scored a personal triumph singing it in the movie *Gold Diggers of 1933*. In 1945, as much as and probably more than ever before, Americans really were in the money or, in the case of most, able to think that tomorrow they would be. They no longer had to make a virtue out of the necessity of settling for nonmaterial rewards. At least those Americans who mattered were in, or about to be in, the money. Those who weren't were bums, and bums were once again pariahs, situated beyond the cultural pale.

Once again, North Americans were ready to hold against Latin Americans their apparent inability, based surely on moral shortcomings, to achieve personal and national material prosperity on any kind of a consistent and sustained basis. America's short-lived cultural revolution was over. So was its Good Neighbor era, at least until the Cold War induced efforts at artificial resuscitation.

Even by the late 1930s, American businessmen were beginning to emerge once again as heroes, as the only persons in the eyes of their fellow citizens with the skill and know-how to lift the country out of its economic doldrums. Bureaucrats and intellectuals did not seem to possess this skill. By 1938 their expedients had met with apparent failure, as the economy took a new dip. Perhaps they should get out of the way, stop harassing the captains of industry and cooperate with them. All the more did this spirit flourish once America entered the war. Prodigies of productivity were what could guarantee victory. And who had the know-how to perform these prodigies? The industrialists and entrepreneurs. They were America's, and the world's, saviors; and increasingly conservative and centrist Democrats joined Republicans in recognizing the titans of industry not as robber barons but as saviors. If Democrats began to join Republicans in this assessment, most of them had been slow to do so. Perhaps that is why Republicans gained forty-four seats in the House and nine in the Senate in the 1942 midterm elections.[3]

In the early '30s Americans reveled in disclosures of congressional investigations about the nefariousness of the armaments makers and big business in general in dragging the country under Woodrow Wilson into what, in retrospect, had become a largely unpopular war. Now, a decade later, Americans hailed business leaders for the know-how that would guarantee victory in an overwhelmingly popular struggle. In a wartime song Irving Berlin called on Americans to look up and see bombers in the sky. "Rockefeller helped to build them," he exulted, and "So did I." The factory hand was allied with the business tycoon. Big business knew what it was doing in discharging its patriotic mission. Let big business have its way, whether in America or in Latin America or in any part of the world. The war, according to a labor historian, "turned out to be the gravedigger of domestic economic and social reform."[4] In its aftermath, it also proved something of a gravedigger of government efforts to tell Yankee entrepreneurs how to behave in Latin America, at least until Cold War diplomacy began to dictate some basic etiquette reeducation.

During the Depression, FDR had experimented with the sort of corporatist economic intervention that since colonial times had been the stock-in-trade of Latin American governments. By 1945, Americans were in no mood to tolerate the Latin Americanization of their institutions. Instead of corporatism, Americans placed their trust in "*corporationism*." Prosperity had returned, and "with it the prestige and power of corporate capitalism." Rising by more than 200 percent between 1940 and 1945, the Gross National Product hit $284 billion in 1950, "compared with only $35 billion in 1935." Unemployment in 1949 stood at less than 5 percent. Capitalism worked! And the major task facing Americans was to ensure its continuation and perhaps increase the privileges and perquisites of those who made it work, both in America itself and wherever Yankee capitalism operated in the world at large.[5]

Ever inclined to juggle and to synthesize opposites, Roosevelt in his late days seemed not altogether to like what he observed. Already in a 1940 Fireside Chat he warned that a "common sense of decency" made it imperative "that no new group of war millionaires shall come into being in this nation as a result of the struggle abroad." Moreover, in his already-cited January 1944 state of the union address Roosevelt delivered what has been called "the most social democratic speech ever made" by a sitting U.S. president. In it, he attacked "selfish pressure groups who seek to feather their nests while young Americans are dying." Roosevelt may have been playing to his leftist constituency. Just as likely, though, he was perturbed by the fact that fifty-six of the largest companies received three-quarters of all federal war contracts. Perhaps in his own way he was anticipating the warning issued by President Dwight Eisenhower near the end of his second term about the rise of a military-industrial complex.

Perhaps, too, he was indicating his unease that capitalism as it ascended once more in America did not appear to be capitalism with a humane countenance.⁶

However that may be, by 1945 it was Time-Life magnate Henry Luce rather than a dying president who had his finger on his country's pulse. Casting an uncritical eye on the resuscitation of U.S. capitalism Luce had, in a February 17, 1942, *Life* magazine essay, proclaimed the advent of the "American Century." Luce's celebratory tone, rather than the doubting voice employed by the expiring wartime leader, appealed to and reflected the public mood as the international struggle approached its end. In articulating his vision of the American Century Luce did not accord even lip service to the inclusion of Latin America as a partner in shaping the century—beyond providing a certain amount of human clay to be remolded. For him, the time had come to discard most of the animating impulses and assumptions of the Good Neighbor policy. The century that Luce foresaw was strictly a North American, i.e., a United States, type of century.

During the Great Depression, with their future apparently in doubt, Americans—nearly one hundred million of them—had flocked to "century of progress" fairs promising, in effect, the advent of a new, richer, more modern, and infinitely more powerful America: an America of material plenty that would become the model for all the rest of the world. This, at least, is how Robert Rydell compellingly interprets the Depression-era phenomenon in his 1993 book *World of Fairs: Century of Progress Expositions*.

In effect, Luce proclaimed that the America anticipated by chauvinistic fair impresarios had arrived. Only at its peril could the rest of the world eschew the culture that had yielded U.S. supremacy.

### The American Century

In his destined-for-fame essay, Henry Luce told *Life* magazine readers "we have some things in this country which are infinitely precious and especially American." These precious things included "a love of freedom, a feeling for the equality of opportunity, a tradition of self-reliance and independence." The time had come, he proclaimed, for Americans to become "the powerhouse" from which these ideals would "spread throughout the world." The time had come for Americans in effect to take up what Kipling had once described as the White Man's Burden, and—as Luce put it—to lift "mankind from the level of beasts to what the Psalmist called a little lower than Angels."⁷

Harking back in some ways to the nineteenth-century spirit of Manifest Destiny, Luce proclaimed the values of conservative Republicans—and also the values of more than a few Democrats—as he raised, in effect, the call for an economic and cultural imperialism that would bring less fortunate beings throughout the world the opportunity to adapt to the American way of life. At the vital core of the values that Americans would spread in *their* century lay free-enterprise, market capitalism, and the Protestant Ethic sort of values needed to make market capitalism function to its full potential.

About two and a half years after Luce proclaimed the American Century, the Bretton Woods Economic Conference made him seem a prophet. Out of this 1944 conference at the Mount Washington Hotel nestled in New Hampshire's White Mountains came an American triumph in setting some of the fundamental ground rules for the world economy for years to come. Bretton Woods "set the seal on America as the world's ruling financial superpower"—if not for a century, at least "for a little while."[8] More than ever, the United States could now claim the "powerhouse" status envisioned by Luce.

Three years after Luce proclaimed the American Century, and about half a year after the Bretton Woods conference, "Will" Clayton along with Spruille Braden and other U.S. delegates had represented their country at the Chapúltepec conference. There Clayton had, in effect, announced to Latin Americans what the American Century would mean to them: it would mean the chance to collaborate with and to learn from American capitalists who took up the White Man's Burden south of the border. And if the Latins spurned the opportunity, then in effect they doomed themselves to perpetuating their existence at the "level of beasts"—although Clayton was too diplomatic to frame the matter so baldly.

Secretary of State Dean Acheson threw himself into the spirit of the American Century when in 1949 he proclaimed that the "great increase in U.S. power," resting on the success of the country's "political and economic system in providing high living standards and civil liberties," should suffice to persuade Latin Americans of their need to dedicate themselves to "democratic ideals and the private enterprise system." In the same year Willard L. Beaulac, a veteran Latin America hand who had served as ambassador in several republics, observed that a sine qua non for Latin American progress was "reliance upon and stimulation of private effort as the principal source of social progress."[9] Had he referred to a principal source of economic progress he would have been on firmer ground.

That Latin Americans resented the suppositions and implications of the American Century as proclaimed by Luce in 1942 is hardly surprising. After all, these suppositions and implications challenged the principal tenets that Latin Americans had been led to associate with the Good Neighbor policy. Moreover, as recently as 1944, Latin Americans had tended by and large to assume that the Good Neighbor policy still thrived and was destined for a long life. Under this assumption they had turned out by the thousands, indeed by the hundreds of thousands, to cheer the First Lady as she proceeded on a triumphal tour that took her, in addition to various Caribbean island republics and possessions (including Cuba, Puerto Rico, and the Virgin Islands), to Guatemala, Panama, Venezuela, Colombia, Ecuador, and Brazil. Everywhere she went Eleanor Roosevelt triumphed as an ambassador of goodwill, even as her husband had in Buenos Aires at the end of 1936. Her primary purpose had been to visit American troops, but wherever she went she received tumultuous welcomes from the local populace, indicating how far her own reputation—not just that of her husband—had spread. Latin Americans mistook her tour as a symbol of the vitality of the Good Neighbor policy, whereas in reality it was a dying gasp. Again misreading reality, wishfully thinking Latin Americans, at least many of them, hoped or even assumed that the coming century would be—as Eleanor Roosevelt and Henry Wallace, among others, predicted—an all-encompassing People's Century, not an ethnocentric American Century. As it turned out, though, the Henry Luce vision of the future was more nearly the correct one. By no means unfortunately, so far as national and even international interests were concerned, by 1945 Eleanor Roosevelt and Henry Wallace had become the odd couple in the United States.

At the time, most Latin Americans who concerned themselves with the issue keenly regretted that the pluralistic, cultural-relativist assumptions of the People's Century had given way to the culturally restrictive desiderata of the American Century. What is surprising is that within about fifty years Latin Americans, having become addicted to American popular culture, decided that the American Century was not to be eschewed. They decided, or at least huge numbers of them decided, that they could savor a steady diet of what American (i.e., norteamericano) culture produced only by adopting the sort of free-enterprise system that had spawned it. Shopping malls and conspicuous consumption and endless distraction for the relatively well-to-do from the mounting social afflictions of the not-so-well-to-do emerged only out of *corporationism*. But, before they succumbed to the lure of (North) Americanism, Latin Americans would have to romance other isms, among them Marxism and traditionalism and corporatism in various guises, thereby currying the contempt of norteamericanos embarrassed in retrospect by their Good Neighbor fling with people who just weren't their kind of people.

## Not Their Kind of People

Already by 1943 Californians had made it clear that many Mexicans and Mexican-Americans living in their midst were not their kind of people. U.S. sailors in June of that year (as described in Chapter 11) went on a rampage in the Chavez Ravine area of Los Angeles, and the mayhem they perpetrated came to be known as the zoot-suit riots. Some Los Angeles law enforcement officers sympathized with the rampaging sailors and in order to justify them revived timeworn stereotypes of Mexicans as social deviants with a basic inclination toward indolence and crime.

Two years later the U.S. Congress made it clear it no longer wanted to defend people who were not the American kind of people when it moved in 1945 to end the Fair Employment Practices Committee (FEPC), established in 1941 to protect the rights of minority workers and thereby contribute to morale among defense workers. Even before the FEPC's demise industries in California and other states had already begun laying off African- and Mexican-American workers "ahead of other employees." [10] With the FEPC eliminated, the trend gathered momentum. Jobs had to be protected for the "right kind of people" and not even returning African- and Native- and Mexican-American decorated war veterans really qualified for this category.

If Latinos in their own midst did not qualify as the right kind of people, real Americans reverted to old and pejorative stereotypes as they assessed south-of-the-border Latins. Already by the end of 1940 a poll conducted by the Office of Public Opinion revealed this turn of events. Respondents were given a choice of nineteen adjectives with which to describe Central and South Americans. Between 40 and 50 percent of the respondents chose "quick-tempered," "emotional," "superstitious," "backward," "lazy," "ignorant," and "suspicious." At the bottom, "selected by just 5 percent of those questioned, came 'efficient.' Above that, in order, were 'progressive,' 'generous,' 'brave,' 'honest,' 'intelligent,' and 'shrewd'— none of which were chosen by more than 16 percent." At the very top of the list came "dark-skinned," the designation chosen by 80 percent of respondents as applicable to Latin Americans.[11] By dint of dark skin, Latins were guilty of what for many Americans was an unforgivable breach of propriety; for as the war came to an end the Negro and all others of less than white complexion had definitely passed out of the vogue that a few had enjoyed during the Harlem Renaissance. Just as much as the zoot-suit riots, wartime race riots—with Negroes as their target—announced that racism would remain a fundamental building block of national identity in the American Century. Black skin remained a sin, as Louis Armstrong once lamented.

Even way-of-life, small-scale, "yeoman" farmers, revered since the time of Jefferson and, in effect, honored as role models during the early days of the New Deal with the attempt to resettle unemployed urbanites on the land, might not qualify as the right sort of people in the American Century. There could be no questioning, though, the character qualifications of the millionaire farmer-entrepreneurs who (as mentioned briefly in Chapter 19) became the principal beneficiaries of the billions of dollars that various New Deal programs lavished on agricultural development projects in the South and West, justified at the time as a means of offering jobs to the unemployed and bringing electricity and other advantages to marginal ruralites.[12]

In his 1941 song "Pastures of Plenty" Woodie Guthrie, employed at the time by the Bonneville Power Administration near Portland, Oregon, recounts his labors on the Grand Coulee Dam in Washington state. Grand Coulee figured among the more ambitious New Deal projects that temporarily helped the poor and dispossessed but ultimately redounded to the benefit of the rich and the powerful by providing them, among other advantages, with the subsidized water and cheap electricity that facilitated the rise of mass-scale, mechanized farming, through which they could increase their haul of seemingly perpetual agricultural subsidies, all the time posing as rugged individualists in the mold of those who had originally settled the American frontier. How ironic that some Americans most lavish in their praise of the American Century's "free-enterprise" system as it emerged in the wake of World War II had reviled FDR for *his* hypocrisy. After the war, moreover, they often reverted to hoary stereotypes as they reviled Latin American caudillos for their "characteristic" hypocrisy and Latin American masses for their dependence on government handouts.

Just as in the railroad-building age, so also in the American Century, U.S.-style "free-enterprise" socialism would be manipulated so as to further advantage the advantaged; and this was well and good, even though not to be talked about too much in public. On the other hand, as the following chapter will show, U.S. statesmen and bureaucrats and the general public regarded as little better than common criminals those accommodated Latin Americans who claimed their share of Washington's largesse when the Good Neighbor administration dispensed public funds to shore up south-of-the-border support for the war effort. These Latin Americans may not necessarily have been very nice people; but they acted very much in the North American style.

As Americans settled into the postwar era subsidized farmer millionaires joined industrial tycoons and wartime profiteers as national heroes. But, farmers who weren't into the modern stage of their profession were old-fashioned rubes and hicks, hardly qualified for honored status in the American Century. As to the pajama-clad peasants of China or Mexico over whom intellectuals and Hollywood moviemakers and all who shared in the cult of primitivism had swooned in the Depression era, they had now become figures of pity and scorn, the antiquated relics of a bygone age. How embarrassing that only a decade or so earlier Americans had accepted them as symbols of the good life, as people who very definitely were their kind of people. Now, as they entered the postwar era, Americans adopted a more normal and rational attitude toward such super-annuated close-to-the-good-earth persons. They must be prodded on their way, whether to oblivion or to salvation, through American Century–style modernization.

The modern type of farmer-cattleman was the one featured in the Johnny Mercer song "I'm an Old Cowhand from the Rio Grande."[13] This "cowhand" learned to ride 'fore he learned to stand; he learned to ride, that is, in the family car. When he grew up, he rode the range in a Ford V-8. That was as far as his riding skills extended. He knew nothing about roping techniques beyond what he had viewed at an occasional ro-deo. He did know the songs that the cowboys sang, 'cause he "learned 'em all on the radio." With his gadgets and machines, he managed to avoid hands-on experience with the good earth. Here was the sort of person who instead of going on roundup would drive to government offices to make certain his subsidies and allotments and public rangeland assignments were in order. Here was the Westerner turned modern; here was the sort of man, ready for the American Century, ready to lecture Latin Americans that it was high time for them to learn the character- and nation-building skills of free-enterprise capitalism.

# 28. Rethinking Good Neighborliness as the American Century Begins

❖ ❖ ❖ ❖ ❖ ❖ ❖ ❖ ❖ ❖ ❖ ❖ ❖ ❖ ❖ ❖ ❖ ❖ ❖ ❖ ❖ ❖ ❖ ❖ ❖ ❖ ❖ ❖ ❖ ❖ ❖ ❖ ❖

### The Withering of Hemispheric Goodwill North of the Border

North American pejorative attitudes toward Latin Americans, as indicated by the 1940 poll cited in the previous chapter, spread and undoubtedly hardened in the aftermath of World War II. Here is one hint: in 1946 singer Peggy Lee, early in the career that would make her a legend, released one of her all-time hits. It was "Mañana (Is Soon Enough for Me)." Written by Lee and her husband at the time, guitarist Dave Barbour, "Mañana" (which provoked considerable outrage below the border) is a song about the "typical" Mexican perpetually relaxing in the sun beneath his sombrero and putting off until tomorrow the work that needs to be done today, and then putting it off again when tomorrow comes. As norteamericanos listened to the song, they were inspired to wonder all the more why the feckless Latins could not develop the moral character, the consistent self-discipline, needed to assure progress and prosperity.

Not only did those North Americans who paid any attention at all to their neighbors tend to find them inadequate to the challenges of the dawning American Century; they also had, or imagined they had, scores out of the recent past to settle with their neighbors. Somehow they suspected, in some cases were even convinced, that the Latins had not proved themselves worthy wartime allies. President Roosevelt himself had come to the point of sharing not so much the suspicion as the conviction.

Perturbed by the situation during the war, FDR found it expedient to avoid telling the public that the United States "was not receiving complete cooperation from the other American republics in ending subversion."[1] To have admitted this would have been to cast doubt on the efficacy of the entire Good Neighbor policy. Foreign service officers were well aware of the situation, and their frustrations and resentments accumulated as they awaited the day when they could bring a halt to the Good Neighbor charade and to the public relations announcements expected of them concerning the splendid cooperation of their Latin allies.

Perhaps as close as the president ever came to hinting at his true feelings about Latin American wartime cooperation came in Fireside Chats of July 1943 and June 1944. On these occasions Roosevelt accorded eloquent praise to people throughout the world who were contributing to the Allied Powers' war effort. He saluted the "heroic armies of Generalissimo Chiang Kai-shek," he referred to "the gallant Canadians," the "fighting New Zealanders," the "courageous French and the French Moroccans, the South Africans, the Poles, and the East Indians." But he spoke not a word in praise of Latin American contributions.[2]

Toward the end of 1943 a British diplomat posted in Washington wrote: "We get certain indications here that the honeymoon of Pan-Americanism may be drawing to a close, leaving behind the problems of day-to-day matrimony." Meantime, he added, the "ardently wooed bride seems to have been so spoilt by the lavish gifts of courtship that she has come to expect them as a matter of course, and is apt to sulk when they are no longer forthcoming. For his part, the new bridegroom may think her a bit *exigente*."[3] Precisely: North Americans whose grasp of hemispheric affairs extended beyond the facade of Good Neighbor public relations blurbs had indeed, rightly or wrongly, come to regard the Latins as shamelessly exigent.

Already in 1941 Baltimore-based pundit H. L. Mencken complained, in print, that New Dealers apparently were planning to spend five hundred million dollars in Latin America in an attempt "to line up the politicians for 'religion and morality.'" Mencken expected little good to come of this expenditure; and clearly he regarded the Latins as excessively greedy. The following year columnist Raymond Clapper expressed the same opinion, privately, in far stronger terms. In a letter to a friend he wrote: "There is a lot of talk about Latin pride and so on, but personally I have felt, without knowing them, unfortunately, they are a pretty cheap sleezy kind of people and are pretty much [ready] to set the money price on anything." Behind the scenes, Sen. Hugh Butler (R., Nebraska) may have been just as outspoken as the columnist. Even for the record he was explicit enough when he returned to Washington from a 1943 visit to Argentina and other Latin American republics. He asserted publicly that the Good Neighbor policy had resulted in the squandering of six hundred million dollars in three years; and for this sum precious few results had been obtained. Butler articulated what many Americans had come to believe. Already by 1943 rapidly accumulating evidence indicated that in government and private circles as well impatience with "indiscriminate largesse to Latin America" was on the upswing. It awaited only the end of the war for U.S. diplomacy to begin to reflect this souring mood.[4]

At the beginning of 1945 "Will" Clayton and his supporters at Chapúltepec reflected general disillusionment with Latin Americans as they insisted that their neighbors must quickly learn to rely on private investment rather than U.S. government grants to address their problems. This insistence arose not only out of ideological convictions but out of the perception that North Americans had been played for suckers by their neighbors. And the mounting eagerness of the State Department and other branches of government to defend private U.S. investors threatened by Latin American governments was tinged by pent-up anger and frustration caused by the perception that wartime exigencies had forced Washington to bow to Latin greed and unscrupulousness.

Back in 1935, with domestic policy in mind, FDR had stated that the lessons of history "show conclusively that continued dependence upon relief induces a spiritual and moral disintegration fundamentally destructive to the national fiber."[5] As World War II entered its final months, not only the president but most of the makers of hemispheric policy in Washington and in the field had concluded that Latin American dependence on what amounted to relief, or in some instances virtual bribe money, also produced moral disintegration. And they were prepared to do what they could to end the circumstances that allegedly nourished that disintegration.

Trouble was brewing in the hemisphere as of 1945. Latin Americans expected the United States to maintain the good neighborliness that circumstances had forced upon it during the war years. But North Americans were anxious to call a halt to the use of government funds in providing "walking-around" money for Latin leaders. Moreover, American political leaders were, by and large, eager to end what they considered the excessive wartime bite that Latin governments had put on U.S. investors operating in their countries. From now on, American officials resolved, they would move more resolutely to defend the interests of private U.S. investors south of the border. Brazil's postwar president Eurico Gaspar Dutra (1946–1950) was given this message quite clearly when, early in his term, he visited Washington. He should, he was told, keep government out of the economic sphere, reserving that sphere for relatively unencumbered private enterprise capital, whether Brazilian or North American.[6]

African-American writer Zora Neale Hurston, extremely sensitive about the feelings of some minorities, expressed mainstream cultural-ethnic prejudices when—just before the Japanese attack on Pearl Harbor—she wrote on the Latin American. Nobody much doubted, she suggested, that the "Latin brother" meant to be a good neighbor. "We know that his intentions are the best. It is only that he is so gay and fiesta-minded that he is liable to make arrangements that benefit nobody but himself." Therefore, he "must be taught to share with big brother before big brother comes down and kicks his teeth in. . . . We are far too moral a people," she added, "to allow poor Latin judgment to hinder good works."[7] Surely by 1945 few Americans who thought about the issue at all doubted that if little brother down south wasn't willing to shape up, and if he got unduly in the way of good works, nation-building works as conceived by can-do gringo capitalists, then big brother would have some teeth-kicking to do.

## Latin Americans React against the Spirit of the American Century

From north of the border, Latin Americans by the mid-1940s had come to be perceived as suffering from a cargo cult mentality. Among various "primitive" peoples messianic hopes of deliverance from misery had focused on the belief that somehow, miraculously, from overseas would come abundant cargos of every imaginable type, thereby assuring lives of carefree plentitude. The only problem was to build adequate facilities for storing the manna that would come not from heaven but from across the sea. Well, so far as more and more Yankees were concerned as World War II came to an end, Latin Americans had come to expect their manna from the United States; and the sooner they were disabused of this expectation, the better.

Latin Americans had an entirely different perspective. So far as they were concerned the gringos had, again and again, made wartime promises about economic assistance that they had subsequently reneged on. Diplomats and even the man in the White House had offered the moon, but then Congress or some Washington agency had withdrawn the offer. If anything, from the Latin perspective, they had been taken advantage of by the Yankees; one time after another they had disrupted their economies in order to supply their northern neighbors with more and more of what they needed for the war effort, and had received relatively little in return. If any Americans had consistently sacrificed financially in contributing to the war effort, they believed it was they, the Latin Americans, who had done so. In large numbers they shared the attitudes that Panamanians had acquired by the mid-1940s. As historian Michael L. Conniff notes, "As far as many Panamanians were concerned, Franklin Roosevelt's Good Neighbor policy had been little more than a public relations ploy. The New Deal had turned out to be a raw deal."[8]

By the end of the '40s and the beginning of the new decade, the American Century idea was not the only idea circulating in the world attesting to delusions of grandeur. Out on the periphery of the international economic order as decolonization shortly got underway, the idea of a Third World Century began to exercise an intoxicating appeal. The idea rested upon perceptions of persecution as well as delusions about the grandeur that Third World countries could achieve by repudiating the political and economic institutions of a predatory First World that had grown rich by plundering its colonies, actual or virtual. From the Third World perspective, cargo cults had flourished all too long; the trouble was, the cargos had passed from the Third to the First World, from the "periphery" to the "center." Now all of that must end. Now the Third World would develop its own economies in its own way, tapping into autochthonous institutions and customs in order to gain both ideological and economic liberation from alien exploiters. As this process unfolded, any aid the periphery might be able to bluster or cajole the center into extending would be accepted as no more than a token downpayment of recompense for what through the years the center had extracted.

Enthusiastically embracing Third World perceptions of past exploitation and expectations of future glory, a new generation of Latin American pensadores and politicians developed a heady brand of nationalism resting on a central article of faith that proclaimed the periphery's historical victimization by the center. For Latin American intellectuals and populist politicos, egged on and applauded by the political left in the United States, there was no doubt that the center by which their periphery had been plundered and exploited and tempted into rejecting authentic traditions and values and identity lay to the north.

Really, North Americans should not have been surprised that the values Latin Americans identified with as they proclaimed the rebirth of authentic traditions had something of a socialist core, regardless of whether the socialism derived from fascism, from Thomistic corporatism, from Marxism-Leninism, or from pre-Columbian institutions. After all, when Americans themselves had briefly faced devastating adversity in the 1930s, many had turned to the socialist persuasion. In doing so, they had turned to the persuasion so often preferred by people living in environments of scarcity that seem to lack adequate resources for group survival—unless the people curb the instincts of the solitary predator and surrender some or all individual freedoms to those elders or wise men (and women) or, in more modern terms, to charismatic dictators thought to be consumed by devotion to the common good.

Depression-era Americans had turned in significant number to socialist values and expedients; and some had even sought salvation from caudillo figures (perhaps including FDR himself). They had acted this way even though to do so was to act in a manner contrary to their country's mainline religions, its civil religion, and its political and economic traditions, all of which enshrined individualism and democracy. How altogether logical and predictable, then, for Latin Americans, continuing to confront harsh adversity in the postwar setting, to turn, along with much of the Third World, to ways that were natural to them: socialist, authoritarian ways, whether associated in modern times with the right or left of the ideological spectrum.

Latin Americans suffered from colossally bad timing as they embarked on the quest to find alternatives to the values of the American Century. And this bad timing beset Latin Americans whether they came ideologically from right or left, whether they identified with a traditionalism tinged with authoritarianism and often with militarism and fascism, or with a socialism that was rooted in the indigenous past and in the teachings of some of the religious orders, to which had been added now an admixture of Marxism, and often a dose of militarism as well. Whether coming from right or left, Latin Americans entered upon their delayed nation-building experiments, upon their endeavor to confound American Century prophets, just as worldwide evidence would begin to accumulate that maintaining any large, "closed, repressive society . . . had become— economically, socially, militarily, and technologically—impossible."[9]

## A Good Neighbor Policy, of Sorts, Reborn

History excels at producing unlikely scenarios; but few recent ones would have seemed more unlikely as of 1945 than the one that unfolded in the Americas beginning in the late 1940s. At that time a largely moribund Good Neighbor policy claimed a new lease on life, at least in some of its aspects, as North Americans devised fresh programs to lavish public funds on Latin American nationalists—whether militarists or not, whether right- or left-leaning—who advocated state-controlled, state-driven economies. All the nationalists had to do to qualify as worthy recipients of U.S. public funds was to present credible evidence that they did not incline toward the Soviet Union. Among those who soon qualified was Juan Domingo Perón, particularly coveted as a friendly neighbor lest otherwise he warm up not only to the Soviet Union but to Britain and seek to revitalize the old economic relationship with that country that historically had left little room for U.S. capital.

Perón exemplified widespread Latin American trends in the sort of nationalism he concocted for Argentina. His way, the way of *justicialismo,* he maintained, was a Third Way: it was neither U.S.-style capitalism nor Soviet-style socialism, but an in-between hybrid. (FDR was not the only American leader who liked to juggle and to mix opposites!) Nor did Perón bother to hide very carefully the fascist elements in the Third Way as he and his fellow justicialista ideologists criticized democracy's "inherent weaknesses," its dissolving effects on discipline and order and moral values, that if not counteracted would open the door to the false remedy of Soviet-style communism.[10] This last point is what mattered to U.S. observers. For all his flaws, Perón did not seem likely to prove soft on communism.

Despite his strong reservations about the United States and much of what it allegedly stood for, Perón never hesitated to arrange a reconciliation of sorts with that country through the good offices of Ambassador George Messersmith (as described in Chapter 25). Throughout much of Latin America his fellow nationalists, generally to their considerable economic advantage, soon followed suit.

Latin America's wildly disparate postwar nationalists by and large rejected what they perceived the United States to represent in its political culture, even as Washington began once more to transfer public funds south of the border. And North Americans who arranged or witnessed the transfer of funds by and large rejected what the ideologically mixed bag of Latin American recipients of these funds represented—insofar as they, the North Americans, understood just what values the recipients did represent. In a perfect world, neither member of the coalition would have chosen to have much to do with the other. But suddenly the world, both from the northern and the southern perspective, seemed to be veering away from perfection.

Brandishing its newfound powers and its own utopian visions of a new century, the Soviet Union posed a threat both to U.S. prophets of the American Century and to Latin American prophets of nationalism shaped purportedly by their region's genuinely endemic traditions. Soon the Latin Americans developed considerable skill at exaggerating the Soviet threat in order to extract more generous contributions from the United States, just as at an earlier time they had, for similar purposes, played with virtuosity on Yankee fears of Nazi and fascist threats.

From both sides of the border during the Cold War came impetus to a renewal of good neighborliness. From both sides of the border came also the realization that refurbished good neighborliness would, even more than its original manifestation, rest on feigned civility and charades of mutual respect.

All in all, the Cold War exerted an enormous influence on hemispheric relations, on the death of old and the birth of new Good Neighbor policies, under circumstances in which the new was very much like the old. A more detailed look at some of the hemispheric implications of the Cold War, so far touched on only sporadically, follows in the next chapter.

# 29. The Cold War and a Hemispheric Marriage of Convenience

❖ ❖ ❖ ❖ ❖ ❖ ❖ ❖ ❖ ❖ ❖ ❖ ❖ ❖ ❖ ❖ ❖ ❖ ❖ ❖ ❖ ❖ ❖ ❖ ❖ ❖ ❖ ❖ ❖ ❖ ❖

### A Reemergent Need for U.S. Good Neighbor Collaborators

In his 1941 book *Inside Latin America* John Gunther had concluded that "We need Latin America just as much as it needs us." By the end of 1944 the partners who had come together on the basis of mutual interest and even empathy beginning in the 1930s began to feel they neither needed nor wanted to continue a close relationship.

North Americans had a few months at best in which to indulge the fancy that, with the world apparently having turned more benign, they could ignore their neighbors. World War II had scarcely ended before U.S. officials were speaking of communism as once they had spoken of Nazism; once again they were invoking continental solidarity and hemispheric defense against a foreign threat. Indeed, with the war against the Axis still underway early in 1945, U.S. intelligence intercepted a communique to the Mexican Foreign Ministry from its ambassador in Moscow to the effect that Stalin was exploring the possibilities of close postwar collaboration between the two countries.[1] This was enough to put Washington insiders on guard. Within two years the Russian bear was prowling far more menacingly.

Responding to a perceived worldwide communist menace President Truman in 1947 announced the doctrine that soon came to bear his name. The Truman Doctrine "implied that Americans possessed the right and the obligation to intervene in behalf of pro-Western anticommunist regimes whenever their survival seemed endangered."[2] In the same year Secretary of State George Marshall announced the European Recovery Program that quickly came to be known as the Marshall Plan. Under its provisions, huge amounts of American public money soon flowed overseas to facilitate and expedite the rebuilding of British and Western European economies.

Latin Americans, it was now clear, would not receive the massive infusion of U.S. development aid that some had anticipated, often encouraged in their anticipation by delusionary Americans like Henry Wallace with a special devotion to the Third World countries and a conviction that with enough no-strings-attached aid from the United States they would readily surmount all problems. Happily, this aid was not forthcoming. Well and good, said many Latin American traditionalists. Making a virtue of necessity, they rationalized that massive infusion of Yankee money would have brought Yankee culture in its wake, thereby undermining authentic national values. Nevertheless, traditionalists, especially the military leaders among them, soon had their hands out for lesser sums of money. After all, they could claim they needed to modernize their armies and navies in order to help resist the spread of communism into the American hemisphere. Internal security was what they talked about; and in order to facilitate it, they claimed a need for U.S. funds—not only to shore up defense capabilities but to address social and economic problems that, if not addressed, threatened to undermine domestic stability.

Strategic planners in Washington tended to agree with Latin American assessments. Thus developments that only a very few of them had foreseen as the struggle against the Axis wound down shortly drove U.S. policymakers to overlook perceived wartime slights and to refurbish a hemispheric marriage of convenience. Like it or not, what John Gunther had written in 1941 seemed more valid than ever four or five years later.

## Communists, Marxists "a la Criolla," and Right-Wing Nationalists in Latin America

Many conservative Latin American pensadores, as previously suggested, had admired certain features of Nazism-fascism because these features overlapped with traditional Iberian distrust of liberal bourgeois democracy and free-enterprise capitalism. North Americans—and for that matter a fair number of Latin Americans—never developed any particular skill at distinguishing between entirely homegrown conservative pensadores and the relatively few all-out partisans of genuine National Socialism and/or fascism. Often unaware of their lack of proficiency in this matter, North Americans understandably enough preferred to err on the side of caution: if Latin Americans looked or acted in any way like Nazis or fascists, then assume that this is what they genuinely were. As the old and simplistic aphorism (more or less) has it, "If they quack like ducks, then they are ducks."

FDR himself had sometimes acted on this assumption. A similar lack of discernment characterized North American actions in the crusade to ferret out reds in Latin America. In short, Cold War North American paranoia about the foreign-inspired threat from the left mirrored World War II paranoia about the foreign-inspired threat from the right. An underlying reason for both forms of paranoia was this: in their mutual dislike of what they took to be the underlying features of Yankee civilization, Latin American defenders of what they deemed their genuine and authentic traditions had much in common *both* with fascists *and* with Marxists.

Like Latin American rightists, whether fascist or not, and also like the Arielists and Krausists (as described in Chapter 9), Latin America's twentieth-century leftists professed that human beings best attained moral grandeur when shaped by societies that pursued nonmaterial rewards above all others. Right and left agreed that Yankees had degraded themselves through their fixation on material rewards. Right and left agreed that democracy of the one-person, one-vote variety had the leveling effect of reducing society to its lowest common denominator and beyond that, given the way liberal capitalism functioned, of encouraging plutocracy rather than genuine democracy. Right and left tended to agree that mass mobilization was preferable to genuine individual participation, that raising consciousness had a higher priority, at least in the early stages of building new patrias, than raising per-capita income; that self-discipline and abnegation took precedence over gratification and self-indulgence, and that people were at their best when surrendering their egos to some transcendent cause or dream. Finally, both right and left agreed that state control of the economy was useful if for no other reason than that it would stifle the competitive, entrepreneurial streak that inevitably reduced moral grandeur among citizens and prevented them from seeking realization through immersion in some transcendent cause or movement.

Like fascism, like Arielism-Krausism, so also Marxism appealed to the vanity of intellectuals. After all, what social-function group would be so essential as intellectuals in formulating and articulating the nonmaterial values and the visions of grandeur that would liberate the masses from obsession with mere pecuniary rewards? The same attraction that postwar French intellectuals found in Marxism flourished in Latin America. What Raymond Aron wrote about his fellow Frenchmen and women applied also to Latin Americans in the postwar era: Marxism was the opiate of the intellectuals. In the postwar era as in the past, Latin Americans of any social standing generally aspired at least to be taken for intellectuals; las letras still conferred nobleza. So did las armas. Mere business acuity counted for little.

However much Latin American leftist intellectuals might sympathize with socialism in its modern guise of Marxism-Leninism, with relatively rare exceptions they were not Communists—by which I mean they did not join the Communist Party (except for just possibly a brief looking-over process) and they did not accept discipline from Moscow or concern themselves over what the party line at any particular moment might be. Showing the same sort of obtuseness they had often demonstrated in World War II when confronting the Nazi-fascist menace, North Americans by and large seldom learned to distinguish Latin Americans who were Marxists in their own way (Marxists *a la criolla,* in a free-wheeling indigenous style) from those who were actual card-carrying members of the Communist Party, ready to accept discipline from Moscow. For that matter, a good number of North Americans, among them congressmen who served on the House Committee on Un-American Activities, established in 1938, never acquired the ability to distinguish between dyed-in-the-wool party-member Communists in the United States and social reformers who doubted that free-enterprise capitalism had been decreed by God or ordained by the very nature of men and women. Nor did North American acuity in this respect improve during the long witch-hunt era that began during the Truman administration.

Still, it was by no means just lack of discernment that caused some North Americans to detect a communist menace in Latin America. There *were* some capital-C Communists in the area. Mainly, though, there were Latin Americans who sought intellectual modishness by playing with new ideas, or who thought there *must* be more attractive formulas for moving countries ahead than grubby, self-seeking individualism, or who recognized the advantage of playing on Yankee fears by wildly exaggerating the Bolshevik menace—just as their on-the-make predecessors had liked to titillate gringos with tales about the fascist menace. By dwelling on the possibility, even the likelihood, of a communist takeover in their particular countries, Latin American rightists as well as nonideological opportunists discovered they could extract more aid and assistance from Washington. Thereby they could rearm their nations and satisfy importunate officers; thereby they could finance social programs and pacify the masses; thereby they could finance state industries to staff and overstaff with their partisans; thereby they could, in general, sate their own greed and indulge their opportunism.

## Saving Latin America from Communism

In their Cold War crusade to prevent Latin Americans from falling under communist or Marxist-a-la-criolla regimes, North Americans supported many south-of-the-border thugs, while arming and pampering many military and civilian leaders who although not necessarily thugs cared little more about democracy and human rights than Genghis Khan. However, North Americans purportedly trying to save Latin Americans from themselves did—so they believed—rescue Guatemalans from rule by a leftist-leaning intellectual lightweight, Jacobo Arbenz—though surely if left to their own devices the Guatemalans would have "saved" themselves. In any event, had Arbenz somehow contrived to remain in power he might well have made Guatemala a worse economic basket case than did the prevailingly corrupt and brutal rulers who came to power in the wake of the barely disguised U.S. intervention that toppled him in 1954: an intervention in large part engineered by the Dulles brothers, John Foster and Allen, who served in the Dwight Eisenhower administration as secretary of state and head of the CIA, respectively. We know what the lamentable alternative to Arbenz was, but we don't know what rule under him or his cronies would have been like. There is nothing in recent Latin American history to inspire confidence it would have been better than the alternative.

Ten years after the Guatemalan adventure, the Lyndon B. Johnson administration abandoned FDR's relatively gentle noninterventionism and supported a military coup that ousted an elected president of Brazil, judged—with some justification—to be so ineffectual in his foggy leftist leanings as to pose the threat of plunging his country into chaos. In the aftermath of the coup, the Brazilian military inaugurated a lengthy period of ineffectual and heavy-handed conservative rule. The following year (1965) President Johnson proved even less gentle—and more paranoid about communist threats—when he ordered the landing of U.S. troops in the Dominican Republic to restore "appropriate" order.

With just a bit of a shove from the United States under President Richard Nixon and national security assistant–Secretary of State Henry Kissinger, but actually operating mainly on their own, Chileans in 1973 rescued their country from Salvador Allende, who had already led it pretty far down the road toward economic chaos and even civil war. Under their military savior and blood-thirsty scourge of leftists Augusto Pinochet, Chileans initiated the process—at first deplorably harsh and brutal—that transformed their country into Latin America's economic "tiger," and ultimately led to a reflowering of democracy. Roughly similar results came to pass in Argentina as the military waged an effective but notoriously vicious "dirty war" against mainly leftist opponents before having to return the country to democratic processes after disgracing themselves in a war against Britain over the Falkland/Malvinas Islands in the early 1980s. Meantime, other trouble spots had developed in Central America.

If in 1979 President Jimmy Carter had been able to figure out a way to prevent the Sandinistas from coming to power in Nicaragua, he would have saved that country several years of colossal economic mismanagement that resulted mainly in the personal enrichment of Sandinista officials, a process that did not end even with their electoral defeat in 1990. If, on the other hand, Ronald Reagan's administration (1981–1989) had not drawn the line in the sand in El Salvador, that country might very well have fallen under Marxist rule as politically heavy-handed and economically incompetent as the Sandinistas initiated in Nicaragua. However, had not the Salvadoran Marxists posed their challenge to the established order, there is no conceivable way in which Washington could have pressured conservative incumbents, as the price for coming to their rescue, into moving toward significant social, economic, and political reforms. Salvadorans, like Latin Americans in general, had only laughed when Yankees during the John F. Kennedy administration (1961–1963) sought to nudge them in this direction through Alliance for Progress inducements.

Only in the case of the former *de facto* Yankee colony just ninety miles from home did it prove impossible to prevent or to reverse a 1959 socialist takeover that soon yielded at least a pretty good approximation of a genuine, party-lining Marxist-Leninist administration. Perhaps in a way it was fortunate that President Kennedy failed with the 1961 Bay of Pigs invasion to oust Cuba's Fidel Castro; for otherwise the hemisphere would not have had the instructive example of the shambles to which a country can be reduced by a regime that sets out to forge new persons whose consciousness has been remade so as to conform to the visions of self-proclaimed prophets and latter-day interpreters of Marx and Lenin.

Arguably, there is something epic, something heroic in the scale of the delusions that led a good number of Cubans to put ideological faith above the material lures of embourgeoisement. But there is also something monumentally tragic in the scale of their delusions. The rest of Latin Americans spared themselves the cataclysmic agony of a *Götterdämmerung,* of a downfall of the gods of ideology that would have brought with it the downfall of all those who had believed in those gods. Well before the end of the Cold War but more decisively and more dramatically than ever after its end, Latin Americans as a whole turned their backs on Marxian messianism and opened their arms to embourgeoisement, as Henry Luce and many a nobler American including Franklin Roosevelt had anticipated they would.

## Assessing the Good Neighbor Policy in Its Cold War Resuscitation

The future as foreseen by some hubris-driven and tunnel-vision American Century advocates may have been tawdry and unheroic and stiflingly materialistic. But that future was certainly preferable to the one envisioned by disciples of Marx and Lenin, whether true believers or a-la-criolla samplers of an international ideological smorgasbord. Even the a-la-criolla Marxists inclined all too often toward withholding freedom from citizens until they had been conditioned and "resocialized" into proper understanding of just what it was that they were free to believe. Even the a-la-criolla Marxist-Leninists, just like the a-la-criolla fascists of a few years earlier, wanted to combine the dogmas of their favorite contemporary prophet figures with traditional authoritarianism deriving (in the case of fascist-leaning types) from the Iberian background of priest and conquistador or (in the case of communist types) from the despotism developed by the highest pre-Columbian civilizations.

To some limited degree at least, the revived and revised Good Neighbor approach into which the Cold War forced Washington helped minimize the appeal among the Latin Americans of either manifestation, right or left, of the totalitarian temptation. Updated Good Neighbor approaches helped make the Yankee Colossus seem just a little less menacing, just a little less necessary to defend against by rallying around delusionary alternatives.

Leftist critics can argue that had it not been for its unparalleled wealth in the postwar era, the United States could not have bribed and coerced most of Latin America's directing classes into eschewing radical social and economic experiments that, so the critics contend, ultimately would vastly have benefited the Latin Americans. The critics undoubtedly are right about the use of bribery and occasional coercion; but from the vantage point of the mid-1990s there seems little likelihood that economic and social radicalism would have benefited many Latin Americans, and therefore much reason to applaud the bribery and perhaps even the relatively rare coercion. Indeed, as of the mid-1990s, it seems more and more obvious that success in holding to a minimum the occasions on which Latin proclivities for the command economy actually grew over into out-and-out Marxism-Leninism stands as one of Washington's greatest hemispheric triumphs and good deeds. And for that particular triumph and good deed a resuscitated Good Neighbor policy ultimately deserves some credit.

Forget for a moment the fact that a Fidel Castro could not have come to power in Cuba in the 1920s because the Yankees would not have permitted this in what was still their *de facto* colony; forget this and assume

Fidel had captured control of Cuba in 1929 instead of 1959. In that earlier year I think it safe to speculate he would have gained far-reaching recognition among Latin Americans as a new Bolívar who would help them shake off the chains of colonialism, in this case of Yankee colonialism. Surely with his charisma and wit and mesmerizing oratory he would have eclipsed the far less prepossessing Sandino, who despite his limitations evoked considerable enthusiasm south of the Rio Grande. In 1959, though, Latin Americans were all too aware of new trends set in motion by the Good Neighbor policy to pay much heed to an island utopianist who promised liberation from the gringos and after that utopia unlimited. What verbal support the Cuban caudillo did elicit outside the island often came from pensadores and politicos who actually had little esteem for Castro but simply sought to bolster their claims to being au courant with intellectual fashions, whether decreed by ideologues in Moscow or in Paris.

In spite of all its shortcomings and inconsistencies and hypocrisy and out-and-out failures the Roosevelt-initiated Good Neighbor policy won a new, however grudging and seldom publicly acknowledged, empathy for the United States in Latin America. Had it not been for that empathy, out of which came a heightened ability to give the gringo's institutions and political-economic culture a bit more of the benefit of the doubt, then the United States might have had to be far more overtly interventionist and heavy-handed, or it might have had considerably to up the requisite bribes, in order to accomplish what must be seen as its most significant deed of good neighborliness in the American hemisphere: the *relatively* nonviolent containment of Marxism in a bewildering array of Cold War guises that ran the fashion gamut from left to right and that even included one style called liberation theology.


When policies work relatively well in addressing the immediate challenges and problems for which they were designed, it has never seemed quite fair to me eventually to condemn those policies because of the unforeseen and unforeseeable complications they led to decades later. Perhaps, then, it is stretching a point to praise the Good Neighbor policy as it originally developed under FDR for having contributed, however indirectly, to success in addressing later problems that could not have been foreseen prior to 1945. Still, fortuitous successes are bound to seem preferable to fortuitous failures.

Without the Yankee's ardent wooing of the Latin in the early stages of an opportunistic neighborhood romance, initiated because at the time the Yankee had virtually no one else to woo, there might never have come about the post–World War II marriage of convenience. That marriage ultimately benefited the mutually suspicious and never very faithful partners, benefited them both enormously.

Ultimately, Latin Americans could in many ways claim as much credit as norteamericanos for preserving a rocky hemispheric marriage. By the 1980s, growing disillusioned in the chronic failures of statism, whether justified ideologically from the right or from the left, Latin Americans had begun to turn toward market rather than command economies. Already they were preparing the way for the virtual explosion of privatization that erupted after the collapse of the Soviet Union. Already in a 1987 book political scientist Lars Schoultz, perhaps the sharpest-eyed observer of hemispheric relations during the period when his fellow North Americans assumed the responsibility of saving their neighbors from communism, had this to say: "Latin America is quickly outgrowing the Cold War."[3]

# SECTION VIII

❖❖❖❖❖❖❖❖❖❖❖❖❖❖❖❖❖❖❖❖❖❖❖❖❖❖❖

*Good Neighbor
Themes and
Variations
Half a
Century Later*

# 30. New Economic Forces Begin to Transform the New World

❖ ❖ ❖ ❖ ❖ ❖ ❖ ❖ ❖ ❖ ❖ ❖ ❖ ❖ ❖ ❖ ❖ ❖ ❖ ❖ ❖ ❖ ❖ ❖ ❖ ❖ ❖ ❖ ❖ ❖ ❖ ❖ ❖

### The Privatization Stampede

Toward the end of Chapter 28 appears a quotation that bears repeating: "[R]unning a huge, closed, repressive, society in the 1980s had become— economically, socially, militarily, and technologically—impossible."[1] The author of these lines, master spy novelist and shrewd international ob- server John le Carré, had Leonid Brezhnev's Soviet Union specifically in mind when delivering this judgment. However, throughout what used to be referred to as the Free World more and more persons assumed, espe- cially in the *immediate* aftermath of the Soviet Union's collapse, that the British novelist's analysis is well-nigh universally applicable: applicable not only to huge and developed but to underdeveloped small and medium- sized societies as well.

Just possibly, though, China, in the early-to-mid 1990s, with its strange concoction of "market Leninism" and its dramatic economic growth, an- nounces that le Carré's appraisal is open to exceptions. Just possibly also the records compiled by several of East Asia's so-called economic tigers demonstrate that controlled economies can yield dramatic growth. For now, though, I choose to ignore such possibilities and to address the de- gree to which a new generation of Latin American leaders has assumed that privatization of the economic structure provides the only secure path to development, all other paths having come to dead ends—especially now with the huge Ronald Reagan–era deficits having effectively ended the likelihood of large-scale government-to-government hemispheric grants in a post–Cold War era.

What began to transpire in Latin America in the early 1990s was, as one of the most distinguished historians of that region notes, part of a worldwide phenomenon. According to Charles Berquist, Marxist social-ism for more than a century not only inspired much of the world labor movement, but deeply influenced "much of the scholarship on labor, es-pecially in the field of labor history." Now, however, in the early stages of the twentieth century's final decade, "neo-liberalism" was sweeping the globe. In its wake came faith in the efficacy of free trade, privatization, and market forces to unleash "the productive potential of all human be-ings and sweep away inefficiencies of the bureaucratic, interventionist, so-cial welfare state."[2]

Trying desperately to regroup in the post–Cold War era, Latin Ameri-ca's left, for a time at least, began to minimize the importance of economic socialism while stressing the desirability of political democracy. If social problems could be solved at all, the reasoning went, they would be solved not by economic means so much as by the political expedient of spreading democracy downward until it finally sank roots among the disadvantaged. Perhaps then, slowly, the benefits of the market economy might begin to disperse themselves throughout society. But any attempt to rush the pro-cess through socialism's command economies seemed doomed. Finding themselves in no position to reverse the privatization tide, even had they so desired, Latin America's demoralized left by and large went tentatively and dubiously along with it, although here and there a few guerrillas re-mained in the field. Meantime more conservative elements tried enthusi-astically to propel the privatization bandwagon more rapidly ahead.

Here is how Mexican poet Octavio Paz, who like the typical Latin American pensador had once wondered if the capitalist system was basi-cally inimical to decency and morality, put the matter in 1991: "It is im-possible to fight against the market economy, or to deny its benefits." All Paz could hope was that "a new political and social way of thinking" might permit that system to result in "less onerous forms of exchange."[3]

Rather than fighting the market economy, Latin Americans—by and large—had begun in the late 1980s a stampede to embrace it. Indeed, be-tween 1988 and 1993, the rush toward privatization had been greatest not in Europe but in Latin America; and in the year 1992 Latin America ac-counted for 35 percent of privatization's "worldwide total, by value." Through privatization, Latin American regimes managed to attract not only foreign private capital but to encourage the repatriation of funds that citizens had shipped abroad during the era when local economic policies had not inspired investor confidence.[4]

With liberal and radical-leaning writers and commentators in relative disarray, at least for the moment, centrist and rightist pundits in the United States since 1990 have jubilantly trumpeted Latin America's rush toward privatization and the economic gains that have accrued in consequence. Not surprisingly, they like to concentrate on what has happened in Chile since the generals threw out Salvador Allende and his Marxist administration and then initiated a dramatic move toward economic privatization—a process that at the end of the 1980s the generals placed in the hands of the democratically elected Christian Democratic Party.

Chilean Christian Democracy originated in the 1950s as a statist, largely corporatist movement that, like the papal encyclicals of 1891 and 1931 that profoundly influenced it, showed a distinct suspiciousness of free-enterprise capitalism. The new Christian Democracy in Chile has taken happily to the free-enterprise spirit initiated by the generals who ousted Allende, and reflects the opening toward economic liberalism evident in the 1991 encyclical of Pope John Paul II: *Centesimus Annus*. If Chile is any indicator, even among Catholic social thinkers John Locke and Adam Smith have begun to replace St. Thomas as sources of political, economic, and social philosophy. Certainly French Thomistic philosopher Jacques Maritain, whose social-justice distributionist thought profoundly influenced the Christian Democratic movement throughout Latin America at midcentury, is no longer deemed relevant.

Even Cordell Hull's old bête noire Argentina began resolutely to move toward privatization under Carlos Saul Menem, elected president in 1988. The leader of his country's Peronist party, Menem totally reversed the policies initiated by the party's eponymous founder. Under Menem, privatization reached out to encompass even the giant oil industry, once the showpiece of a statist economy. The entire economy, in fact, was opened to private investment, both foreign and domestic, while a stabilization program reduced inflation from triple-digit figures to about 17 percent in 1992. Under the new approach, the economy grew in that year at a 9 percent rate, thereby rivaling growth rates in Chile. In its first five years, Menem's push to dispose of government enterprise had "netted beyond $10 billion." Meantime, in a transition that would cause the founder of Peronism to turn in his grave, the movement's new man in the Casa Rosada referred to the United States as "the greatest country in the world, like it or not."[5] Spruille Braden and Henry Luce could not have hoped for more. To them, the charismatic Menem would have seemed heaven-sent.

Had it not been for political-economic scandals so egregious as to result in the impeachment of a president, and after that to tarnish numerous national and local politicians, Brazil might have progressed as rapidly as its neighbor in the move toward privatization. At least that country did put behind it the old rivalries with Argentina (that had threatened to extend even into atomic weaponry research) and those with other neighbors that in the past had impaired economic growth. Throughout Latin America, in fact, a new spirit of economic cooperation based on market principles served to dampen the old nationalistic and ideological disputes that in the past had thwarted development, whether within individual countries or within regional blocs. Economic pragmatism rather than ideological commitment became the order of the day, and the economic rewards for the change were little short of spectacular—at least in the upper reaches of the social order.

Around the turn of the twentieth century a Colombian writer had commented on his country's devotion to truth as defined by philosophers. In consequence of this devotion, he observed, Colombia perishes but the truth is saved. By the 1980s, Colombian mainstream politicians, even if not a few die-hard revolutionaries, concerned themselves with economic pragmatism, with policies that resulted in development, rather than with so-called truth, on the essence of which philosophers could never agree anyway. The same transition was evident in neighboring Venezuela, where economic privatization acquired some momentum—unfortunately, along with some of the political corruption that had vitiated market reform endeavors in Brazil and elsewhere in the rapidly privatizing countries that comprise what once was designated the Third World. At least the new spirit of economic pragmatism both in Colombia and Venezuela served to blunt the old nationalistic and ideological contentiousness that had for many years, since independence in fact, soured relations between the two republics, often causing national leaders to think more about the glories of yesterday's wars and their generals than about cooperative future quests for prosperity.

Meantime Bolivia, long mired in the economic doldrums and ideologically tied to a revolutionary "reform" movement dating back to the 1950s that had for a time delighted socialist-leaning observers both in the United States and Latin America, had moved resolutely toward privatization. In the process its leaders had begun to improve the health of a chronically ailing economy. Moreover, Bolivian President Gonzalo Sánchez de Posada, elected in 1993, surrounded himself with advisers trained in economics in the United States. This, too, reflected a new trend in Latin America. Instead of philosophers educated at the Sorbonne, the new breed of Latin American presidents wanted advisers trained in economics at Harvard or the University of Chicago. The day of the pensador was giving way to the age of the economist and technocrat; at the same time the penchant for economic philosophy gave way to a concern for applied economics.

Mutual concern with pragmatic economics brought Bolivia into line with Chile, the country that previously it had not begun to forgive for having plundered it of its coast in the War of the Pacific (1879–1884). Now, in the 1990s, convergence in economic thought and in dreams of a common market began to turn attention from a bitter past to a hopeful future, presaging the sort of transition that some observers believed underway in all Latin America: the transition of underdeveloped traditional societies looking backward into modern republics focused on the future, the transition from people resigned to relive their history to people determined to escape history.

By the early '90s Peru, the third party to the War of the Pacific, seemed caught up in the hemispheric metamorphosis. Although President Alberto Fujimori reverted half-heartedly and justifiably to the ways of the dictator in seeking to suppress a long-festering and singularly vicious old-style Marxist millennialist insurrection, he moved at the same time to bring his country into line with the privatization craze sweeping the continent. Also by the early 1990s, Ecuador, a country that in the past had developed a nationalism based on brooding over military defeats and territorial despoilment inflicted by Colombia and Peru, had begun to focus on the future: on the economic resurgence it hoped to achieve by following the laws of the market and on the vast gains that would accrue to it through unencumbered trade with Colombia and Peru.

In no Latin American country has escape from the past and the shift toward privatization been more pronounced than in Mexico under its Harvard-trained President Carlos Salinas de Gortari (1988–1994). Writing in 1993 Santiago Levy, a highly placed official in the Salinas administration, gloated: "We have found that judicious deregulation can foster prosperity. In addition, the process of trade liberalization and deregulation has brought about a radical change of mind-set among public administrators regarding the overall role of market regulation." Making the case for a seat-of-the-pants, pragmatic approach to the economy, Levy observed that government bureaucrats and regulators lack the complete information and understanding required to formulate feasible market controls. Therefore, they should have the sense, and the humility, to leave the markets largely alone. Bowing, in effect, to the sort of wisdom "Will" Clayton had vainly preached at Chapúltepec in 1945, Levy confessed that Mexicans really should have had the sense many years ago to recognize the market's built-in logic. Instead, it took them an inordinate amount of time to learn what for them was an unpleasant truth: "that the market, despite its shortcomings, is the most efficient mechanism to allocate resources."[6]

The Salinas administration delivered the coup de grace to many of the statist reforms introduced during the Cárdenas years (1934–1940) that had elicited such enthusiastic approval from liberal New Dealers, especially those who were romantic agrarians, which to some considerable degree Ambassador Josephus Daniels had been. The collectivist approach to farming, based in large part on the ejido, which had been as sacred to utopianist Mexicans as the kibbutz to visionary Zionists in the 1930s, was gradually abandoned in favor of agrarian privatization. Even in the nationalized petroleum industry, long regarded as the crowning glory of the Cárdenas reform era, a few tentative openings were made to private, even foreign, investors.

What will happen to displaced campesinos as the agrarian sector undergoes privatization? Reporting in generally glowing terms on the transitions underway in Mexico, London's *Economist* observed in 1993 that the only viable long-term solution was industrialization and the development of a larger service industry to provide greater urban employment opportunities. This will not happen overnight, the *Economist* conceded; in the short term, the immediate impact of "the double blow struck by agricultural reform [aimed at privatizing communal lands] and falling tariff barriers will be to cause many to leave the countryside—and often the country, as they head north for the United States."[7] By the beginning of the following year, though, the *Economist* was reporting on another response to agricultural reform (and also to political corruption and anti-Indian prejudice in Mexico's official party): rebellion by campesinos in the southern state of Chiapas. In a way, this was a case of history repeating itself. In the nineteenth century liberal reformers out to "rationalize" the economy in line with U.S. models often seized individual and communal Indian properties. Invariably they stirred up indigenous revolutionary ferment, which then led to attempts by traditionalists to restore social peace by reverting to "irrational" patterns of village ownership and of paternalism, both private and public.

The uprising of the Chiapas "Zapatistas" (a topic that reappears toward chapter's end) was abetted by nonindigenous and possibly even non-Mexican socialist visionaries desperately seeking new fields in which to rekindle old hopes. Beyond that, the uprising responded in part to the conviction among many Mexican leftists that the North American Free Trade Agreement (NAFTA) among the United States, Mexico, and Canada would only exacerbate the plight of Mexican underlings.

In theory, and if all goes well, NAFTA (which went into effect on the first day of 1994, precisely when the Zapatistas arose) should produce the sort of stimulus to the Mexican economy that will ultimately furnish jobs for citizens and enough relatively well-off purchasers to create markets for an increasing flow of American imports. Indeed, even without NAFTA these results might, albeit more slowly, have come to pass in the wake of Mexico's economic revolution under President Salinas that in its consequences already, as of the early 1990s, had in some ways eclipsed the consequences of the bloody revolution that began in 1910.

Already by 1993 Mexico had become the third-largest trade partner for the United States, after Japan and Canada; already by then Mexico's growing internal markets attracted ever greater attention from U.S. manufacturers and providers of services; already by then American companies were investing considerably more in Latin America than overseas in Europe and Asia, with the lion's share of the investments going to Mexico. And Mexicans seemed ever more intent upon increasing the lion's share, and thereby besting some of Asia's tigers in the developmental sweepstakes.

Foreign Enterprise Institute resident scholar Mark Falcoff has drawn attention to the fact that "one-party rule and economic nationalism, once seen as obvious responses to the Yankee threat, now seem antiquated to many Mexicans. . . . Mexico," he concludes, with just a touch of condescension, "is ceasing to be Mexico." Another observer notes that Mexico's traditional fear of American dominance has faded as realization has mounted that national development depends on U.S. investment. "Gringophobia is, for now at least, a shadow of its former self." And this, the observer concludes, "is a sign of maturity in a young country, with enough self-confidence to deal with a vastly more powerful neighbor."[8] Just possibly it is also a sign of naive belief that the United States has truly learned how to enter the American Century as envisioned by Henry Luce.

During the Franklin Roosevelt administration, good neighborliness depended upon U.S. toleration and even approbation of Mexican endeavors to distance itself as far as possible from traditional North American social, political, and economic models. Toward the end of the century, good neighborliness apparently had come to depend on Mexico's voluntary welcoming of some of the social and economic models traditionally most dear to the gringo heart, and also on the sort of commercial ties in which Cordell Hull had placed so much hope. Indeed, as of the early 1990s Mexicans seemed more devoutly to desire those ties than the North American heirs of Cordell Hull. It remained only for Mexico to steer toward political reform: toward the democracy that the Latin American left now generally extols, and away from the political corruption and rigged elections of one-party rule.

China may be able to get away with "market Leninism" for some time to come (though that is not certain); but in Mexico time may be running against the marriage of authoritarian, corrupt, one-party politics and open-market economics—running against the hopes of the ruling party to have Mexico cease to be Mexico, economically, but continue to be Mexico, politically.

In the rest of Latin America, where in many countries a democratizing trend more pronounced than in Mexico has accompanied the move toward economic privatization, is the nationalist, interventionist, protectionist, corporatist past *really* past? If not, North Americans in the future may have to relearn some of the hemispheric lessons that FDR learned about tolerating differences among neighbors while putting on hold expectations about future similarities.

## *Is the Past Really Past in Latin America?*

In the Reagan administration one of the hardest-nosed of all the hard-nosed hemispheric cold warriors was Elliott Abrams, assistant secretary of state for inter-American affairs (1985–1989). While some of the policies with which Abrams was involved remained controversial, he could by mid-1993 take great personal pleasure in the remarkable economic progress that Latin Americans had begun to achieve through the free-market reforms he had privately and in his official capacity urged upon them. And yet, Abrams sounded a note of caution. Displaying a solid grasp of history, he observed that populism, in the form of corporatism (he prefers the word "corporativism") and statist intervention, "has returned to Latin America again and again because the benefits of development have been siphoned off by a small elite that used the government to protect its privileges."

Conceivably, Abrams concedes, history could repeat itself. But he remains hopeful that this time Latin America may be out of the statist woods. This time, he believes, equality of opportunity has genuinely begun to replace "government of, by, and for the rich"; this time, he hopes, nationalism may have come "to mean investing in the nation's human capital rather than blaming foreigners for the nation's ills." If that is so, then, he concludes, "populism will recede into Latin history."[9]

Whatever the future may hold, one development clearly discernible as of the early 1990s is especially striking to those who attend to the hemisphere's past. Back in 1933 when Herbert Eugene Bolton in his presidential address to the American Historical Association argued (as mentioned in Chapters 2 and 20) that the Americas shared a common history and were advancing toward ever greater convergence, Latin American pensadores overwhelmingly rejected the thesis; some, in fact, found the thesis downright offensive. Nowadays, the Bolton thesis of a common past that will yield a common future produces less indignation among Latin Americans—especially in its prophecy of future convergence. On the whole Latin Americans may not incline to go as far as Carlos Menem in publicly hailing the United States as the greatest country in the world. But they might well be hard pressed to name one they consider greater; and despite the leanings of a few toward East Asian development models, most Latin Americans concede the attraction of the U.S. economic system. At the same time, most Latin Americans concede the positive features of the triumph of the bourgeoisie in the United States (ignoring the fact that as of the early 1990s that triumph seemed threatened by emergent plutocracy above and increased pauperization below). No longer, as of the early 1990s, did some of those traits (listed toward the end of Chapter 11) that Latins used to associate, disdainfully, with Yankees necessarily suggest character flaws. Increasingly, Latins saw little wrong with admitting openly to being themselves "materialistic" and "utilitarian," to recognizing the pragmatic benefits of a "lack of idealism," to celebrating the developmental wonders facilitated by a certain "worship of money."

The Bolton thesis and the tenets of the Western Hemisphere Idea (as described in Chapter 20), with their shared insistence on the common values and aspirations of all the Americas, seem regnant, for now, throughout the New World. Below the border, talk about Third World socialism as the wave of the future has become barely audible. For better or worse, for the moment at least, the surging tide of the American Century as foreseen by Henry Luce seems to have reduced Latin American doubters to the role of frustrated Canutes. And yet, symptoms remain even now, in the mid-'90s, of the old longing to find a Third Way between capitalism and various varieties of socialism and/or traditionalism.

So, is the past really past?

As of the mid-'90s it was becoming clear that privatization yields bitter social fruits along with its succulent economic fruits. Just possibly the bitter fruits (some of which are scrutinized in Chapter 32) may make it difficult for governments to cope with mounting social unrest short of turning armed forces loose against poverty-stricken multitudes, in the sort of law-and-order campaign that actually seems to attract some hardcore rightists in the United States itself. Without proceeding all the way to this worst-case scenario, Latin America's leaders could begin before century's end to have second thoughts about Americanization, about embourgeoisement, about full-fledged entry into the American Century. Just possibly they might be tempted to retreat again into a living past, into what Elliott Abrams describes as a past of corporativism and populism.

### Is the Latin American Past a Living Past?

A one-time Soviet official observed in 1993: "In our society the supremacy of ideology over everything else did in fact always exist"—at least until the demise of communism.[10] In many ways, throughout much of its past, this statement was applicable to Latin America. Nowadays, the age of the pensador seems to have given way to the age of the entrepreneur, whether the large-scale, well-financed, well-connected entrepreneur, or the penny-capitalist who functions within the so-called informal economy, seeking his or her livelihood by operating beyond the reach of government regulators and tax collectors in providing goods and services to a small number of local clients.

Here is another quote, this time from British labor historian E. P. Thompson: "There is no such thing as economic growth which is not at the same time, growth, or change of culture."[11] What seems to have occurred recently in Latin America is a change in culture that in turn has produced a jump in economic growth rates. In the new culture, it is no longer letras and armas that confer nobleza, but rather economic expertise and the habits that result in achievement as measured in wealth and goods. On a massive scale, Latin America, for better or for worse, seems to have undergone embourgeoisement, to have become a beneficiary or a victim of North Americanization.

Political scientist Howard Wiarda, a lifelong observer of Iberian traditions, referred in 1993 to a theme that has long fascinated him: the Iberian world's ingrained "authoritarian organicist [or corporatist], elitist, Rousseauian and mercantilist [i.e., economic interventionist] principles and institutions."[12] Professor Wiarda is looking at the Iberian past, though I take him to believe he is also looking at its present and future. Perhaps, though, cultures *do* change and thereby produce changes in economic and social attitudes that in turn, as E. P. Thompson argues, can yield changes in economic growth rates. What, though, if—as Wiarda's extensive oeuvre suggests—Latin America's culture change represents decidedly less than a sea change? What if the past really is, still, a living past? What if, in the face of mounting socioeconomic problems within newly privatized societies, prophets of a better life find it useful—even as some have begun to do within the former Soviet Union—to attribute malaise to the aping of "materialistic, utilitarian" North Americans, with their "lack of idealism" and their "worship of money"?

Is Latin America, or part of it at least, still caught up in a living past?

In Chapters 6 and 15 I referred briefly to Latin America's turn-of-the-twentieth-century attempt to introduce more liberal, more market-oriented economic practices and to discard its old corporatist traditions. However, this endeavor exacerbated social problems and caused the ruling classes to fear revolutionary pressure from below. In response, they reverted to statist social programs that quickly closed the opening to the ways of the Yankee. Might the past still assert itself and curtail, even if not snuffing out so completely as at the turn of the century, Latin America's embrace of untrammeled free enterprise? After all, leaders to the south remain sensitive to what historian E. Bradford Burns, in the title of a 1980 book dealing with nineteenth-century Latin America, has called *The Poverty of Progress.*

The poverty-of-progress phenomenon helps explain the already-mentioned Zapatista uprising of 1994 in southern Mexico. In a way, it can be seen as a justified reaction against new social injustices inflicted in the name of economic liberalism's privatization. If still alive, John Collier, FDR's commissioner of Indian affairs, would have sympathized with the Zapatista protesters; and once again he would have used issues involving the Indian as a springboard for attacks against some of the most clear and obvious abuses of market capitalism. However, through the lens of cynicism the Zapatista challenge, which quickly became something of a public relations sensation as self-styled champions of the downtrodden throughout Mexico rushed to embrace it, can be seen as populism at its worst—precisely the type of populism Elliott Abrams hoped was dead. Clearly, the Chiapas phenomenon includes the use of Indian issues by non-Indians in order to enhance not necessarily the cause of Indians but the cause of certain non-Indians hoping to rise higher within the national power structure.

Seen through the lens of cynicism (or at least suspiciousness), the Zapatista movement presages a new chapter in the sort of non-Indian use of indigenista rhetoric that preceded and accompanied the Good Neighbor era in the 1920s and '30s: not only in Mexico but in much of Latin America. It presages a new instance in which the sincerity and naivete of a few high-minded white and mestizo reformers become enveloped in the ambitions of a horde of nonindigenous opportunists hoping to dramatize the suffering of the Indian in order to facilitate their own ascent in the light-skinned realm of power wielders. Above all, the Zapatista movement and the cult it quickly developed throughout the country among the politically sophisticated suggest that Mexico may not have ceased to be Mexico after all; for this is the sort of complex, multifaceted populism that has emerged periodically since colonial times—and sometimes yielded, on balance, eminently worthwhile consequences.

For all their self-serving motives, Zapatistas and Latin American populists in general—from the time of the Spanish military conquest on up to the Yankee cultural conquest—should not evoke automatic disparagement. The populists emerge out of persisting conditions of generalized exploitation and desperate poverty. They emerge out of refusal, whether idealistic or self-serving or both, to accept exploitation and poverty as inevitable.

Out of widespread perceptions of exploitation and an incontrovertible reality of poverty in the United States, Franklin Roosevelt emerged. He emerged in the midst of socially and economically precarious circumstances with a desire to help himself and his party politically, but also with a desire to help others survive temporary adversity—or even chronic adversity, if matters should come to that. That sort of mixed-motivation desire can still make a difference in the American hemisphere, north and south of the border. In spite of all its propensity for phoniness and its tendency to produce at least short-term negative effects on corporate balance sheets, populism (or whatever term one wants to attach to the quest for institutionalized social decency) promises to endure.

As presiding eminence over the Good Neighbor policy, FDR's great challenge was to distinguish Latin America's sincere if sometimes naive and deluded populists from self-seeking frauds, to differentiate between south-of-the-border Harold Ickes– and John Collier– and Eleanor Roosevelt–types on one hand, and Father Coughlin– and Huey Long–types on the other; and sometimes he and his crew met the challenge successfully, as with Cárdenas on one hand and Perón on the other. A similar challenge continues to confront U.S. policy-makers at century's end as Latin America, or much of it, moves toward the market economy.

Roosevelt might sometimes have been taken in by impractical visionaries and rank poseurs among Latin American reform mongers, or at least have found it useful to the hemispheric solidarity demanded by security needs to pretend he had been taken in. However, he also knew that poverty could indeed issue out of free-enterprise progress, and that sometimes populists were sincere and justified in demanding reform. That is why he could sympathize with the need occasionally to put restraints on those who profited the most from progress in order to protect those who suffered actual or relative decline in its wake. Otherwise, as he well knew, dangerous visionarist and populist poseurs would only proliferate.

## Fifty Years Later: FDR's Acuity and Fallibility as Hemispheric Prophet

Franklin Roosevelt assumed that ultimately Latin America would take up the attitudes and values (in short, the culture) that had shaped the United States. Fifty years after his death, it seems possible, perhaps even likely, but by no means certain that he was right. Quite possibly the Good Neighbor policy had, as he anticipated it would, helped speed the process of cultural change in Latin America by making the gringo appear less the ogre whose ways had at all costs to be rejected.

On the other hand, Roosevelt did not foresee, indeed could not have foreseen, the degree to which cults of Third World socialism cum fascism spawned during the Cold War would impede the "Americanization" of Latin America. Nor, I suspect, did FDR foresee, any more than he would necessarily have liked, the type of privatization convergence that seemed by the 1990s, after the collapse of the Soviet Union, to bind the two halves of the hemisphere together.

Roosevelt always envisioned a system for the United States, and for Latin America as well, in which communitarian values somehow would merge with those of individualism, in which neither set of values would cancel out the other. Could he have glimpsed the fin-de-siècle hemisphere he might well have hoped that he was seeing it in a passing phase; he might have hoped that the past was not altogether past, and that Latin America's historical openness to communitarian traditions would somehow reappear and in the process strengthen those same traditions that, however muted, had always existed in the United States and that he had sought to safeguard, even to strengthen.

Something else would have given Roosevelt pause had he been able to view the hemisphere at century's end: the extent to which New World ties seemed to be eclipsing Atlantic-community bonds. By 1992 the United States provided 57 percent of Latin America's imports, compared with 22 percent of Europe's. Whether or not other south-of-the-border republics realize their hopes to enter into the North American Free Trade Agreement, the importance of Latin American markets to U.S. producers of goods and services seemed destined to grow—especially in view of European Common Market barriers that impede the flow of U.S. goods into member countries.[13] "Dinky little countries," quite as much as the European bastions of culture that Roosevelt, following in the steps of Woodrow Wilson, had joined a world war to save, seemed to have assumed a crucial role in shaping North America's destiny.

In the mid-1980s while serving as vice president, George Bush remarked "that while France might be a more important country than Mexico, Mexico was much more important to the United States."[14] FDR could scarcely have imagined such a development arising out of the forces that his Good Neighbor policy had helped unleash. Some fifty years after his death, the big time, the big leagues, had come to the American hemisphere. In cultivating Latin American ties, he had, as it turned out, done far more than just create a minor league farm system. In some ways Henry Clay, along with other prophets of the Western Hemisphere Idea back in the 1820s, may have looked ahead more presciently than FDR to the eventual importance of Latin America to the United States.

# 31. *Expanding Potentials for Good (and Bad) Neighborliness Toward Century's End: Religion and Immigration*

❖ ❖ ❖ ❖ ❖ ❖ ❖ ❖ ❖ ❖ ❖ ❖ ❖ ❖ ❖ ❖ ❖ ❖ ❖ ❖ ❖ ❖ ❖ ❖ ❖ ❖ ❖ ❖ ❖ ❖ ❖

### The Religious Scene in the Americas

By the time of the New Deal, as suggested in Chapter 6, religion had lost some of its old potential to fan mutual discord, misunderstanding, even hatred, between North Americans and Latin Americans. By the 1930s, instead of growing up to hate Catholics, American Protestants had become accustomed to a large Catholic presence in their country, resulting in part from massive immigration from such countries as Ireland, Italy, and Poland. Even more than when Catholic Al Smith had run unsuccessfully for the presidency in 1928, American Catholics found acceptance in the age of Roosevelt. In fact, FDR went out of his way to court Catholics and to make them one of the basic props of his administration.

By the 1930s it had become politically safe to exhibit benevolent tolerance of Catholics in America. Moreover, American Protestantism, riven by serious internal disputes, could not have presented a united front in opposition to Catholics even had the old religious biases still obtained in their nineteenth-century intensity—which they did not. At last, religious pluralism, despite the objections of dyed-in-the-wool bigots on all sides, was beginning to become a reality. Along with cultural relativism, religious toleration was one of the Good Neighbor policy's essential building blocks. In a way, religious toleration fed on the religious indifference spawned at a time when secular humanism enjoyed a considerable vogue not only in the United States but in much of the western world—and in parts of the Islamic world as well.

South of the border, the secular and anticlerical spirit harking back in some ways to colonial times soared to new heights, especially in revolutionary Mexico. And Latin America's burgeoning secularism and anticlericalism facilitated a new opening toward the United States in the New Deal era. Secularism-anticlericalism below the border helped to blunt some of the traditional hysteria with which Latin America's purported defenders of genuine Catholic principles had once condemned the United States as a lair of godlessness and sinfulness.

By and large, though, changes occurring north of the border during Good Neighbor days made the principal contribution to removing religion as a major source of hemispheric divisiveness. In contrast, fifty years later religious changes taking place *south* of the border were primarily responsible for expanding the possibilities of good neighborliness. Fifty years after FDR's Good Neighbor era the old Catholic-Protestant animosities that once soured hemispheric relations were disappearing because Latin Americans in unprecedented numbers were converting to Protestantism.

Earlier in this book I referred to the Belgian Jesuit Roger Vekemans, who at mid-twentieth century spent considerable time in Chile. Specifically, I referred to his conviction that there was no hope for Latin American economic development on a scale adequate to address its burgeoning social problems unless its overwhelmingly Catholic citizenry basically made a commitment to the socioeconomic tenets of the "Protestant Ethic"—with its stress on individual initiative and probity in waging the struggle for material security and for eternal salvation.[1]

Not long after Vekemans made his observation in the early 1960s, the movement known as liberation theology began to score sweeping advances among Latin American Catholics. Essentially, liberation theology saw the solution to temporal, socioeconomic ills not so much in a Protestant Ethic approach of individual effort as in redistributionist schemes and various forms of state socialism. Arguably, liberation theology produced consequences counterproductive to Latin American development. Most definitely, by the end of the 1970s its tenets elicited the stern disapproval of the Polish-born pope, John Paul II. Midway through the 1980s, liberation theology seemed little more than a part of Latin America's historical past of failed millennialist movements. Even more than the conservative pope, the rush to privatization that became a stampede following the collapse of the Soviet Union dealt what for the moment at least appear mortal blows to liberation theology.

Already by the mid-to-late 1980s, the new religious style in Latin

American Catholicism had come more and more to be set by Opus Dei, a Catholic lay order especially dear to the heart of John Paul II. In many ways the Opus Dei represents what Roger Vekemans had looked forward to (even though most Jesuits remain highly skeptical about the young religious order, founded, like their own, by a Spaniard). Opus Dei associates the habits of hard work and denial of the instinct for instant gratification not only with temporal but also with eternal, supernatural success. Departing from the old Iberian Catholic line that poverty is the estate richest in the means of salvation, the Opus Dei, echoing the Protestant Ethic, counsels that economic success manifests the virtues that result in salvation. A sampling of this approach finds its way into John Paul II's 1991 encyclical *Centesimus Annus*. In this encyclical, John Paul was by no means original in making the connection between avenues to worldly success and to otherworldly redemption. Quite to the contrary, the pope simply picked up "on the vast literature generated by Max Weber's thesis that capitalism" flowed out of a "Protestant ethic" that was at the same time assumed to assure eternal salvation.[2] Unlike the situation in Poland when its native son ascended the throne of St. Peter, more and more Latin Americans have found the essence of a "Protestant Ethic" not in the Catholic Church's shifting temporal attitudes but in Protestantism itself.

Beginning especially in the 1960s, Latin Americans had witnessed dramatic breakaways from Protestant churches established decades earlier in their midst by, among others, Lutheran, Presbyterian, Methodist, Baptist, Moravian, Christian Science, and Brethren of Christ missionaries. Many of the breakaway Protestants joined evangelical churches. In the process they helped initiate an unprecedented rise in Protestant influence and conversions. The process gained momentum as a wave of new missionaries, especially from the United States, led by Seventh Day Adventists, Mormons, and a broad assortment of evangelicals, won masses of converts, often from the rural and urban poor, especially in Chile, Brazil, and Guatemala. By and large the new wave of Protestant missionaries stressed personal reform based on the individual's eradication of sinfulness. Eternal salvation depended on individual effort and initiative, not on passive reception of grace conferred by a supernaturally endowed priesthood—just as temporal rewards depended on personal initiative rather than the largesse of set-apart governing classes.

Through a complex, multifaceted rather than a monolithic advance, Protestantism is changing the religious and also the temporal scene in Latin America. As of 1993, two Protestant fundamentalists had served (with gross incompetence, as it turned out) as presidents of Guatemala, while in El Salvador an evangelical movement had gained influence not only among the country's poor but among military officers, businessmen, and university students. For a time, especially in Central America, many conservative citizens concluded that Protestantism offered a firmer bastion against communism than did Catholicism, with its numerous leftist-leaning clergy. But this was only one among many reasons that attracted Latins in Central America and elsewhere to new faiths. Throughout Latin America the influence of Protestantism and the numbers of its converts have continued their ascent following the collapse of international communism.

In South America the Protestant ascent has been especially pronounced in Brazil, where branches of the Universal Church of the Kingdom of God have often led the way. A 1991 survey showed that only 72 percent of Brazilians described themselves as Roman Catholic, down from 89 percent in the 1980 census. Moreover, the Catholic Church estimated that in 1991 it would lose another 600,000 of its faithful to Protestant churches. By the early 1990s, some 20 million Brazilians, about 20 percent of the population, identified themselves as Protestant—up from a mere 4 percent in 1960. Furthermore, common estimates suggest that on any particular Sunday the roughly 15-to-20 percent of Brazilians present at Protestant services outnumber those in the pews at Catholic churches.[3]

Throughout Latin America, Catholics retain their traditional reluctance to go to church—a habit that horrified U.S. Catholics sixty years ago but one into which they have increasingly fallen themselves as they take to the Latin style of being Catholics in their own way. Toward century's end even in traditionally devout Colombia, only 18 percent of the people go to church on Sundays, while in Chile the figure is 12 percent; in Mexico and Bolivia, respectively, the figures are 11 percent and 5 percent. In contrast Protestants, although a minority (Guatemala may soon become the first Protestant-majority Latin American republic), are "an enthusiastic one." Indeed, enthusiasm for the evangelical churches among Peru's Andean Indians in the 1980s and early '90s may have held back the spread of that country's variant of Marxism-Leninism that called itself the Shining Path (Sendero Luminoso). Referring to the spread of evangelical Protestantism among his country's *indios,* Peruvian ethnohistorian Nathan Wachtel observed: "[F]inally, after 500 years, the extirpation of idolatries."[4] Among the doomed idolatries may figure not only the worship of pre-Columbian idols but of political saviors, such as Marx and Lenin, as well.

In some instances, Latin America's Catholic hostility to the "invasion" of Protestantism, spearheaded by North American missionaries financed by North American dollars, helps to keep alive old sources of aversion to gringos and their religious culture. On the whole, though, contemporary religious animosities focus on what is occurring *within* a particular Latin American country, while the hemispheric dimensions of religious animosities, that used to extend northward to encompass the United States, are receding. This reflects the situation that prevails within the United States, where religiously inspired hatreds have for some time now been directed more at fellow citizens of the "wrong" faith than at people south of the border.

So, on both sides of the border the religious scene has become a kaleidoscope, one that encourages intranational animosity but not the sort of theologically justified cross-border hatreds that once prevailed. Furthermore, the tendency of North Americans until quite recent times to focus on the real and alleged abuses and scandalous personal lives of the Latin American clergy has all but disappeared as a rationale for the Yankee's religiously justified ethnocentric prejudices. In the early 1990s, the preponderance of known scandals involving both Protestant and Catholic clergy seems to occur within the United States itself, not south of the border.

The removal of the religious issue as a major source of contentiousness between the United States and Latin America became discernible during the Good Neighbor era and vastly facilitated Roosevelt's attempt to establish amicable hemispheric relations. I suspect, though, that FDR would have felt mixed emotions if able to assess the hemisphere's religious scene toward century's end. My guess stems from the fact that to the extent that he was a religious man at all, Roosevelt was attracted to mainline Episcopalianism with its ecumenical leanings and strong Social Gospel orientation. Moreover, he had taken to heart the communitarian, corporatist approach of some of the Catholic clergy who had helped him devise and implement the New Deal's social policies.

Given the religious influences that had appealed to him, Roosevelt could hardly have welcomed uncritically the competitive individualism unreservedly proclaimed as Christ's way, both north and south of the border, by armies of modern-day Babbitts with their emphasis on the dollars-and-sense value of Christianity; nor could he have sympathized with their narrow sectarianism that made a virtue of excluding, rather than including, the Other—however otherness was defined. Undoubtedly, though, he would have taken religiously justified intolerance in stride. After all, in his time Roosevelt had dealt with Father Coughlin and men of his ilk.

I should like to think that Franklin, and Eleanor, Roosevelt would have responded not with surprise, then, but with some element of regret, to the way in which the religious convergence of the American hemisphere was taking place at century's end. As the inveterate synthesizer of opposites he, perhaps rather more than she, would have hoped that the hemisphere-wide clash between secularism and religious fundamentalism might have left to both camps, whether located north or south of the border, a greater ability to tolerate, if not necessarily to admire, what the other had to offer.

Be that as it may, fifty to sixty years after the flowering of the Good Neighbor policy the minimizing of religion as a point of hemispheric contentiousness had proceeded further than most persons on either side of the border would have dared predict in the 1930s. To the extent that Henry Luce's American Century had a religious dimension, a Protestant Ethic sort of dimension, then the American Century had by the 1990s assumed hemisphere-wide proportions. Meantime, something else that very few Americans on either side of the north-south divide had foreseen in Good Neighbor days had come to pass half a century or so later: the American—meaning the U.S.—population in America's Century had taken on a Latin tinge.

### Immigration: The U.S. Population Acquires a Latin Tinge

At the beginning of the twentieth century, as they contemplated the news delivered by scholars, statesmen, and journalists that their own frontier had come to an end, North Americans looked forward to economic expansion—even if not population expansion—into what they regarded as their next frontier: Latin America. To some considerable degree in the decades ahead, that economic expansion indeed took place more or less as North Americans had foreseen. What came as a surprise, though, was that by century's end America, meaning the United States, had become a frontier for Latin Americans: not just for their capital but, more importantly, for their people as well.

The new immigrants flooding northward into the United States differed, as we shall see, among themselves—if for no other reason than that they came from different parts of Latin America. In consequence of differences, they differed among themselves over what they should be called. Most of them disliked such pan-ethnic labels as Hispanic or Latino. They preferred to be known as Cuban Americans or Mexican Americans or Haitian Americans. One can sympathize with their preferences. Still, for the sake of simplicity I will use primarily, and interchangeably, the denominations Hispanic and Latino in referring to the new immigrants— even though some of them come from Caribbean island republics and have no Hispanic or Latin roots whatever.

The so-called "fourth wave" of immigration into the United States got underway in 1965; and Latinos, followed by Asians, have predominated in that fourth wave. Since 1965, 14 million people, not counting illegals, have entered the United States. The immigration wave they comprise has been eclipsed in U.S. history only by the "third wave" of some 16 million who arrived between 1890 and 1920. "But while the earlier wave ended in about a generation, the current one," according to a 1992 report, "is already 27 years old and shows no signs of letting up." Moreover, it was swelled by the "2.5 million illegals of Mexican origin who have been legalized under the 1986 Immigration Reform and Control Act."[5]

The 1990 U.S. census revealed that "Hispanic people" totaled over 22 million nationally. Already in Los Angeles and Houston they outnumbered African Americans, and were rapidly pulling even in New York City and Dallas. Furthermore, according to demographic projections, Hispanics will overtake African Americans overall as the nation's largest minority group at some point between 1997 and 2005.[6]

In some ways the fourth wave can be viewed as one of the great success sagas in American history. The new arrivals have benefited from the civil rights movement of the 1960s, which eased the way for the assimilation of nonwhites. However, the darker their skin color, the more difficulty fourth wavers encounter in achieving true integration. Still, the browning of America currently underway may ultimately result in a country that is far more color-blind than in the past, and a country that is far better morally, and economically, for the fact. As one gushingly optimistic commentator wrote in 1993 about California, the state was "leading the nation into a more Hispanicized culture. And multi-racial Hispanic culture is the obvious bridge across the nation's racial chasms."[7]

Already the fourth-wave phenomenon has undermined FDR's assumption, shared by the majority of his fellow citizens, that America's true foreign affairs interests centered on Europe. With the arrival of Latinos and Asians in unprecedented numbers, Americans may cease to focus on Euro-Israeli issues and turn their attention increasingly to the South and to the East. Moreover, with more and more of their own people living in *El Norte,* Latin Americans may pay decreasing attention to the European countries whence came their nineteenth- and early-twentieth-century immigrants and focus their interest instead on the United States. Very possibly, then, the Good Neighbor purpose of turning Latin attention northward and U.S. attention southward may be realized to a far greater extent than FDR and the leaders of his generation could either have conceived or desired.

Already in the early 1930s as FDR laid the foundations of the Good Neighbor policy, some Mexican Americans had become unofficial ambassadors of goodwill in Texas, even as huge numbers of Mexican citizens deemed superfluous in the Depression era were shipped back to their country of origin. Already in the early 1930s, as indicated in Chapter 11, many Mexican Americans were realizing the American dream, and gaining acceptance among Texans, notoriously hard-bitten at the time in their attitudes toward "greasers." Often active participants in the League of United Latin American Citizens (LULAC), Mexican Americans gained acceptance by undergoing embourgeoisement, by becoming successful middle-class citizens impelled by the capitalist success drive and by the tenets of the Protestant Ethic—even though in most instances they remained Catholic.

In a way, the process that would bring San Antonian Henry Cisneros into President Bill Clinton's cabinet as secretary of housing and urban development originated with Mexican-American success stories as they began to accumulate in the 1930s. At that time, as Richard A. García writes, the Mexican community, with the approval of Anglo society, "was being intricately woven" into San Antonio's economy, and, "ultimately, into its political life." [8]

Fifty years after the Depression, in a process fed by the fourth wave, more and more Latinos provided examples of the Horatio Alger rags-to-riches success formula. Thereby they offered fresh proof of the enduring validity of cherished national myths and garnered the plaudits of old-line native sons and daughters. True, there had been an interlude in the 1960s when many native (and nativist) Americans had found cause to wonder about the assimilability of strangers from below the border. Caught up in that decade's counterculture, young Mexican Americans had undergone a certain antibourgeois radicalization as they formed the Chicano Student Movement and the La Raza Unida party. In these and other associations they railed against assimilation into allegedly corrupt and decadent bourgeois capitalist society and talked about re-creating an Aztlán utopia that allegedly had once flourished on land now belonging to the rapacious gringos. [9] But that movement had proved short-lived, and by and large educated, middle-class Mexican Americans had returned to conventional bourgeois society by the end of the 1970s. A fair number of them even voted for Ronald Reagan and George Bush. But their support for conservative American values, for private enterprise, and in some cases for the Republican Party was as nothing compared to that exhibited by a newly arriving group of Spanish-speaking immigrants: the Cuban Americans.

Ironically, in trying to win the Latin American continent for Marxism Fidel Castro struck a tremendous blow toward projecting Latin America into the age of free-enterprise capitalism as envisioned by "Will" Clayton and like-thinking norteamericanos back in 1945 at Chapúltepec. The million or so Cubans who either fled the island or were expelled, because of their unregenerate bourgeois mentalities, settled primarily in and around Miami, where quickly they compiled chapter after new chapter of American success stories. In fact, as Earl Shorris writes, "no group of newcomers in the United States has ever moved so quickly from penury to prosperity; Fidel Castro had given the middle-class engine of the Cuban economic system to his worst enemy." [10] If Yankee capitalist exploitation of Cuba had been as devastating as many leftist writers assert, it is difficult to understand how so many Cubans would have developed the skills and the overwhelming desire to construct an American-style "middle-class" engine in the first place.

Prospering to a degree unprecedented among Latino fourth wavers, the Cubans built what Shorris calls "an economic fortress" in Miami. Perhaps it would be more accurate to describe what they built, in their Spanish-language state within a state, as a shopping mall and banking enclave. Their shopping and banking facilities assumed hemispheric significance, attracting customers and clients from virtually every part of Latin America. Miami as remade by Cubans fanned the bourgeois dreams of countless Latin American visitors, and sent them home more dedicated than ever to the capitalist credo, and to the gospel of privatization, which lay at the heart of the "Cuban paradigm" as it emerged in Miami.[11]

Thanks in no small part to expatriate Cubans and the "paradigm" they fashioned, Latin America was dragged into the American Century as envisioned by Luce, not into the communist utopia that Castro had talked about while managing only to construct one of the most glaring examples of dystopia in the history of the Americas: a dystopia shaped not only by Marxist-Leninist ideology but also by some of the allegedly paternalistic, interventionist, antimaterialistic ideologies that at various times have beguiled Latin Americans, going all the way back to sixteenth-century Franciscan missionaries and even to the Incas and Aztecs.

So impressed are some old-stock Americans by the success sagas being written in the Southwest and in Florida by Latinos that they have stood on its head one of the great national myths as they urge more and more immigration from south of the border. The old immigration myth—which just like the frontier myth centered on regeneration—held that the destitute from lands afar would be reborn in America. The stood-on-its-head immigration myth holds that the new arrivals, with their work ethic, their need to achieve, their family values, and religious faith, will reanimate Americans grown torpid and dissolute. In short, it is the new arrivals who will bring about regeneration among faltering native sons and daughters.[12]

A precedent exists for turning immigration mythology on its head, a precedent that extends back at least to the 1920s. At the time when the Sacco-Vanzetti issue divided Americans (see Chapter 9), a good number of American liberals and radicals tended to see immigrants as a source of moral and ideological regeneration for a sick, mainstream, bourgeois society. As of the early 1990s, it was primarily conservatives who employed the reverse frontier mythology of regeneration, hoping that from abroad would come the impetus to cure domestic society of the ills that liberalism purportedly had spawned.

Occasionally in the 1990s the argument in behalf of unimpeded fourth-wave immigration ties in with antiblack prejudices. Ignoring the dramatic growth of a black middle class, U.S. advocates of unlimited immigration sometimes imply that African-American inner-city residents may be incapable of pulling themselves up by their bootstraps, as Latino immigrants purportedly are doing. Moreover, immigration advocacy sometimes reflects antigay, antifeminist, and antiabortion sentiments, rooted in the assumption that Latin Americans by and large share these sentiments and will bolster them within the United States if they enter in sufficient numbers.

Regeneration-through-immigration mythology sometimes serves as a mask to disguise what basically are economic concerns. By perpetuating the fourth wave, some Americans hope simply to keep labor costs low and union strength at a minimum. At the same time, regeneration mythology can serve to mask other eminently practical concerns. For example, a huge influx of newly arriving workers will make it less urgent to undertake the expensive projects of training and "resocializing" inner-city African Americans—projects that to many accommodated citizens smack of failed New Deal socialism and of Lyndon Johnson's "Great Society" delusions. Moreover, a steady stream of new workers could be counted upon to relieve upward pressure on wages, thereby enabling the well-to-do to continue to increase the economic distance between themselves and socioeconomic underlings. Whatever their motivation, those Americans who want the fourth wave to continue unabated ignore many aspects of its downside.

As of 1992 (according to nationwide U.S. press releases appearing in August of 1993) Hispanics accounted for a cheap labor pool precisely because 29 percent of them lived below the poverty level, compared to 9 percent of "non-Hispanic whites." At the same time, unemployment rates for Hispanic men stood at higher than 12 percent, compared to 7.5 percent for non-Hispanic whites; for Hispanic women jobless rates stood at nearly 10 percent, compared to 5.4 percent for non-Hispanic white women.

Obviously, if the current immigration wave continues many of the new arrivals will live in circumstances hardly conducive to preparing them to accomplish the moral regeneration of America. What has happened is that defenders of immigration tend to base their optimism not on what new-wave immigrants (aside from Cubans who began to arrive in the 1950s) are accomplishing but rather on the embourgeoisement achieved, beginning in the 1930s, by small numbers of immigrants during an era when overall immigration was minuscule.

## Immigration as a Potential Source of Hemispheric Friction

Up to this point, the present chapter has focused mainly on positive developments of recent years that have helped expand the potential for good neighborliness that the Roosevelt administration tapped into in the 1930s. As viewed from south of the border, fourth-wave immigration into the United States is one of those positive developments. Indeed, many Latin American leaders (including Catholic prelates anxious to escape the consequences of their church's anti-birth-control fixation) perceive the export of surplus population to the United States as a providentially supplied opportunity to mitigate domestic social and economic problems. However, from the U.S. side of the border, fourth-wave immigration is a complex issue fraught with contradictions.

Some of the contradictions were on display in Los Angeles in 1992. In the melee that ensued after police officers accused of beating African American Rodney King were found not guilty in their first trial, conducted by the state of California, the relatively well-off Mexican Americans concentrated in East Los Angeles refrained from joining the rioters. Not only that, they condemned the mainly South Central Los Angeles Hispanics who did join in the riots.

The presence of Hispanics (mainly Mexican Hispanics) among the rioters hints at the downside of the immigration tale. These Hispanics, who make up about 45 percent of the population of South Central Los Angeles (which used to be overwhelmingly African-American), typify in many instances not the relative success stories of their East Los Angeles ethnic counterparts, but rather the all-too-common socioeconomic failure stories of the blacks among whom they live. Often they feel no real stake in their community and, having nothing to lose, take lightly to violence and looting. Throughout the United States, there are many Hispanic counterparts to the Los Angeles inner-city marginals; and many of the Los Angeles marginals and their counterparts elsewhere are illegals who strain the social budgets of the states in which they live while at the same time swelling the profits of native-born American entrepreneurs and farmers and employers of every type.

In the early 1940s, Anglo resentment in Los Angeles and elsewhere against zoot suiters originated not just in race prejudice but also in fear. Zoot suiters carried pistols, razors, blackjacks, and daggers. They terrorized citizens, and they shot, slugged, and slashed their opponents in gang warfare.[13] Yet their pranks were child's play in comparison to the violence in which Hispanic gangs throughout the Southwest, to say nothing of New York and New Jersey and Illinois and Michigan (among other states), engage half a century later. In California and elsewhere (as in the case of Dominican immigrants on the East Coast), many Hispanics even contrive somehow to direct street-gang activities from their prison cells.

The truth is, a large percentage of Hispanics in the United States do *not* succeed (at least not in terms of middle-class traditional values), although it remains unclear if their failure rate is appreciably greater than that of some third-wave immigration groups that have subsequently managed to establish themselves in American society every bit as successfully as old-line stocks. For the moment, though, Hispanics cannot, by and large, be seen as providing an example that will inspire old-line Americans to undergo moral regeneration. And, for the moment at least, many of the most troubling indications of social dysfunction come from the most numerous group of Latinos in the United States: from Mexican Latinos, who comprise about two-thirds of the entire Latino population and whose numbers grew during the 1980s at five times the rate of the national population overall.

As of March 1990 (according to Census Bureau figures as reported in the January 19, 1992, *New York Times*) Mexican Americans were much worse off than non-Hispanic white Americans and considerably worse off than the aggregate of non-Mexican Hispanics. Statistics on median income, on percentage of those living below the poverty line, on school performance and dropout rates all told the same tale about the comparatively poor performances of Mexican-origin Hispanics.

For Latinos as a whole, the high school dropout rate as of 1990 stood somewhere between 35 and 40 percent, depending on which set of statistics one credits (contrasted with dropout rates of 12.7 and 14.9 percent for non-Hispanic whites and for blacks, respectively). Moreover, the new decade quickly produced a dramatic increase in fatherless Latino families. More and more, the Latino dream of upward social mobility was proving empty. More and more the high school dropout rates, combined with "the multiplier effect of dropouts marrying dropouts and producing children who will drop out promises a twenty-first century Latino underclass of enormous size."[14]

In many social indices, Puerto Ricans (who of course are citizens of the United States) ranked even below Mexican Americans. Indeed, among all the ethnic groups that make up the U.S. citizenry, the highest rates of illegitimacy and welfare dependency occur among Puerto Ricans: a people who have been under America's semicolonial custody since the turn of the century and who seem to have derived singularly little benefit from the opportunity to mingle traditional culture with Yankee civilization.[15] Why Puerto Ricans have been so much slower than Cubans, another people subject to strong doses of Yankee domination and cultural infusion, to respond to the bourgeois ethic awaits a convincing explanation.

Judging by the Puerto Rican precedent, and by that of Hispanics in general, one can only question the likelihood that the new wave of Spanish-speaking immigrants will have an easy time escaping the conditions of poverty that sometimes encourage the sort of antisocial behavior that leads America's "solid" citizens to have misgivings about the fourth wave. And to the degree that Americans develop prejudices against Latinos in their midst, they are also apt to entertain doubts about the overall virtue of Latin Americans who remain in their native republics. This is not the sort of situation out of which good neighborliness grows.

As high-paying jobs become more scarce in the United States, its citizens are apt to look for scapegoats on whom to lay the blame. Latin American immigrants seem increasingly likely to be assigned this role. Already indications abound that African Americans tend increasingly to attribute the economic dead ends in which they feel trapped to the rising tide of Hispanic immigrants, legal and illegal. White resentment also is on the rise, especially among lower-middle-class sectors. Obviously, immigrants with a "multi-racial Hispanic culture" are not building a "bridge across the nation's racial chasms," as anticipated by the rosy forecast quoted toward the beginning of the preceding section.

Back in New Deal days as the Depression tightened its grip, the United States simply rounded up and shipped back to Mexico virtually all that country's nationals living in the Southwest. It may be a mark of progress toward equality in hemispheric relations that nowadays the United States can no longer act with such unilateral high-handedness. Yet it is not comforting to most North Americans to contemplate the fact that they have lost control of their borders, and can no longer block the flow of illegal immigrants any more effectively than they can halt the infusion of cocaine and other illegal substances. Nor is it comforting to many Americans that as the twentieth century draws toward a close Mexicans are beginning to avenge the 1848 loss of territory to the United States. Increasingly, Mexicans and also a fair number of Salvadorans and other Central Americans have begun to make southern California more and more their territory, even if not yet to the extent that Cubans have made Miami theirs. South of the border, many observers regard these developments as poetic justice meted out to gringos whose ancestors stole Florida from Spain and much of the Southwest from Mexico. But this viewpoint is not going to find many adherents among North Americans.

In one of its manifestations, the old American frontier myth posited the virtue and ingenuity, daring, and superior entrepreneurial qualities of the intrepid overlanders who left the security of their native regions to seek fortunes in the frontier. There's another version of that myth, though, as found in—among myriad other sources—the movie referred to in Chapter 5: Clint Eastwood's *The Unforgiven*. In this version, it is the lawless elements from the settled cities who were likely to make their way west, bringing with them all their antisocial traits. Nowadays Americans wonder if their land has become a frontier for lawless Latinos, for those who care nothing about violating immigration laws and who are willing if not indeed predisposed to continue living beyond the law after settling among the gringos.

Many Americans, including Abraham Lincoln, once dreamed of relocating "undesirable" African Americans somewhere in a Central American frontier. Nowadays, a considerable number of North Americans keenly resent what they see as the ability of Latin Americans to send their undesirables into a U.S. frontier. In years to come, this resentment will operate against hemispheric solidarity. So, with all the promise for enhanced good neighborliness in the hemisphere that burgeoned fifty or so years ago, there now appears a mounting potential for friction. And if confidence (on both sides of the border) in the economic miracles to be achieved throughout Latin America by means of privatization proves unfounded, the potential for hemispheric discord will only grow.

Rather than setting the pace for the Old World, the New World could fall prey to the same sort of antiforeigner phobias that gripped both Western and Eastern Europe in the wake of the Cold War's end. In the New World, moreover, an excess and rapidly growing population that may outstrip job-creation capabilities and even the environment's carrying capacity could intensify the potential for chaos: a chaos far less gentle than FDR presided over in less complex times. So, at least, say the Cassandras and the Jeremiahs, whose past predictions of impending calamity have happily been wrong as often as right.

# 32. Toward Century's End: Problems in Privatized Paradises

❖ ❖ ❖ ❖ ❖ ❖ ❖ ❖ ❖ ❖ ❖ ❖ ❖ ❖ ❖ ❖ ❖ ❖ ❖ ❖ ❖ ❖ ❖ ❖ ❖ ❖ ❖ ❖ ❖ ❖ ❖ ❖ ❖

### Privatization in Latin America: Profits and Penury

Dreams of encountering paradise in the New World have a long history. Perhaps the dreams have abounded more in the southern than the northern half of that world, although the matter is debatable. Be that as it may, pre-Columbian Indian civilizations from Caribbean islands and Mexico and Guatemala all the way down to Chile's Araucanians chased the dream. So did Catholic missionaries in the early days of conquest. Again and again, throughout the colonial period and on up through the modern era, pursuit of paradise activated visionaries and sometimes inspired vast social movements, violent as well as pacific. For some Latin Americans in the late twentieth century, once Marxism-Leninism and its various a-la-criolla offshoots had demonstrated their futility, privatization loomed as the latest, most modern and up-to-date route to a secular utopia. At last the day long foreseen by Yankee free-enterprise proselytizers seemed to have dawned. And that day soon bore witness to prodigies of profit-making, as briefly suggested already, in Chapter 30.

Unhappily, Latin Americans playing by the new rules of privatization developed a game in which there were more losers than winners. In this game, staggering gains for the few (especially those well enough connected to make deals for the purchase of what once had been state monopolies) contrasted with declining living standards for the masses. Practical and realistic elements among Latin America's chastened and dispirited left scarcely doubt that free-enterprise capitalism is the wave of the future. But they hope for at least the partial curbing of the wholesale graft and fraud and corruption to which piratical privatization has opened the gates, combining the worst features of state-run and private-enterprise economies.[1]

Even the London *Economist,* that staunch advocate of privatization virtually any time and any place, concedes that whereas one in four Latin Americans lived in absolute poverty in 1980, by the end of the decade "it was the lot of nearly one in three." At the same time the distribution of income, "already hideously skewed, grew even less equal." While some countries could point to spectacular 1992 growth rates (10.4 percent in Chile, 9 percent in Argentina, 7.3 percent in Venezuela), the area's economies as a whole grew only a bit more than 2 percent in that year. And as social problems intensified, even administrations in countries with the fastest-growing economies found it increasingly difficult to augment social welfare spending lest they worsen budget deficits and inflation, and turn investors nervous.[2]

Even in Chile, home of the economic miracle to which privatization prophets point with greatest satisfaction, signs of socioeconomic malaise persist along with, to be fair, signs of amelioration. According to one observer, the income share for the top and bottom fifths of the population went from 44.5 percent and 7.6 percent, respectively, in 1969 to 54.6 percent and 4.4 percent in 1989. The same observer frets about the underside of Mexico's economic miracle, claiming that more than half the population lived below the poverty line as of 1990—partially in consequence of a decline from 43 to 35 percent of labor's share of national income that occurred in the '80s.

By no means is the picture entirely bleak. In Chile, while the percentage of citizens living in poverty as 1992 ended was up in comparison to 1984, it was down in comparison to 1987. This was the result of increasing attention paid by a democratic administration to social problems, beginning in the late '80s. And the trend seemed certain to continue under the center-left Eduardo Frei administration that voters overwhelmingly elected in December of 1993. Meanwhile in Mexico President Salinas, for all his advocacy of privatization, did not turn his back on the country's social problems. Through his *Solidaridad* program he sought to alleviate some of Mexico's most pressing social ills. And he signaled his party's dedication to future reforms by choosing as the candidate to succeed him in office the man who had served as head of the Solidaridad program: Luis Donaldo Colosio. In spite of this, the Zapatista uprising in Chiapas at the beginning of 1994 is taken as a sign by many Mexicans, from the president on down, that much more must be done to address social problems.

In Latin America as a whole, indications of future trouble abound. For one thing, much of the growth that is apparent when one looks high enough in the social order results not so much from the effectiveness of internal reforms as from foreign investment, "attracted by low wages and devalued currencies" and the perceived chance to wheel-and-deal with on-the-make bureaucrats.[3]

Looking on Latin America as a whole during the early-to-mid 1990s, conditions in some ways seemed most disheartening in Brazil. For the past half century or so that country has been depicted as Latin America's slumbering giant. As the giant entered the fin-de-siècle decade, some observers detected signs of awakening. In fact, at the beginning of the '90s Brazil had emerged as the world's third-largest exporter. But the old symptoms of drowsy malaise remained, and even worsened. For example, the number of Brazilians living in hunger grew during the 1980s from 25 million to 35 million—in a total population of about 150 million. In a country where per-capita income stood at $2,920 by 1993, the number of Brazilians living on less than a dollar a day increased, according to United Nations statistics, by 40 percent, rising to 35 million during the 1980s. Moreover, "the portion of the population living on less than two dollars a day increased from 34 percent to 41 percent in that decade." As sociologist Herbert Jose de Souza puts it, "Brazil has moved straight from feudalism in this century to *savage capitalism.*"[4]

By the early 1990s Brazilians had taken to calling their country "Belindia": a little bit of Belgium surrounded by India. In Belindia more than a fifth of the overall population simply lacked the means to purchase adequate food. In Belindia, moreover, the richest 20 percent of the population at the beginning of the '90s earned 32.5 times as much as the poorest 20 percent, "an inequality greater even than Bangladesh's."[5] Under these conditions, Brazil's dispirited left showed new vitality in 1994, though not nearly enough to prevail in that year's presidential election, won by a centrist promising to tame inflation.

Brazil's problems were exacerbated by political corruption on a scale unusual even among the worst of Third World kleptocracies. At least corruption had ceased to go unpunished. The mammoth scale on which he practiced it led late in 1992 to the impeachment and removal from office of President Fernando Collor de Mello, throwing into disarray the sweeping privatization programs he had launched, many of which in essence possessed considerable merit and promise. The fault lay perhaps not so much with the programs as with methods of implementation. In Brazil, as in many other parts of Latin America and indeed of the whole world, "neoliberalism is not so much distorted as it is defined by an explosive mixture of gross official corruption, economic fragility, and social despair."[6] The same might well be said of the region that once comprised the Soviet Union.

Sociologist Daniel Bell, scholar in residence at the American Academy of Arts and Sciences, points out that corruption in totalitarian societies "is the arbitrary use of power." In democratic capitalist nations, however, "corruption is money."[7] With its collapse the Soviet Union provided new confirmation to Lord Acton's dictum that power corrupts. But the triumphant Free World, within which Latin Americans and many one-time Soviets now seek their rendezvous with destiny, seemed intent upon proving that money can corrupt just as badly. Indeed, many Free World privatizers seemed bent upon confirming the old adage that money *is* power, even while rejecting the hoary Yankee dictum that time is money. In the new yet really very old order, not time but sweetheart deal-making is money—big money, at least.

"Neoliberals" in the United States, perhaps more accurately dubbed neoconservatives, like to believe that problems of corruption lie not with the market system they advocate, but rather with the perverse genius of Latin Americans to undermine that system by clinging to the governmental and private corruption that marked the bad old days of traditional corporatism, later permeated by neofascist and neocommunist germs. The neoliberals or neoconservatives can also mutter darkly about national character, resorting to old stereotypes about Latin chicanery while overlooking the symptoms of moral malaise in the U.S. privatized paradise attested to by a long history of financial and political corruption. Perhaps the underlying truth is that we simply do not clearly understand what lies behind the shortcomings of Latin America's new attempt to implement market reforms, or behind the social deterioration so evident in the United States itself toward century's end—but only at midpoint in the Henry Luce–projected American Century.

One possible explanation for the shortcomings is this: neoconservatism (or neoliberalism or whatever name one wants to attach to ideological justification for the market economy) may very well provide Latin Americans with the best rationalization for ignoring social problems they have ever had at their disposal—a possibility that prescient and conscionable neoconservatives worry about, as the Elliott Abrams quotation included in Chapter 30 indicates.[8] Their traditional, interventionist ideologies, as well as Marxism-Leninism, at least compelled Latin Americans to apologize for conditions of social deterioration. So did the whole approach of the Good Neighbor era, in which FDR sought to give a gentle edge to the workings of capitalism both below and above the border. Neoconservatism or neoliberalism, however, at least in incautious or calloused hands, readily enough lends itself to calm acceptance of social deterioration as the inevitable result of a market system that will eventually outgrow such little imperfections. The process only requires time—which happens to be among the commodities Latin American regimes may now be running out of.

Liberated at last from the communist menace, it is almost as though the Free World, both in its secular and in some of its religious institutions, is moving to exacerbate the social suffering that helped call communism into being in the first place. Certainly in Latin America the rapid increase in population creates huge numbers of people who simply cannot be absorbed even by fairly rapidly expanding economies. Even with the touted "miracles" of development accomplished by Mexican privatization in recent years, the number of people unable to find adequate economic opportunities in that country is increasing. It seems almost as if a neo-Malthusian virus stalks much of the world, threatening the sort of catastrophe that countervailing catastrophes—some of them now resurgent—helped keep in check in the premodern world: the catastrophes of plague and pestilence and war and undernourishment. Whether or not it is readily possible to establish a direct, causal connection between social conditions and population numbers, one should regard with a cautious eye the fact that, at about 470 million, "the Latin American population has roughly trebled since 1950 and is still rising at 1.8 percent a year."[9]

In much of the world today with more hands available than there are decent employment opportunities, wages confront downward pressures. All the while social problems mount, not only because of low wage levels but because government social services are swamped by the demands of the masses: legitimate demands, sometimes, yet demands that can scarcely be met without taxes so high as to stifle initiative among society's most productive sectors. Faced with mounting problems that their governments could no longer address even if they had the will to do so, marginalized masses seek survival by crowding into the nearest-at-hand developed country. In the American hemisphere the result is that the United States seems unable to halt the flood of illegal immigration.

So far, the U.S. economy has made room for most of the new arrivals, both the legals and the illegals. But there is no proof it can continue to do so; and already indications suggest that the sweet life in America for its old-line citizens is not nearly as sweet as it used to be. In the United States itself, almost as much as in the lands to its south, wages confront downward pressures even as social costs mount and as middle classes find it more and more difficult to cope with tax burdens necessitated by social costs.

## Privatization in the United States: Profits and Pauperism

One of the few positive consequences—beyond hastening the USSR into bankruptcy and collapse—of the huge deficit into which President Ronald Reagan plunged the country between 1981 and 1989 was that the United States could no longer expend lavish amounts of money on problematic

Latin American aid programs. For literally the first time since the middle years of the Good Neighbor era, hemispheric diplomacy shed some of the stresses and tensions that inevitably complicate relations between bribe givers and bribe takers. Meantime, budgetary restraints produced profound effects within the United States.

For better or for worse, depending on political and social perspective, the U.S. deficit curtailed government ability to run a welfare state. Undoubtedly the deficit in many ways weakened the so-called social safety net first established during New Deal days. The Reagan-era deficit, accumulated both in order to deal the coup de grace to international communism and to eliminate domestic "give-away" and "socialist" programs, left the United States simultaneously as the only true superpower in the world and as the largest and wealthiest Third World power in history. The second consequence, of course, cannot by any means be attributed just to the policies of Presidents Reagan and Bush or to the thrust of their neoconservative supporters. Creeping symptoms of Third World status have become the badge of most developed democracies throughout the western world as deteriorating social conditions overwhelm old protective mechanisms and render developed countries more and more like Dickensian England.

It used to be that by moving north across an international boundary, Latin Americans entered a country relatively free of the sort of slums that blighted their own nations. Nowadays residents in the American hemisphere have to move northward across the border that separates the United States from Canada in order to find an ambience relatively free of "Third World" slums that eat away at human dignity and hope. Moreover, recent U.S. travelers to Chile have found its capital, Santiago, far less the typical Third World metropolis than New York City. More and more, within the United States, the number of homeless who comprise part of the population of all inner-city slums has grown massively and has come to include an increasing number of families with children. Moreover, against a background of ossified racial antagonism, there has taken place a clearer "delineation of spaces of wealth and spaces of poverty, and a hardening in the boundaries of each." What is more, the sheer misery of the poor has increased, with many elderly persons finding themselves too impoverished to pay for heating and adequate food. Perhaps these conditions will make it easier for their similarly afflicted successors in fifty years or so to accept the sort of state-decreed euthanasia-induced departure from this life at, say, age ninety that some futurologists predict.[10]

The statistics that point to the impoverishing of the United States are sometimes ambivalent, and consistently contested by champions of free enterprise who take it as an article of faith that by operating within the market paradigm the United States is achieving ever greater prosperity.

Still, the statistics are too compelling and too diverse in their sources to ignore. A study by the Federal Reserve finds that the share of wealth held by the top 1 percent of families, "a ratio long stable at around 31 percent, surged to 37 percent between 1983 and 1989." From the Bureau of the Census comes word that "the fraction of workers whose wages are too low to bring them above the poverty line even if they can find full-time work jumped from 12.1 percent in 1979 to 18 percent in 1990." A Budget Office study finds that in 1990 the top fifth of the population received as much after-tax income as the remaining 80 percent, while the growth in the incomes of the richest 1 percent of Americans between 1980 and 1990 was equal to the total income of the poorest 20 percent of the population. Budget Office statistics also show that by 1988 the richest 9 percent of Americans owned half of the nation's wealth, while the other half was owned mostly in the form of the family home and automobile. Against the background of burgeoning poverty comes the estimate of a recognized authority on the matter that while compensation of America's top Chief Executive Officers (CEOs) "was about 35 times the pay of the average employee in the mid-1970s" the ratio by 1990 had climbed to 120.[11]

Ably summing up some of the recent findings on America's deteriorating social structure, findings that in New Deal days might have elicited far more than the yawn that they prevailingly provoke today after wars on poverty that rightly or wrongly Americans tend to see as lost wars, one authority drew these conclusions in 1993: life "has become bleaker, more stressful, less hopeful, and more atomized" within American cities. Changes have been not only material, but cultural and familial. "It is not simply that many people have become poorer, but they have become poorer in the context of declining opportunities for ever attaining a better life." Furthermore, material prospects have not only dimmed for the young and the poor, but "they have dimmed just when there has been an explosion of affluence and a growing celebration of material consumption at the other end."[12] Even if wars on poverty have been lost, it is a new phenomenon in human affairs to abandon warfare altogether just because of past defeats.

Political scientists in the United States used to take satisfaction in describing their society as one based on achievement, while Latin Americans, so they said, clung to superannuated structures in which ascription (circumstances of birth) determined one's life chances. By the 1990s, the United States and Latin America seemed more and more to be losing their distinctiveness. Latin American social and economic structures came a bit more to resemble those north of the border; and U.S. social and economic structures came a great deal more to resemble those south of the border. Both in Latin America and the United States, a burgeoning underclass created doubt as to the brightness of the future; both in Latin America and the United States the underclass was differentiated from accommodated sectors partially by color; and within the United States itself the underclass was increasingly made up of people who had recently escaped from the underclass in Latin America.

On both sides of the border, despite all the talk about the vibrancy of U.S. democracy and the growth of democratic institutions and market forces in Latin America, one fact remains unassailable: "differences in wealth add to differences in power. This is *the* central fact of the contemporary world, and any approach which ignores it and even denies it is worthless."[13]

Before, during, and immediately after FDR's Good Neighbor era, many North Americans looked forward to the convergence of the Americas. They assumed, though, that in consequence of convergence Latin Americans would gradually move up to the sort of prosperity that typified the United States—when it was not in a depression or recession, that is. In the fin-de-siècle era, hemispheric convergence more and more becomes a reality. All too often, though, it is convergence based on declining standards for North Americans rather than rising standards for Latin Americans. All too often convergence rests, also, on growing disparities between rich and poor. This is hardly what those North Americans, whether they subscribed to the Western Hemisphere Idea or to Herbert Eugene Bolton's thesis of the hemisphere's common history, had in mind when they predicted the coming together of the Americas in a shared culture and destiny.

There is a brighter side, though, to the convergence phenomenon. In the following chapter I hope to suggest this brighter side, after initially dwelling a bit longer on some of the darker aspects. First, though, I end this chapter's treatment of convergence with a glance at some of the symbolism of the hemisphere's shared tradition of political assassination.

### A Near and an Actual Assassination: The United States in 1933, Mexico in 1994

In February of 1933, just as Michigan became the first state to close its banks (referring to the closure as a "holiday"), Franklin Roosevelt interrupted a cruise on Vincent Astor's yacht *Nourmahal* to spend a bit of time in Miami. There an unemployed bricklayer named Joe (or Giuseppe) Zangara sought to assassinate the president-elect, using a revolver he had recently bought in a local pawnshop. Roosevelt escaped unscathed. Less fortunate was a member of the Roosevelt entourage. Former mayor of Chicago Anton Cermak was mortally wounded by a wild bullet that Zangara fired.

After being taken into custody, Zangara explained he did not hate Roosevelt personally. He simply hated everybody who was rich and powerful[14]—the two odious qualities inseparably intertwined in his view of things.

In a way, Zangara's act symbolized the apparent breakdown of North America's traditional free-enterprise capitalist system. In consequence of that breakdown, Americans by the hundreds of thousands, even by the millions, had ceased to be rich, or even to imagine that they might become rich, and thereby powerful. The tiny minority who remained wealthy and powerful could no longer count on widespread respect. Instead, their wealth and power threatened to jeopardize their moral standing, even to render them hateful, among the swollen ranks of impoverished Americans, only a minuscule handful of whom shared Zangara's anarchist proclivities.

In March of 1944 Luis Donaldo Colosio, the candidate of Mexico's official party for the presidential election due in August and therefore virtually his country's president-elect, was fatally shot in Tijuana. The shots that ended his life were fired not far from a staging area used by indigent compatriots preparing to sneak across the Rio Grande in quest of more secure lives, in quest of—if nothing else—some of the social services once dispensed in their native country but now, like guns, more readily obtainable in El Norte.

With the purchased-in-Los Angeles gun that he used, Colosio's assassin, Mario Aburto Martínez, may simply have served as the triggerman for a plot hatched either by left-wing radicals or by right-wing extremists, depending on one's taste in conspiracy theories. What matters as much as obscure background facts is the readily discernible symbolism of the assassination—a symbolism that implies far more than the fatigue of Mexican voters with rigged elections.

Colosio was killed just in front of a two-story brick meeting house built by Solidaridad, the already-mentioned national antipoverty program that he had headed up at the time President Salinas chose him as his successor.[15] Underfunded and understaffed, Solidaridad whether in Tijuana or elsewhere in Mexico had not managed to roll back the grinding poverty that lapped at its meeting halls and other facilities. Just as the near assassination of Roosevelt symbolized and dramatized the apparent breakdown of U.S. capitalism, so the Colosio assassination symbolized and dramatized the collapse of traditional corporatist-populist social safety nets not only in Mexico but in much of the rest of Latin America as well. On these safety nets both sincere reformers *and* self-seeking caudillos had customarily relied. However, these safety nets could not withstand the stampede toward Yankee-style free-enterprise capitalism, as it actually functions or as it is perceived to function from below the border.

Just as much as during the Great Depression, the hemisphere-wide need somehow to synthesize the New World's conflicting private and corporatist, its self-reliant and its paternalistic traditions, retains its urgency. And therefore FDR retains his timeliness for the Americas. He retains his timeliness both because of the warning that issues from his failures to concoct syncretic reforms and because of the appeal that radiates from his apparent successes—with failures and successes alike lying largely in the eyes of beholders.

# 33. The Enduring Potential of FDR's Gentle Chaos

❖ ❖ ❖ ❖ ❖ ❖ ❖ ❖ ❖ ❖ ❖ ❖ ❖ ❖ ❖ ❖ ❖ ❖ ❖ ❖ ❖ ❖ ❖ ❖ ❖ ❖ ❖ ❖ ❖ ❖ ❖ ❖ ❖ ❖ ❖ ❖

## The Dark Side of Hemispheric Trends toward Century's End

This concluding chapter consists largely of variations on old themes. It begins by re-sounding one of the themes heard in the opening section.

Debussy's haunting, operatic treatment of social malaise that included a scene of starving beggars lurking in the shadows disturbed early-twentieth-century audiences. Sixty years after the Great Depression that kind of scene, in real life, haunts Americans and Latin Americans even more than it did in the 1930s. Sixty years after the Great Depression, Berg's symbolic depiction of the underclass, broken man is more timely than when it first shocked operatic audiences in 1925. Both in the United States and Latin America, Wozzecks slink about in the backwaters of society, reviled and ridiculed by those in the mainstream. Sixty years after the Great Depression, frontier violence of the type depicted in *The Unforgiven* has reached epidemic proportions, both in the United States and in Latin America. More often than not, of course, the contemporary frontier is located in inner cities rather than in such remnants of old-style frontiers as Amazonian jungles and forests—although ample violence occurs there, too. Sixty years after the Depression, there is more need than ever, north and south of the border, for Simon Boccanegras to shame national consciences into the quest for social harmony. Sixty years after the Great Depression, some of the graphics issuing out of the WPA Artists' program provide a more revealing glimpse of inner-city and rural misery, both in the United States and in Latin America, than when originally produced. All of this suggests that hemispheric convergence has indeed taken place, but not the type of convergence hoped for by FDR and the shapers of the Good Neighbor policy.

Throughout the New World, pessimists might well conclude that the Western Hemisphere Idea—positing convergence of the Americas, South and North—has reached fulfillment in an all-pervasive "savage capitalism": a capitalism in which success for members of accommodated society often depends on the same savage traits that enhance survival possibilities for urban-jungle dwellers. South and north of the border, the market mechanisms praised by Adam Smith *have* produced the abundance of goods he had foreseen. It seems, though, that these market mechanisms are not producing the moral refinements that he, like so many of the neo-Calvinists who once helped shape the values of U.S. culture, believed would emerge along with wealth.

Perhaps if FDR were alive today he would address both to his fellow citizens and to Latin Americans a radical message along the lines of his 1944 state of the union address, urging, in effect, the compelling need to curb the practitioners of "savage capitalism." Thereby he could demonstrate anew that while he might like capitalism as a system he cared no more for its practitioners than did Latin American patricians and pensadores of fifty years ago—no more for them than Herbert Hoover did when, after the Depression began, he complained about the greed of businessmen. On the other hand, having had the chance to observe the savagery of bureaucrats and to meditate more profoundly on the fact that New Deal expedients of social intervention had failed to accomplish their anticipated goals, he might have refrained from such a speech. One can hope, though, that a series of setbacks would not necessarily have prevented Roosevelt from urging another go at a worthy cause, at an impossible dream. At the very least, one can hope that FDR might have sought to revise the type of "capitalism" that, throughout the hemisphere, had transformed government entitlement programs into instruments more for the benefit of the privileged than of the needy—thereby rendering capitalism savage as regards the powerless but benign as regards the powerful.

### Corporatism, Capitalism, and Chaos Theory

Already by 1938, as the Depression actually tightened its grip on the country, an increasing number of Americans concluded that corporatist expedients did not work. Since then, for over half a century, Latin Americans, clinging to their traditional corporatism in one guise or another and in the process generally failing dismally to achieve hoped-for progress, tended to confirm the conclusion that Americans had begun to reach before the end of 1938, and to which they accorded virtually unprecedented acceptance in the 1970s and '80s: the conclusion that corporatism, whether inspired by left- or right-wing ideology, does not yield the economic and social payoffs expected of it.

All the while, however, evidence has accumulated that laissez-faire and market economics do not produce the cures for suffering humanity that devotees once promised, whether in good faith or not. Perhaps it all goes to show that no system, after all, really works, except during brief and rare moments in history when fortuitous circumstances operate in a particularly benign manner.

In human affairs, perhaps the wisest policy is to take to heart the FDR example and never to abandon the endeavor to borrow and to fuse together what appear to be the best elements from disparate, opposite systems. The process will never produce comprehensive and permanent solutions, for these seem to lie beyond what the human condition yields. But attempts at fusion and synthesis may soften the periodic crises and render more gentle the moments of creative destruction that the human condition so unfailingly does yield.

Notions of periodic crises and moments of creative destruction suggest in a way the chaos theory that became fashionable in the early 1990s, in some small part at least because it underlay the Michael Crichton book *Jurassic Park,* even if not necessarily the enormously popular Steven Spielberg–directed movie of the same name that derived from the book. A principal character in Crichton's book announces that things will never go as planned, for the world is "inherently unpredictable. We have soothed ourselves into imagining sudden change as something that happens outside the normal order of things. . . . We do not conceive a sudden, radical, irrational change as built into the very fabric of existence."[1] In a way FDR *did* seem to have conceived this. And that is why he sought to include as many elements as possible, however contradictory, in the fabric of existence he sought to fashion for America, for Latin America, indeed for the world. The more elements there were that fused together into a system, the less likely it might be for that system totally to crash. But, as FDR found out, hitting upon just the right mix of elements is tricky business.

### Issues of Convergence: The Brighter Side of the Picture

Statesman-savant George Kennan was quite right when he wrote in 1992 that the United States was becoming, "with every day that passes, less European in the composition of its population and in the relative importance of Europe among its various interests and concerns."[2] Franklin Roosevelt, as already suggested in Chapter 30 and elsewhere in the preceding pages, did not foresee and would not have welcomed this development had he been able to foresee it. Nevertheless, Roosevelt himself helped set in motion the very forces that contributed to the waning significance of Europe in America. He did this by helping to focus the thought of Americans, from all of the Americas, on their mutual importance to each other.

Beyond this, Roosevelt indirectly and unintentionally challenged the very idea of the paramountcy of an Atlantic connection by paying eloquent lip service to the concept of a North–South connection: an American hemisphere connection. He preached a doctrine of hemispheric convergence, one that admittedly was chauvinist because it assumed that they, the Latins, must become like us, the true Americans. To some degree, Latins have fulfilled Roosevelt's expectations. All too often, though, they have emulated some of the worst traits of norteamericanos. But law-of-the-jungle capitalism is not the whole story of hemispheric convergence toward century's end. Convergence has a brighter side as well.

Neither in the United States nor in Latin America does "savage capitalism" proceed uncontested. In both parts of the hemisphere, as the last decade of the twentieth century unfolds, the quest for social palliatives has retained some support. Latin American leaders, for example, often raise the call not just for a market economy but for a "*moral* market economy," or a "*social* market economy." They have begun to urge a swing of the political pendulum back to the center-left. While these developments in themselves may or may not be desirable, depending on one's perspective, they suggest a pattern, a process, that surely has much to commend it. The swing of the pendulum suggests that Latin Americans have settled into not one but two political, social, and economic value systems: the old corporatist system at one end of the pendulum's swing and the new free-market system at the other end.

In the Franklin Roosevelt era, Americans accustomed themselves to pendulum swings of their own. In the nineteenth century, they had tended to form a strong consensus in favor of the essentially individualistic, private market economy. But the social-compact chorus remained audible, even if only barely so. By the time Roosevelt died, it was secure against being drowned out, at least for any long interval. Just as frequently and just as compellingly as the opposite-end-of-the-spectrum chorus, the social-compact voices could demand that the pendulum swing their way.

By the time Roosevelt died, only extremist partisans of either the market economy or the social market economy expected to obliterate the other side. Bigots and ideologues on both sides might hope for total victory; but realists and pragmatists, by and large, understood that the two camps should pursue tactical victories over their antagonists but not the latter's unconditional surrender. And, like Roosevelt himself, realists and pragmatists hoped for, even expected, at least occasional moments when opposites joined.

Latin America followed in reverse order the process that unfolded in the United States. Beginning from ingrained state interventionist proclivities Latin American republics had by some point in the second half of the twentieth century, the precise date of which differed substantially from country to country, added an individualistic, market element as an authentic ingredient of national identity—thereby bringing to fruition tender, vulnerable seeds that had been planted in the nineteenth and even in the eighteenth centuries. Henceforth, each of Latin America's two, equally legitimate, poles of national identity will attract partisans. Henceforth, barring overwhelming crises, there may be grounds for hope that these partisans will engage not only in dialogue-of-the-deaf combat but in genuine discussion about how best to address the basic needs of citizens— at least to the degree necessary to keep those citizens relatively tranquil.

As a sort of sideshow to accompany the main drama of a triumphant U.S. entry into the Old World, FDR had all along hoped, even anticipated, that the Americas, North and South, would coalesce in his "let's-mingle-opposites" style. He might feel vindicated could he view some facets of the hemispheric experience toward century's end. However, the sort of New World convergence that FDR had desired and that half a century after his death had come to pass had nothing to do with the expectations of old-time believers in the Western Hemisphere Idea. They had foreseen a *unique* kind of convergence among Americans. In fact, little if anything was unique about the convergence that Americans, North and South, had actually attained in their similar pendulum swings toward century's end. Throughout vast parts of the world, societies had begun to oscillate between their own, distinctive traditional styles and the style prevailingly recognized as modern and, more often than not, as made in America—the United States of America, that is.

U.S. observers must be on guard lest they mistake signs of a creeping resurgence of traditionalism in Latin America during the coming years for a burgeoning of neofascism or neo-Marxism. However, the dark reality is that an upsurge of genuine neofascism or neo-Marxism is not outside the realm of possibility in Latin America, any more than it is in Europe when exaggerated hopes of capitalist miracles are dashed. On the fringes of Europe, moreover, the dashed hopes on which extremism always feeds nowadays nourish Islamic fundamentalism. And Latin America itself may not yet be entirely out of the woods of religious extremism, as the not-so-long-ago confrontation between liberation theology and Polish-style conservative Catholicism may suggest.

## The Melding of Opposites and the Roosevelt Style

At the conclusion of an admirable book on the Mediterranean world, British journalist Robert Fox makes this observation: "With the movement of peoples from the southern shores into the north, and the need for their work and skills there, the Mediterranean is now becoming an integral part of Europe itself. No longer can it be dismissed as Europe's inconvenient annex. . . . The new Mediterraneans and Mediterranean ways are firmly with us." [3]

A similar process has been at work in the American world. The Latins and their ways have established an unmistakable and ineradicable presence in the United States, just as the United States has established an irreversible presence—cultural and material—in Latin America. And yet the two half-worlds of North and South, both in Europe and America, retain much of the distinguishing features of their old and separate identities. If the North-South synthesis in the Old World and the New is to endure, it will have to be constantly re-created, in new and as yet unforeseeable ways. And this will require leadership of the sort that FDR brought to bear in the American hemisphere.

In personalizing and dramatizing a Good Neighbor policy that certainly he did not conceive or even necessarily believe in very profoundly, FDR simply followed his nature as he strove for the sort of gentle chaos that results from blending opposites. Thereby he hoped to avoid in the hemisphere the sort of cataclysmic implosions and explosions likely to result from steadfast loyalty to just one idea or "timeless" system. This, after all, is the way of the trickster. It is the way also of Isaiah Berlin's celebrated fox, with its many ideas, in contrast to the hedgehog, with its one, fixed idea. Is this not also the way of the United States, at least as revealed in some of the country's better moments and in many of its noblest seers?

And yet, the way of compromise can also lead to calamity, as FDR himself realized when he confronted Hitler, but as he did not at first seem to know when he encountered Stalin. The greatest statesmen are those with an instinct that permits them to understand when, on rare occasions, compromise is utterly unacceptable, however tragic the immediate consequences, and when, as is generally the case, compromise is worth a try.

In domestic and in hemispheric matters, FDR's instincts for compromise more often than not did not fail him. Consistently, he intuited the need and as often as not summoned the skill, as circumstances and political expediency permitted, to curb U.S. capitalism's potential for savagery, both domestically and in its Latin American operations. But he did this without trying to crush the system itself; for he realized that statism could be fully as brutal and bestial, and also more all-encompassing in its evil, than capitalism at its worst. So, I've circled back to the plutocrats-bureaucrats standoff theme sounded first at the beginning, in the preface.

Because he realized how good and how bad both sides were, FDR—perhaps better than any other American president—sought conciliation between capitalism and statism, between dedicated, above-board, hard-working wage earners together with calculating, devious hustlers, on one hand, and duty- and public-service-driven, self-effacing civil servants together with underhanded, on-the-make, power-hungry politicos, on the other hand. His influence penetrated both sides of the dividing line between the United States and Latin America. Therefore, he was able to contribute toward the gentleness of chaos in the New World and to reduce, however unintentionally, the significance of the dividing line.

## The Trickster Departs, Leaving a Grin Behind

For all his accomplishments, FDR will remain a figure of controversy: in the United States, in the American hemisphere, in the world as a whole. The trickster inevitably is a figure of controversy. He, or she, can be seen, from different perspectives, as a "culture-hero" able to confer great boons and as a "chaos-maker" who "sows discord among human beings by wantonly breaking the taboos" that heretofore had helped maintain social cohesion. Tricksters may lack a moral center, but they can also provide images and visions that can inspire among many who experience them "a more tolerant and comprehending psychological world-view"—one that transcends mere rationality. Tricksters respond to the persisting human need "to imagine the socially unimaginable and thus to envisage the possibility of social change." In this function tricksters altogether transcend the identifying gift of the vast majority of political leaders: mere trickiness.

Tricksters, it bears repeating one final time, specialize in reconciling opposites; and under FDR the opposites of the New World's North and South were resolved—in many instances, at least, and for a few moments—as they have seldom if ever been, before or since. Ironically, given what bordered on disdain for the relatively weak republics to the south, FDR—at least during most of the 1930s—performed the trickster role more successfully for the American-hemisphere than for the Atlantic-community audience.

The trickster tales of many societies and many cultures have, it has been observed, one thing in common. They deal with figures who, when they depart or disappear, leave behind their grin, "like the Cheshire Cat."[4] Can anyone who has experienced it, even if only in old photographs, forget the Roosevelt grin?

Thomas McAvoy, *Life* Magazine, © Time Warner, Inc.
*F.D.R. at Jackson Day dinner, January 1939.*

Maybe FDR grinned because he relished the obfuscation he knew he was going to leave behind him as a trickster president who was both a trans-actional *and* a transformational leader.[5] Certainly, the American hemi-sphere that FDR left behind was largely the same as he had found it, and yet it would never be quite the same again. Here was the sort of legacy to set any trickster smiling.

If—unlikely thought—the Roosevelt persona is ever adequately cap-tured and set down on paper or in some new medium, the feat will have to be accomplished by a someone who, among his or her other qualities, is at the same time a novelist and poet of genius: a novelist, say, in the Saul Bellow mold, a poet in the Walt Whitman tradition, and therefore capable of dealing unflappably with diversity of existences within the same in-dividual. Meanwhile, FDR can continue to flash his impish grin, leg-slappingly delighted by the teasing contradictions through which he hid his identity.

Looking back on the Good Neighbor policy, many North Americans—assuming they know anything at all about it—perceive it as a success story, insofar at least as it fostered goodwill below the border. Sometimes Americans of this persuasion attribute perceived success to a president who, in his affable, trickster, Dionysian rather than Apollonian style, was in the stereotyped Latin American mold. That was why the Latins, pre-sumably, understood and warmed to FDR: he was their kind of man. Depending on their own point of view and prejudices, North Americans regard presumed Latin American acceptance of their protean leader as symptomatic either of a plus or a minus in his own character and in the character of his Latin observers.[6]

Just what perceptions of FDR from below the border actually were and are remains largely to be discovered—and taken into account in assessing the Good Neighbor policy. Probably, though, the task of divining Latin perceptions is too complex to yield clear results, in which case FDR will remain, even as among his compatriots, an enigma and a source of contro-versy. Indeed, on both sides of the border the trickster may leave behind, along with his grin, the question as to whether he himself understood or even consistently cared very much about precisely who he was. If, as has been said, the unexamined life is not worth living, it may also be true that, as FDR seemed to believe, the overexamined life adds up to a narcissistic waste of time.

Roosevelt's enigmatic qualities served him well as a hemispheric states-man. All too often in the past Latin Americans had, rightly or wrongly, felt certain that U.S. leaders cared nothing about their neighbors. With FDR, the Latins found it monumentally difficult to be sure.

# Notes

## Preface

1. See, among others, J. Ethan Ellis, *Republican Foreign Policy, 1921–1933* (New Brunswick, N.J.: Rutgers University Press, 1968); William E. Leuchtenburg, *Franklin D. Roosevelt and the New Deal, 1932–1940* (New York: Harper and Row, 1963); Frederick W. Marks III, *Wind over Sand: The Diplomacy of Franklin Roosevelt* (Athens: University of Georgia Press, 1988); and William Appleman Williams, *The Tragedy of American Diplomacy*, 2d ed., rev. and enl. (New York: Dell Publishing, Delta Books, 1972).

2. See Bryce Wood, *The Making of the Good Neighbor Policy* (New York: Columbia University Press, 1961).

3. See Lloyd C. Gardner, *Economic Aspects of New Deal Diplomacy* (Madison: University of Wisconsin Press, 1964); and David Green, *The Containment of Latin America: A History of the Myths and Realities of the Good Neighbor Policy* (Chicago: Quadrangle Books, 1971).

## Chapter 1

1. Blanche Wiesen Cook, "Eleanor—Loves of a First Lady," *Nation*, July 5, 1993, 24.

## Chapter 2

1. Robert Reich quoted by Dennis Farney, "Turning Point: Even U.S. Politics Are Being Reshaped by a Global Economy," *Wall Street Journal*, October 28, 1992.

2. See "The World in Our Image," *Wilson Quarterly,* 16 (Summer 1992): 7, reporting on a 1992 American Enterprise Institute conference on "The New Global Popular Culture."

## Chapter 3

1. Roger Biles, *A New Deal for the American People* (DeKalb: Northern Illinois University Press, 1991), 207. The contrast between the spotty prosperity of the 1920s and the well-nigh universalized Depression of the following decade is skillfully sketched by Michael E. Parrish, *Anxious Decades: America in Prosperity and Depression* (New York: W. W. Norton, 1992).

2. See Pare Lorentz, *FDR's Moviemaker: Memoirs and Scripts* (Reno: University of Nevada Press, 1992), 125, 165, 173, 181, 210.

3. Alan Dawley, *Struggles for Justice: Social Responsibility and the Liberal State* (Cambridge, Mass.: Harvard University Press, 1991), 335, 351.

4. Biles, *A New Deal,* 209.

5. See editorial comments, *FDR's Fireside Chats,* ed. Russell D. Buhite and David W. Levy (Norman: University of Oklahoma Press, 1992), 11.

6. Richard M. Ketchum, *The Borrowed Years, 1938–1941: America on the Way to War* (New York: Random House, 1989), 20, 28, 32, 108; Frederick W. Marks III, *Wind over Sand: The Diplomacy of Franklin Roosevelt* (Athens: University of Georgia Press, 1988), 14.

7. Page Smith, *Redeeming the Time: A People's History of the 1920s and the New Deal* (New York: McGraw-Hill, 1987), 296.

8. Richard Wright quoted by David P. Peeler, *Hope among Us Yet: Social Criticism and Social Solace in Depression America* (Athens: University of Georgia Press, 1987), 170–171.

9. See James Gregory, *American Exodus: The Dust Bowl Migration and Okie Culture in California* (New York: Oxford University Press, 1989), 68, 87.

10. Ibid., 14; Robert Athearn, *The Mythic West in Twentieth Century America* (Lawrence: University Press of Kansas, 1986), 97.

11. Nicholas Natanson, *The Black Image in the New Deal: The Politics of FSA Photography* (Knoxville: University of Tennessee Press, 1992), 203, 3–4; Athearn, *The Mythic West,* 95.

12. Walter Prescott Webb quoted by Athearn, *The Mythic West,* 83.

13. Gregory, *American Exodus,* 105.

14. Smith, *Redeeming the Time,* 293–294.

15. Webb quoted by Gerald D. Nash, *The American West Transformed: The Impact of the Second World War* (Bloomington: Indiana University Press, 1985), 3.

## Chapter 4

1. Page Smith, *Redeeming the Time: A People's History of the 1920s and the New Deal* (New York: McGraw-Hill, 1987), 266–267, 309; Richard M. Ket-

chum, *The Borrowed Years, 1938–1941: America on the Way to War* (New York: Random House, 1989), 22.

2. "Introduction: A Statement of Principles," *I'll Take My Stand: The South and the Agrarian Tradition* (1930; reprint, Baton Rouge: Louisiana State University Press, 1962), xli; Ferdinand Lumberg quoted by T. H. Watkins, *Righteous Pilgrim: The Life and Times of Harold L. Ickes, 1874–1952* (New York: Henry Holt and Company, 1990), 628.

3. Andrew Bergman, *We're in the Money: Depression America and Its Films* (New York: New York University Press, 1971), 15, 23–24, 140–144.

4. The Jim Garland song was published by Stormking Music, Inc., and is included in the Smithsonian Collection of Recordings, *Folk Songs of America: A Twentieth-Century Revival* (Washington, D.C., 1990). The Mellon-Hoover ditty is cited by Charles A. Jellison, *Tomatoes Were Cheaper: Tales from the Thirties* (Syracuse, N.Y.: Syracuse University Press, 1977), 65.

5. Richard N. Sheldon, "The Pujo Committee 1912," in *Congress Investigates: A Documentary History, 1729–1974,* ed. Arthur M. Schlesinger, Jr., and Roger Bruns (1975; reprint, New York: Chelsea House, 1983), 3:303; Donald A. Ritchie, "The Pecora Wall Street Exposé, 1934," *Congress Investigates,* 4:174.

6. Reinhold Niebuhr, *Moral Man and Immoral Society: A Study in Ethics and Politics* (New York: Charles Scribner's Sons, 1932), 144.

7. See Ritchie, "The Pecora Wall Street Exposé, 1934," *Congress Investigates,* 4:173–210; Roger Biles, *A New Deal for the American People* (DeKalb: Northern Illinois University Press, 1991), 31, 34; and broadcast of June 28, 1934, *FDR's Fireside Chats,* ed. Russell D. Buhite and David W. Levy (Norman: University of Oklahoma Press, 1992), 47–48.

8. See Roosevelt statement of May 17, 1942, on the origins of the Good Neighbor policy, in *Franklin D. Roosevelt and Foreign Affairs,* ed. Edgar B. Nixon (Cambridge, Mass.: Harvard University Press, 1969), 1:20.

9. Ketchum, *The Borrowed Years,* 136–137.

10. Walt Whitman, "Democratic Vistas," in *Complete Poetry and Collected Prose* (New York: Library of America, 1982), 950–951.

11. Caffery quoted by Stephen J. Randall, *Colombia and the United States: Hegemony and Interdependence* (Athens: University of Georgia Press, 1992), 135.

12. See *Congress Investigates,* 4:341, referring to the views of New Deal critic John T. Flynn.

13. The John Burke song "I've Got a Pocketful of Dreams" was featured in the 1938 movie *Sing You Sinners.*

14. Bing Crosby recorded the John Burke–Arthur Johnston song "Pennies from Heaven" in 1936. He made the classic recording of the E. Y. Harburg–Jay Gorney song "Brother, Can You Spare a Dime?" in 1932.

15. Frederick W. Marks III, *Wind over Sand: The Diplomacy of Franklin Roosevelt* (Athens: University of Georgia Press, 1988), 38–39.

16. Studs Terkel, *Hard Times: An Oral History of the Great Depression* (New York: Pantheon Books, 1970), 443.

17. See David G. Haglund, *Latin America and the Transformation of U.S. Strategic Thought, 1936–1940* (Albuquerque: University of New Mexico Press, 1984), 86, 119.

## Chapter 5

1. See David M. Wrobel, *The End of American Exceptionalism: Frontier Anxiety from the Old West to the New Deal* (Lawrence: University of Kansas Press, 1993), 57.
2. Ibid., 80.
3. Roosevelt quoted in ibid., 133.
4. See Richard Slotkin's superb book *Gunfighter Nation: The Myth in Twentieth-Century America* (New York: Atheneum, 1992).

## Chapter 6

1. Ray Allen Billington, *The Protestant Crusade, 1800–1860: A Study of the Origins of American Nativism* (New York: Macmillan, 1938), 345, 347.
2. See Forrest G. Wood, *The Arrogance of Faith: Christianity and Race in America from the Colonial Era to the Twentieth Century* (New York: Alfred A. Knopf, 1990), 220, 210–211.
3. Martin E. Marty, *Modern American Religion,* vol. 2, *The Noise of Conflict, 1919–1941* (Chicago: University of Chicago Press, 1991), 313. Marty develops his thesis on the fragmenting of the Protestant synthesis especially in chap. 5, "The Protestant House Divided."
4. Ibid., 213, 253–254.
5. Thomas Stritch, *My Notre Dame: Memories and Reflections of Sixty Years* (Notre Dame, Ind.: University of Notre Dame Press, 1991), 69.
6. Elizabeth Kendall, *The Runaway Bride: Hollywood Romantic Comedy of the 1930s* (New York: Alfred A. Knopf, 1990), 263. See also Clayton R. Koppes and Gregory D. Black, *Hollywood Goes to War: How Politics, Profits, and Propaganda Shaped World War II Movies* (Berkeley: University of California Press, 1990), 14; and Robert Sklar, *Movie-Made America: A Cultural History of American Movies* (New York: Random House, 1975), 174–175.
7. See Page Smith, *Redeeming the Time: A People's History of the 1920s and the New Deal* (New York: McGraw-Hill, 1987), 710, 878.
8. See Nathan Miller, *F.D.R.: An Intimate History* (Lantham, Md.: Madison Books, 1983), 60–61; Patrick J. Maney, *The Roosevelt Presence: A Biography of Franklin Delano Roosevelt* (New York: Twayne Publishers, 1992), esp. pp. 5, 56, 79; broadcasts of September 30, 1934, and April 28, 1935, *FDR's Fireside Chats,* ed. Russell D. Buhite and David W. Levy (Norman: University of Oklahoma Press, 1992), 57, 70.
9. Alan Dawley, *Struggles for Justice: Social Responsibility and the Liberal State* (Cambridge, Mass.: Harvard University Press, 1991), 389; broadcast of June 5, 1944, *FDR's Fireside Chats,* 295, 296.
10. Quoted by Sidney E. Mead, *The Lively Experiment* (New York: Harper and Row, 1976), 160.
11. The Methodist pledge is quoted by Richard Brookhiser, *The Way of the Wasp: How It Made America, and How It Can Save It, So to Speak* (New York: Free Press, 1991), 107. For the Reinhold Niebuhr material, see his *Moral Man*

*and Immoral Society: A Study in Ethics and Politics* (New York: Charles Scribner's Sons, 1932), xxii.

12. See Robert E. Sherwood, *Roosevelt and Hopkins: An Intimate History* (New York: Harper, 1948).

## Chapter 7

1. See Peter J. Kuznick, *Beyond the Laboratory: Scientists as Political Activists in 1930s America* (Chicago: University of Chicago Press, 1987), 110, 210.

2. Ibid., 28–29, 331, 32; George H. Douglas, *Edmund Wilson's America* (Lexington: University of Kentucky Press, 1983), 116.

3. Quoted by David P. Peeler, *Hope among Us Yet: Social Criticism and Social Solace in Depression America* (Athens: University of Georgia Press, 1987), 8. See also Robert S. McElvaine, *The Great Depression: America, 1929–1941* (1983; reprint, New York: Times Books, 1993), 139.

4. See McElvaine, *The Great Depression,* 8, 28, 167; and Linda W. Wagner, *Dos Passos: Artist as American* (Austin: University of Texas Press, 1979), 98, 168.

5. See Fredrick B. Pike, *The United States and Latin America: Myths and Stereotypes of Civilization and Nature* (Austin: University of Texas Press, 1992), 243–248.

6. Steven Fraser, *Labor Will Rule: Sidney Hillman and the Rise of American Labor* (New York: Free Press, 1991), 78, 94.

7. See Michael Ogorzaly, *Waldo Frank: Prophet of Hispanic Regeneration* (Lewisburg, Pa.: Bucknell University Press, 1994).

8. Geoffrey C. Ward, *A First-Class Temperament: The Emergence of Franklin Roosevelt* (New York: Harper and Row, 1989), 254.

9. Ross Gregory, *America 1941: A Nation at the Crossroads* (New York: Free Press, 1989), 154–155; Bruce F. Pauley, *From Prejudice to Persecution: A History of Austrian Anti-Semitism* (Chapel Hill: University of North Carolina Press, 1992), xviii; Istvan Deak, "Strategies of Hell," *New York Review of Books,* October 8, 1992, 8 n.4; Nathan Miller, *F.D.R.: An Intimate History* (Lantham, Md.: Madison Books, 1983), 489.

10. On the tragic saga of the *St. Louis* see Robert M. Levine's splendid study *Tropical Diaspora: The Jewish Experience in Cuba* (Gainesville: University of Florida Press, 1993).

11. Mariana Torgovnick, *Gone Primitive: Savage Intellects, Modern Lives* (Chicago: University of Chicago Press, 1990), 188.

12. Ward, *A First-Class Temperament,* 254, 255 n.8.

## Chapter 8

1. Page Smith, *Redeeming the Time: A People's History of the 1920s and the New Deal* (New York: McGraw-Hill, 1987), 797–798.

2. See Richard M. Ketchum, *The Borrowed Years, 1938–1941: America on the Way to War* (New York: Random House, 1989), 57.

3. Thomas Fleming, "The Past Is What Catches Up with Us," *New York Times*

*Book Review,* January 12, 1992, 12. Fleming's essay is a review of Michael Kammen's important book *Mystic Chords of Memory: The Transformation of American Culture* (New York: Alfred A. Knopf, 1991).

4. Broadcast of September 6, 1936, *FDR's Fireside Chats,* ed. Russell D. Buhite and David W. Levy (Norman: University of Oklahoma Press, 1992), 81; Smith, *Redeeming the Time,* 806.

5. Erika Doss, *Benton, Pollock, and the Politics of Modernism: From Regionalism to Abstract Expressionism* (Chicago: University of Chicago Press, 1991), 135–136.

6. See Vivian Green Fryd, *Art and Empire: The Politics of Ethnicity in the U.S. Capitol, 1815–1861* (New Haven, Conn.: Yale University Press, 1992), passim; Dore Ashton, *The New York School: A Cultural Reckoning* (Berkeley: University of California Press, 1992), 18; and David P. Peeler, *Hope among Us Yet: Social Criticism and Social Solace in Depression America* (Athens: University of Georgia Press, 1987), 206.

7. Ashton, *The New York School,* 41.

8. Robert Hughes, "Art, Morals, and Politics," *New York Review of Books,* April 23, 1992, 22.

9. For a sample of some of the vast literature on these matters see James H. Billington, *Fire in the Minds of Men: Origins of the Revolutionary Faith* (New York: Basic Books, 1980); Donald C. Hodges, *Sandino's Communism: Spiritual Politics for the Twenty-First Century* (Austin: University of Texas Press, 1992); Fredrick B. Pike, *The Politics of the Miraculous in Peru: Haya de la Torre and the Spiritualist Tradition* (Lincoln: University of Nebraska Press, 1986); and James Webb, *The Harmonious Circle: The Lives and Work of G. I. Gurdjieff, P. D. Ouspensky, and Their Followers* (New York: G. P. Putnam's Sons, 1980).

10. Walt Whitman, *Complete Poetry and Collected Prose* (New York: Library of America, 1982), 1147.

## Chapter 9

1. On Krausism and Arielism, see Fredrick B. Pike, *Hispanismo, 1898–1936: Spanish Conservatives and Liberals and Their Relations with Spanish America* (Notre Dame, Ind.: University of Notre Dame Press, 1971), passim; and Pike, *The United States and Latin America: Myths and Stereotypes of Civilization and Nature* (Austin: University of Texas Press, 1992), esp. pp. 193–201.

2. Robert Hughes, "Art, Morals, and Politics," *New York Review of Books,* April 23, 1992, 23.

3. See Paul Avrich, *Sacco and Vanzetti: The Anarchist Background* (Princeton, N.J.: Princeton University Press, 1991), 56.

4. Ibid., 3.

5. Jim Seymour quoted by Louis Joughin and Edmund M. Morgan, *The Legacy of Sacco and Vanzetti* (1948; reprint, Princeton, N.J.: Princeton University Press, 1976), 338.

6. Quoted in ibid., 338.

## Chapter 10

1. Robert Ferguson, *Henry Miller: A Life* (New York: W. W. Norton, 1991), describes Miller's doctrine of spontaneity as "the religion of instinct." It has also been called the "new instinctivism." See Perry Meisel, "A Dirty Young Man and How He Grew," *New York Times Book Review,* June 23, 1991, 1.

2. Page Smith, *Redeeming the Time: A People's History of the 1920s and the New Deal* (New York: McGraw-Hill, 1987), 972.

3. Robert Dallek, *Franklin D. Roosevelt and American Foreign Policy, 1932–1945* (Oxford, England: Oxford University Press, 1979), 329.

4. Smith, *Redeeming the Time,* 515; Waldo Frank, *South American Journey* (New York: Duell, Sloan and Pearce, 1943), 47–57.

5. See Arnold Rampersad, *The Life of Langston Hughes,* vol. I, *1902–1941: I, Too, Sing America* (New York: Oxford University Press, 1986), 47–49.

6. See Fredrick B. Pike, *The United States and Latin America: Myths and Stereotypes of Civilization and Nature* (Austin: University of Texas Press, 1992), 239–240.

7. Helen Delpar, *The Enormous Vogue of Things Mexican: Cultural Relations between the United States and Mexico, 1920–1935* (Tuscaloosa: University of Alabama Press, 1992), 122.

8. George H. Douglas, *Edmund Wilson's America* (Lexington: University of Kentucky Press, 1983), 75.

9. Delpar, *The Enormous Vogue,* 143–146.

10. Ibid., 195.

11. Bertram D. Wolfe, *A Life in Two Centuries: An Autobiography* (New York: Stein and Day, 1981), 291.

12. Nicholas Natanson, *The Black Image in the New Deal: The Politics of FSA Photography* (Knoxville: University of Tennessee Press, 1992), 26, referring to the 1937 book of photographs by Margaret Burke-White with text by Erskine Caldwell, *You Have Seen Their Faces.*

13. Mariana Torgovnick, *Gone Primitive: Savage Intellects, Modern Lives* (Chicago: University of Chicago Press, 1990), 99.

14. Carl N. Degler, *In Search of Human Nature: The Decline and Revival of Darwinism in American Social Thought* (New York: Oxford University Press, 1991), 145; Margaret M. Caffrey, *Ruth Benedict: Stranger in the Land* (Austin: University of Texas Press, 1989), 131–132.

15. See Nancy Leys Stepan, *The Hour of Eugenics: Race, Gender, and Nation in Latin America* (Ithaca, N.Y.: Cornell University Press, 1991), passim.

16. Degler, *In Search of Human Nature,* 131.

17. Elazar Barkan, *The Retreat of Scientific Racism: Changing Concepts of Race in Britain and the United States between the World Wars* (Cambridge, England: Cambridge University Press, 1992), 260.

18. Ibid., 85.

19. Ibid., 266–267.

20. Stepan, *The Hour of Eugenics,* passim.

21. Degler, *In Search of Human Nature,* 80.

22. Regna Darnell, *Edward Sapir: Linguist, Anthropologist, Humanist* (Berkeley: University of California Press, 1990), 233.

23. Ruth Benedict, *Patterns of Culture* (Boston: Houghton Mifflin, 1934), 209.

24. Barkan, *The Retreat of Scientific Racism,* 1.

## Chapter 11

1. Quoted by Patricia Nelson Limerick, *The Legacy of Conquest: The Unbroken Past of the American West* (New York: W. W. Norton, 1987), 247.

2. See Gary R. Mormino and George E. Pozzetta, *The Immigrant World of Ybor City: Italians and Their Latin Neighbors in Tampa, 1885–1985* (Urbana: University of Illinois Press, 1987), chap. 8, passim.

3. Ross Gregory, *America 1941: A Nation at the Crossroads* (New York: Free Press, 1989), 100, 171.

4. Kenneth Roberts quoted by Helen Delpar, *The Enormous Vogue of Things Mexican: Cultural Relations between the United States and Mexico, 1920–1935* (Tuscaloosa: University of Alabama Press, 1992), 17; Studs Terkel, *Hard Times: An Oral History of the Great Depression* (New York: Pantheon Books, 1970), 55.

5. Earl Shorris, *Latinos: A Biography of the People* (New York: W. W. Norton, 1992), 219; Arnoldo D. León, *Ethnicity in the Sunbelt: A History of Mexican Americans in Houston* (Houston: University of Houston Mexican American Studies Program, 1989), 27, 47; Richard A. García, *The Rise of the Mexican American Middle Class: San Antonio, 1929–1941* (College Station: Texas A & M University Press, 1991), 184, 36. For background see Arnoldo De León, *They Called Them Greasers: Anglo Attitudes toward Mexicans in Texas, 1821–1900* (Austin: University of Texas Press, 1983); Thomas E. Sheridan, *Los Tucsonenses: The Mexican Community in Tucson, 1854–1941* (Tucson: University of Arizona Press, 1986); and *Foreigners in Their Native Land: Historical Roots of the Mexican Americans,* ed. David J. Weber (Albuquerque: University of New Mexico Press, 1973).

6. Peter J. Kuznick, *Beyond the Laboratory: Scientists as Political Activists in 1930s America* (Chicago: University of Chicago Press, 1987), 96.

7. Lorena Hickock quoted by Richard Lowitt, *The New Deal and the West* (Bloomington: Indiana University Press, 1984), 17.

8. Bernice Reagon quoted by Martin Gottlieb, "On the White Side of Crossover Dreams," *New York Times,* February 14, 1992.

9. Delpar, *The Enormous Vogue,* 81–82.

10. De León, *Ethnicity in the Sunbelt,* 60.

11. García, *Rise of the Mexican American Middle Class,* 6. See also Benjamin Márquez, *LULAC: The Evolution of a Mexican American Political Organization* (Austin: University of Texas Press, 1983).

12. García, *Rise of the Mexican American Middle Class,* 260.

13. Vekemans develops his thesis in, among other sources, "Economic Development, Social Change, and Cultural Mutation in Latin America," in *Revolution and Reform: New Forces for Change in Latin America,* ed. William V. D'Antonio and Fredrick B. Pike (New York: Praeger, 1964), 129–142.

14. Dana Polan, *Power and Paranoia: History, Narrative, and the American Cinema, 1940–1950* (New York: Columbia University Press, 1986), 123–124.

15. Gerald D. Nash, *The American West Transformed: The Impact of the Second World War* (Bloomington: Indiana University Press, 1985), 110–115; De León, *Ethnicity in the Sunbelt,* 107–108; Shorris, *Latinos,* 97.

16. Shorris, *Latinos,* 97.

17. Roy L. Garis quoted in ibid., 153.

18. Elizabeth Kendall, *The Runaway Bride: Hollywood Romantic Comedy of the 1930s* (New York: Alfred A. Knopf, 1990), 94–95. For general coverage of Hollywood's changing treatment of Latin American themes see Alfred Charles Richard, Jr., *The Hispanic Image on the Silver Screen: An Interpretive Filmography from Silents into Sound* (Westport, Conn.: Greenwood Press, 1992).

19. Robert Wohl, "Republic of the Air," *Wilson Quarterly* 17 (Spring 1993): 115.

20. See William S. Stokes, "Democracy, Freedom, and Reform in Latin America," in *Freedom and Reform in Latin America,* ed. Fredrik B. Pike (Notre Dame, Ind.: University of Notre Dame Press, 1959), 123.

## Chapter 12

1. Juan Montalvo, *Siete tratados* (Besançon, France: Impr. de J. Jacquin, 1882), 2:121–123.

2. Merl E. Reed, *Seedtime for the Modern Civil Rights Movement: The President's Committee on Fair Employment Practice, 1941–1946* (Baton Rouge: Louisiana State University Press, 1991), 15. Quoting Gunnar Myrdal on the issue, Robert S. McElvaine, *The Great Depression: America, 1929–1941* (1983; reprint, New York: Times Books, 1993), 188, argues that the whole configuration of the "Negro problem" changed for the better during the New Deal. If this is true, Roosevelt had little to do, personally, with the change.

3. See Arnold Rampersad, *The Life of Langston Hughes,* vol. I, *1902–1941: I, Too, Sing America* (New York: Oxford University Press, 1986), 276.

4. Interview with Horace Cayton in Studs Terkel, *Hard Times: An Oral History of the Great Depression* (New York: Pantheon Books, 1970), 437.

5. See Joel Williamson, *New People: Miscegenation and Mulattoes in the United States* (New York: New York University Press, 1941), passim.

6. See Rampersad, *I, Too, Sing America,* 132–135, and passim.

## Chapter 13

1. April 22, 1912, letter to his mother, *F.D.R.: His Personal Letters,* ed. Elliott Roosevelt (New York: Duell, Sloan and Pearce, 1947–1950), 2:185, 187, 189.

2. August 24 and 25, 1915, letters to his wife and mother, respectively, ibid., 2:285, 287.

3. Geoffrey C. Ward, *A First-Class Temperament: The Emergence of Franklin Roosevelt* (New York: Harper and Row, 1989), 206, 222, 240–242. Ward's account is critical, objective, and massively researched. For a friendly, impressively

researched single-volume biography of Roosevelt see Frank Friedel, *Franklin D. Roosevelt: A Rendezvous with Destiny* (Boston: Little, Brown, 1990). Friedel has also written a widely acclaimed four-volume study of the young Roosevelt. Arthur M. Schlesinger, Jr., inclines occasionally toward hero worship in his beautifully written and carefully documented three-volume study *The Age of Roosevelt* (Boston: Houghton Mifflin Company, 1957–1960). Kenneth S. Davis is more critical, but never uncharitable, in his splendid, ongoing biography of Roosevelt, now up to its fourth volume: *FDR: Into the Storm 1937–1940. A History* (New York: Random House, 1993).

4. Michael L. Conniff, *Panama and the United States: The Forced Alliance* (Athens: University of Georgia Press, 1992), 76–77.

5. Patrick J. Maney, *The Roosevelt Presence: A Biography of Franklin Delano Roosevelt* (New York: Twayne Publishers, 1992), 18; Warren F. Kimball, " 'The Juggler': Franklin D. Roosevelt and Anglo-American Competition in Latin America," in *Argentina between the Great Powers, 1939–1946,* ed. Guido di Tella and D. Cameron Watt (Pittsburgh: University of Pittsburgh Press, 1990), 21.

6. Ward, *A First-Class Temperament,* 329–333.

7. Ibid., 334.

8. Ibid., 328.

9. Nathan Miller, *F.D.R.: An Intimate History* (Lantham, Md.: Madison Books, 1983), 176; James MacGregor Burns, *Roosevelt: The Lion and the Fox* (New York: Harcourt, Brace, Jovanovich, 1956), 75–76.

10. The quoted section from Roosevelt's aborted history comes from *F.D.R.: His Personal Letters,* 2:550.

11. Quoted by Frederick W. Marks III, *Wind over Sand: The Diplomacy of Franklin Roosevelt* (Athens: University of Georgia Press, 1988), 8.

12. Quoted by Ward, *A First-Class Temperament,* 333.

13. See Fredrick B. Pike, *The United States and Latin America: Myths and Stereotypes of Civilization and Nature* (Austin: University of Texas Press, 1992), 266.

14. Godfrey Hodgson, *The Colonel: The Life and Wars of Henry Stimson, 1867–1950* (New York: Alfred A. Knopf, 1991), 172; Brenda Gayle Plummer, *Haiti and the United States: The Psychological Moment* (Athens: University of Georgia Press, 1992), 211.

15. Quoted by Lester D. Langley, *The Banana Wars: An Inner History of American Empire, 1900–1934* (Lexington: University of Kentucky Press, 1983), 216.

16. Irwin F. Gellman, *Good Neighbor Diplomacy: United States Policies in Latin America, 1933–1945* (Baltimore: Johns Hopkins University Press, 1979), 119.

17. Quoted by Miller, *F.D.R.,* 333.

18. Burns, *Roosevelt,* 164; Marks, *Wind over Sand,* 245; Gellman, *Good Neighbor Diplomacy,* 227.

19. See David G. Haglund, *Latin America and the Transformation of U.S. Strategic Thought, 1936–1940* (Albuquerque: University of New Mexico Press, 1984), esp. chap. 1; and Gellman, *Good Neighbor Diplomacy,* 17.

20. D. Cameron Watt, "All-American," *Times Literary Supplement,* July 3, 1992, 31; Bullitt quoted by Marks, *Wind over Sand,* 256.

## Chapter 14

1. Patrick J. Maney, *The Roosevelt Presence: A Biography of Franklin Delano Roosevelt* (New York: Twayne Publishers, 1992), 4; Geoffrey C. Ward, *A First-Class Temperament: The Emergence of Franklin Roosevelt* (New York: Harper and Row, 1989), 76.

2. Quoted by James MacGregor Burns, *Roosevelt: The Lion and the Fox* (New York: Harcourt, Brace, Jovanovich, 1956), frontispiece.

3. Helmut Sonnenfeldt, writing in *Economist*, October 3, 1992, 97.

4. See Robert S. McElvaine, *The Great Depression: America, 1929–1941* (1983; reprint, New York: Times Books, 1993), 119.

5. Page Smith, *Redeeming the Time: A People's History of the 1920s and the New Deal* (New York: McGraw-Hill, 1987), 816.

6. Godfrey Hodgson, *The Colonel: The Life and Wars of Henry Stimson, 1867–1950* (New York: Alfred A. Knopf, 1991), 372.

7. Robert Dallek, *Franklin D. Roosevelt and American Foreign Policy, 1932–1945* (Oxford, England: Oxford University Press, 1979), 88.

8. July 5, 1934, letter to Eleanor Roosevelt, *F.D.R.: His Personal Letters*, ed. Elliott Roosevelt (New York: Duell, Sloan and Pearce, 1947–1950), 3:305. Emphasis is in the original.

9. Burns, *Roosevelt*, 228–229.

10. See William Ivy Hair, *The Kingfish and His Realm: The Life and Times of Huey P. Long* (Baton Rouge: Louisiana State University Press, 1991), 270–271.

11. Lyrics for "How About You?" are by Ralph Freed, the melody by Burton Lane. Copyright 1941, renewed in 1969 by Lee Feist, Inc.

12. See Dana Polan, *Power and Paranoia: History, Narrative, and the American Cinema, 1940–1950* (New York: Columbia University Press, 1986), 66–67.

13. July 10, 1934, letter to Eleanor Roosevelt, in *F.D.R.: His Personal Letters*, 3:406. Emphasis is in the original.

14. Quoted by Frank Friedel, *Franklin D. Roosevelt: A Rendezvous with Destiny* (Boston: Little, Brown, 1990), 217.

15. On FDR's reception in Rio, Buenos Aires, and Montevideo, see: David G. Haglund, *Latin America and the Transformation of U.S. Strategic Thought, 1936–1940* (Albuquerque: University of New Mexico Press, 1984), 43, 48; and Frederick W. Marks III, *Wind over Sand: The Diplomacy of Franklin Roosevelt* (Athens: University of Georgia Press, 1988), 218.

16. Friedel, *Franklin D. Roosevelt*, 217.

17. Roosevelt's loss of touch with reality, initially resulting far more from his landslide 1936 reelection than his triumphant Latin American visit, receives masterful treatment from Kenneth S. Davis, *FDR: Into the Storm 1937–1940. A History* (New York: Random House, 1993), esp. chap. 2.

## Chapter 15

1. On corporatism, in theory and in practice, see *The New Corporatism: Social-Political Structures in the Iberian World*, ed. Fredrick B. Pike and Thomas Stritch (Notre Dame, Ind.: University of Notre Dame Press, 1974).

2. This was the appraisal of *Fortune* magazine in a 1934 edition devoted to analysis of the Italian system; it is quoted by John A. Garraty, "The New Deal, National Socialism, and the Great Depression," *American Historical Review* 74 (1973): 914.

3. Steven Fraser, *Labor Will Rule: Sidney Hillman and the Rise of American Labor* (New York: Free Press, 1991), 293.

4. Geoffrey C. Ward, *A First-Class Temperament: The Emergence of Franklin Roosevelt* (New York: Harper and Row, 1989), xvi.

5. James MacGregor Burns, *Roosevelt: The Lion and the Fox* (New York: Harcourt, Brace, Jovanovich, 1956); William Phillips quoted by Patrick J. Maney, *The Roosevelt Presence: A Biography of Franklin Delano Roosevelt* (New York: Twayne Publishers, 1992), 81; FDR quoted by Warren F. Kimball, *The Juggler: Franklin Roosevelt as Wartime Statesman* (Princeton, N.J.: Princeton University Press, 1991), 7.

6. See Whitman's observations on visiting the grave of Emerson, included in *Emerson in His Journals,* selected and edited by Joel Porge (Cambridge, Mass.: Harvard University Press, 1982), xvii.

7. Tugwell quoted by Page Smith, *Redeeming the Time: A People's History of the 1920s and the New Deal* (New York: McGraw-Hill, 1987), 389, 370–371; Frederick W. Marks III, *Wind over Sand: The Diplomacy of Franklin Roosevelt* (Athens: University of Georgia Press, 1988), 204. Due to Marks's confusing (to me) endnote, I am unable to identify the source he credits on Roosevelt's "almost feminine intuition."

8. This is the description of Max Weber's concept of charisma as described by Talcott Parsons, *The Structure of Social Action* (1949; reprint, New York: Free Press, 1968), 2:669.

9. See Fredrick B. Pike, *The Politics of the Miraculous in Peru: Haya de la Torre and the Spiritualist Tradition* (Lincoln: University of Nebraska Press, 1986), 201.

*Chapter 16*

1. Anderson quoted by Benjamin T. Harrison, *Dollar Diplomat: Chandler Anderson and American Diplomacy in Mexico and Nicaragua, 1913–1928* (Pullman: Washington State University Press, 1988), 120.

2. See Page Smith, *Redeeming the Time: A People's History of the 1920s and the New Deal* (New York: McGraw-Hill, 1987), 169–170.

3. Ibid., 102.

4. See Godfrey Hodgson, *The Colonel: The Life and Wars of Henry Stimson, 1867–1950* (New York: Alfred A. Knopf, 1991), 5, 99. For an outstanding essay reviewing the most important literature on and by Stimson, see Alan Brinkley, "The Good Old Days," *New York Review of Books,* January 17, 1991, 24–30.

5. Hodgson, *The Colonel,* 120; Brenda Gayle Plummer, *Haiti and the United States: The Psychological Moment* (Athens: University of Georgia Press, 1992), 120; Alan Dawley, *Struggles for Justice: Social Responsibility and the Liberal State* (Cambridge, Mass.: Harvard University Press, 1991), 359; Irwin F. Gellman,

*Good Neighbor Diplomacy: United States Policies in Latin America, 1933–1945* (Baltimore: Johns Hopkins University Press, 1979), 10–11, 34.

6. The negative aspects of my appraisal of Sandino issue in part from Donald C. Hodges, *Sandino's Communism: Spiritual Politics for the Twenty-First Century* (Austin: University of Texas Press, 1992). Professor Hodges, however, arrives at a final assessment of Sandino that is vastly more positive than mine.

7. See Fredrick B. Pike, *The Politics of the Miraculous in Peru: Haya de la Torre and the Spiritualist Tradition* (Lincoln: University of Nebraska Press, 1986), 179–182; and Cole Blasier, *The Hovering Giant: U.S. Responses to Revolutionary Change in Latin America* (Pittsburgh: University of Pittsburgh Press, 1976), 127.

8. See Frederick W. Marks III, *Wind over Sand: The Diplomacy of Franklin Roosevelt* (Athens: University of Georgia Press, 1988), 33; Gellman, *Good Neighbor Diplomacy,* 18–22; Robert Dallek, *Franklin D. Roosevelt and American Foreign Policy, 1932–1945* (Oxford, England: Oxford University Press, 1979), 86–87; Louis A. Pérez, Jr., *Cuba and the United States: Ties of Singular Intimacy* (Athens: University of Georgia Press, 1990), 191–196.

9. Gore Vidal, "The Essential Mencken," *Nation,* August 26–September 2, 1991, 233.

10. Pérez, *Cuba and the United States,* 201.

11. Gellman, *Good Neighbor Diplomacy,* 39.

12. James Tanner, "Change of Heart: Venezuela Now Woos Oil Firms," *Wall Street Journal,* October 2, 1991. The president quoted in the text is Carlos Andrés Pérez, serving a second term shortly to be aborted by his removal from office on charges of malfeasance.

## *Chapter 17*

1. Walter L. Creese, *TVA's Public Planning: The Vision, the Reality* (Knoxville: University of Tennessee Press, 1990), 52.

2. Timothy Egan, "The Things That Get Left Out in the Fight for the Wild Northwest," *New York Times,* May 30, 1993.

3. Stephen Fox, *The American Conservation Movement: John Muir and His Legacy* (Madison: University of Wisconsin Press, 1985), 199.

4. Roger Biles, *A New Deal for the American People* (DeKalb: Northern Illinois University Press, 1991), 211.

5. T. H. Watkins, *Righteous Pilgrim: The Life and Times of Harold L. Ickes, 1874–1952* (New York: Henry Holt and Company, 1990), 580, 202, 331.

6. See Richard Lowitt, *The New Deal and the West* (Bloomington: Indiana University Press, 1984), 205; Creese, *TVA's Public Planning,* 16, 65; Studs Terkel, *Hard Times: An Oral History of the Great Depression* (New York: Pantheon Books, 1970), 25; October 12, 1937, broadcast, *FDR's Fireside Chats,* ed. Russell D. Buhite and David W. Levy (Norman: University of Oklahoma Press, 1992), 102.

7. See David P. Peeler, *Hope among Us Yet: Social Criticism and Social Solace in Depression America* (Athens: University of Georgia Press, 1987), 99; Linda W.

Wagner, *Dos Passos: Artist as American* (Austin: University of Texas Press, 1979), 115; Meryle Secrest, *Frank Lloyd Wright* (New York: Alfred A. Knopf, 1992), 385; and Arthur M. Schlesinger, Jr., "Aggressive Progressive," *New York Review of Books,* April 25, 1991, 51.

8. See Jim Bob Tinsley, *For a Cowboy Has to Sing* (Orlando: University of Central Florida Press, 1991), 94, 140–141. As for the song "Don't Fence Me In," Cole Porter bought it in 1944 from Bob Fletcher for $25. Fletcher wrote the song in 1935 for a proposed film (*Adios Argentina*) that was never produced.

9. See Thomas Stritch, *My Notre Dame, Memories and Reflections of Sixty Years* (Notre Dame, Ind.: University of Notre Dame Press, 1991), 40; William C. Havard and Walter Sullivan, "Introduction," *A Band of Prophets: The Vanderbilt Agrarians after Fifty Years,* ed. Havard and Sullivan (Baton Rouge: Louisiana State University Press, 1982), 5; and John Crowe Ransom, "Reconstructed but Unregenerate," the lead essay in *I'll Take My Stand: The South and the Agrarian Tradition* (1930; reprint, Baton Rouge: Louisiana State University Press, 1962), 14.

10. William Faulkner, *Absalom, Absalom!* (1936; reprint, New York: Viking Books, 1967), 14, 15.

11. See Nicholas Lemann, *The Promised Land: The Great Black Migration and How It Changed America* (New York: Alfred A. Knopf, 1991).

## Chapter 18

1. "South of the Border" (1939) is by Jimmy Kennedy and Michael Carr. Copyright is held by Peter Maurice Music Co., Ltd., London.

2. See Geoffrey C. Ward, *A First-Class Temperament: The Emergence of Franklin Roosevelt* (New York: Harper and Row, 1989), 303, 338–340, 355–357; and Irwin F. Gellman, *Good Neighbor Diplomacy: United States Policies in Latin America, 1933–1945* (Baltimore: Johns Hopkins University Press, 1979), 10.

3. August 6, 1920, letter to Daniels, *F.D.R.: His Personal Letters,* ed. Elliott Roosevelt (New York: Duell, Sloan and Pearce, 1947–1950), 2:489. For valuable background, see *Roosevelt and Daniels: A Friendship in Politics,* ed. Carroll Kilpatrick (Chapel Hill: University of North Carolina Press, 1952).

4. See Joseph P. Lash, *Eleanor and Franklin* (New York: New American Library, 1971), 408, 522–524, 544–545, 549; and Walter L. Creese, *TVA's Public Planning: The Vision, the Reality* (Knoxville: University of Tennessee Press, 1990), 29, 51, 247, 250, 526–527.

5. Stuart Chase, *Mexico: A Study of Two Americas,* written in collaboration with Marian Tyler (New York: Macmillan, 1931), 327, 199, 16, 9.

6. Ibid., 314–315.

7. Ibid., 311, 323, 327.

8. Carleton Beals, *Mexican Maize* (N.p.: Book League of America, 1931), 117, 158.

9. Frank Tannenbaum, *Peace by Revolution: An Interpretation of Mexico* (New York: Columbia University Press, 1933), 6.

10. Quoted by Helen Delpar, *The Enormous Vogue of Things Mexican: Cultural Relations between the United States and Mexico, 1920–1935* (Tuscaloosa: University of Alabama Press, 1992), 122.

11. Warren F. Kimball, *The Juggler: Franklin Roosevelt as Wartime Statesman* (Princeton, N.J.: Princeton University Press, 1991), 76.

12. See Frederick W. Marks III, *Wind over Sand: The Diplomacy of Franklin Roosevelt* (Athens: University of Georgia Press, 1988), 30.

13. See David G. Haglund, *Latin America and the Transformation of U.S. Strategic Thought, 1936–1940* (Albuquerque: University of New Mexico Press, 1984), 74.

14. Robert Dallek, *Franklin D. Roosevelt and American Foreign Policy, 1932–1945* (Oxford, England: Oxford University Press, 1979), 176.

15. Jesse H. Stiller, *George S. Messersmith: Diplomat of Democracy* (Chapel Hill: University of North Carolina Press, 1987), 171; and Gellman, *Good Neighbor Diplomacy*, 53.

16. See Josephus Daniels, *Shirt-Sleeve Diplomat* (Chapel Hill: University of North Carolina Press, 1947), 258.

17. Adolf A. Berle, Jr., *Navigating the Rapids, 1918–1971: From the Papers of Adolf A. Berle, Jr.*, ed. Beatrice Bishop Berle and Travis Beal Jacobs (New York: Harcourt, Brace, Jovanovich, 1973), 212, 561.

18. Daniels quoted by Kenneth S. Davis, *FDR: Into the Storm 1937–1940. A History* (New York: Random House, 1993), 273.

19. See ibid., 405–407.

20. Gellman, *Good Neighbor Diplomacy*, 54.

21. Stiller, *George Messersmith*, 172.

22. See Bryce Wood, *The Making of the Good Neighbor Policy* (New York: Columbia University Press, 1961), passim.

23. Malcolm Richardson, "Review: 'The Buried Mirror,'" *American Historical Association Newsletter* 30 (October 1992): 9–10.

24. Stiller, *George Messersmith*, 188–189.

25. Ibid., 195–196.

26. Ibid., 175.

27. "Frenesi," with Spanish words and lyrics by Alberto Domínguez, bears a 1939 copyright. English-language lyrics by Ray Charles and S. K. Russell hold a 1941 Peer International Corporation copyright. The words "bungalow in Mexico" do not appear in the Charles-Russell translation, but I remember them well from a contemporary recording I cannot now track down.

## Chapter 19

1. See Fredrick B. Pike, *The United States and Latin America: Myths and Stereotypes of Civilization and Nature* (Austin: University of Texas Press, 1992), 273–274.

2. Curt Gentry, *J. Edgar Hoover: The Man and the Secrets* (New York: W. W. Norton, 1991), 307.

3. Ibid., 307–310; Loch K. Johnson, "Spies in Pinstripes," *New York Times Book Review*, June 14, 1992, 25.

4. Perón letter of 1952 to President Carlos Ibáñez of Chile, cited in Fredrick B. Pike, *Spanish America, 1900–1970: Tradition and Social Innovation* (New York: W. W. Norton, 1973), 125.

5. Sumner Welles, *Where Are We Heading?* (New York: Harper and Brothers, 1946), 236–237.

6. Geoffrey C. Ward, *A First-Class Temperament: The Emergence of Franklin Roosevelt* (New York: Harper and Row, 1989), 473 n.25.

7. Warren F. Kimball, *The Juggler: Franklin Roosevelt as Wartime Statesman* (Princeton, N.J.: Princeton University Press, 1991), 119–120.

8. See David G. Haglund, *Latin America and the Transformation of U.S. Strategic Thought, 1936–1940* (Albuquerque: University of New Mexico Press, 1984), 86, 94, 119.

9. See Godfrey Hodgson, *The Colonel: The Life and Wars of Henry Stimson, 1867–1950* (New York: Alfred A. Knopf, 1991), 49, 56–57.

10. See, for example, Richard M. Ketchum, *The Borrowed Years, 1938–1941: America on the Way to War* (New York: Random House, 1989), 221, 224, 664; and Kimball, *The Juggler,* 44–45, 118–119, 120, 188. For valuable background see Cordell Hull, *The Memoirs of Cordell Hull,* 2 vols. (New York: Macmillan, 1948); and the classic account by Julius W. Pratt, *Cordell Hull, 1933–1944,* 2 vols. (New York: Cooper Square Publishers, 1964).

11. Paul Gigot, "Potomac Watch," *Wall Street Journal,* March 19, 1993.

12. Quoted by Benjamin T. Harrison, *Dollar Diplomat: Chandler Anderson and American Diplomacy in Mexico and Nicaragua, 1913–1928* (Pullman: Washington State University Press, 1988), 120.

*Chapter 20*

1. See Arthur P. Whitaker, *The Western Hemisphere Idea: Its Rise and Decline* (Ithaca, N.Y.: Cornell University Press, 1954).

2. See *Do the Americas Have a Common History? A Critique of the Bolton Theory,* ed. Lewis Hanke (New York: Alfred A. Knopf, 1964).

3. Warren F. Kimball, *The Juggler: Franklin Roosevelt as Wartime Statesman* (Princeton, N.J.: Princeton University Press, 1991), 10.

4. See Richard A. Reiman, *The New Deal and American Youth: Ideas and Ideals in a Depression Decade* (Athens: University of Georgia Press, 1992), 137.

5. On the inter-American cartel idea see William L. Langer and S. Everett Gleason, *The Challenge to Isolation: The World Crisis of 1937–1940 and American Foreign Policy* (1952; Gloucester, Mass.: Peter Smith reprint ed., 1970), 2: 630–635.

*Chapter 21*

1. See Alec Campbell, "Anglo-American Relations, 1939–1946: A British View," in *Argentina between the Great Powers, 1939–1946,* ed. Guido di Tella and D. Cameron Watt (Pittsburgh: University of Pittsburgh Press, 1990), 6.

2. Irwin F. Gellman, *Good Neighbor Diplomacy: United States Policies in Latin America, 1933–1945* (Baltimore: Johns Hopkins University Press, 1979), 73. See also David G. Haglund, *Latin America and the Transformation of U.S. Strategic Thought, 1936–1940* (Albuquerque: University of New Mexico Press, 1984), esp. chap. 2. On Roosevelt's struggle to swing the country away from iso-

lationism and toward internationalism see two classic accounts by Robert A. Divine: *The Illusion of Neutrality* (Chicago: University of Chicago Press, 1962), and *Second Chance: The Triumph of Internationalism in America during World War II* (New York: Atheneum, 1971).

3. See Samuel Flagg Bemis, *The Latin American Policy of the United States: An Historical Interpretation* (New York: Harcourt, Brace and Company, 1943), 68.

4. See Robert Dallek, *Franklin D. Roosevelt and American Foreign Policy, 1932–1945* (Oxford, England: Oxford University Press, 1979), 326; James Rhodes, "Chipping at the Churchill Memorial," *Times Literary Supplement,* January 8, 1993, 7; and Frederick W. Marks III, *Wind over Sand: The Diplomacy of Franklin Roosevelt* (Athens: University of Georgia Press, 1988), 214–215, and passim. While I tend to be put off by what strikes me as his tiresome anti-Roosevelt bias, I nevertheless think Marks provides one of the best published accounts of Roosevelt's ill-starred attempts to save the Old World through expedients he thought he had perfected in America.

5. One of the many sources that quotes Churchill's magnificent speech inspired by the Dunkirk catastrophe is Richard M. Ketchum, *The Borrowed Years, 1938–1941: America on the Way to War* (New York: Random House, 1989), 351–353.

6. Roosevelt quoted by William L. Langer and S. Everett Gleason, *The Challenge to Isolation: The World Crisis of 1937–1940 and American Foreign Policy* (1952; Gloucester, Mass.: Peter Smith reprint ed., 1970), 2:83.

7. Warren F. Kimball, *The Juggler: Franklin Roosevelt as Wartime Statesman* (Princeton, N.J.: Princeton University Press, 1991), 110.

8. Ibid., 182.

9. September 21, 1943, letter to George W. Norris, in *F.D.R.: His Personal Letters,* ed. Elliott Roosevelt (New York: Duell, Sloan and Pearce, 1947–1950), 4:1446–1447.

10. On this see the concluding sections of the classic study by J. Lloyd Mecham, *A Survey of United States–Latin American Relations* (Boston: Houghton Mifflin Company, 1965).

*Chapter 22*

1. Frances Perkins quoted by Edward M. Bennett, *Franklin Roosevelt and the Search for Security: American-Soviet Relations, 1933–1939* (Wilmington, Del.: Scholarly Resources, Inc., 1985), 95; Robert Dallek, *Franklin D. Roosevelt and American Foreign Policy, 1932–1945* (Oxford, England: Oxford University Press, 1979), 112.

2. "Quarantine speech," quoted by Bennett, *Franklin Roosevelt and the Search for Security,* 98. For a reliable general account of FDR's security concerns triggered by Germany, see Robert E. Herzstein, *Roosevelt and Hitler: Prelude to War* (New York: Paragon House, 1989).

3. William L. Langer and S. Everett Gleason, *The Challenge to Isolation: The World Crisis of 1937–1940 and American Foreign Policy* (1952; Gloucester, Mass.: Peter Smith reprint ed., 1970), 2:623.

4. Forrest G. Wood, *The Arrogance of Faith: Christianity and Race in America*

*from the Colonial Era to the Twentieth Century* (New York: Alfred A. Knopf, 1990), 215.

5. David G. Haglund, *Latin America and the Transformation of U.S. Strategic Thought, 1936–1940* (Albuquerque: University of New Mexico Press, 1984), 184, 196.

6. Broadcasts of December 29, 1940, and May 27, 1941, *FDR's Fireside Chats,* ed. Russell D. Buhite and David W. Levy (Norman: University of Oklahoma Press, 1992), 167–168, 175. For a study of the Nazi threat to Latin America (real and imagined) that has retained its value through the years, see Alton Frye, *Nazi Germany and the American Hemisphere* (New Haven, Conn.: Yale University Press, 1967).

7. Broadcast of September 11, 1941, *FDR's Fireside Chats,* 192–193; Irwin F. Gellman, *Good Neighbor Diplomacy: United States Policies in Latin America, 1933–1945* (Baltimore: Johns Hopkins University Press, 1979), 114; Warren F. Kimball, *The Juggler: Franklin Roosevelt as Wartime Statesman* (Princeton, N.J.: Princeton University Press, 1991), 118; Patrick J. Maney, *The Roosevelt Presence: A Biography of Franklin Delano Roosevelt* (New York: Twayne Publishers, 1992), 132.

8. See Ronald C. Newton, *The "Nazi Menace" in Argentina, 1931–1947* (Stanford, Calif.: Stanford University Press, 1992), 167, and passim; Dallek, *Franklin Roosevelt and American Foreign Policy,* 235–236; and Gellman, *Good Neighbor Diplomacy,* 113.

9. See Haglund, *Latin America,* esp. pp. 15, 55, 79, 132–134.

10. Frederick W. Marks III, *Wind over Sand: The Diplomacy of Franklin Roosevelt* (Athens: University of Georgia Press, 1988), 223; Carlos Baker, *Ernest Hemingway: A Life Story* (New York: Macmillan, 1969), 372; Stephen J. Randall, *Colombia and the United States: Hegemony and Interdependence* (Athens: University of Georgia Press, 1992), 162; Langer and Gleason, *Challenge to Isolationism,* 1:41, 273–274.

11. See Curt Gentry, *J. Edgar Hoover: The Man and the Secrets* (New York: W. W. Norton, 1991), 264–268, 295–296, 415, 664.

12. Richard M. Ketchum, *The Borrowed Years, 1938–1941: America on the Way to War* (New York: Random House, 1989), 484.

*Chapter 23*

1. Robert Dallek, *Franklin D. Roosevelt and American Foreign Policy, 1932–1945* (Oxford, England: Oxford University Press, 1979), 176–177; David G. Haglund, *Latin America and the Transformation of U.S. Strategic Thought, 1936–1940* (Albuquerque: University of New Mexico Press, 1984), 108–109.

2. Haglund, *Latin America,* 109; Dallek, *Roosevelt,* 177.

3. William L. Langer and S. Everett Gleason, *The Challenge to Isolation: The World Crisis of 1937–1940 and American Foreign Policy* (1952; Gloucester, Mass.: Peter Smith reprint ed., 1970), 1:83.

4. On the complex issues of U.S. relations with Brazil during the World War II era (and in some instances before and beyond), see John W. F. Dulles, *Vargas of Brazil: A Political Biography* (Austin: University of Texas Press, 1967); Stanley E.

Hilton, *Brazil and the Great Powers, 1930–1939: The Politics of Trade Rivalry* (Austin: University of Texas Press, 1975); Frank D. McGann, Jr., *The Brazilian-American Alliance, 1937–1964* (New York: Oxford University Press, 1973).

5. For a superb treatment of some of the origins and early development of inter–Latin American rivalry and checkerboard diplomacy, see Robert N. Burr, *By Reason or Force: Chile and the Balancing of Power in South America, 1830–1905* (Berkeley: University of California Press, 1965). See also Bryce Wood, *The United States and Latin American Wars* (New York: Columbia University Press, 1966); and David H. Zook, Jr., *The Conduct of the Chaco War* (New Haven, Conn.: Yale University Press, 1961).

6. See Frederick C. Adams, *Economic Diplomacy: The Export-Import Bank and American Foreign Policy, 1934–1939* (Columbia: University of Missouri Press, 1976).

7. Irwin F. Gellman, *Good Neighbor Diplomacy: United States Policies in Latin America, 1933–1945* (Baltimore: Johns Hopkins University Press, 1979), 169.

8. See Jesse H. Stiller, *George S. Messersmith: Diplomat of Democracy* (Chapel Hill: University of North Carolina Press, 1987), chap. 3.

## Chapter 24

1. See Mark Falcoff, "Argentina," in *The Spanish Civil War, 1936–1939: American Hemispheric Perspectives,* ed. Falcoff and Fredrick B. Pike (Lincoln: University of Nebraska Press, 1982), 291–348; and Raanan Rein, *The Franco-Perón Alliance,* trans. Martha Grenzeback (Pittsburgh: University of Pittsburgh Press, 1993), passim.

2. William L. Langer and S. Everett Gleason, *The Challenge to Isolation: The World Crisis of 1937–1940 and American Foreign Policy* (1952; Gloucester, Mass.: Peter Smith reprint ed., 1970), 2:695.

3. David G. Haglund, *Latin America and the Transformation of U.S. Strategic Thought, 1936–1940* (Albuquerque: University of New Mexico Press, 1984), 219.

4. See Samuel Flagg Bemis, *The Latin American Policy of the United States: An Historical Interpretation* (New York: Harcourt, Brace and Company, 1943), 369–370.

5. Robert Dallek, *Franklin D. Roosevelt and American Foreign Policy, 1932–1945* (Oxford, England: Oxford University Press, 1979), 235.

6. Langer and Gleason, *The Challenge to Isolation,* 2:724.

7. See Frank A. Ninkovich, *The Diplomacy of Ideas: U.S. Foreign Policy and Cultural Relations, 1938–1950* (Cambridge, England: Cambridge University Press, 1981), 35–49.

8. See Paul H. Nitze, *Tension between Opposites: Reflections on the Practice and Theory of Politics* (New York: Charles Scribner's Sons, 1993), 93–94, 110–111.

9. Irwin F. Gellman is especially astute in dealing with Rockefeller and his Latin American program. See his *Good Neighbor Diplomacy: United States Policies in Latin America, 1933–1945* (Baltimore: Johns Hopkins University Press,

1979), 143–154. See also Joe Alex Morris, *Nelson Rockefeller* (New York: Harper, 1960).

10. Nicolas Shumway, *The Invention of Argentina* (Berkeley: University of California Press, 1991), passim.

11. See Thomas F. O'Brien, "AHR Forum: The Revolutionary Mission: American Enterprise in Cuba," *American Historical Review* 98 (1993): 785.

## Chapter 25

1. Berle is quoted by Irwin F. Gellman, *Good Neighbor Diplomacy: United States Policies in Latin America, 1933–1945* (Baltimore: Johns Hopkins University Press, 1979), 121. See also p. 115, and Warren F. Kimball, *The Juggler: Franklin Roosevelt as Wartime Statesman* (Princeton, N.J.: Princeton University Press, 1991), 115–116.

2. Bryce Wood, *The Dismantling of the Good Neighbor Policy* (Austin: University of Texas Press, 1985), 2.

3. On wartime issues and their effect on U.S.-Brazilian relations, see Stanley E. Hilton, *Hitler's Secret War in South America, 1939–1945: German Military Espionage and Allied Counterespionage in Brazil* (Baton Rouge: Louisiana State University Press, 1981).

4. Samuel Flagg Bemis, *The Latin American Policy of the United States: An Historical Interpretation* (New York: Harcourt, Brace and Company, 1943), 379; Richard M. Ketchum, *The Borrowed Years, 1938–1941: America on the Way to War* (New York: Random House, 1989), 37.

5. Bemis, *Latin American Policy,* chap. 22. For valuable coverage of troubled U.S.-Argentine relations preceding and during World War II, see Alberto Conil Paz and Gustavo Ferrari, *Argentina's Foreign Policy, 1930–1962,* trans. John J. Kennedy (Notre Dame, Ind.: University of Notre Dame Press, 1966). Unsurpassed is Michael J. Francis, *The Limits of Hegemony: United States Relations with Argentina and Chile during World War II* (Notre Dame, Ind.: University of Notre Dame Press, 1977), while persuasive insights abound in Randall Bennett Woods, *The Roosevelt Foreign-Policy Establishment and the "Good Neighbor": The United States and Argentina, 1941–1945* (Lawrence: University of Kansas Press, 1979).

6. Merwyn K. Bohan, Economic Counsellor to the U.S. in Buenos Aires, 1942–1944, quoted by Paul B. Goodwin, Jr., "Comment on 'Foreign and Domestic Policy in Argentina,'" *Argentina between the Great Powers, 1939–1946,* ed. Guido di Tella and D. Cameron Watt (Pittsburgh: University of Pittsburgh Press, 1990), 106. See also Alec Campbell, "Anglo-American Relations, 1939–1946: A British View," *Argentina between the Great Powers,* 3.

7. Ketchum, *The Borrowed Years,* 613.

8. John Major, "A Northern Summing-up," *Argentina between the Great Powers,* 202–203.

9. Carlos Escudé, "U.S. Political Destabilization and Economic Boycott of Argentina during the 1940s," *Argentina between the Great Powers,* 59–60, 69; Ronald C. Newton, "Disorderly Succession: Great Britain, the United States and the 'Nazi Menace' in Argentina, 1938–1947," *Argentina between the Great Powers,* 114; Warren F. Kimball, "'The Juggler': Franklin D. Roosevelt and Anglo-

American Competition in Latin America," *Argentina between the Great Powers,* 23; Cole Blasier, *The Hovering Giant: U.S. Responses to Revolutionary Change in Latin America* (Pittsburgh: University of Pittsburgh Press, 1976), 54; Wood, *Dismantling the Good Neighbor Policy,* 30; Fredrick B. Pike, *Chile and the United States, 1880–1962* (Notre Dame, Ind.: University of Notre Dame Press, 1963), 206–207, 272.

10. Campbell, "Anglo-American Relations," 4.

11. Breckinridge Long quoted by Gellman, *Good Neighbor Diplomacy,* 135. See also *The War Diary of Breckinridge Long,* ed. Fred L. Israel (Lincoln: University of Nebraska Press, 1966), passim.

12. Wood, *Dismantling the Good Neighbor Policy,* 26.

13. Ibid., 4.

14. February 19, 1942, letter to Getulio Vargas, *F.D.R.: His Personal Letters,* ed. Elliott Roosevelt (New York: Duell, Sloan and Pearce, 1947–1950), 4:1495; Stanley E. Hilton, "The United States and Argentina in Brazil's Wartime Foreign Policy, 1939–46," *Argentina between the Great Powers,* 171–173.

15. July 14, 1944, letter to Winston Churchill, *F.D.R.: His Personal Letters,* 4:1521.

16. Callum A. MacDonald, "The Braden Campaign and Anglo-American Relations in Argentina, 1945–46," *Argentina between the Great Powers,* 138; Elizabeth A. Cobbs, *The Rich Neighbor Policy: Rockefeller and Kaiser in Brazil* (New Haven, Conn.: Yale University Press, 1991), passim.

17. For background, see Spruille Braden, *Diplomats and Demagogues: The Memoirs of Spruille Braden* (New Rochelle, N.Y.: Arlington House, 1971). See also Braden and Ellis O. Briggs, *Our Inter-American Policy* (Washington, D.C.: Government Printing Office, 1971).

18. Ronald C. Newton, *The "Nazi Menace" in Argentina, 1931–1947* (Stanford, Calif.: Stanford University Press, 1992), 348–349. See also Gary Grank, *Juan Perón vs. Spruille Braden: The Story behind the "Blue Book"* (Lantham, Md.: Madison Books, 1980).

19. MacDonald, "The Braden Campaign," 142.

20. See Nathaniel West, "Argentina Faces Some Evil History, But Not All," *New York Times,* February 16, 1992; and West, "Argentina Files Show Huge Effort to Harbor Nazis," *New York Times,* December 14, 1993.

21. See Sumner Welles, *Where Are We Heading?* (New York: Harper and Brothers, 1946), 236–237.

## Chapter 26

1. Alan Cassels, "Communications," *American Historical Review* 84 (1979): 1232; and A. James Gregor, "African Socialism, Socialism and Fascism: An Appraisal," *Review of Politics* 29 (1967): 124–153. See also Gregor, *The Fascist Persuasion in Radical Politics* (Princeton, N.J.: Princeton University Press, 1979), *Italian Fascism and Developmental Dictatorship* (Princeton, N.J.: Princeton University Press, 1979), and *Young Mussolini and the Intellectual Origins of Fascism* (Berkeley: University of California Press, 1979). Also valuable is Zeev Sternhell with Mario Sznajder and Maia Asheri, *The Birth of Fascist Ideology: From Cul-*

*tural Rebellion to Political Revolution,* trans. David Maisel (Princeton, N.J.: Princeton University Press, 1993). Sternhell and his collaborators stress that fascism when it burst upon the world emphasized socialism just as much as nationalism, and that its aberrations were not necessarily any greater than those of contemporary liberalism or of various forms of socialism professedly antithetical to nationalism.

2. Jesse H. Stiller, *George S. Messersmith: Diplomat of Democracy* (Chapel Hill: University of North Carolina Press, 1987), 220.

## Chapter 27

1. A sympathetic biography is Gregory Fossedal, *Our Finest Hour: Will Clayton, the Marshall Plan and the Triumph of Democracy* (Stanford, Calif.: Hoover Institution Press, 1993). See also Ellen Clayton Garwood, *Will Clayton: A Short Biography* (Austin: University of Texas Press, 1958).

2. For background, see *Americanizing the American Indians: Writings of the "Friends of the Indian",* ed. Francis Paul Prucha (Cambridge, Mass.: Harvard University Press, 1973).

3. See Louis Galambos, *The Public Image of Big Business in America, 1880–1940* (Baltimore: Johns Hopkins University Press, 1975), 262–263.

4. The words of the Irving Berlin song are quoted by George Will, "Familiar Narrative of Top Race Wants," *Gainesville Sun,* September 7, 1992. The "gravedigger" quotation comes from Steven Fraser, *Labor Will Rule: Sidney Hillman and the Rise of American Labor* (New York: Free Press, 1991), 441.

5. "Corporationism" is the term used by Alan Dawley, *Struggles for Justice: Social Responsibility and the Liberal State* (Cambridge, Mass.: Harvard University Press, 1991), 325. The statistics are from Erika Doss, *Benton, Pollock, and the Politics of Modernism: From Regionalism to Abstract Expressionism* (Chicago: University of Chicago Press, 1991), 280, 333.

6. Broadcast of May 26, 1940, in *FDR's Fireside Chats,* ed. Russell D. Buhite and David W. Levy (Norman: University of Oklahoma Press, 1992), 160; *Economist,* July 31, 1993, 30; Robert Dallek, *Franklin D. Roosevelt and American Foreign Policy 1932–1945* (Oxford, England: Oxford University Press, 1979), 443.

7. See Henry Luce, "The American Century," *Life* magazine, February 17, 1942, esp. pp. 61–63; and Ross Gregory, *America 1941: A Nation at the Crossroads* (New York: Free Press, 1989), 23. For a basically unfriendly assessment see John B. Judis, *Grand Illusion: Critics and Champions of the American Century* (New York: Farrar, Straus and Giroux, 1992).

8. Dennis Farney, "Turning Point: Even U.S. Politics Are Being Reshaped by a Global Economy," *Wall Street Journal,* October 28, 1992.

9. Dean Acheson and Willard L. Beaulac quoted by Bryce Wood, *The Dismantling of the Good Neighbor Policy* (Austin: University of Texas Press, 1985), 133, 136.

10. Merl E. Reed, *Seedtime for the Modern Civil Rights Movement: The President's Committee on Fair Employment Practice, 1941–1946* (Baton Rouge: Louisiana State University Press, 1991), 322.

11. See George Black, *The Good Neighbor: How the United States Wrote the History of Central America and the Caribbean* (New York: Pantheon Books, 1988), 61.

12. See Gerald D. Nash, *The American West Transformed: The Impact of the Second World War* (Bloomington: Indiana University Press, 1985), esp. pp. 17–25; and Richard Lowitt, *The New Deal and the West* (Bloomington: Indiana University Press, 1984), passim.

13. "I'm an Old Cowhand," music and lyrics by Johnny Mercer, copyright Leo Feist, Inc., 1936.

## Chapter 28

1. Irwin F. Gellman, *Good Neighbor Diplomacy: United States Policies in Latin America, 1933–1945* (Baltimore: Johns Hopkins University Press, 1979), 115.

2. Broadcasts of July 28, 1943, and June 5, 1944, *FDR's Fireside Chats,* ed. Russell D. Buhite and David W. Levy (Norman: University of Oklahoma Press, 1992), 263, 295, 296.

3. Sir Ronald Hugh Campbell, quoted by Bryce Wood, *The Dismantling of the Good Neighbor Policy* (Austin: University of Texas Press, 1985), 40–41.

4. *The Impossible H. L. Mencken: A Selection of His Best Newspaper Stories,* ed. Marion Elizabeth Rodgers (New York: Anchor Books/Doubleday, 1991), 676; Raymond Clapper quoted by Gellman, *Good Neighbor Diplomacy,* 170; Wood, *Dismantling the Good Neighbor Policy,* 40; Frederick W. Marks III, *Wind over Sand: The Diplomacy of Franklin Roosevelt* (Athens: University of Georgia Press, 1988), 230–231.

5. Roger Biles, *A New Deal for the American People* (DeKalb: Northern Illinois University Press, 1991), 104.

6. See Gerald K. Kaines, *The Americanization of Brazil: A Study of U.S. Cold War Diplomacy in the Third World, 1945–1954* (Washington, D.C.: Scholarly Resources, 1989), 131.

7. Zora Neale Hurston, *Dust Tracks on a Road: An Autobiography* (1942; reprint, Chicago: University of Chicago Press, 1984), 341.

8. Michael L. Conniff, *Panama and the United States: The Forced Alliance* (Athens: University of Georgia Press, 1992), 95.

9. John le Carré quoted by David Remick, "Le Carré's New War," *New York Review of Books,* August 12, 1993, 20.

10. Frederick M. Nunn, *The Time of the Generals: Latin American Professional Militarism in World Perspective* (Lincoln: University of Nebraska Press, 1992), 170, 259–260.

## Chapter 29

1. See Tim Weiner, "U.S. Spied Extensively on Allies in World War II," *New York Times,* August 11, 1993. On the Cold War and its specific implications for hemispheric relations, see Norman A. Bailey, *Latin America in World Politics*

(New York: Walker, 1967); John Moors Cabot, *Toward Our Common American Destiny* (Freeport, N.Y.: Books for Libraries Press, 1955); Gordon Connell-Smith, *The United States and Latin America: An Historical Analysis of Inter-American Relations* (London: Heinemann, 1974); and Laurence Duggan, *The Americas: The Search for Hemispheric Security* (New York: Holt, 1949). Most useful of all are Stanley E. Hilton, *Brazil and the Soviet Challenge, 1917–1947* (Austin: University of Texas Press, 1991); and two books by Lars Schoultz: *Human Rights and United States Policy toward Latin America* (Princeton, N.J.: Princeton University Press, 1981), and *National Security and United States Policy toward Latin America* (Princeton, N.J.: Princeton University Press, 1987). On the origins of the Cold War in general, see John Lewis Gaddis, *The United States and the Origins of the Cold War, 1941–1947* (New York: Columbia University Press, 1972); and Melvyn P. Leffler, *A Preponderance of Power: National Security, the Truman Administration, and the Cold War* (Stanford, Calif.: Stanford University Press, 1992).

2. Richard H. Pells, *The Liberal Mind in a Conservative Age: American Intellectuals in the 1940s and 1950s* (New York: Harper and Row, 1985), 66.

3. Schoultz, *National Security and United States Policy,* 330.

## Chapter 30

1. See chap. 28, n. 9.

2. Charles Berquist, "AHR Forum: Labor History and Its Challenges: Confessions of a Latin Americanist," *American Historical Review* 98 (1993): 757.

3. Octavio Paz quoted by John Butt, "The Visionary and the Ironist," *Times Literary Supplement,* July 24, 1992, 6.

4. *Economist,* August 21, 1993, 19.

5. *Economist,* March 13, 1993, 54, and August 21, 1993, 19.

6. Santiago Levy, "Mexican Regulators Humming the Deregulation Rag," *Wall Street Journal,* May 30, 1993.

7. *Economist,* February 13, 1993, 13.

8. Mark Falcoff, writing in the January–February 1939 *American Enterprise,* quoted in *Wilson Quarterly* 17 (Spring 1993): 126–128; *Economist,* February 13, 1993, 4.

9. Elliott Abrams, "How to Avoid the Return of Latin Populism," *Wall Street Journal,* May 21, 1993. In his thought-provoking book *Utopia Unarmed: The Latin American Left after the Cold War* (New York: Alfred A. Knopf, 1993), Jorge C. Castañeda unerringly picks out the major flaws in Latin America's post–World War II varieties of populism, while arguing in behalf of a new reformist populism, shorn of its statist inefficiencies, its counterproductive anti-Americanism, and its contempt for constitutional, democratic rule.

10. Nicolai Ryzhkov, the penultimate prime minister of the USSR, quoted by Robert Conquest, "Red for Go," *Times Literary Supplement,* July 9, 1993, 9.

11. E. P. Thompson quoted by Gary R. Mormino and George E. Pozzetta, *The Immigrant World of Ybor City: Italians and Their Latin Neighbors in Tampa, 1885–1985* (Urbana: University of Illinois Press, 1987), 12.

12. Letter of Howard J. Wiarda, *Wilson Quarterly* 17 (Winter 1993): 155. See also *The Iberian–Latin American Connection: Implications for U.S. Foreign Policy,* ed. Wiarda (Boulder, Colo.: Westview Press, 1986).

13. See Nathaniel C. Nash, "A New Rush into Latin America," *New York Times,* April 11, 1993.

14. George Bush quoted by Adam Watson, "Vanishing Values," *Times Literary Supplement,* May 21, 1993, 15.

## Chapter 31

1. See chap. 11, n. 13.

2. Richard John Neuhauss, "Tightening the Bible Belt," *Times Literary Supplement,* March 5, 1993, 24. For an analysis that may or may not read too much of the Protestant Ethic and defense of capitalism's spirit of private initiative into the thought of Pope John Paul II, see Michael Novak, *The Catholic Ethic and the Spirit of Capitalism* (New York: Free Press, 1993). Perhaps more perceptive in outlook is Michael L. Budde. In his book *The Two Churches: Catholicism and Capitalism in the World System* (Durham, N.C.: Duke University Press, 1993), he suggests that complaints against unchecked, trickle-down-theory capitalism will intensify within the Church of Rome as Third World Catholics come to comprise the majority of its faithful.

3. For a review of timely literature on the topic, see David Martin, "Faiths Escaping the Hierarchies," *Times Literary Supplement,* December 18, 1992, 22.

4. See *Economist,* April 17, 1993, 14; and David Lehmann, "The Shining Path to Terror," *Times Literary Supplement,* July 26, 1991, 10.

5. Daniel James, "Big Immigrant Wave Swamps Assimilation," *Wall Street Journal,* July 2, 1992.

6. Douglas Martin, "As the Hispanic Presence Grows, So Does the Resentment of Blacks," *New York Times,* June 20, 1993.

7. Richard Carlson, "As California Grows," *World Monitor,* May 1993, 21.

8. Richard A. García, *The Rise of the Mexican American Middle Class: San Antonio, 1929–1941* (College Station: Texas A & M University Press, 1991), 31. For an excellent general treatment of the topic, see Peter Skerry, *The Mexican Americans: The Ambivalent Minority* (New York: Free Press, 1993). Good insights are plentiful in *Barrios and Borderlands: Cultures of Latinos and Latinas in the United States,* ed. Denis Lynn Daly Heyek (New York: Routledge, 1994); Lester D. Langley, *MexAmerica: Two Countries, One Future* (New York: Crown Publishers, 1988); and David M. Reimers, *Still the Golden Door: The Third World Comes to America* (New York: Columbia University Press, 1985).

9. See Alejandro Portes and Ruben C. Rumbaut, *Immigrant America: A Portrait* (Berkeley: University of California Press, 1990), 128.

10. Earl Shorris, *Latinos: A Biography of the People* (New York: W. W. Norton, 1992), 68.

11. Ibid., 322.

12. For a succinct and properly suspicious analysis of the thesis that immigrants will bring about moral regeneration among Americans, see Michael Lind,

"Aliens among Us: The Right's New Immigration Gambit," *New Republic,* August 23 and 30, 1993, 22–23.

13. Arnoldo D. León, *Ethnicity in the Sunbelt: A History of Mexican Americans in Houston* (Houston: University of Houston Mexican American Studies Program, 1989), 107–108.

14. Shorris, *Latinos,* 134, 179, 228.

15. See Fredrick B. Pike, *The United States and Latin America: Myths and Stereotypes of Civilization and Nature* (Austin: University of Texas Press, 1992), 354.

## Chapter 32

1. See Jorge G. Castañeda, *Utopia Unarmed: The Latin Left after the Cold War* (New York: Alfred A. Knopf, 1993), passim.

2. See *Economist,* July 17, 1993, 16, 18.

3. Catherine Orenstein, "Latin America's Dark Side," *New York Times,* May 16, 1993. Orenstein provides an accurate, succinct picture of the downside of privatization in Latin America. The hopeful developments of Chile and Mexico are indicated by Michael C. Nash, "Candidate's Easy Campaign Reflects Chileans' Satisfactions," *New York Times,* December 5, 1993; and *Economist,* December 11, 1993, 44.

4. James Brooke, "A Hard Look at Brazil's Surfeits," *New York Times,* July 10, 1993. Emphasis is added.

5. *Economist,* July 10, 1993, 35, 38.

6. Ken Silverstein, "Tropical Thatcherism: Marketing Misery in Latin America," *Nation,* December 21, 1992, 766.

7. Daniel Bell, "The Old War," *New Republic,* August 23 and 30, 1993, 18.

8. See chap. 30, n. 9.

9. *Economist,* August 14, 1993, 39.

10. See *Economist,* July 10, 1993, 38, and September 11–17, 1993, 83; and Saskia Sassen, "Hard Times in the City," *Times Literary Supplement,* September 18, 1992, 11. See also William W. Goldsmith and Edward J. Blakely, *Separate Societies: Poverty and Inequality in U.S. Cities* (Philadelphia: Temple University Press, 1992); and Enzo Mingione, *Fragmented Societies: A Sociology of Economic Life beyond the Market Paradigm* (Oxford, England: Blackwell Press, 1992).

11. Paul R. Krugman, "Like It or Not, the Income Gap Yawns," *Wall Street Journal,* May 21, 1992; and Sassen, "Hard Times in the City."

12. Gene Guerrero, "Beyond the Drug War," *Nation,* July 19, 1993, 114, quoting from Elliott Currie's book *Reckoning: Drugs, the Cities, and the American Future* (New York: Hill and Wang, 1993).

13. Ernest Gellner, "What Do We Need Now?" *Times Literary Supplement,* July 16, 1993, 4.

14. See Arthur M. Schlesinger, Jr., *The Age of Roosevelt: The Crisis of the Old Order, 1919–1933* (Boston: Houghton Mifflin Company, 1957), 464–466.

15. "Mexicans Struggle to Cope with Shock of Candidate's Killing," *Wall Street Journal,* March 25, 1994, an article to which David Wessell and Neal Templin contributed.

## Chapter 33

1. See Stephen Jay Gould, "Dinomania," *New York Review of Books,* August 12, 1993, 52.

2. George Kennan, *Around the Cragged Hill: A Personal and Political Philosophy* (New York: W. W. Norton, 1992), quoted by Adam Watson, "Vanishing Values," *Times Literary Supplement,* May 21, 1993, 15.

3. See Robert Fox, *The Inner Sea: The Mediterranean and Its People* (New York: Alfred A. Knopf, 1993).

4. All quoted material under the final heading to this point comes from Denys Potts, "The Trickster as Hero," *Times Literary Supplement,* February 18, 1994, 28, a review of *Mythical Trickster Figures: Contours, Contexts and Criticisms,* ed. William J. Hynes and William G. Doty (Tuscaloosa: University of Alabama Press, 1993).

5. On transactional and transformational qualities and other aspects of leadership, often with specific reference to FDR, see James MacGregor Burns, *Leadership* (New York: Harper-Torch, 1982); and two books by Bernard Bass: *Leadership and Performance beyond Expectations* (New York: Free Press, 1985), and *Leadership, Psychology and Organizational Behavior* (Westport, Conn.: Greenwood, 1973).

6. Had they become available or known to me perhaps six months earlier, there are several recent books pertaining to diplomatic history that could have strengthened my treatment of various topics in this book, including cross-border perceptions of strengths and weaknesses of FDR as a hemispheric leader and statesman. Perhaps above all others, Doris Kearns Goodwin's *No Ordinary Time: Franklin and Eleanor Roosevelt: The Home Front in World War II* (New York: Simon and Schuster, 1994) would have helped to flesh out my portrayal of FDR's multidimensional and ER's less protean (but often enigmatic) personalities.

# Index

Fair Employment Practices Committee (FEPC), 108, 117, 287
Falcoff, Mark, 314
Farm Security Administration (FSA), xxiii, 22–23, 76, 179
Farrell, Gen. Edelmiro J., 261–262
Fascism, 231, 249, 260, 261, 266–271, 294–296, 298–300, 303, 319
Faulkner, William, 182
Faye, Harold, *17*
FBI, 233–234, 242, 262
Federal Art Project (FAP), 70
Federal Bureau of Investigation (FBI), 233–234, 242, 262
Federal Theater Program, 69–70
Federal Writers' Project, 68–69
FEPC. *See* Fair Employment Practices Committee (FEPC)
Fields, W. C., 162
Films. *See* Movies
Fitzgerald, Barry, 50
Forbes, Cameron, 169
Ford, Henry, 187
Forrestal, James, 252–253
Fox, Robert, 350
France, 166, 215, 222, 230, 258
Franco, Francisco, xx, 49, 52, 88, 122, 247–248
Frank, Waldo, 65, 89, 193, 202, 203
Freeman, Don, *20*
Frei, Eduardo, 336
Freud, Sigmund, 86, 92, 158, 160
Freyre, Gilberto, 99
Frontier myth, 36–44, 83–84, 132, 205–206, 333–334, 345
FSA. *See* Farm Security Administration (FSA)
Fuentes, Carlos, 196
Fujimori, Alberto, 312

García, Mario T., 106–107
García, Richard A., 328
Gardner, Lloyd, xii
Gargan, William, 50
Garis, Roy L., 109
Garland, Jim, 28
GATT, 208
Gellman, Irwin F., 136, 174, 232
General Agreement on Tariffs and Trade (GATT), 208

Germany, 190–192, 215, 229–233, 239, 246, 247, 250, 257
Gershwin, George, 78
Gillis, James M., 52
Gómez, Juan Vicente, 244
Good Neighbor policy: author's rationale for assessment of, xiv–xxv; and Cold War, 295–305; cultural program of, 251–254; decline of, 270–295; Depression's impact on, 15, 25, 32–33, 38; disillusionment of U.S. with, 250–251, 261–265, 290–293; diverse approaches to, 241–244; economic motivations for, 36–38, 41, 174–176, 205–209, 236–251, 265; and FDR's aspirations for international leadership, 223–226, 273–274; FDR's hard versus soft approaches to, 211–218, 224; and FDR's personality, 137, 138, 161, 162, 273, 353; hard approach to, 200, 205–210; inclusionist vision of, 84; and isolationism, 31–32; and Mexico oil crisis, 192–196; motivations for, xii–xiv, 136–137, 225–226, 228; and nonintervention, 164–176; operatic comparisons with, 2–10; origins of, xi, 42, 135–136; overview of FDR's approach to, xii–xiv, 135–136, 267–268; and reciprocity, 267–268; and religious toleration, 321–322; and security issues in Latin America, 228–251; soft approach to, 199–205; targeting of, 199–201. *See also* Latin America; and names of specific countries
Grau San Martín, Ramón, 171, 173
Green, David, xii
Gregor, A. James, 271
Guatemala, 241, 286, 301, 323, 324
Guevara, Ernesto (Che), 36, 159
Gunther, John, 232, 297, 298
Gurdjieff, Georges I., 74
Guthrie, Woody, 178, 288

Haas, Francis, 52
Hackett, Charles Wilson, xv–xvi
Haiti, 17, 122, 130–134, 143, 159, 169
Halifax, Lord, 261
Hanson, Howard, 78
Harding, Warren, 139
Harlem Renaissance, 89, 92, 121, 287
Harris, Roy, 78, 181

Havana Conference of 1940, 247–250, 251, 258, 261
Haya de la Torre, Víctor Raúl, xix, xxii, 7, 92, 159, 161, 170
Helfond, Riva, *155*
Hemingway, Ernest, 64, 232–233
Hepburn, Katharine, 112
Herbst, Josephine, 64
Hernández Martínez, Maximiliano, 159
Hickock, Lorena, 104
Hillman, Sidney, 65
Hispanics: Cuban Americans, 102–103, 328–329, 330; deportation of Mexicans, 105, 333; embourgeoisement of, in Southwest, 105–111, 327–328; employment and unemployment of, 330; as ethnic label, 326; as immigrants, 326–327, 331–333; in Los Angeles riot in 1992, 331; prejudice and discrimination against, 102–105, 109, 111, 287; Puerto Ricans, 332; social problems of, 331–333; statistics on, 106, 327, 332; U.S. citizenship for, 106; in World War II, 109; zoot suiters and pachucos, 108–109, 287, 331
Hitler, Adolf, 67, 97, 99, 148, 149, 221–224, 229–232, 247, 250, 350
Hodgson, Godfrey, 207–208
Hollywood movies. *See* Movies
Hoover, Herbert: *American Individualism* by, 42; cabinet of, 133; and the Depression, 19, 26, 37; and economic success of U.S., 18, 26, 165; on FDR, 138; and Good Neighbor policy, xi; humor on, 28; Latin American policy of, 169; and noninterventionism, 172; and tariffs, 208
Hoover, J. Edgar, 66, 67, 201–203, 233–234, 242, 262
Hope, Bob, 112
Hopkins, Harry, 55, 68, 104, 114, 203
House Committee on Un-American Activities, 69, 300
Howe, Louis, 148, 187
Huerta, Victoriano, 129
Hughes, Langston, 89, 117, 120, 122, 124
Hughes, Robert, 73, 79
Hull, Cordell: and Argentina, 173, 237, 255, 258–263, 273; conflicts with Welles, 203, 208, 242, 268; evaluation of, 208–209; and free trade, 208–209,

221; and Havana Conference of 1940, 247–249, 261; and *indigenismo*, 93; and Lima Conference of 1938, 236–238; and Mexican oil expropriation crisis, 191–194, 197; and Mexico, 243, 314; and Montevideo conference, 172, 173; and Nazi menace, 266; personality of, 140; retirement of, 263; and Rio Conference of 1942, 258; as traditionalist, 5–6, 213, 256, 271
Hurston, Zora Neale, 89, 292–293

Ickes, Harold, 90, 93, 179, 181, 203, 242
Immigration, 105, 321, 326–334
Indians. *See* American Indians
*Indigenismo*, 90, 91, 92–93, 318
Individualism, 39–44
Intellectuals: African American "talented tenth," 119–123; American intellectuals, 57–67, 79, 156; and Democratic Party, 252; and FDR, 74–76; and *indigenismo*, 92–93; Jews as, 64–67, 122; and Krausism-Arielism, 76–78, 87–88, 255, 299; Latin American intellectuals, 57–61, 63, 69, 79, 92, 115, 120–123, 156, 294, 299–300; and Marxism, 299–300; and noninterventionism, 165; on Sacco-Vanzetti case, 82, 84
Inter-American Bank, 243
Irigoyen, Hipólito, 159
Isolationism, 30–32, 37, 40–41, 136, 219–220, 229, 273, 281
Italy, 88, 215, 229, 232, 247, 257, 258, 321

James, William, 96
Japan, 215, 232, 243, 257, 258, 313
Jews, 48, 49, 64–67, 81, 94–95, 99, 100, 121, 181, 190, 202
John Paul II, Pope, 310, 322, 323
Johnson, Hugh, 154
Johnson, Lyndon B., 142, 301, 330
Jones, Jesse, 242, 243, 246, 279
Josephson, Matthew, 63
Jung, Carl, 158, 160

Kennan, George, 347
Kennedy, John F., 146, 302
Kennedy, Joseph, 78, 131

Kertesz, Steve, xxi–xxii
Keynes, John Maynard, 153
King, James M., 46–47
King, Martin Luther, Jr., 119
King, Rodney, 331
Kipling, Rudyard, 284
Kissinger, Henry, 140–141, 162, 301
Klemperer, Otto, xvii
Knox, Frank, 230, 242
Koussevitsky, Serge, 78
Krause, Karl Christian Friedrich, 77
Krausism, 76–79, 87–88, 299

Labor movement, 51, 65, 66, 117, 154, 156
LaFeber, Walter, xii
Laing, R. D., 7
Langley, Lester D., xix, xxv–xxvi
Latin America: and American popular culture, 286; Catholicism of, 46–47, 49–52, 56, 65–66, 107, 151, 158, 267, 321–325; caudillos in, 146, 148, 159, 294; and Cold War, 295–305; communism in, 92, 167, 268–269, 270–271, 281, 294–295, 299–304; compared with U.S. during Depression, 13–25; compared with U.S. in 1990s, 341–342, 347–349; complexity in Americans' judgments of, 111–115; corporatism in, 150–153, 346–347; Democrats' views of, 42–44; disillusionment of U.S. with, 250–251, 261–265, 290–293; and economic issues, 36–38, 41, 55–56, 112–113, 174–176, 205–209, 228–251, 265; empathy for, 29–31, 67; and fascism, 231, 249, 260, 261, 266–271, 294–296, 298–300, 303, 319; FDR's early impressions of, 128–134; FDR's mature perspectives on, 134–137, 319–320; FDR's trips to, during presidency, 147–148, 220–221; goodwill tours in, 124–125, 286; imports from U.S. to, 320; *indigenismo* in, 90, 91, 92–93, 318; intellectuals in, 57–61, 63, 69, 79, 92, 115, 120–123, 156, 294, 299–300; and isolationism, 31–32; Krausism-Arielism in, 76–77; landowners in, 113; light-skinned ruling classes in, 118, 133; music in, 79; nonintervention in, 164–176, 236; past in, 315–319; population of, 339; populism in, 143, 144; poverty in, 336–339; privatization in, 271–272, 280, 305, 308–315, 335–339; Protestantism in, 107, 323–325; racism in, 118–119, 123–124, 133; and racism in U.S., 116–125; reactions of, to American Century, 285–286, 293–295; reassessment of, 32–33; Republicans' views of, 42–44, 234; rivalry among countries of, 237, 240–241; and Theodore Roosevelt, 39–40; and Sacco-Vanzetti case, 84; and security issues, 149, 174–176, 228–251; spiritualism in, 74, 158–160; stereotypes of norteamericanos, 115, 275, 316; supermadres in, 56, 140; and Third World Century, 294–295; torture and civil rights violations in, 233; U.S. bureaucratic infighting about, 241–243; U.S. economic assistance to, 29–30, 251, 279–280, 285, 291–292, 298, 308–309, 339–340; U.S. intervention in, 129–133, 165, 167, 171–172, 186, 265–266, 279, 301; U.S. neglect of, 281–282; U.S. public opinion polls on, 134–135, 193, 287, 290; U.S. stereotypes of, 114, 133, 193–194, 233–234, 251, 282, 287–288, 290, 292–293; University Reform movement in, 254–255; urbanization in, 151; walking-around money to, 251, 279, 292; and World War II, 257–260, 290–292. *See also* Good Neighbor policy; and names of specific countries
Lawrence, D. H., 190
League of Nations, 131, 226
League of United Latin American Citizens (LULAC), 106–109, 327–328
Le Carré, John, 308
Lee, Peggy, 290
Leo XIII, Pope, 49, 52
Levy, Santiago, 312
Lewis, Sinclair, 27
Lima Conference of 1938, 236–238
Lincoln, Abraham, 334
Lindbergh, Charles, 94
Lippmann, Walter, 31, 167
Locke, Alain, 89
Locke, John, 310
London Economic Conference, 37, 220
Long, Breckinridge, 67, 261
Long, Huey, 141, 144, 192

NAFTA, xx, 313, 320
Native Americans. *See* American Indians
Nativists, 83–84
Navarro, Ramón, 112
Nazism. *See* Fascism; Germany
Neoconservatism/neoliberalism, 271, 338
New Deal, xxiii, 13, 22, 32, 48, 51, 52, 55,
    68–76, 117, 122, 149, 154, 203–204,
    206, 239, 250, 252, 256, 288, 325. *See
    also* Depression; and specific agencies
Newton, Ronald C., 232
Nicaragua, 74, 128, 131, 159, 167–171,
    241, 302
Niebuhr, Reinhold, 28, 54–55
Niemeyer, Vic, xvii
Nixon, Richard, 301
Nonintervention, 164–176, 236
Noriega, Manuel, 159
Norris, Frank, 27
Norris, George W., 225
Norteamericanos, stereotypes of, 115, 275,
    316
North American Free Trade Agreement
    (NAFTA), xx, 313, 320
Nye, Gerald P., 30–31

O'Brien, Patrick, 50
O'Connell, Father Marvin R., xxi
O'Connell, William Cardinal, 52
Office for Coordination of Commercial and
    Cultural Relations between the Ameri-
    can Republics, 252–254
Ogorzaly, Michael, 193
Oil industry, 166, 191, 192–196, 243, 244,
    259, 312–313
Operas, 2–10, 159, 280, 345
Opus Dei, 107, 323
Orozco, José Clemente, 71
Ortiz, Roberto M., 245, 247, 248
Other, the, 81–84, 91, 96, 204, 212
Ouspensky, P. D., 74

Pachucos, 108, 109
Panama, 40, 128–130, 131, 159, 212, 231,
    241, 286, 293
Panama Canal, 128–129, 173, 233, 247
Panama Conference of 1939, 245–247
Paraguay, 144, 209, 221, 240
Parish, Betty Waldo, *110*

Parks, national, 178–179
Paz, Octavio, 309
Peabody, Endicott, 51, 142
Pecora, Ferdinand, 29
Pecora hearings, 29, 31
Perkins, Frances, 55, 56, 70, 114, 203, 228,
    242
Perkins, Susanna, 70
Perón, Eva, 140, 147, 265
Perón, Isabel, 159
Perón, Juan D., 147, 152, 203, 261–262,
    264–266, 273, 278, 295–296, 319
Peronistas, 269, 310
Persichetti, Vincent, 78
Personalism, 145–147, 148
Peru: author's research in, xix; conflicts
    with other Latin American countries,
    240; corporatism in, 152; *indigenismo*
    in, 92; Krausism in, 77; populism in,
    144; privatization in, 312; religion in,
    324; request for U.S. intervention in,
    170; skin color in, 116; spiritualism in,
    74, 159; Wallace in, 202; and War of
    the Pacific, 312; and World War II, 261
Petroleum industry. *See* Oil industry
Pike, Pachita Tennant, xv, xvii
Pinochet, Augusto, 301
Pius XI, Pope, 49, 52
Populism, 143–145, 148, 192, 316, 318–319
Porter, Cole, 181, 198
Potter, David, 13
Poverty, 336–342, 345–346. *See also*
    Depression
Pragmatism, 96–97
Prejudice. *See* Racism
Primitivism, 86–96, 177, 289, 293
Privatization: in Latin America, 271–272,
    280, 305, 308–315, 335–339; in
    United States, 339–342
Protestantism, 5–6, 46–51, 54, 107, 321–
    326
Puerto Ricans, 332
Puerto Rico, 147, 158, 213–214, 222, 286
Pujo, Arsene, 28
Pujo Committee, 28, 30
Pumarejo, Alfonso López, 152

Raboy, Mac, *23*
Racism, 100–106, 116–125, 133, 287,
    329–330

Verdi, Giuseppe: *Simon Boccanegra*, 9–10, 280
Vidor, King, 114
Villa, Pancho, 90, 114
Villa-Lobos, Heitor, 79

Wachtel, Nathan, 324
Wagner, Richard, 159, 160
Wallace, Henry, 29, 74, 93, 160, 195, 197, 202, 203, 242, 243, 286
Waller, Thomas (Fats), 118
Ward, Geoffrey C., 156–157
Ward, Lester Frank, 96
Warren, Harry, 282
Washington, Booker T., 105–106
Watt, D. Cameron, 136
Wayne, John, 42
Webb, Albert James, *34, 81*
Webb, Walter Prescott, 24–25
Weber, Max, 323
Weldon, Casey Bill, 117
Welles, Sumner: as ambassador to Cuba, 171–172; conflicts with Hull, 203, 208, 242, 268; and Daniels, 186; dismissal of, 203, 262; and Gunther, 232; homosexual scandal involving, 203, 262; and *indigenismo*, 92–93; as journalist, 263; and Latin American policy, 6, 202–205, 213, 255, 256, 262, 268; and Mexican oil expropriation, 195–196, 197; and Mexico, 186, 243; and Panama Conference of 1939, 245, 246; and Pan American conference plans, 230; personality of, 6, 204; recall of, from Cuba, 172, 173, 266; at Rio Conference of 1942, 258–259; security risk allegedly posed by, 202–203
Western Hemisphere Idea, xix–xx, 211–212, 217–218, 320, 342, 346

Wheeler, Burton K., 30
Whitaker, Arthur P., xix, xx, 211
Whitman, Walt, 32, 158, 217, 353
Wiarda, Howard, 317
Wilkie, Wendell, 252
Williams, William Appleman, xii
Wilson, Edmund, 63
Wilson, Woodrow: Daniels in administration of, 185–186; and delusions of grandeur, 148; FDR in administration of, 129; Latin American policy of, 172, 206, 209, 213, 215, 216, 217; personality of, 139; and reform of American business, 168, 209; and World War I, 30, 148, 162, 283
Wolfe, Bertram, 94–95
Wolfe, Ella, 95
Wood, Bryce, xi, 196
Wood, Gen. Robert E., 37
Woodin, William H., 135
Works Progress Administration (WPA), xxiii, 69, 70, 76, 117, 345–346
World War I, 30–31, 283
World War II, 109, 118, 124, 157, 190–191, 222–225, 230–234, 245–247, 249, 255, 257–260, 290–292, 300
WPA. *See* Works Progress Administration (WPA)
Wright, Frank Lloyd, 74, 181, 187
Wright, Olgivanna, 74
Wright, Richard, 21, 69
Writers, 63–64, 68–76, 78, 88, 89, 122, 292–293. *See also* specific writers

Zangara, Joe (Giuseppe), 342–343
Zapatista movement, 313, 317–318
Zionism, 201, 313
Zoot suiters, 108–109, 287, 331

## DATE DUE